Understanding *and* Using Statistics *for* Criminology *and* Criminal Justice

Jonathon A. Cooper
Indiana University of Pennsylvania

Peter A. Collins
Seattle University

Anthony Walsh
Boise State University

New York   Oxford
OXFORD UNIVERSITY PRESS

Oxford University Press is a department of the University of Oxford.
It furthers the University's objective of excellence in research,
scholarship, and education by publishing worldwide.

Oxford   New York
Auckland   Cape Town   Dar es Salaam   Hong Kong   Karachi
Kuala Lumpur   Madrid   Melbourne   Mexico City   Nairobi
New Delhi   Shanghai   Taipei   Toronto

With offices in
Argentina   Austria   Brazil   Chile   Czech Republic   France   Greece
Guatemala   Hungary   Italy   Japan   Poland   Portugal   Singapore
South Korea   Switzerland   Thailand   Turkey   Ukraine   Vietnam

For titles covered by Section 112 of the US Higher Education
Opportunity Act, please visit www.oup.com/us/he for the
latest information about pricing and alternate formats.

Published by Oxford University Press
198 Madison Avenue, New York, New York 10016
http://www.oup.com

Oxford is a registered trademark of Oxford University Press.

Library of Congress Cataloging-in-Publication Data
Cooper, Jonathon A., 1982-
   Understanding and using statistics for criminology and criminal justice /
Jonathon A. Cooper, Peter A. Collins, Anthony Walsh.
      pages cm
   Includes bibliographical references and index.
   ISBN 978-0-19-936446-6
   1. Criminology--Methodology. 2. Criminal justice, Administration
of--Research--Methodology. 3. Criminal statistics. I. Collins, Peter A.
(Peter Alan) II. Walsh, Anthony, 1941- III. Title.
   HV6018.C665 2016
   519.5--dc23
                                                          2015011390

Printing number: 9 8 7 6 5 4 3 2 1

Printed in the United States of America
on acid-free paper

The authors dedicate this book to the following individuals:

Sancheen, Kaiya, and Lucas
—PC

Kammi
—JC

"His drop-dead gorgeous wife, all his children, grandchildren, and great grandchildren,
and his co-authors."
—TW

Brief Table of Contents

Contents

Preface

The goal of our textbook on probability statistics is to introduce criminology and criminal justice students to a wide range of analytic tools and help them to develop the skills necessary to critically examine the use and interpretation of statistics in criminology, criminal justice, and other social service fields. We want to help our readers create a mindset of **statistical thinking** and to help them become **good consumers of research**. The knowledge and skills associated with being a good consumer of research will serve students and practitioners as well as future (or current) criminal justice decision makers, whether in law enforcement, courts, corrections or forensics, law, or many other social service and public service fields. At the end of a course that uses this text, readers will possess the tools to make more informed decisions about how to incorporate the results of empirical research into new or existing policies, as well as a better understanding of how statistical information impacts their own thinking about justice issues.

Students often approach statistics with much fear, largely because of the perception that "statistics" is code for "difficult math." This fear is largely unnecessary. To attenuate such concerns, this textbook assumes zero exposure to statistics from a classroom setting and minimal exposure to mathematics at a college setting. Students should be familiar with basic mathematical operations (addition, subtraction, multiplication, division, fractions, etc.), be able to use formulas to solve problems, and be able to "find for the unknown," for example, "if $x + 6 = 7$, what does x equal?" In addition, because criminology and criminal justice students come from a spectrum of backgrounds, including active duty and prior service military men and women, current criminal justice practitioners and other social service agents, and traditional college students, we have strived to make this book as accessible as possible to all college audiences.

Our approach to accessibility can best be described in the following manner: we present the statistic conceptually *first*, and *then* we discuss its underlying mathematics. Further, the math is presented step by step, rather than assuming that students can intuitively follow the often convoluted and intimidating statistical formulae. Although we believe it is incorrect to say that statistics are *not* math, it is also wrong to say that they are *only* math. Throughout the following pages, we hope to help students bridge the gap between math and art so that they feel confident in their ability to grasp the (seemingly) complex nature of probabilistic statistics. Indeed, we believe that the strength of our textbook is the fact that it provides a conceptual approach to statistics for criminology and criminal justice students, while teaching them not only the basics, but also the most important probabilistic statistics that criminologists and criminal justicians need to understand as our justice system continues to move forward in the evidenced-based and intelligence-lead paradigms that are coming to define the administration of justice in the twenty-first century.

Finally, we hope that students *and* instructors find our text useful. It seems to us that statistical textbooks are often written with a hope and wish that the instructor will be able to explain the textbook to the students. Our approach is different: we want students to be able to learn from our text, and we want instructors to be able to see it as a tool, rather than a required nuisance. To say that we *love* statistics may be a bit strong, but we certainly enjoy the challenge of statistics. It is the challenge of abstracting the social world to numbers, using those numbers to ascertain the reality of the social world, and then looping back to talk about that world. It is a fascinating and, we argue, an enjoyable exercise. We sincerely hope that this textbook, in the hands of inquisitive students and capable instructors, conveys our excitement of this process and provides students with a glimpse into the prospect of using statistics to better understand the world around them.

Our text is divided into two parts. Part 1 we call "The Building Blocks of Probabilistic Statistics." This section outlines those parts of statistics most essential for understanding probabilistic statistics: measurements of central tendency and dispersion, the normal curve and probability, the central limit theorem, and hypothesis testing, beginning with the Student *t* test. These topics are essential for students to learn to knowledgeably calculate and interpret the linear model, which is the focus of part 2, which we call "Hypothesis Testing with Probabilistic Statistics." This section combines all of the elements covered in the previous part and teaches students statistical operations that will be important for analysis and graduate school. In this section, we distinguish between parametric and nonparametric statistics and introduce the linear model. We start with ANOVA because this can be introduced with relative ease as a comparison to the *t* test students will have just covered. We then spend several chapters discussing measurements of association before returning to the parametric linear model, which teaches students correlation and multiple regression.

Each chapter includes the following elements: learning objectives, which help students know from the start what they should be focusing on and getting out of the chapter; step-by-step instructions on calculating specific statistics; examples of computer printouts; examples of tables from actual journal articles, along with explanations; and exercises. In addition, there are multiple graphs and call-out boxes to help students better and more deeply understand the statistics under question. The call-out boxes are particularly geared toward more detailed explanation and so can be safely ignored if professors want to keep things lighter for their students. Our approach in each chapter is to introduce the *concepts* underlying each statistic, then demonstrate how to calculate the statistic, and conclude by connecting the concept with the math and providing students with directions on conventional ways of interpreting the particular statistic in question. We have aimed to provide explanations that are the least technical as possible, without watering down the discussions. We do so with the belief that our students are up to the task of engaging with the challenging yet accessible text.

Chapter 1 serves two purposes. First, it provides an introductory primer on probabilistic statistics. After reading this chapter, students should therefore readily apprehend the overarching concept of statistics, how it applies to science, and how it applies to the administration of justice. Second, this chapter provides a methodological review of those elements most pertinent to statistics. In this way, students, after reading this chapter, are on firm ground to begin learning statistics for criminal justice and criminology. This chapter essentially sets the tone for our textbook's purpose of providing students with a conceptual approach to statistics.

Chapter 2 builds on the idea of a conceptual approach by introducing students to ways of graphically representing statistical output. Students are therefore introduced to the importance of summarizing and visualizing raw data; how to calculate and interpret raw counts, percentages, and rates; how to calculate and interpret bar, pie, and line charts; and the nature of distributions and how to graph distributions as histograms. This chapter is replete with graphical illustrations.

Chapter 3 considers the two most elementary yet arguably most important statistical families: measurements of central tendency and dispersion. To fully understand how probabilistic statistics work, students need an immediate grounding in these most basic of descriptive statistics. All probabilistic statistics build on these simple operations. In addition, they are intuitive to calculate and to interpret, thus providing students with confidence in their ability to "do" statistics. By the end of this chapter, students will know how to calculate and interpret the mode, median, mean, range, standard deviation, variance, and variation.

Whereas chapter 3 provided the two most important statistical building blocks leading up to hypothesis testing, central tendency and dispersion, chapter 4 continues this theme by introducing students to basic probability and its relationship to the normal curve. This chapter will make considerable use of examples and graphs to better help students understand what can be perceived as a complex subject. By the end of chapter 4, students will understand the normal curve and how it is created and will be ready for the next step: sampling distributions and what they mean for statistics.

Chapter 5 is the final chapter in preparing students to engage in hypothesis testing. In it, students learn how important sampling is to statistics and are taught the central limit theorem. This chapter completes the picture of "how statistics work," both conceptually and analytically, and provides students with all the necessary tools to engage in hypothesis testing.

Part 1 ends with chapter 6, which covers basic hypothesis testing for continuous data. It first introduces students to the concept and steps of hypothesis testing (in keeping with our conceptual approach) and finishes with two examples of simple hypothesis tests: the z and t tests. Having read this chapter, students will understand degrees of freedom, the role of distributions in hypothesis testing, alpha levels, and the distinction between one- and two-tailed tests.

Part 2 begins with chapter 7 on analysis of variance, more commonly referred to as ANOVA. ANOVA is the hallmark of the general linear model; it is therefore introduced first in part 2 of the textbook. Students learn about assumptions of the linear model and are then taught the logic behind ANOVA. Once the concept has been presented, students are taught how to calculate and interpret model F, effect size, and tests of multiple comparisons. Finally, students are introduced to interactions and factorial models.

Chapter 8 teaches students how to perform hypothesis tests for variables that break the assumptions required by ANOVA. They are introduced to a new distribution (the chi square distribution), how to calculate a test statistic using this distribution, and how to calculate and interpret effect sizes. This chapter is used as a springboard for chapters 9 and 10, which consider more nonparametric statistics and basic measures of association. By the end of chapters 9 and 10, students will know what bivariate statistical tests are appropriate for binary, nominal, ordinal, and categorical variables, how to find *causation* using such data, and how to control for intervening variables using tabular data. Chapter 10 also serves as an introduction to correlation and regression.

A brief digression concerning these three chapters (8, 9, and 10) is necessary. First, chapters 9 and 10 are more complicated mathematically than previous chapters. They remain, nevertheless, accessible. But because of the complexity, instructors may consider liberally picking and choosing what they wish to cover and what they wish to provide as merely cursory reviews from these chapters. Because we introduce hypothesis testing using the linear model (ANOVA, chapter 7), students will still be prepared for bivariate and multivariate regression (chapters 11 and 12, respectively). Second, although chi square may be a more easily grasped example of hypothesis testing, we believe that introducing students to this subject via chi square sets them up to fail. Specifically, because it is nonparametric, chi square makes no assumptions about the population. To this end, the distribution it uses to establish statistical validity is empirical, rather than hypothetical, as with the rest of the linear model family. We therefore move forward under the assumption (supported by our experience in teaching classes on statistics at both the undergraduate and the graduate level) that it is better to begin with a member of the linear model, complete with its suite of parametric assumptions, rather than the weaker and nonparametric chi square statistic when introducing the idea of hypothesis testing.

Regardless of whether the instructor wishes to cherry-pick from chapters 9 and 10 or avoid them altogether, by now students will be ready for correlation and regression. Students are first introduced to these topics using only two variables. Chapter 11 therefore serves two purposes. First, it teaches students how to measure association with two continuous variables, something inappropriate for all of the statistical functions so far covered. It covers both correlation coefficients and bivariate regression coefficients. Second, it prepares students for chapter 12, which discusses multiple regression. It does this by introducing important concepts that distinguish correlation from regression: error terms and partial coefficients. Chapter 12, dealing with multivariate regression, is therefore the culmination for students: conceptually and mathematically it puts all of the pieces so far covered together so students fully understand the linear model, its assumptions, and the concept of control variables. More specifically, students will learn how the ANOVA F test is used for the model fit of multiple regression; how the t tests are used to distinguish b coefficients from 0; and how to fully interpret β coefficients. After reading this chapter, students will be prepared to understand the most common statistics in social science journals and professional publications.

In addition to these main chapters, we offer two appendices that we believe both students and instructors will find useful. Criminology and criminal justice researchers and analysts rarely work with raw dependent variables that are normally distributed and therefore appropriate for the linear model. Fortunately, criminologists and justicians now have enough statistical sophistication to work with these measurements on their own terms, rather than transforming them. Appendix A therefore considers the use of statistical models that employ limited dependent variables because such statistics do a better job of modeling criminal justice outcomes. This is an introductory treatment, but it is one that will provide students with the tools to: (a) understand conceptually what is going on in the generalized linear model; and

(b) successfully interpret model fit and coefficients. Appendix A therefore covers a general introduction to the generalized linear model, with specific notes on models with binary, multinomial, ordered categorical, and count outcomes.

What's more, students are now presented with a multitude of statistical software packages. Although SPSS may be considered the conventional package for learning and doing social statistics, we believe that there is more variation than that among scholars and analysts. It is for this reason that the computer printouts provided throughout the main chapters are generic. Anyone familiar with statistical software knows that their printouts are relatively similar; our generic examples capitalize on that lack of uniqueness so that, again, we can reach the largest audience possible. Nevertheless, we agree that students should have at least a cursory knowledge of the major statistic programs. Therefore, Appendix B offers a brief primer on the most common statistical software packages: SPSS, SAS, Stata, and R. In this fashion, instructors who want to use a statistical package can, whereas others who do not still have the opportunity of introducing their students to at least four of their options.

Last, in addition to the main text we also provide several ancillaries both within and attached to our book: a glossary of terms; a test bank; PowerPoints; a formula index; and typical statistical tables.

We thank all the good folks at Oxford University Press (past and present) for making this book a reality. We would especially like to express our gratitude to the following individuals: Sarah Calabi, Caroline Osborne, John Challice, Olivia Geraci, and Steve Helba, among many others. Additionally, we thank Roxanne Klaas and everyone else involved in the book's production, from copyeditors to cover designers.

Tony acknowledges the love and support of his drop-dead gorgeous and nicer than nice wife, Gracie. She has been a constant source of wonder, inspiration, and comfort to me. Love you, sweetpea!

Pete thanks, first and foremost, Seattle University Criminal Justice graduate student Elisabeth Jandro for her invaluable help with the chapter study questions/problem sets. Second, thanks to Loreli Smith, who also provided help with some of the end of chapter materials as well as teaching assistance in Pete's undergraduate statistics course. Last, a special thanks to Sancheen, Kaiya, and Lucas and the rest of the Collins/Fraser clan for their unwavering love and support.

Jon acknowledges the support of his colleagues and the staff in the Department of Criminology and Criminal Justice at Indiana University of Pennsylvania, as well as the work undertaken for this book by his graduate assistants, Samantha Gavin, Kweilin Pikciunas, Lori Wiester, Lindsey Smathers, and Myunghee You. Thanks are further due to Dr. Reneè Lamphere (University of North Carolina at Pembroke) for her invaluable insights. Jon also acknowledges the formative role that all of his previous statistics professors played throughout his undergraduate and graduate career, including Drs. Anthony Walsh, Jeremy Ball, Leona Aiken, Roger Millsap, Gary Sweeten, and Eric Hedburg. Last, a thanks to Kammi for her patience, kindness, and love.

Finally, Jon and Pete both acknowledge the enormously influential role that Tony has played in our academic and personal life: as our instructor, our reference, our mentor, our example, and our friend. We are humbled and proud to know you, Tony; drinks on us.

Part 1

The Building Blocks of Probabilistic Statistics

CHAPTER 1

Introduction to Statistical Analysis

LEARNING OBJECTIVES:

After reading this chapter, the student should understand the following concepts:

- The purpose of statistics and how they are used in contemporary criminal justice practice
- The difference between descriptive and inferential statistics
- Levels of measurement and their implications for probabilistic statistics
- The importance of validity and reliability for statistical analysis
- The relationship among sample statistics, population parameters, and error

WHY STUDY STATISTICS?

As civilizations become more complex and technical, it becomes increasingly necessary for our thinking to also become more complex and technical. The Industrial Revolution was the beginning of the end of a long period in history in which people could make a living with only a strong back. It eventually became necessary to understand, interpret, and analyze the written words of our cultures, that is, to read. People who did not have the opportunity or the ability to adjust to this new cultural requirement were, by and large, condemned to lives of poverty and exploitation. H. G. Wells, writing in the nineteenth century, stated that "statistical thinking will one day be as necessary for efficient citizenship as the ability to read or write."

The founder of modern nursing, Florence Nightingale, similarly stated that "[s]tatistics is the most important science in the whole world: for upon it depends the practical application of every other science and of every art; the one science essential to all political and social administration, all education, all organization based upon experience, for it only gives the results of our experience." We agree—and we believe that we have long ago arrived at the day spoken of by H. G. Wells.

Many people have an aversion to statistics—some people even call statistics sadistic—and students may have a tendency to mask their fears by belittling the topic. It is a lot easier to think of some sharp and witty reasons to avoid our fears than to confront and master them. British Prime Minister Benjamin Disraeli's famous dictum that "there are three kinds of lies: lies, damned lies, and statistics" and W. H. Auden's admonition to his fellow poets, "[t]hou shalt not with statisticians sit, or commit a social science," may give us a chuckle, but they are not to be taken seriously because they are attempts to dignify ignorance. We do not deny that people lie with statistics, and we will give you several examples, but this is precisely why one should understand their possibilities and limitations. In short, people often mistrust and caricaturize what they do not understand. But you will do well to ignore them and look to the headline of a 2009 *New York Times* story regarding the most useful area of study for acquiring good jobs in today's economy: *"For Today's Graduate, Just One Word: Statistics"* (Lohr, 2009: A1).

In addition, the criminal justice, legal, and general social science professions continue to use statistics in new and innovative ways. For example, the New York Police Department developed and employed COMPSTAT, short for computer statistics, to hold officers accountable in their jurisdictions and as a crime control and reduction measure. COMPSTAT, by its very name, makes overt use of statistical computations. Additionally, more police departments are using early-intervention systems: data-mining software that analyzes a host of variables related to police work, such as citizen complaints, use of force incidents, and sick days, to pinpoint officers who are underperforming or have not yet crossed the line in their interactions with civilians, but may be on their way to doing so. Such software helps prevent good officers from becoming bad ones, it ultimately helps protect citizens who interact with the police, and it helps to restore credibility in departments where relationships with citizens have been less than ideal. As a final example, most state correctional institutions will no longer employ a treatment program just because it sounds good. Thanks to Martinson's (1974) statement that "nothing works" in regard to a host of correctional treatment programs, correctional agencies today require statistical and empirical evidence that the programming and services they deliver demonstrate some measurable impact. In other words, they are relying on statistics to do their job better. Clearly, it is in your best interest as a criminal justice, criminology, or social science student or the like to be equipped with the knowledge necessary to increase your performance throughout your career. Thus, the statistical methods you will learn and be exposed to within this text will provide you with a variety of practical and powerful tools that will aid in problem solving, policy formation, and management, as well as the decision-making processes within every possible career path in the criminal justice, criminology, and public health/social service fields.

THINKING STATISTICALLY

Statistics is the language of science. It is a mathematical language that enables us to draw logical conclusions within known boundaries of error from a set of data. **Data** (singular, datum) are simply a set of numerical scores relating to the phenomenon under investigation. Statistics enables us to reduce thousands of separate pieces of numerical information to a few easily understood summary statements. For example, one database that was recently used by one of the authors of this text contained information related to roughly 3,000 juvenile offenders. There were 2,500 variables, or pieces of information, associated with each juvenile and their case(s), for a total of $(3,000 \times 2,500) = 7,500,000$ data points—far too many points to make any sense of underlying patterns by simply looking at the raw data. Once we have organized these data using statistical techniques, however, the analyses and findings enable us to make a multitude of statements about, for example, the sample of juvenile offenders noted above.

Statistics are numbers that allow us to analyze, evaluate, and summarize large quantities of data. Essentially, statistics abstract real life into patterns and numbers. Think about what a single statistic—your GPA for instance—can say about you. Each semester's GPA allows analysis of your progress over time, an evaluation of your overall scholastic ability, and a summarization of your intellectual performance over many different subjects, professors, and semesters. You may object by saying that a single number cannot possibly serve to evaluate a person's intellectual abilities: GPA indicates what you *have done*, not what you *can do*. True enough, there is always room for additional information to help those who must evaluate intellectual ability. However, that information will probably be in numeric form also and may include IQ scores, SAT scores, hours spent studying or at work, and so on. Taken as a whole, these numbers may provide an accurate account of an individual's intellectual performance when compared to, for example, the "average" person's performance.

Although statistics is not just another math class, one of the first things you will do is to perform some simple calculations. Knowing how to come up with the right numbers is an essential part of statistics, but it's only the beginning. Quite honestly, computing statistics is the easiest part of a statistics class. The most difficult part of learning statistics is developing an understanding of *when* to use and *how to apply* certain statistical techniques and then how to *interpret* the results from your calculations. Statistics are numbers representing some form of reality, such as everything that makes your GPA what it is. When those numbers are subjected to computational procedures, the result (which will be, of course, numeric) must be translated back into the reality the raw numbers were supposed to represent. If you get the calculations right but misinterpret what they mean (or vice versa), the exercise is useless.

The following are some of the types of erroneous statistical findings we run into almost every day as consumers of information, both inside and outside the university. After reading these findings, see if you can think of ways in which the conclusions based on them could be in error. All of the below examples have actually appeared in print in one place or another.

1. It appears that gender is a substantial cause of TV watching. We found that women watch significantly more TV than men (up to 50 percent more).
2. Researchers from "Fundamentalist Church University" have found a highly significant relationship between a preference for a mix of death metal music and unwed motherhood. The researchers suggest that death metal be banned from the home as detrimental to the morals of young people.
3. Race-based sentencing disparities are declining in our criminal justice system. Findings indicate that, on average, nonminority defendants receive significantly more severe sentences than do minority defendants.
4. Fifty percent more teachers in 1996 said that U.S. educational standards were declining than said so in 1995. It is a sad fact that U.S. education standards continue to fall behind those of other industrialized and postindustrial nations.

Did you find any flaws in these research findings? The first three statements are examples of what social scientists call *misspecified models*. **Misspecification** is the omission of crucial explanatory variables from the model. No doubt women may have watched more TV than men in the 1960s when this study was conducted, but not because they were women: women were less likely to be employed outside the home than men and thus may have had more time to watch TV. Similarly, we would not argue with a finding that reports a strong link between a preference for death metal and unwed motherhood. However, a preference for both death metal and unwed motherhood is also strongly associated with age. So age can be said to "cause" both musical preference and unwed motherhood. Nor would we particularly agree with the finding that race-based sentencing disparities are absent or declining in our criminal justice system. But before we start talking about racism we need to know whether the researchers had taken into account additional factors, such as whether there were differences in the severity of the crime and number of prior offenses between the groups or differences in the quality of legal representation.

Note that we have no argument with any of the simple statements of the findings— that is, the facts. They are what they are. Many of these problems arise with faulty interpretations based on incomplete information. We avoid this type of predicament by including other theoretically relevant variables in our statistical models: employment status in the first case, age in the second, and severity of the crime, prior record, and private or public legal counsel in the third. Statistics allow us not only to measure reality with numbers, but also to rule out the possibility that any relationship we might observe between two variables is actually based on chance.

The problem with the fourth example, the one on educational standards, is the way it is presented. As presented it tells us absolutely nothing. What were the answer categories? Perhaps 10 percent said they were declining, 50 percent said they were not declining, and 40 percent actually said they were improving. What were the sample sizes? Perhaps the number of people who responded (sample respondents) to the 1996 questionnaire had considerably increased compared to the number of respondents that made up the 1995 sample and this alone accounted for the additional 50 percent. If we don't know the answers to these questions, the statement is meaningless. Understanding statistics and how they operate help us catch fallacious conclusions such as these.

To interpret statistics properly you must know the origin of the data and how statistics are computed. If the person or group presenting the findings has an agenda, such as the need to prove how bad our schools are, that we live in a racist or nonracist society, or how sinful death metal music is, the findings may be suspect. We also need to know how the statistics underlying reported findings are computed and whether they were appropriate for the task to which they were applied.

DESCRIPTIVE AND INFERENTIAL STATISTICS

A major function of all statistics is to describe the phenomenon under investigation. By convention, statisticians have reserved the label **descriptive statistics** for information, which usually describes or summarizes something about a single measure or variable that can be organized and presented in simple and direct ways. We are all familiar with such basic descriptive statistics as baseball batting averages, the annual rainfall in an area, the number of cars on American roads, and marriage and divorce rates. Percentages, ratios, proportions, frequencies, charts, tables, and graphs are some of the ways we organize, summarize, present, and describe these data. Descriptive statistics are limited to the data at hand and do not involve any inferences or generalizations beyond them; however, they remain useful. For example, if it wasn't for simple descriptive statistics, we would not be aware of one of the most important findings in criminal justice: the dramatic decline in crime in the 1990s. From World War II to the 1970s, crime increased alongside population growth. In the 1970s, crime began to increase faster than population growth, and then in the 1980s this increase in crime skyrocketed. Just as suddenly, crime plummeted in the mid-1990s and has continued to fall, or at least level out, ever since. Without descriptive statistics, we would not even be able to distinguish this important pattern (see Box 1-2 below for more details).

Inferential statistics are statistical techniques that enable us to make inferences or generalizations about a large group of subjects or objects called a **population** on the basis of data taken from a subset of that population called a **sample**. This is possible by use of **probability** and is the subject of this textbook, namely **probabilistic statistics**. Probability, as applied to inferential statistics, is the likelihood or chance that what we observe statistically with our sample represents what is actually going on in the population. When we have sample data we are not really interested in the sample per se; we are interested in the population from which the sample came. If we have data on an entire population (i.e., a complete tabulation of some characteristics of interest from all elements in a population) we have a **census**.

Census refers to not only the enumeration of the populace that the government undertakes every decade but also any comprehensive tabulation of many different

---

Box 1-1
Galton's Quincunx

A tip from Sir Francis Galton: for a graphical illustration regarding error and sample size, type the word "quincunx" into your Internet browser. Search around until you find an interactive graphic/machine and hit play (an example can be found at http://www.mathsisfun.com/data/quincunx.html/).

kinds of populations. The term population does not necessarily mean a body of people, although it almost always does in social science. Population refers to all cases about which a researcher wishes to make inferences. If we want to make general statements about adult Americans, the entire adult population of the United States is the population. If we are interested in the religious practices of Mormons, all Mormons are the population. If we are interested in the recreational activities of members of the New York City Police Department, the NYPD is the population.

For virtually all statistical research in the social sciences, including criminology and criminal justice, the intention is to use information derived from a representative sample to make statements about the population from which the sample was drawn. We use **sample statistics** (like the mean or average of a variable within a sample) to estimate population parameters, or summary descriptions about particular variables in a population: for example, the average age of all inmates in prison. Both a statistic and a parameter are numbers, the former being a proxy for the latter. We all make decisions based on samples even if we are not aware that we are doing so. Many students go to two or three different sections of an introductory course to sample the teaching style and class requirements of different professors. On the basis of the sample, the student decides which section he or she will enroll in. The student infers from the sampling of classes what the remainder of the classes will probably be like in terms of subject matter, requirements, and level of difficulty. Likewise, it is hardly necessary to eat a whole cow before deciding that the meat is tough. This is the point of scientific research and inference: we do not need to take the time or endure the cost necessary to obtain information relevant to our research from all elements of the population before we can draw conclusions. Statistical techniques allow us to estimate population parameters, like averages within precisely known margins of error (probability).

The relationship among samples, parameters, populations, and statistics is presented graphically in Figure 1-1. In the example shown in Figure 1-1, we are attempting to estimate the average job satisfaction score of all NYPD officers (the parameter) from the average job satisfaction score of a random sample of those officers (the statistic). Keep in mind that a statistic is to a sample as a parameter is to a population. We measure job satisfaction with a simple question: "On a scale of 1 to 3, with 1 being not satisfied at all and 3 being completely satisfied, how satisfied are you with your job?" Assuming that our sample of NYPD officers is representative of all such officers in the NYPD, we can say that our best prediction of the average level of job satisfaction is 2.711, and we can then place some margin of error around this prediction.

FIGURE 1-1

The relationship among
populations, samples,
parameters, and
statistics

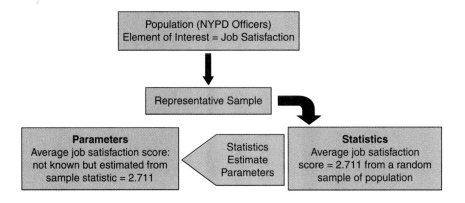

STATISTICS AND ERROR

Any time we measure some element of interest in the social sciences, some degree of **error** is inevitable (see Box 1-1). By error we mean the degree to which our estimate is off—in other words, the extent to which our sample statistic does *not* reflect the population parameter. Error in measurement is basically a function of two things: the accuracy of our instruments and the size of our samples. The instrument used in the above example to measure job satisfaction is not as reliable as a well-calibrated scale used to measure weight or even a yardstick used to measure height—or even a job satisfaction scale with more than three options for the respondent. A person's feelings about his or her job vary from time to time and are more nuanced than what can be captured in a simple three-point scale. Fortunately, these fluctuations tend to cancel one another out. That is, we might reasonably assume that for every person we catch on a bad day, we catch another on a good day.

Sample size is the other factor influencing the degree of error. All other things being equal, the larger the sample the smaller the error will be. If we want to determine the height of all men in the U.S. Marine Corps, a sample size of 1,000 would be better than one of 150, which is better than a sample of 50. Populations always have more variability than do samples. Populations, by definition, contain all common and all rare cases. The larger the sample, the more likely it is to represent the situation as it exists in the population. Thus a larger sample of Marines is more likely to include some rare or atypical cases (such as male Marines shorter than 5 feet 2 inches or taller than 6 feet 2 inches). But whatever the sample size, there will always be error associated with the sample statistics used to estimate population parameters. Recognizing this, we place some margin of error around the estimates. We might conclude from our study of job satisfaction among NYPD officers that the average job

> *Box 1-2*
> *How Do We Know the Drop in Crime Really Happened?*
>
> There are two major sources of national crime data: the FBI's Uniform Crime Reports (UCR) and the Census Bureau's National Crime Victimization Survey (NCVS). The UCR reports on arrests and clearances from police agencies, and the data come directly from participating police agencies (of which there are a lot—almost all police agencies report data to the FBI for use in the UCR). The NCVS, on the other hand, is a probability sample of all households in the United States. Its data come from household residents and cover questions of victimization.
>
> Both the UCR and the NCVS have problems with reliability and validity. The UCR, for example, assumes that all police officers and all police agencies are reporting the same crimes under the same definitions. The NCVS, on the other hand, assumes that victims can accurately recall when they were victimized. Despite their problems, however, *both* the UCR and the NCVS agree: crime did go down in the 1990s. Whether we are talking about the number of arrests or the number of victimizations per household, we see the same pattern emerge in the last decade of the twentieth century: crime went down.
>
> *Explore the FBI's Crime in America UCR data here: http://www.fbi.gov/about-us/cjis/ucr/ucr*
> *Explore the NCVS data here: http://bjs.ojp.usdoj.gov/index.cfm?ty=dcdetail&iid=245*

satisfaction score is 2.711, plus or minus 0.5, or between 2.211 and 3.211. Statistical procedures for assessing the degree of error are addressed later in this book.

OPERATIONALIZATION

The measurement of such physical constructs as height and weight is relatively unproblematic, but what about such social science concepts as criminality, socioeconomic status, or even gender? If we are serious about the social science enterprise, first we must be clear about what we want to measure. Then we must design a series of operations that yield suitable measurements of it. In short, we are concerned with the **operationalization**, or how we define and measure our concepts.

Let us first distinguish between a conceptual definition and an operational definition. A **conceptual definition** is a verbal statement relating our understanding of a phenomenon. For instance, we can conceptually define blood pressure as "the pressure exerted on the arterial walls by the pumping action of the heart." This is an accurate verbal definition, but what if I want to compare the blood pressure of a number of individuals in an attempt to determine whose pressure is higher (more) or lower (less)? The ideas of *higher* and *lower* and *more* and *less* are at the heart of measurement. As you may or may not know, there is a well-established series of operations used to measure blood pressure, which is measured by a sphygmomanometer. The operational definition of blood pressure is "the height of a column of mercury in standard units recorded at the first Korotkoff phase (the first audible sounds of the heartbeat) and the fifth Korotkoff phase (termination of audible sounds)." The Korotkoff phases give us systolic and diastolic readings, respectively. We now have measured numbers that we can compare and contrast with other numbers obtained by the same operations. Thus, an **operational definition** is *the definition of a concept in terms of the operations used to measure it.*

Consider the concept of recidivism—how do social scientists go about measuring recidivism? We can measure it as re-arrest, reconviction, violation of probation/parole, re-offense, re-incarceration, technical violation, and many more. Or consider something more difficult to measure, like low self-control. How do we know someone has low self-control, as opposed to only impulsive behavior? Are impulsivity and lack of self-control the same thing? Is impulsivity part of the picture of low self-control? Should we measure low self-control attitudinally, with answers to a survey, or should we measure it behaviorally, by putting respondents in scenarios and observing how they react to specified stimuli? Our answers to these questions would affect any study on low self-control. It is imperative, therefore, that we are always extremely clear regarding how we are measuring our phenomenon, no matter how much we think the operational definition is "obvious."

Figure 1-2 shows how the courts in Ohio operationalize the concepts of crime seriousness and prior record. Note that numbers have been assigned to different

FIGURE 1-2

An example of operationalization

Felony Sentencing Worksheet

Defendant's Name: _____ Case No. _____

OFFENSE RATING

1. Degree of Offense
Assess points for the one most serious offense or its equivalent for which offender is being sentenced, as follows: 1st degree felony = 4 points; 2nd degree felony = 3 points; 3rd degree felony = 2 points; 4th degree felony = 1 point.

2. Multiple Offenses
Assess 2 points if one or more of the following applies: (A) offender is being sentenced for two or more offenses committed in different incidents; (B) offender is currently under a misdemeanor or felony sentence imposed by any court or (C) present offense was committed while offender on probation or parole.

OFFENDER RATING

1. Prior Convictions
Assess 2 points for each verified prior conviction, any jurisdiction. Count adjudications of delinquency for felony as convictions.

Assess 1 point for each verified prior misdemeanor conviction, and jurisdiction. Count adjudications of delinquency for misdemeanor as convictions. Do not count traffic or intoxication offenses as disorderly conduct, disturbing the peace, or equivalent offenses.

2. Repeat Offenses
Assess 2 points if present offense is offense of violence, sex offense, theft offense, or drug abuse offense, and offender has one or more prior convictions for same type of offense.

3. Actual or Potential Harm

Assess 2 points if one or more of the following applies: (A) serious physical harm to a person was caused; (B) property damage or loss of $300 or more was caused; (C) there was a high risk of any such harm, damage, or loss, though not caused; (D) the gain or potential gain from theft offense(s) was $300 or more or (E) dangerous ordinance or a deadly weapon was actually used in the incident, or its use was attempted or threatened.

4. Culpability

Assess 2 points if one or more of the following applies: (A) offender was engaging in continuing criminal activity as a source of income or livelihood; (B) offense was part of a continuing conspiracy to which offender was party, or (C) offense included shocking and deliberate cruelty in which offender participated or acquiesced.

5. Mitigation

Deduct 1 point for each of the following, as applicable: (A) there was substantial provocation, justification or excuse for offense; (B) victim induced or facilitated offense; (C) offense was committed in the heat of anger, and (D) the property damaged, lost or stolen was restored or recovered without significant cost to the victim.

Net Total = Offender Rating

INDICATED SENTENCE

3. Prison Commitments

Assess 2 points if offender was committed one or more times to a penitentiary, reformatory or equivalent institution in any jurisdiction. Count commitments to state youth commission or similar commitments in other jurisdictions.

4. Parole and Similar Violations

Assess 2 points if one or more of the following applies: (A) offender has previously had probation or parole for misdemeanor or felony revoked; (B) present offense committed while offender on probation or parole; (C) present offense committed while offender free on bail; or (D) present offense committed while offender in custody.

5. Credits

Deduct 1 point for each of the following, as applicable: (A) offender has voluntarily made bona fide, realistic arrangements for at least partial restitution; (B) offender was age 25 or older at time of first felony conviction; (C) offender has been substantially law-abiding for at least 3 years; and (D) offender lives with his or her spouse or minor children or both and is either a breadwinner for the family or, if there are tinier children, a housewife.

Net Total = Offender Rating

-Circle the box on the chart where the offense and offender ratings determined on the previous page intersect. This indicates a normal sentencing package.

FIGURE 1-2
Continued

		OFFENDER RATING				
		0–2	3–5	6–8	9–11	12 or more
Offense Rating	6 or More	Impose one of three lowest minimum terms No probation	Impose one of three highest minimum terms No probation	Impose one of three highest minimum terms No probation	Impose one of two highest minimum terms. Make at least part of multiple sentences consecutive. No probation	Impose highest minimum term. Make at least part of multiple sentences consecutive. No probation
	5	Impose one of three lowest minimum terms Some form of probation indicated only with special mitigation	Impose one of three lowest minimum terms No probation	Impose one of three highest minimum terms No probation	Impose one of three highest minimum terms No probation	Impose one of two highest minimum terms. Make at least part of multiple sentences consecutive. No probation
	4	Impose one of two lowest minimum terms Some form of probation indicated	Impose one of three lowest terms Some form of probation indicated only with special mitigation	Impose one of three lowest minimum terms No probation	Impose one of three highest minimum terms No probation	Impose one of three highest minimum terms No probation
	3	Impose one of two lowest minimum terms Some form of probation indicated	Impose one of two lowest minimum terms Some form of probation indicated	Impose one of three lowest minimum terms Some form of probation indicated only with special mitigation	Impose one of three lowest minimum terms No probation	Impose one of three highest minimum terms No probation
	0–2	Impose lowest minimum term Some form of probation indicated	Impose one of two lowest minimum terms Some form of probation indicated	Impose one of two lowest minimum terms Some form of probation indicated	Impose one of three lowest minimum terms Some form of probation indicated only with special mitigation	Impose one of three lowest minimum terms No probation

aspects of the crime and to the offender's criminal history. Those numbers are then summed to give each individual a crime seriousness and prior record score. The felony sentencing worksheet is the operational definition of these two variables.

No matter how many indicators we use to measure a concept, we never exhaust its meaning. For instance, an IQ test is an operationalization of the concept of intelligence, but it doesn't necessarily get at the essence of the concept of intelligence. You may be an excellent student in all respects, but you won't get an A in most courses unless you achieve a cumulative score of 90 percent or more (the operational definition of the concept of academic excellence) on your examinations. Being clear about our operationalizations—and being careful to operationalize our variables—is key to understanding and interpreting statistics.

VALIDITY AND RELIABILITY

Researchers wish to be sure that the instruments used to measure their concepts are both valid and reliable (see Box 1-2). **Validity** refers to how well the measures derived from the methodological/statistical operation reflect the conceptual focus of the study. That is, are we measuring what we intend to measure? Does it reflect reality? **Reliability** refers to the consistency with which the same measure produces the same results across time and across observers. The validity of a blood pressure gauge is determined pragmatically. That is, individuals whose blood pressure is consistently high, say 180/95, have different cardiovascular histories than individuals whose blood pressure is normal or low, say 120/75, for instance. Note that the concepts *high* and *low* in this context have definite numbers attached to them. A blood pressure gauge is reliable if two or more health workers obtain the same reading with the same patient or if the same researcher obtains identical readings from the same person with a different gauge.

The assessment of reliability and validity of a social science instrument, such as a scale to measure job satisfaction or low self-control, is usually done mathematically. Other times, social scientists engage in qualitative research to assess the validity of a quantitative instrument. If quantitative research—the domain of statistics—is using numbers to explore social phenomena, then qualitative research is using nonquantifiable or nonnumeric methods of studying social phenomena. Rather than reducing social phenomena to numbers, qualitative criminologists attempt to understand the nature, etiology, and consequences of crime through means that are not easily quantifiable, such as direct observation and interviews. Such methods are also useful for testing the validity of a given quantitative measurement: if an officer indicated that his or her job satisfaction was a satisfied "4" of a scale of "5," yet in an interview complained vehemently about the NYPD, the validity of that job satisfaction scale may be called into question. Other social science variables, such as race, biological sex, number of children, or whether an immigrant is a U.S. citizen, are straightforward and measured by simple observation or by a single question. Whatever the concept we are operationalizing is, for it to be included in a quantitative model or as a statistic or parameter, it must be given a numeric value that validly expresses its core concept.

VARIABLES

Observations that we measure are called **variables**, which refer to anything that can change in value from case to case; that is, it varies. Gender is a variable because cases vary from male to female. Job satisfaction is a variable because responses to a job satisfaction scale can be arranged on a continuum from those scoring lowest to those scoring highest. What if *all* participants in a particular study on violent offending are male? In this case, although *male* is an attribute of the variable *gender*, gender is not a variable in the data set because all offenders are male. For this particular case, gender of offender is a **constant** because gender does not vary from case to case. We will explain the details behind this later, but for now, it is imperative for you to understand that only variables can be analyzed statistically.

Dependent and Independent Variables

The role variables play in research is one of the ways variables can be classified. A **dependent variable** is a variable that depends on the value of another variable or variables for its own values. The variables on which the dependent variable depends for its values are called **independent variables**. Independent variables "cause" changes in dependent variables; dependent variables are "affected" by independent variables. In the examples under the *Thinking Statistically* section at the beginning of the chapter, gender was the independent variable said to affect variation in TV watching, the dependent variable; a liking for death metal music (independent variable) was said to affect the rate of unwed motherhood (dependent variable); and race—or perhaps prejudice toward one race (independent variable)—was said to affect sentencing severity (dependent variable). Many variables can be independent or dependent variables in different contexts. Gender and race obviously cannot be dependent variables in the sense that they can be thought of as caused by some antecedent social variable, but liking death metal could be a dependent variable and unwed motherhood could be an independent variable in some contexts. For example, perhaps one's peer group enjoys listening to death metal music, thus influencing one's own musical preferences. In this case, peer group is the independent variable, whereas death metal preference is the dependent variable.

Variables can be discrete (often referred to as *categorical*) or continuous. **Discrete or categorical variables** classify observations according to the kind or quality of their characteristics. Yes/no, black/white, and male/female are examples of discrete and dichotomous (division of two) variables. Discrete variables can take on more divisions than two: religious affiliation, ethnic origin, and income categories are examples of multicategory discrete variables. We can also rank some discrete variables, such as first, second, or third place or first- and second-degree murder and manslaughter.

Continuous variables can theoretically take on any value between two points on a scale and be classified according to the magnitude and quantity of their characteristics. What this means is simpler than it first appears: you can do math with continuous variables, which you cannot for discrete variables. You cannot, for example, make the statement that Catholic + Protestant = Hindu. You can, however, make the statement that the average level of job satisfaction is 2.711. An average is a statistic that is calculated by dividing the sum (represented by the Greek letter *sigma*, Σ) of all responses (represented by the letter x) by the total number of responses (represented by the letter n; we will get into statistical notation later, but for now, know that we can write this same statement with fewer figures: $\Sigma x/n$—statistics is also a language—a thrifty language!).

In addition, we can create (or recode) categorical variables from continuous variables, *but not the other way around*. For example, it is possible to divide age into any number of values on a continuum of years, months, days, hours, and seconds, for example, ages 0–12, 13–18, and 19 or older. If we began with these categories, however, we could not ascertain one's exact age. Discrete variables have sharply demarcated distinct values—you cannot have 1.5 yes answers or 2.45 males, nor can you have sold 25.35 cars last year.

The rules we use to assign numbers to observations result in various **levels of measurement**. Information comes to us in many forms, ranging from crude to refined. The statistics we use in our research depend greatly on the relative crudeness or refinement of our measures. There are four levels of measurement with different properties that are important to understand: nominal, ordinal, interval, and ratio. These levels are hierarchical and cumulative in that each higher level incorporates the characteristics of those levels beneath it as well as having its own special characteristic. Nominal and ordinal variables are qualitative variables and are discrete or categorical. Although they may differ in kind, they cannot be expressed numerically except in an arbitrary fashion. Interval and ratio measures are quantitative and continuous and can be expressed numerically.

Nominal Level

The **nominal level** is the crudest form of measurement and is used only to classify, that is, to name observations that are different in some qualitative way. The categories of the classification scheme should be *mutually exclusive* and *exhaustive*. To be mutually exclusive means that if an observation can be placed in any one category, it cannot be placed in another category. For example, if a researcher is interested in religious affiliation and a particular respondent to the survey question answers "Catholic," we could not say of that person that he or she is anything but Catholic when it comes to religious affiliation. To be exhaustive means that the categories cover all possible categories of a variable that could be included. For example, if we are interested in the variable of biological sex, the three categories of "male," "female," and "intersex" should be included, and being placed in any one of these three categories automatically excludes the respondent from being placed in one of the other categories. Thus, the list of possible answers or categories is both mutually exclusive (only one answer can be given) and exhaustive (all possible answers are available).

The numbers assigned to nominal-level data are arbitrary. The researcher may assign the number 0 to nonminority and 1 to minority. A nominal variable, such as race, that includes only two categories (nonminority/minority) is called a **dichotomous variable** (sometimes referred to as a **binary** variable), meaning it only has two possible categories (such as either male or female, black or white, old or young). If the researcher is interested in religion, he or she might numerically code Catholics = 1, atheists = 2, and Jews = 3 or any other sensible coding system. As explained above, we cannot perform mathematical operations such as adding, subtracting, dividing, and multiplying with nonquantitative data (you cannot multiply Catholics by Jews and arrive at some meaningful third value). Numbers assigned to categories in this way are nothing more than labels and are used for later statistical analysis. Statistical formulas for variables measured at this level make use of category frequencies (how many males, females, Catholics, etc., are in the data), not the numeric code value used to identify a particular category of the variable. For further explanation, see chapter 2.

Ordinal Level

Variables measured at the **ordinal level** can be ranked as well as classified. That is, we can put the data in an order that ranges somewhere from bottom to top, low to high, or less to more. For example, we can ask all students in the classroom to stand. We can then arrange them in a line based on descending order of height. Note that when we do this we have a rank order, but we do not have the precise measures of the differences among the heights of the individuals. We know that the tallest person is at the top and the shortest person is at the bottom and that every other person is located in his or her proper ascending or descending location. We do not have the precise heights of the tallest person or the shortest person or any person; we just have the right order.

Examples of ordinal-level data are class standing. For example, if we're studying college students by years in college, we would have to include freshman, sophomore, junior, and senior (categories that, incidentally, are more often determined by credits completed—a continuous variable—than by actual years completed). Or we could measure social class as lower, middle, or upper or even rank order the seriousness of crime (less to more serious). These categories can be perceived only as *more* or *less* since we cannot validly assign an arithmetic interval separating them. That is, first-degree murder is, statistically speaking, not twice as serious as manslaughter because manslaughter + second-degree murder ≠ first-degree murder.

Interval Level

The **interval level** is the next highest level of measurement. At this level, in addition to classification and order, we have equal units of measurement; that is, there are precisely defined intervals between and among the observations. For instance, the interval between 5 and 10 is exactly the same as the interval between 25 and 30, and both are identical in magnitude to the interval between 1,155 and 1,160. An example of an interval-level variable is IQ. Consider four individuals with IQ scores of 70, 140, 75, and 145. We can say that the differences between 70 and 140 and between 75 and 145 are exactly the same, but we cannot say that the second person is twice as intelligent as the first. All we can say is that those with the higher scores are more intelligent than those with the lower scores. Almost any measurement scale in the social sciences (self-esteem, alienation, delinquency, etc.) is an interval-level measurement. What we lack with an interval scale is a stable starting point. Typically, this is considered an absolute zero, which is when a zero is considered to mean an absence of the phenomenon. Consequently, the scale values cannot be interpreted in any absolute sense. This limits the suite of mathematical operations available to us in theory (although, in practice, we often break this rule). However, we can perform a large number of mathematical operations with interval data not possible with nominal and ordinal data.

Ratio Level

The **ratio level** has all the properties of the lower measurement scales in addition to an absolute zero point. We can classify it, we can place it in proper order, the numbers we use to measure it are of equal magnitudes, and it has a meaningful zero. Examples include height, years of education, income, and years sentenced to prison. We can use all sorts of mathematical procedures with ratio-level variables, including multiplication and division. Someone with an income of $50,000 makes precisely twice as much as someone with an income of $25,000, which produces a meaningful ratio of 2:1.

It is important to be aware of the level at which you have measured your variables because the choice of statistical analysis depends on it. However, we must point out that there are arguments among statisticians regarding level of measurement issues. The main bone of contention is whether it is permissible to treat certain ordinal variables as continuous-level variables to take advantage of superior statistical techniques. An alienation scale ranging from a possible low of 0 to a possible high of 40 would be treated by most researchers as continuous, although such a scale only approximates the equidistant functions of true continuous scales. That is, although scores on an alienation scale are continuous, they have properties that lie somewhere between ordinal and interval levels of measurement.

This does not mean that all ordinal variables can be properly treated as continuous variables. Generally, the greater the number of ranks or categories of the measured ordinal variable, the greater confidence we may have in treating the variable as being continuous. Scores on an alienation scale ranging from 0 to 40, for example, can be much more validly treated as a continuous variable than if they were divided into low, medium, and high levels of alienation. A further consideration is the approximation to the equidistant function. A scoring system that looks like 0, 1, 2, 3, 4, 5 is much better than one that looks like 0, 8, 9, 16, 28, 42. The latter scoring system is far from being equidistant and begins to look much like discrete ordered categories. Table 1-1 illustrates the cumulative and hierarchical character of the four levels of measurement.

TABLE 1-1. *Characteristics of Levels of Measurement*

USE THE ACRONYM *NOIR* TO HELP REMEMBER THE LEVELS OF MEASUREMENT: **N**OMINAL, **O**RDINAL, **I**NTERVAL, AND **R**ATIO

Measurement	Classify	Order	Equal Units	Absolute Zero
Nominal	Yes	No	No	No
Ordinal	Yes	Yes	No	No
Interval	Yes	Yes	Yes	No
Ratio	Yes	Yes	Yes	Yes

THE ROLE OF STATISTICS IN SCIENCE

As you know by now, many other considerations take place before researchers actually apply statistical techniques to their data. Figure 1-3 illustrates the place of statistical analysis in the scientific enterprise. Almost all research starts with the researcher's immersion in theory related to the proposed research. We begin with theory because theory tells us not only what is already known in a given area, but also where and how to look for new information about it. To begin a research project without a thorough knowledge of theories pertaining to the subject matter of the project is like taking a trip into unknown territory without either a guide or a map—but much less exciting. Rather, it quickly becomes a frustrating enterprise. A theory is similar to the major premise in logical argumentation—"*if* this is true, *then* this should be true." Philosophers use these kinds of "if/then" statements to arrive at a logical conclusion derived from what is assumed to be a self-evident premise. If the major premise is true ("All men are mortal"), and if the minor premise is also true ("Plato is a man"), then the conclusion ("Plato is mortal") is logically correct. This is a **deductive** process—arguing from the general to the particular—from a theory to conclusions.

However, the conclusion for the philosopher is only the beginning for the scientist. The philosopher's conclusion based on reason is formally known as a **hypothesis** by scientists, who demand more proof than logical reasoning alone affords, because logic is only as good as the premise it is based on. Simply put, the hypothesis is a *testable statement* about the relationships between or among the variables that are to be studied. For example: we can argue that *The Andy Griffith Show* was originally broadcast as a black-and-white television show. Further, we know that some species of penguins are black and white. *Ipso facto*, we must conclude that penguins are,

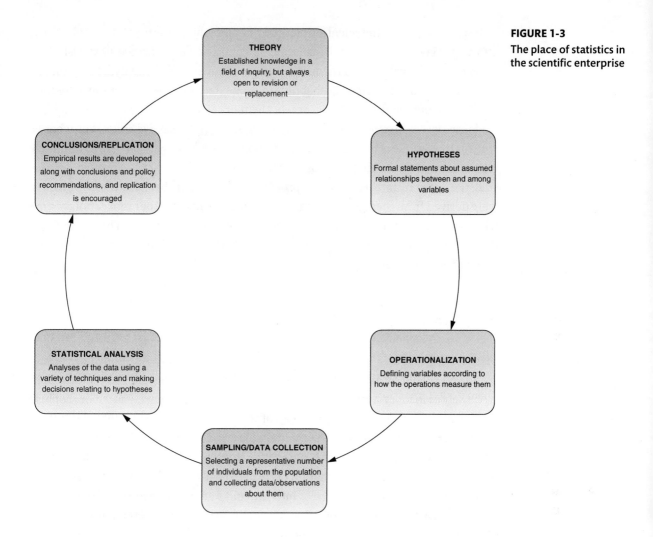

FIGURE 1-3
The place of statistics in the scientific enterprise

in fact, reruns of *The Andy Griffith Show*. The reasoning process for scientists proceeds from theory to hypothesis, rather than from premise to conclusion. The hypothesis must then be put to the test.

The next step is the operationalization of the concepts contained in the hypothesis. As we have seen, this entails defining concepts in terms of the operations used to measure them. The next step is to take a representative sample of individuals from the population of interest and apply our measuring instruments and/or collect data/observations about the sample elements (sample elements consist of units of analysis, which much of the time consist of people, but can also consist of other elements such as police departments, neighborhoods, cities, states, and so on).

It is at this point in the scientific method that the subject matter of this book comes into play. Having taken our measurements/collected our data, the next task is to apply our statistical tools to them. The results of our statistical analyses will enable us with a certain degree of probability to make decisions regarding our hypothesized assumptions; that is, do we accept them or reject them? If we decide that the evidence derived from the sample supports our hypothesis, we infer that what is true for the sample is probably true in the population from which it came, although we are always aware that the possibility exists that it may not be (remember: the statistics covered in this book are *probabilistic*). Further, because the hypotheses were derived from theory, we may also conclude, through further replication of similar analyses in different contexts, that the theory is supported. The circle from theory and back again is therefore completed. The journey is a fascinating one, but one that is never as neat and tidy as we have presented it.

SUMMARY

Statistics is becoming an increasingly important field of study. As a consumer of statistics you should be aware of the many ways that the producers of statistics, either purposely or inadvertently, can mislead you. This book will make you a more sophisticated consumer, as well as a producer, of statistics.

Descriptive statistics describe data in simple and direct ways using graphs, charts, percentages, proportions, ratios, and rates. Inferential statistics make inferences about a population from information derived from a sample. A population is the totality of all observations that are of interest, and a sample is a subset of the population. We estimate population characteristics, called parameters, from sample characteristics, called statistics. In our estimation of parameters there will always be a certain amount of error, although we can quantify this error and take it into account. However, before we can estimate any parameter, such as the average level of job satisfaction of a population of police officers, we must be able to measure it. Before we can measure it we must define it operationally, that is, in terms of the operations used to measure it.

Measurement is the assignment of numbers to observations according to rules. We measure variables, defined as some characteristic or trait that takes on different values across observations, at four different levels of measurement. Nominal-level variables, the crudest level, have mutually exclusive and exhaustive categories that differ from one another only qualitatively. There is no implied order or equality of distance between the categories. The ordinal level of measurement allows for the rank ordering of categories, but not with respect to equal distance. The interval level of measurement has categories of equal distance between continuous variables, but they lack a true zero point. The ratio level of measurement is the highest form of measurement in that it contains all the attributes of the lower levels in addition to having a true zero point. Only interval- and ratio-level variables are amenable to mathematical operations. Each level of measurement has the attributes of lower levels as well as its own.

At the end of the day, statistics are part math, part interpretation. Throughout this book we will draw a clear line between what is math and what is analytic interpretation, but we do this only as a teaching tool: the fact is that in statistics, the interpretation is made in light of the underlying math. We hope that you keep this in mind as you progress through this book and that you apply this to the practice problems as well.

PRACTICE APPLICATION: VARIABLES AND LEVELS OF MEASUREMENT

A researcher decides to generate a statistical description of a class of 11 students on four variables: sex, class standing, IQ, and the number of days this academic year that the student has skipped class—that is, a status offense, truancy. These measurements are made and placed in Table 1-2.

The first variable, sex, is a discrete, dichotomous, qualitative variable measured at the nominal level. It has no quantitative value, and all we can do arithmetically is count the numbers of males and females in the sample. The second variable, class standing, is a discrete, ordered, qualitative variable measured at the ordinal level. Isaac and Jillian are of higher class standing than Lucas, Jacari, Sam, Makenna, David, and Daniel, who are themselves of higher standing than Justin, Kaiya, or Reyna. Here we can talk about higher and lower, but nothing else. If there were a direct one-to-one relationship between the number of years spent in college and class standing, we could conceptualize this variable as ratio level and make statements such as "Lucas has been in school twice as long as Kaiya." However, as the variable is currently conceptualized, we cannot even assume that Lucas has been going to school as long as David. His superior IQ, especially in relation to David's, makes it possible that he could have passed more classes than David in less time.

The third variable, IQ, is a continuous, quantitative variable measured at the interval level. Since we have equal units, we can say that the difference between David's and Daniel's IQ scores (five points) is exactly the same as the difference between

TABLE 1-2. *Description of College Students in Criminal Justice 201*

| Student | VARIABLE AND LEVEL OF MEASUREMENT | | | |
	Sex (nominal)	Class Standing (ordinal)	IQ (interval)	Truant (ratio)
Justin	0	1	120	1
Jillian	1	3	115	0
Lucas	0	2	125	2
Jacari	1	2	132	0
Samuel	0	2	108	4
Kaiya	1	1	130	5
Reyna	1	1	103	8
Makenna	1	2	165	0
Isaac	0	3	111	6
David	0	2	85	18
Daniel	0	2	90	15

Coding: Sex: 0 = male, 1 = female. Class standing: 1 = freshman, 2 = sophomore, 3 = junior, 4 = senior. IQ = continuous. Truant = continuous (count).

Sam's and Reyna's. However, although Makenna's IQ score is numerically almost twice that of David's, we cannot say that she is almost twice as intelligent because IQ scales lack a precise absolute zero.

The final variable, number of days truant, is a continuous, quantitative variable measured at the ratio level. Since truant has an absolute zero, we can validly say that Kaiya was truant five times as much as Jillian and Jacari. Note again that the ratio level of measurement contains all the attributes of the lower levels (name, order, equal units) in addition to having an absolute zero point.

REFERENCES

Lohr, S. (2009). For today's graduate, just one word: Statistics. *New York Times*, August 5: A1.

Martinson, R. (1974). What works? Questions and answers about prison reform. *The Public Interest* (Spring): 22–54.

CHAPTER 2

Presenting Data

LEARNING OBJECTIVES:

After reading this chapter, the student will understand the following concepts:

- The importance of summarizing and visualizing raw data
- How to calculate and interpret raw counts, percentages, and rates
- How to calculate and interpret bar, pie, and line charts
- The nature of distributions and how to graph distributions as histograms

INTRODUCTION

Prior to getting into the meat of this book, we want to spend some time talking about how to present data. *Data* is the plural of the word *datum*, which is simply a piece of information. For our purposes, it is most often a piece of *numerical* information that we can combine with other pieces of numerical information and submit this collection of datum to statistical analysis. When we have several pieces of datum we have a data set—and data sets can often become extremely large. Trying to understand a data set by just scanning the raw numbers for patterns and relationships is overwhelming, inefficient, and in many cases simply impossible. This chapter therefore provides an overview of several common and elementary techniques for presenting your data, or more specifically, the summary patterns and relationships found *within* your data, in a meaningful fashion.

Cogently presenting data is an incredibly important tool for the statistical analyst. As we've already suggested, how we present our data can aid in how it's later interpreted by other people. A data set left in its raw form can readily tell us very little—we must take some steps to make all those numbers comprehensible. Even a simple ordering of the data (for example, from lowest score to highest score) can go a long way toward helping us get a handle on what's going on in a data set. In addition to making a data set easier to consume, how we present the data can help us actually analyze it. When we rearrange the data in understandable forms—such as the forms we discuss in this chapter—we begin to see patterns that are not quickly or even easily apparent. This is the first step in any statistical analysis.

To this end, we cover a number of basic techniques for how to meaningfully present your data or, more correctly, summaries of your data. We will start with numerical presentations, including simple counts, then percentages, and finally rates. Although we move from the most simple technique to the most complex, you'll see that even rates hardly merit the word "complex" here, either in terms of the math involved or in their interpretation. Then, we'll discuss some visual ways to present data, where we'll cover bar, pie, and line charts and graphs. These are simple yet powerful tools that not only help the analyst understand their data, but also help others quickly and simply grasp the story that complex statistics can tell us. Finally, we conclude this chapter by talking about frequency distributions. Frequency distributions are at the heart of probabilistic statistics, and understanding how they are constructed and interpreted is essential. We will consider both their numeric construction and how to present them graphically.

STANDARDIZING DATA

In one sense, all statistics are trying to do one thing: standardize some raw number so that we can compare it to other standardized raw numbers. To **standardize** means to render a number comparable to other numbers or, essentially, to remove the *scale* behind the number. Consider, for example, if city A experienced 10,000 arrests last year and city B experienced 100,000. At first glance, it appears that city B is in dire straits when compared to city A. These are what we would call the raw data or the raw numbers or, more formally, count data. We present more information on count data in a moment, but what matters now is how deceptive these raw numbers might be. For example, imagine that city A only has a population of 100,000 and city B has a population of 100,000,000. Knowing this information, does that change your opinion about which city is in dire straits? It should. With the population as an anchoring point, we can standardize these counts into what are known as rates, such as the number of arrests (numerator) per 1,000 occupants (denominator) in any given city. For example, the arrest rate for city A is 100 arrests per 1,000 people, compared to city B at 1 arrest per 1,000 people (arrest rate = number of arrests/

population × 1,000). Clearly, city A has the graver crime concern. In this section, we first consider counts, then discuss percentages, and conclude with rates. Much of this should be review—we use these quotients regularly in everyday parlance. Let us now formalize our use of these terms.

Counts

Count data is precisely what it sounds like: it is a numerical count of the data. In the preceding paragraph, we compared count data to raw data, and although this is true, it can be a bit misleading. For example, imagine that we have a data set that includes the variable *type of crime*, with the options of either *property* or *violent*. We can then *count* the raw data according to *type of crime*.

The data set may look something like this:

ID	TYPE
1	1
2	1
3	0
4	0
5	1
6	0
7	0
8	0
.	
.	
.	
134	1

Box 2-1
Coding Data

Coding is the process of assigning numerical values to categories of data and comes in handy for analyzing categorical data (we discuss this process in later chapters). To code a simple binary variable, such as whether someone is a police officer, we could say that everyone who is a police officer is coded as 1 and everyone who is not a police officer is coded as 0. We can do the same thing with more categories, too. For example: line officer = 0, sergeant = 1, and brass = 2.

Box 2-2
When to Use N *and* n

Researchers generally use two symbols when referring to the number of "units" such as people, jails, and neighborhoods, in the samples that are being studied. Generally, the use of "N" refers to the entire sample or total number of units in a given sample, such as $N = 134$ people (people are our unit of analysis here). On the other hand, "n" refers most often to the use of a "subgroup" within our total sample. For example, let's say that of the $N = 134$ people in our sample, there are $n = 75$ males and $n = 59$ females. That way you can differentiate between the entire sample and subgroups within that sample, which ultimately leads to less confusion amongst your readers.

In this data set, we have coded *type of crime* such that 0 = property crime and 1 = violent crime (see Box 2-1). Note in this data set that there are 134 subjects (in statistical terms, we would write $N = 134$, which is read as "an N of 134"; see Box 2-2 for the general rules surrounding the use of N or n). Without organizing the data into categories of 0's (property crimes) and 1's (violent crimes), we are left with a handful of data that vary between 0 and 1. By putting things into categories, we can get a better idea of what's going on. For example, we might find that of 134 criminals, 87 were property offenders and 47 were violent offenders.

But this is as far as count data will let us go. In this particular data set, we can compare the number of property offenders to the number of violent offenders, but that's it. If we had another data set of property and violent offenders, we might not be able to compare them. This would be the case, for example, if their N's were different. Imagine a second data set where we had $N = 3,047$, with 1,793 property offenders and 1,254 violent offenders. Certainly, the numbers of offenders in *either* category are larger in the second data set compared to the first. But this should be evident: there are *more* people in data set 2 than in data set 1. So although counts help us organize and wrap our heads around the basic structure of the data, we must take further steps before we can present the data in both a meaningful and a logical way.

Percentages

One such method is to calculate percentages. **Percentages** are quotients: something that is divided by something else. The resulting value is then often multiplied by 100 so that we can say things like "*x* percent." By way of example, let's take data set 1 from above. In this example, we'd like to see what percentage of offenders in the data set are property offenders compared to violent offenders. The numerator for each category will be the raw count of type of offenders (either property or violent), and the denominator will be the N, or total number of observations, or in this case people, in our sample. In other words, the math behind a percentage takes some category and pits it against the total of all categories and then standardizes it (if we did not multiply it by, say, 100, we would have a proportion, not a percentage). So we'd calculate our first data set like this: property offenders: $87/134 = 0.6492$ and for violent offenders: $47/134 = 0.3507$. We can make the interpretation of these proportions easier by multiplying these quotients by 100: 0.6492 becomes 64.92 percent and 0.3507 becomes 35.07 percent. This allows us to say that, for data set 1, about 65 percent of the offenders committed property crimes compared to only 35 percent who committed violent offenses. Giving some leeway for rounding error, these two percentages should add up to 100.

Percentages also allow us to compare *different data sets*. We can now, therefore, meaningfully compare the two data sets from above. Since we have already completed the math for data set 1, let's jump right to the math for data set 2: $1,793/3,047 \times 100 = 58.84$ percent are property offenders and $1,254/3,047 \times 100 = 41.16$ percent are violent offenders. Thus we can safely say that data set 1 is composed of *more* property offenders (64.92 percent) and *fewer* violent offenders (35.07 percent) when compared with data set 2 (58.84 percent and 41.16 percent, respectively). With just the raw numbers, this wasn't as evident—if it was evident at all.

Rates

When we multiply our proportion quotient by 100, thereby transforming it into a percentage, we are doing two things. First, we are standardizing *by* 100. That is, we are anchoring our raw numbers by the value 100. Doing so allows us to discuss the counts with a nice round 100. Percentages make intuitive sense to us: the question, "what percentage" requires little explanation. In the same way that we know what a jar that is about 75 percent full of peanut butter looks like, we understand what we mean when we say that 65 percent of offenders in data set 1 are property offenders. Multiplying by a constant such as 100 also allows us to discuss the raw count data in another way: as the number of persons per 100. That is, saying that 65 percent of offenders from data set 1 are property offenders is the same thing as saying "for every 100 offenders, 65 are property offenders." This can also be stated as "65 in every 100 offenders are property offenders" or written as 65:100 (which we can, of course, reduce to 13:20 if we wanted to or if it makes sense to).

In some respects, the choice of 100 as a constant is quite arbitrary. We can pretty much choose *any* number. Convention dictates that we choose multiples of 10, however; values such as 100, 1,000, or even 100,000 work well (the standard the U.S. Census and many other governmental agencies use) because of how intuitively interpretable they are. We typically interpret the rate/ratio as "*x* in *n*" or "*number of events* per/in *n*" or the constant (but see Box 2-3). Let's return to the first example of this section:

> Consider, for example, if city A experienced 10,000 arrests last year and city B experienced 100,000. At first glance, it appears that city B is in dire straits when compared to city A . . . Imagine that city B has a population of 100,000,000, and city A only has a population of 100,000. Knowing this information, does that change your opinion about which city is in dire straits? It should. With the population as an anchoring point, we can standardize these counts into what is known as a rate. The crime rate for city A is 10:100, compared to city B at 0.1:100 (arrest rate = number of arrests/population × 100).

Those two values, 10:100 and 0.1:100, are *rates*. They were calculated by dividing the total number of arrests for each city by that city's population. So for city A, 10,000/100,000 = 0.10. When we multiply this by the constant 100, we get 10. We would therefore say that the arrest rate for city A is 10 in 100, or for every 100 persons we would expect 10 arrests. And for city B, 100,000/100,000,000 = 0.001,

---

Box 2-3
The Difference between a Rate and a Ratio

Many of us often confuse rates with ratios and vice versa. A ratio is simply a comparison of two numbers measured with the same unit/type; such as 3 beers to 6 beers, or simply 3:6. Sometimes ratios are expressed as proportions and percentages. On the other hand, a rate implies a relationship between two non-identical measured units, such as your rate of speed, which is calculated by dividing distance (numerator) by time (denominator). To follow our example above, you might compare the differences in the rates of beers imbibed by a sample of college students on a Saturday night after watching their favorite football team win and another sample of students prior to taking a midterm stats exam. The rate for either would be calculated as the following: drinking rate per hour = number of beers ingested (numerator) divided by time in hours (denominator).

> **Box 2-4**
> **A Cautionary Note**
>
> According to the *individualistic fallacy*, we cannot analyze individuals to make conclusions about groups—groups act differently than people (observed behavior moves from the individual to the group). Likewise, we cannot take group level statistics, such as those reported above, and apply them to individuals; a similar error referred to as the *ecological fallacy*. An example of the individualistic fallacy would be: student A, who goes to Acme University, is lazy and sleeps in class; therefore all students who attend Acme University are lazy and sleep in class. An example of the ecological fallacy would be: a majority of Acme University students drink root beer, therefore student A drinks root beer.

multiplied by 100 is 0.1, or for every 100 persons we would expect one-tenth of an arrest. This is how we know that crime in city A is more prevalent than in city B.

But "1/10 for every 100 persons" doesn't make much sense—which is the point of converting raw counts to rates in the first place. Remember that the constant we choose is arbitrary. So long as it makes sense (as most multiples of 100 do) and we apply it to all the quotients we are interested in comparing, we are on safe ground. So rather than multiply by 100, let's use 1,000 as our constant. This renders an arrest rate for city A of 100 arrests for every 1,000 people and an arrest rate of 1 for every 1,000 people in city B.

Using rates, especially crime rates, is extremely important because of **units of analysis**. In this example, our unit of analysis is the city, rather than individual arrestees; we therefore need a statistic that represents crime at the "city" level. Rates are an excellent representation of arrests at the city level because they consider all of the crime in the city independently of individual offenders (see Box 2-4 for a cautionary note on logical fallacies). Rates are a hallmark of criminal justice and criminological research.

VISUALIZING DATA

Graphical displays of data, such as figures (charts and graphs) and tables, are a quick way to visualize the information that can be presented in the numerical formats we discussed above. As with the methods above, they help us tease out patterns and potential relationships that may not be as obvious by just scanning the raw data. Because they do so visually, they tend to be more easily consumed by readers. There are many ways to display statistics visually; in this section, we present the most common ones, including bar, pie, and line charts.

Bar Charts

Figure 2-1 presents a simple bar chart, based on the 2010 Uniform Crime Reports. The data are the total arrests, by state. We have randomly chosen four states—each bar represents the total number of arrests for that state. In other words, we are using a bar chart to visualize count data. Bar charts can be vertical, as in Figure 2-1, or horizontal, as in Figure 2-2.

Both figures indicate that Texas had the most arrests—by far. But as we learned above, these are only the raw numbers. To more meaningfully compare these four states, we can convert the raw counts to a rate (say, arrests per 100,000 persons) and then plot these values on a bar chart. This has been done in Figure 2-3.

When displayed in this way, it is clear that *Wyoming* actually has the highest per capita arrest rate and that Virginia and Texas are quite close, with Pennsylvania having the lowest crime rate in 2012. This demonstration should be enough to convince you of just how important it is to consider standardization when comparing and presenting data.

FIGURE 2-1

An example of a bar graph—vertical

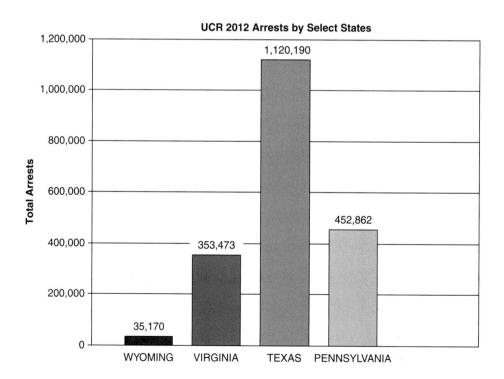

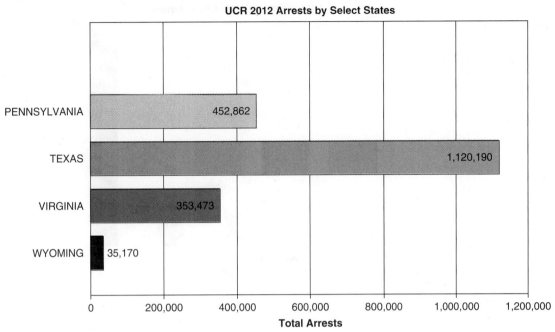

FIGURE 2-2
An example of a bar graph—horizontal

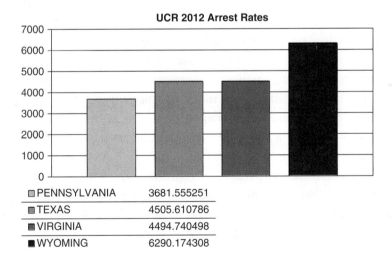

FIGURE 2-3

An example bar graph with ratios per 100,000 pop

Pie Charts

Like bar charts, pie charts are a handy way to quickly understand data. Although they can be used to display any kind of data—including raw counts and rates—we find them most useful to display percentages. Pie charts work so well for

FIGURE 2-4
Raw data for a pie chart

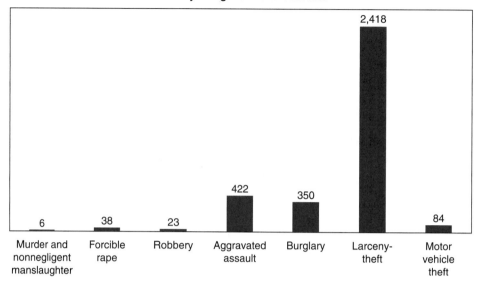

2012 Wyoming Index Crime Arrests

percentages because they present data "as a whole"—which is a nice analog for what *x* percent actually means—that is, a part of a whole. Let's consider the arrests from Wyoming one more time, but this time, let's break them down into the seven Part I index crimes: murder and nonnegligent manslaughter, forcible rape, aggravated assault, robbery, burglary, larceny-theft, and motor vehicle theft. First, let's look at the raw numbers, as displayed in a bar chart (Figure 2-4).

Because Figure 2-4 relies on the raw numbers, it actually tells us very little, beyond that there are more larceny-thefts than anything else. Therefore, we can convert these to percentages and display them in a handy pie chart, as shown in Figure 2-5.

Although we knew larceny-theft would fill the bulk of the pie, it's incredible to consider just how *much* of a bulk it fills—nearly three fourths of all arrests in Wyoming (for index offenses) can be attributed to larceny-theft. The next highest category, weighing in at merely 10 percent, is aggravated assault. (Rounding error forces the percentage attributable to murder and nonnegligent manslaughter to be listed as simply 0 percent.) As with rates, it pays to do some simple arithmetic to get a better handle on what the data look like.

Line Charts

Sometimes we are interested not only in comparing groups, but also in comparing changes in a single group (or multiple groups, for that matter) *across time*. When we are interested in temporal (time-based) changes, line charts are a powerful yet

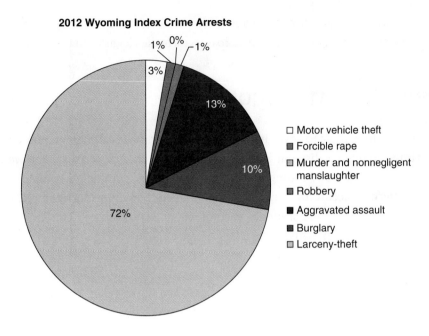

2012 Wyoming Index Crime Arrests

Legend:
- ☐ Motor vehicle theft
- ■ Forcible rape
- ☐ Murder and nonnegligent manslaughter
- ■ Robbery
- ■ Aggravated assault
- ■ Burglary
- ☐ Larceny-theft

FIGURE 2-5

An example of a pie chart

simple tool that, as with the graphs above, help us tease out patterns and relation-ships. One of the most important changes we have seen in modern criminal justice history is the dramatic drop in crime during the 1990s in the United States (and in other countries as well). Let's consider the crime drop using the rate of offenses known to police per 100,000 people as our units of observation/analysis. Such a line graph is presented in Figure 2-6.

Using arrest statistics such as this, you can see a distinct pattern of an increase in arrests followed by a sudden drop in arrests—a drop that is so dramatic that by the

Homicide Rates in the United States 1960–2013

— Homicide Rate (per 100,000)

FIGURE 2-6

An example of a line chart

(Source: FBI UCR)

late 1990s we are below the early 1980s' levels. Although we could have gleaned this by looking at the rates, plotting them across years makes it easier to distinguish.

FREQUENCY DISTRIBUTIONS

We have one final topic to cover in this chapter and it is a vital one: **frequency distributions**. Frequency distributions are the heart and soul of statistics, and we will refer to them continually throughout the book. In essence, a frequency distribution arranges the data according to category and frequency. Imagine, for example, if you have 100 Criminology 101 students, each of whom just took an exam. Their scores may look something like this:

82	79	50	96
72	79	74	78
74	73	77	64
69	82	96	80
73	74	60	63
53	68	59	81
74	64	52	73
62	77	87	78
77	65	99	79
80	94	71	76
88	74	65	72
69	59	80	62
68	72	82	96
76	85	66	91
73	71	83	85
73	68	82	60
91	61	73	64
75	78	60	80
74	73	85	76
93	81	83	75
69	69	71	77
88	72	68	56
75	78	84	72
74	72	78	66
91	77	81	65

We can make more sense of these scores if we order them:

50	69	74	81
52	69	74	81
53	69	75	81
56	69	75	82
59	71	75	82
59	71	76	82
60	71	76	82
60	72	76	83
60	72	77	83
61	72	77	84
62	72	77	85
62	72	77	85
63	72	77	85
64	73	78	87
64	73	78	88
64	73	78	88
65	73	78	91
65	73	78	91
65	73	79	91
66	73	79	93
66	74	79	94
68	74	80	96
68	74	80	96
68	74	80	96
68	74	80	99

Ordering them reveals a number of duplicates. We can create a table that summarizes how many students scored in each category:

The column labeled "Bin" represents our categories, whereas "Frequency" represents how many students can be placed in that category, according to their grade. Even a quick glance would indicate that most students earned C's, fewer students earned B's and D's, and even fewer students earned A's or F's. We can use the manner in which we organized these data in Table 2-1 to create a distribution chart (Figure 2-7).

TABLE 2-1. *Bins for a Frequency Distribution*

Bin	Frequency
0–59	6
60–69	23
70–79	42
80–89	20
90–100	9

FIGURE 2-7

An example of
a histogram

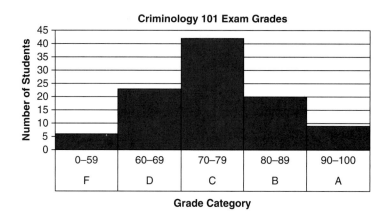

When we graph distributions, such as in Figure 2-7, we refer to them as **histograms** (see Box 2-5). Histograms help us get a handle on how the data are distributed by breaking them into meaningful categories. In our example here, the categories would include the typical grade setup of A, B, C, D, and F. The histogram

Box 2-5
The Difference between a Bar Chart and a Histogram

There is a distinction that must be made between a bar chart (as illustrated in the first few figures) and a histogram (illustrated in Figure 2-7). As you may have noticed, the bar charts had gaps between the bars, whereas the histogram did not. This is the main *visual distinction* between bar charts and histograms, but it also represents an important difference in how our variables are measured—recall our discussion of levels of measurement in the prior chapter. Generally speaking, bar charts are used for nominal/ordinal-level data and the separation of the columns implies separation of the *categories* tied to the x-axis, such as the States in our example. On the other hand, histograms are used when we have a *continuum of data* (data measured at the interval or ratio level) tied to the x-axis, like we have in Figure 2-7, or the grouped frequency distribution of grades on the Criminology 101 exam. You might be scratching your head right now, asking the question, Well, aren't letter grades categories? You'd be right to think this, and this might be an example of where you could go either way, depending on how you collected and wish to present your data graphically. Perhaps a better example might be a grouped frequency distribution of age, where there is continuity between the age categories of 16–20, 21–15, 16–30, and so on (i.e., there are no "real" gaps between 20 and 21, 15 and 16, etc.).

presented in Figure 2-7 is particularly important because it represents a **normal distribution**—one that is symmetrical, with equal respondents on either side of the center category (in this case, a C). We will revisit the normal distribution shortly.

SUMMARY

In this chapter, we covered methods of meaningfully presenting data. Data by itself—which we called raw data or count data—are important, but rarely useful in describing things. Further, using these techniques, we are better able to discern patterns and relationships within the data that, when left with only the raw data, we can rarely achieve. To this end, we discussed both numerical and visual ways of presenting the data.

Numerically, we learned how to calculate and interpret percentages and rates. Both are quotients multiplied by some constant. For percentages, that constant is 100, and thus our percentage represents the fraction that the particular category takes up of the whole. For example, in Wyoming we learned that 72 percent of all arrests for index crimes in 2010 could be considered larceny-theft. A rate, on the other hand, is any variable of interest divided by the total population and multiplied by any constant that is a multiple of 10. Most commonly this 1000, 10,000, or 100,000. A rate is interpreted as the number of events per 100,000 population.

We used bar, pie, and line charts to better visualize such summary, or frequency, statistics. Bar charts help us look at categories, especially rates, whereas pie charts help us visualize percentages. Line charts are best for observing differences within the same category across time. Such changes are termed *trends*. Finally, we learned how to construct a histogram using the distribution of data. A histogram is a special kind of chart that we can create by organizing our continuous data into meaningful categories, such as grades. The histogram that we observed in this chapter is a special kind of distribution known as a normal distribution.

CHAPTER 3

Central Tendency and Dispersion

LEARNING OBJECTIVES:

After reading this chapter, the student will understand the following concepts:

- How measurements of central tendency are calculated and when to use which ones
- How measurements of dispersion are calculated and when to use which ones
- The nature of the sum of squares, variation, and standard deviation and their promise for future statistics
- A basic concept of the normal curve and its relationship to the mean, mode, median, and standard deviation

INTRODUCTION

In studying social phenomena, scientists collect and evaluate data in numerous ways. Organizing the data into frequency distributions, charts, graphs, and tables is a useful way of visualizing the shape and scope of the data for a single variable, but if we wanted to compare Idaho homicides with California homicides, American suicides with Swedish suicides, and so on, we would find visual inspection of frequency distributions cumbersome and not very precise. When beginning to make such comparisons it would be more useful to have mathematically precise summary statements that would tell us the center of each distribution and how the data in each are dispersed or scattered away from their centers—in other words, the extent to which the data are similar and different. We call such techniques measures of central tendency and measures of dispersion, respectively.

Measures of central tendency indicate the center of the data, where we find the preponderance of values in a distribution, in other words, the degree to which the data are similar. For example, researchers use statements such as "the average case" or "the typical case looks like . . ." or "the most frequently occurring case is. . . ." **Measures of dispersion** indicate the spread of the data away from the center, in other words, the degree to which the data are different. These measures sacrifice the overall view of the data provided by a frequency distribution, but more than make up for it by providing useful numeric summaries that can be compared with distributions of other populations and samples. Further, as you will see throughout this book, probability statistics are largely built on measures of central tendency and dispersion. We turn first to measures of central tendency. There are three measures of central tendency: the mode, median, and mean; we begin with the mode.

MEASURES OF CENTRAL TENDENCY

Mode

The **mode** (which we will symbolize with *Mo*) is defined as the score that occurs most frequently in a distribution of scores. It is possible to have more than one mode in a frequency distribution; in such cases the distribution is bimodal or even multi-modal. The mode is the only valid measure of central tendency for nominal data, but it may also be validly used for all other levels of measurement. For example, suppose we asked 20 known burglars to reveal the number of burglaries they committed last month and we organize their responses into ungrouped and grouped distributions as shown in Table 3-1. In looking at the ungrouped section on the left of the table first, the mode of these data is 5 because it is the number-of-burglaries category that occurs most often (five times). For the grouped data on the right, the modal interval is 1–5, which represents the class interval that occurs most frequently (eight times). The mode is the least frequently used measure of central tendency in statistics because it does not lend itself to mathematical operations. It is purely a descriptive statistic that provides useful information regarding the typical case. Note, also, how the data behave similarly, yet in unique ways, when we force a continuous variable (number of burglaries) into a categorical variable (class intervals). Recall from chapter 1 that we always lose information when we move down the levels of measurement, or recode from ratio/interval, to ordinal or nominal (categorical).

TABLE 3-1. *Number of Residential Burglaries over the Past Month; in Ungrouped and Grouped Form,* N = 20

UNGROUPED				GROUPED		
Value*	Freq.	Value	Freq.	Class	Freq.	Cum. freq.**
1	1	12	1	1–5	8	8
1	1	14	1	6–10	7	15
3	1	16	1	10–15	3	18
5	5	25	1	16–20	1	19
6	1			21–25	1	20
7	2					
8	1	Total	20		Total	20
9	2					
10	1					
11	1					

*Note: "Value" here refers to the number of observations occurring during the study period, such as 1 burglary, 3 burglaries, or 10, and so on; **cum. freq., cumulative frequency.

Median

The **median** (symbolized here as *Md*) is defined as that score in the range that divides the scores into two equal parts: it is the middle score of a set of scores that have been arranged from lowest to highest. Consider the following range of scores:

5 6 8 9 10 11 **12** 13 15 16 18 21 33

The median score is 12 since half of the values are above that number and half are below it. Because there are 13 scores, 6 of the scores will be above the median and 6 will be below. If there is an even number of scores, the median is determined by interpolating between the two middle scores by taking their average. For example:

5 6 8 9 10 11 **12 13** 14 15 16 18 21 33 $Md = (12 + 13)/2 = 12.5$

To take our previous monthly burglary example, because there are 20 observations or scores in our data, we must interpolate between the two middle scores, which are

1 1 3 5 5 5 5 5 6 **7 7** 8 9 9 10 11 12 14 16 25

The 10th score is 7 and the 11th is 7. Thus, $(7 + 7)/2 = 7$; the median number of burglaries of this group of observations is 7 burglaries.

The Mean

The **mean** is symbolized in two different ways, depending on whether we are describing the population mean (μ read *mu*) or the sample mean ($\bar{x}$ read *x-bar*). Recall from chapter 1 that this is the difference between the population parameter (μ) and the sample statistic ($\bar{x}$). The mean is the measure of central tendency that most of us think about when we hear the term *average*. It is simply the average of a distribution of scores. Among all measures of central tendency, the mean is most commonly used. Unlike the mode and the median, it is suited only to interval- and ratio-level data. The mean is the focal point and entrance to more advanced statistics because before we can calculate the interval- and ratio-level statistics we will be discussing later, we must first know the means of the variables with which we are working. Another nice characteristic of the mean is that it is quite stable across repeated random samples from the same population. The modes and medians of repeated random samples from the same population tend to fluctuate more than the means. Therefore, any statistical conclusions drawn from modes and medians will be more likely to contain larger degrees of error compared to the mean.

The common formula for the mean is given in formula 3-1, which simply informs us to add all the individual scores or values together (this is what the Greek symbol Σ, *sigma*, or "sum," tells us to do) and divide the total sum by the sample size.

3-1

$$\bar{x} = \frac{\Sigma x}{n}$$

$\bar{x}$ = the sample mean
Σ = the sum of
x = represents each individual value in the set of values
n = sample size (the total number of values to be summed)

The mean number of burglaries is obtained from Table 3-1 by the following process:

STEP 1. Sum (Σ) all of the numbers in the burglaries distribution:

$$\Sigma x = 1 + 1 + 5 + 5 + \text{.......} + 25 = 164$$

STEP 2. Divide this number by the total number of observations (n), 20.

$$164/20 = 8.2$$

STEP 3. Interpret our answer: The mean or average number of burglaries reported by our sample ($n = 20$) is about 8.

Choosing a Measure of Central Tendency

Choosing a measure of central tendency depends on the kind of information you want to convey to the readers of your research. You should use the mode if you are referring to a variable measured at the nominal level. It makes no sense to talk about the mean sex of a sample, but we can say that the modal sex was male. You also use the mode when you wish to point out the typical case. For instance, a researcher is interested in the "typical" opinion regarding the death penalty (the modal opinion between the following three categories, "for," "against," or "not sure") rather than any "mean level" of opinion, which in this case, really makes no sense.

The median is used when the variable to be described is measured at the ordinal level or higher. It is useful when extreme scores distort the mean. The mean is exceptionally sensitive to extreme scores, both low and high. This is why median household income is reported more often than the mean household income: the mean household income is disproportionately affected by the relatively small percentage of individuals who make an extremely large amount of money. The income of billionaires pulls the mean in the direction of the higher incomes. Using the median gives us a better picture of incomes that fall in the middle of the distribution and more accurately reflects the "average" American household. Consider the following numbers:

1 1 2 4 5 5 7 7 8 8 9 9 34 40

Looking at this simplified distribution, the median is 7, whereas the mean is 10. But 10 clearly does not reflect what is average or normal about these data: 7 is a more

TABLE 3-2. *Relationship Between Measures of Central Tendency and Measurement Levels*

Measurement	Mean	Median	Mode
Nominal	No	No	Yes
Ordinal	No	Yes	Yes
Interval	Yes	Yes	Yes
Ratio	Yes	Yes	Yes

appropriate number in this case. In such cases the median better reflects central tendency than does the mean because it is less affected by extreme scores.

We use the mean only with interval- or ratio-level measures. It is the only measure of central tendency that uses all the information in a distribution. Variables measured at the interval or ratio levels are not limited to the mean for description, however; it is valid to report all measures of central tendency for such variables. Table 3-2 summarizes the relationship, or when it is appropriate to use each statistic, between the measures of central tendency and levels of measurement.

Statisticians refer to the mean as the *center of deviations*, or the *center of gravity*. By this it is meant that deviations from the mean in a distribution of scores, both above and below the mean, will balance each other out. To illustrate, suppose we have the distribution of scores given in Table 3-3. We calculate the mean, median, and mode for these data and find them to be 9, 10, and 6, respectively. We first calculate the deviation scores for the mean. A **deviation score** is the raw score minus the mean ($x - \bar{x} = y$), where y = the deviation score. As illustrated, the sum (Σ) of y will always be equal to zero. However, the deviations from the mode and the median will not be zero unless the distribution is perfectly symmetrical (the mean, median, and mode are identical).

As noted earlier, there is one significant problem regarding the mean. Although we have said that it is the most stable measure of central tendency across random samples from the same population, it is affected more than the mode or median by extreme scores in a distribution. In this sense it is less stable than the median. For instance, if we had a twenty-first respondent in our residential burglary data set who reported 38 burglaries in the last month, it would change the mean considerably (from 8.2 to 9.6), would not change the median (it stays at 7), and would also leave the mode unchanged (5 would still be the modal category). Bear this in mind as we progress through the statistics covered in this book: the distribution of your data has serious ramifications on how the statistics will behave.

TABLE 3-3. *Deviations from the Mean, Mode, and Median of a Distribution of Scores*

	MEAN			MEDIAN			MODE	
x	$\bar{x}$	$x - \bar{x}$	*x*	Md	*x* − Md	*x*	Mo	*x* − Mo
3	9	−6	3	10	−7	3	6	−3
6	9	−3	6	10	−4	6	6	0
6	9	−3	6	10	−4	6	6	0
6	9	−3	6	10	−4	6	6	0
10	9	+1	10	10	0	10	6	+4
10	9	+1	10	10	0	10	6	+4
12	9	+3	12	10	+2	12	6	+6
13	9	+4	13	10	+3	13	6	+7
15	9	+6	15	10	+5	15	6	+9
	$\Sigma(x - \bar{x}) = 0$			$\Sigma(x - Md) = -9$			$\Sigma(x - Mo) = +27$	

Note: the symbol *x* represents each individual score.

Figure 3-1 presents four distributions (from an infinite number of possible distributions) with the mean, mode, and median in different positions relative to each other. A distribution is similar to the histogram discussed in chapter 2; however, these distributions are presented as **curves**. We will have more to say about curves in chapter 4. By way of a brief introduction, the **normal curve** is perfectly symmetrical, with the mean, mode, and median all being exactly in the center of the distribution. A curve is considered nonnormal if it is **skewed**. Skewness is measured on a scale where the closer to 0, the less skew is present. The normal curve has no skew, with a skewness value of 0.0. A curve skewed to the right is called a positive skew, and a curve skewed to the left is called a negative skew. A rough-and-ready indication of the skewness is the difference between the mean and the median. If that value is negative, the curve has a negative skew; if positive, it has a positive skew. Atypical cases pull the mean toward one of the tails of the distribution, which creates the skew. Another measure of the shape of a distribution is called **kurtosis**, which is a measure of the relative peakedness of a curve. Like skewness, a distribution's kurtosis is measured using a scale where the closer to 0 the kurtosis is, the more normal is its distribution. The normal curve has a kurtosis of 0.0. If kurtosis is positive, the curve is more peaked or narrow than the normal curve; if it is negative it is flatter than the normal curve.

FIGURE 3-1
Four distributions

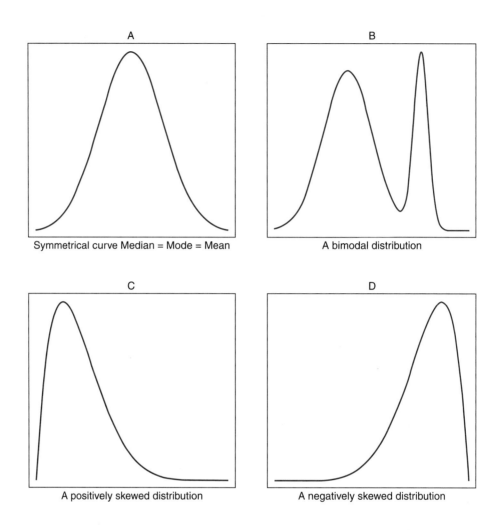

A
Symmetrical curve Median = Mode = Mean

B
A bimodal distribution

C
A positively skewed distribution

D
A negatively skewed distribution

These concepts are covered in more detail in chapter 4. For now, note that in a positively skewed distribution the mean is greater than the median and the median is greater than the mode. In a negatively skewed distribution the mean is less than the median and the median is less than the mode. Our original ($N = 20$) burglary data would be distributed approximately like curve C, with a mode of 5, a median of 7, and a mean of 8.2.

A Research Example

We expand on our previous example of self-reported residential burglaries by increasing the sample size to $n = 439$. Additionally, instead of using a one-month time frame, we expand it to the past three months. From chapter 1, you learned that larger samples

TABLE 3-4. *Number of Residential Burglaries Reported over the Past Three Months (n = 439)*

Mean	16.26	Range	71.00
Median	14.00	Standard deviation	9.13
Mode	12.00	Skewness	2.34
		Kurtosis	8.77

are more representative of the population because they carry more variation—more on this later. The hypothetical question we asked each of the known offenders was, "Over the last three months, how many residential burglaries did you commit?" Here, we are simply interested in providing a descriptive analysis of the data; we want to provide a summary of observations in a way that is easily communicated to our audience. The variable we are measuring is *number of burglaries* over the last three months, which is self-reported by each offender. From the **frequency table** (see Table 3-4) above we see that the mode is 12, the median is 14, and the mean is 16.26. We will defer discussion of the other printed values until our discussion of dispersion. For now, we can see that our distribution is most likely *not* normal: the skewness is 2.34, indicating a strong positive skew. The rightward skew of this distribution is a function of a few highly atypical cases at the high end of the distribution. As is usual in such skewed distributions, the median falls between the mode and the mean, and the mean lies closest of the three measures to the tail of the distribution. In a situation such as this, a researcher would most likely report both the mean and the median, given how skewed the data are.

MEASURES OF DISPERSION

The measures of central tendency are useful in relating indices of typicality for a group of scores. However, it is also useful to gain some idea of how the individuals or objects in a distribution differ from one another or spread away from the average. A measure of dispersion or variability, coupled with the mean, allows us to compute measures indicating how different two or more individuals or groups are with regard to a variable of interest. Think of it this way: let's say we have a sample of monetary earnings from 50 social science professors and 50 drug-dealing kingpins. Now, suppose that the mean annual income for both a sample of college professors and a sample of drug dealers is found to be $55,000. One could draw the conclusion that employing oneself as a drug lord is as lucrative a venture as becoming a college professor! Such information standing alone, however, conveys a false impression without a measure of the variability within the respective samples. For example, the median income for drug lords is probably more like $5,000 (if even that), but one drug lord in the sample nets $250,000 annually, which heavily skews the distribution. Compare that to the median income of college professors in our sample, at $53,000, and the seemingly apparent similarities between the two group's earnings begin to reveal their true patterns. There are three measures of dispersion that will aid us in deciphering patterns in our data beyond mere central tendency: range, variance, and standard deviation.

Range

The **range** is the simplest measure of dispersion. Unlike the other measures we will be discussing, the range is not a measure of the dispersion from the mean; rather it is simply the difference between the lowest and highest scores in the distribution. In our first burglary example distribution ($n = 20$) the lowest score is 1, the highest is 25, and the range is 24 ($25 - 1 = 24$). Some researchers might simply report the lowest and highest scores, called the minimum and maximum, thus 1 to 25. Even this simple measure of dispersion gives us a better feel for the data than we would have with the mean alone. In our professors/drug lords example, suppose the lowest income is $50,000 and the highest is $115,000 for the professors and $1,000 and $250,000 for the drug lords. The range for the distribution of salaries for professors is $65,000 and for the drug lords it is $249,000. We know there is a ton of variability among the drug lords and a moderate amount in comparison among the professors' salaries. Among the professors, the highest paid person receives about 2.3 times more money than the lowest paid person, whereas the highest paid drug lord receives 250 times more than the lowest paid drug lord—talk about income inequality!

However, the range is a crude measure of sample variation that depends entirely on the two most extreme values (the lowest and the highest). One or both of these values may be so atypical as to render the range most untrustworthy as a measure of dispersion. A somewhat better measure of dispersion is the **interquartile range** (IQR). The term *quartile* refers to the division of a distribution into four equal quarters. The first quartile (Q1) contains the first 25 percent of the cases, Q2 contains the 25 percent of the distribution from the end of Q1 to Q2 (the median), Q3 contains the 25 percent from the end of Q2 to Q3, and Q4 contains the final 25 percent of cases. Another way of putting it is to say that Q1 lies at the 25th percentile, Q2 at the 50th percentile, Q3 at the 75th percentile, and Q4 at the 100th percentile. The IQR is obtained by the formula IQR = Q3 − Q1, that is, the score at the 75th percentile minus the score at the 25th percentile. Imagine that, for our professors, Q1 = $17,133 and Q3 = $85,896.

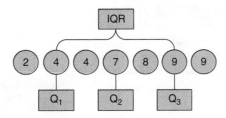

FIGURE 3.2
How to Calculate the Interquartile Range (IQR)
Find the midpoint; here it would be 7. Excluding the median, or 7, find the midpoints of the upper and lower quartiles. Here, the lower quartile is 4 and the upper is 9. To calculate the IQR = Q3 − Q1 or 9 − 4 = 5. The IQR = 5 (the range between the lower and upper midpoints). Note: Q2 is the median.

This means that the IQR is $68,763. The advantage of the IQR over the range is that the IQR reports the range of scores in the middle 50 percent of the distribution, where the great majority of cases typically fall, thus eliminating much of the bias imposed by extreme scores lying at the ends of the distribution. This is clearer if you consider Figure 3-2: If we cut a normal curve into four equidistant parts, the majority of cases fall within the middle two panels—that is, within Q1 and Q3, or the IQR.

The range and the IQR are quick and dirty measures of dispersion that are unsatisfactory if we want to go beyond describing a distribution. Note that the range and IQR use only two values to report dispersion. A more satisfactory measure of dispersion is one that utilizes every score in the distribution in its calculation, which minimizes the effects of any extreme scores. Such a measure is the standard deviation.

The Sum of Squares, Variance, and the Standard Deviation

Although there are a number of other rarely used measures of dispersion, we will concentrate on the three major indices of variability used to assess the spread of interval and ratio data in a distribution about their mean. Although they are different measures, they are only made so by mathematical transformations. The most basic of the three is the **sum of squares**. A measure called the **variance** is derived from the sum of squares, and the **standard deviation** is derived from the variance. All three measures are used in their various transformations in statistical analysis of interval- and ratio-level data. The relationship among the sum of squares, variance, and the standard deviation, along with their symbols and formulas, is illustrated in Figure 3-3.

A good measure of dispersion should utilize all the scores in the distribution and describe the typical or average deviation of the scores around their mean. Such a measure would be small in a distribution in which the scores are closely clustered around the center and get larger as they become more scattered away from it. The standard deviation is such a measure. As the observations become more different from one another, the standard deviation becomes progressively larger. The standard deviation, in effect, reflects the extent to which the mean represents the entire set of observations in a population or sample.

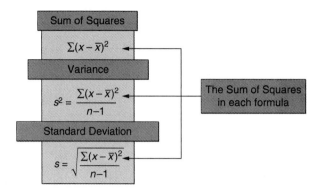

FIGURE 3.3

Examining the importance of the sum of squares

The sum of squares portion of the formula $[\Sigma(x - \bar{x})^2]$ is central to calculating variance and standard deviation (as well as other statistics you will use later). It is important because it provides the distance of one observation or data point, relative to the mean of the entire sample/group. Because we are balancing the data using the mean, the distances from each observation can be either negative or positive. In fact, if we were to sum these scores at this point, the result should always be 0. This is why we then square the respective differences—to get rid of the negative values. Next these values are added together to produce the "sum" of the "squared differences" from the mean. This "anchoring" (each score to the mean) effect is an integral to assessing the spread or distribution of your data. Interestingly, as you can see, the only difference between variance and standard deviation is the addition of the square root term. The issue with variance is that the score itself is hard to interpret because it is not returned in the same metric of the variable that is being measured; therefore, we take the square root of the variance to return it to its original metric, for example, "age" or "IQ." As you will see, there are a few other distinctions that can be made, but it is essential to understand the role that the sum of squares plays in these formulas.

Like the mean, there are two symbols for the standard deviation. When we talk about the population standard deviation, the lowercase Greek letter sigma (σ) is used, and when we are referring to a sample standard deviation, which is used to estimate the population standard deviation, we use the letter s. The formulas for the population and sample standard deviations are as follows:

3-2. Population standard deviation formula

$$\sigma = \sqrt{\frac{\Sigma(x - \mu)^2}{N}}$$

Where

N = the number of cases (the population)

x = each individual score

Σ = the sum of

μ = the population mean

3-3. Sample standard deviation formula

$$s = \sqrt{\frac{\Sigma(x - \bar{x})^2}{n - 1}}$$

Where
$\bar{x}$ = the sample mean
n = the sample size

Because we rarely have a population to work with, we will focus on the sample standard deviation, or formula 3-3. Both formulas work the same, however. They are calculating the *average deviation* scores. Indeed, if you compare the standard deviation formula with that of the mean, you will see striking similarities: Both sum a certain value (either all x's or all deviation scores—that is, the difference between the mean and each of those x's) and standardize that sum by dividing it by n (or, in the case formula 3-3, $n - 1$). Formula 3-3 instructs us to subtract the mean from each case or observation. Doing this will result in some negative and some positive values. Because the positive and negative deviations cancel each other out, the sum of $(x - \bar{x})$ will always be 0, as we demonstrate on step 3 in Table 3-5. A measure of dispersion that always sums to 0 is obviously no use to us. To avoid this inconvenience, we square each difference before we sum (which cancels out all of the negative values). Note also that when the standard deviation of a sample is calculated we use $n - 1$ rather than N, as we do when calculating a population standard deviation. We do this because s^2 (the sample variance) is a biased estimator of σ^2 (the population variance), and subtracting 1 from n corrects for that bias or error. The bias reflects the fact that a sample has less diversity (variance) than is found in its parent population. The correction factor is particularly important for small samples, but the difference between N and $n - 1$ becomes more and more trivial as the sample size gets larger and larger.

Box 3-1
N or n?

A note on usage: Remember, when reading research within the social sciences, you may note that when referring to a population many researchers use a capital N and when referring to a sample they use a small n.

Let's compute the standard deviation with a small data set of randomly selected high school seniors and ask them to indicate how many times in the past month they had taken some illicit drug, including alcohol. Each individual case (x) represents the number of times each student reported doing so. After taking the mean from each observation, squaring the difference, and summing, we have a value known as the sum of squares, which is the numerator under the radical in the standard deviation formula $[\Sigma(x - \bar{x})^2]$, which is equal to 56.5. The next step is to divide the sum of squares by $n - 1$, which provides us with the variance (s^2). The variance is the complete term under the radical in the standard deviation formula and is equal to 6.278 for these data. Let's go through this step by step, using Table 3-5 to help us out.

STEP 1: Fill out the A column with all the values provided by our respondents and then fill out the B column with the sample mean. In this case, high school seniors admitted to taking mind-altering substances over the past month an average of 5.5 times (the mean is reported in column B).

TABLE 3-5. *Computing the Standard Deviation of Number of Times High School Seniors Have Used Mind-Altering Substances over the Past Month (n = 10)*

A	B	C	D
x	$\bar{x}$	$(x - \bar{x})$	$(x - \bar{x})^2$
2	5.5	−3.5	12.25
4	5.5	−1.5	2.25
4	5.5	−1.5	2.25
4	5.5	−1.5	2.25
5	5.5	−0.5	0.25
5	5.5	−0.5	0.25
6	5.5	0.5	0.25
6	5.5	0.5	0.25
8	5.5	2.5	6.25
11	5.5	5.5	30.25
*Σ = 55		**Σ = 0.0	***Σ = 56.50

Note: * = sum of x; ** = sum of each individual score (x) minus the mean $(x - \bar{x})$, which will always sum to zero; *** = the sum of squares, or $\Sigma(x - \bar{x})^2$.

STEP 2: Subtract the A column from the B column, or $(x - \bar{x})$. Fill in the differences in the C column.

STEP 3: Sum values in column C, or $\Sigma(x - \bar{x}) = 0$. This is a good check to make sure that your math in the C column was correct. Remember: the mean is the average around which all other scores deviate—half of the distribution is above it and half is below it. Thus, all deviation scores must cancel each other out.

STEP 4: Square the values in column C and place those values in column D, or $(x - \bar{x})^2$.

STEP 5: Sum the values in column D, or $\Sigma(x - \bar{x})^2$. You now have all the tools you need to calculate the standard deviation.

STEP 6: Reconsider formula 3-3:

$$s = \sqrt{\frac{\Sigma(x - \bar{x})^2}{n - 1}}$$

You can now plug the numbers from above into this formula:

$$\sqrt{\frac{56.5}{9}} = \sqrt{6.278} = 2.50$$

The standard deviation for our sample of high school drug users is therefore 2.50. That is, on average, respondents differed from the mean by ($\pm$)2.5 uses per month, or the majority of the sample reported using drugs between 3 and 8 times per month (5.5 − 2.5 and 5.5 + 2.5).

Within the formula are two other statistics: the sum of squares and the variance. The sum of squares is simply $ss = \Sigma(x - \bar{x})^2$, whereas the variance is $s^2 = \Sigma(x - \bar{x})^2 / n - 1$. Both are used in statistics we will be covering in future chapters. The variance is an important and vital statistic that will be used in many subsequent calculations. However, it is somewhat difficult to conceptualize because it represents the square of whatever it is we're measuring. If we performed the calculation on a distribution of the number of children in a neighborhood's households and told you that the typical deviation from the mean number of children is 3.5 *squared* children, your mind might rebel. In fact, such statements are not easy for anyone to understand. What we need to do is to get these values back to the same metric in which they were originally measured by taking the square root of the variance to arrive at the standard deviation, which has a value of 2.5. Referring back to our example, we might say that a random sample of high school seniors reported using drugs/alcohol 5.5 times on average over the past month, with a standard deviation of 2.5—meaning the bulk of those cases or scores reported in this sample fell between 3 and 8 uses (5.5 ± 2.5).

Computational Formula for *s*

Formula 3-4 is the definitional formula for the standard deviation, presented to give you an intuitive appreciation of what is going on mathematically. With a large number of cases it is a cumbersome and time-consuming method. Fortunately, there is a computational formula that requires far less time and effort. As you will note from the computational formula for the standard deviation (formula 3-4), you don't have to compute the mean, you don't have to bother too much with decimals, and you will only make one subtraction rather than *N* subtractions. Let's take a look at an example:

3-4. Computation formula for sample standard deviation

$$s = \sqrt{\frac{\Sigma x^2 - (\Sigma x)^2 / n}{n - 1}}$$

where
Σx^2 = the sum of the squared individual scores
$(\Sigma x)^2$ = the sum of the individual scores squared

The Table 3-6 for solving this calculation is much less intimidating than Table 3-5.

STEP 1: Fill in column A with the values from each respondent (*x*).
STEP 2: Square each of the values in column A; fill in column B with these values.
STEP 3: Sum column A, then square that value, then divide it by *n*.
STEP 4: Sum column B to get Σx^2. (Note that $\Sigma x^2 - (\Sigma x)^2 / n$ is the sum of squares.)
STEP 5: You are now ready to plug these numbers into formula 3-4:

$$s = \sqrt{\frac{359 - 3{,}025 / 10}{9}}$$

TABLE 3-6. *Computation Formula Table for the Standard Deviation of a Sample (n = 10)*

A	B
x	*x²*
2	4
4	16
4	16
4	16
5	25
5	25
6	36
6	36
8	64
11	121
$\Sigma x = 55$	$\Sigma x^2 = 359$

$$s = \sqrt{\frac{359 - 302.5}{9}} = \sqrt{6.25} = 2.5$$

The mean and the standard deviation (along with its cousins the sum of squares and the variance) constitute the computational bedrock of statistics. The usefulness of the standard deviation will become more apparent when we use it to compute more advanced statistics later on. For now, let us say that it serves as a summary of the dispersion of a single variable. A small *s* (relative to how our variable is measured and compared to the mean) tells us that there is little variability among the observations (they are clustered rather tightly around the mean); a large *s* tells us the opposite. The mean and the standard deviation comprise the basis for the calculation of many of the statistics we will be examining that are applied to variables measured at the interval and ratio levels of measurement. Additionally, because the mean is the reference point for computing the standard deviation, the standard deviation is viewed as the expected (average or typical) amount of error we would make in attempting to guess any score in a distribution from its expected value (the mean). When we discuss the normal curve in the next chapter we will see that more than two-thirds of all observed values will be within 1 standard deviation on either side of their mean.

More on Variability and Variance

The idea of variance (s^2) is of great importance to us because the whole point of the vast majority of social and behavioral research, including criminology and criminal justice, is to *explain* or *account for* variance in dependent variables. Whenever we measure observations of any kind we are bound to find a degree of variability or difference in the measures from case to case. When we observe a distribution of scores and note that they are not all the same, we want to know why. We then look for theoretically meaningful variables that may help us to find out (recall the scientific process described in chapter 1). Let's look at an example that should make the idea of *variance explained* intuitively more understandable.

We begin with a class of 10 rookie police officers training at the police academy of a major city in 1999. Since they all share the same rank and seniority, they all are paid the same salary of $36,000 per year. What will the mean, standard deviation, and variance be? Because there is no variability in salary, the mean will be $36,000, and *ss* (the sum of squares), s^2 (the variance), and *s* (the standard deviation) will all be zero. Since there is no variance, there is none to explain or to be accounted for. Ten years later, we return to the same police department and to the same group of officers. We find that their salaries differ considerably this time, ranging from $48,000 to $69,000. Now we have variability, and thus variance, to be accounted for. We put these data in a table so that we can calculate the variance (Table 3-7). We have rounded to the nearest $1,000 and eliminated the last three zeros for ease of computation.

Following the steps above and plugging our values into formula 3-4, we can calculate the variance by *not* returning things to scale—that is, by not taking the square root:

$$s^2 = \frac{\Sigma x^2 - (\Sigma x)^2 / N}{N - 1}$$

$$\frac{30,547 - 301,401 / 10}{9} = \frac{406.9}{9} = 45.21$$

TABLE 3-7. *Police Officer Salary 10 Years Posthire (n = 10)*

x	x^2
48	2304
48	2304
50	2500
51	2601
52	2704
54	2916
57	3249
58	3364
62	3844
69	4761
$\Sigma x = 549$	$\Sigma x^2 = 30{,}547$

$(\Sigma x)^2/n = 30{,}140.1$

The variance is 45.21. This is the number that we want to explain, mathematically, using statistics. What do you think would explain or account for this variance, that is, account for the differences in salary? Rank (patrol officer, sergeant, lieutenant, etc.) would certainly account for a big proportion. Other variables might include overtime pay, specialist assignments, and pay given for special skills such as bilingualism or statistical knowledge. In the behavioral and social sciences, explaining variance is a major objective for researchers. We should be able to account for all of the variance (100 percent—that is, all 45.21) in salary here because salary levels are predetermined. However, since many variables, including pure chance, affect social behavior (which is a quite different kettle of fish from salary), researchers often fall short of being able to account for even 50 percent of the variance in many if not most dependent variables. Explaining variance is the goal of probabilistic statistics and will be revisited again and again throughout these pages. As you read on, contemplate how a number as abstract as the squared sum of deviation scores is the key to explaining the behavior of individuals and organizations.

Box 3-2
The Coefficient of Variation and the Index of Qualitative Variation

There are two other measures of variation that may be helpful in your own research: the coefficient of variation and the index of qualitative variation.

The *coefficient of variation* (CV) is used to assess relative rather than absolute variation. It is useful for comparing variation in two distributions of the same variable having different means or for comparing two distributions in which the variable of interest is measured in different units. CV standardizes s by multiplying it by 100 and dividing the product by the mean:

3-5

$$CV = s100/\bar{X}$$

For instance, let's say we have IQ data from two different samples. One sample is composed of juvenile delinquents and the other of adult offenders. The mean IQ for the juveniles is 92.2 with a standard deviation of 10.5. The mean for the adults is 93.56, with a standard deviation of 12.18. Let us see which sample has the most relative variation.

$$\text{Juvenile CV} = \frac{(10.5)(100)}{92.2} = 11.39 \quad \text{Adult CV} = \frac{(12.18)(100)}{93.56} = 13.0$$

There is more variation in the adult offender population.

The *index of qualitative variation* (IQV) measures variation in nominal and ordinal data. If all the values of a variable are in one category of a nominal or ordinal variable, there is no variation, and the IQV will be zero. If the values are distributed evenly across the categories, IQV will be 1, its maximum value. The formula for IQV is as follows:

3-6

$$IQV = \frac{k(N^2 - \sum f^2)}{N^2(k-1)}$$

Where
k = the number of categories
N = the number of cases
$\sum f^2$ = the sum of the squared frequencies

Let us compute and compare the IQV using a hypothetical example. Say we are interested in the difference of marital status between offenders and nonoffenders.

IQV for Marital Status (Offender Data)

Marital Status	f	f^2
Married	230	52,900
Divorced	117	13,689
Single	285	81,225
Widowed	5	25
	$\Sigma = 637$	$\Sigma = 147,839$

$$IQV = \frac{k(N^2 - \Sigma f^2)}{N^2(k - 1)}$$

$$\frac{4(405,769 - 147,839)}{405,769(3)} = \frac{1,031,720}{1,217,307} = 0.847$$

Now do the same for the nonoffender data.

IQV for Marital Status (Nonoffender Data)

Marital Status	f	f^2
Married	87	7,569
Divorced	28	784
Single	8	64
Widowed	12	144
	$\Sigma = 135$	$\Sigma = 8,561$

$$IQV = \frac{k(N^2 - \Sigma f^2)}{N^2(k - 1)}$$

$$\frac{4(18,225 - 8,561)}{18,225(3)} = \frac{38,656}{54,675} = 0.707$$

Thus, there is more variation in marital status among the offenders than among the nonoffenders.

SUMMARY

Measures of central tendency indicate the centrality of the data, and measures of dispersion indicate the spread of the data away from the center. The mode, median, and mean each report a summary value of a typical or representative value of the data. The mode is the most frequent value found in the data, the median is the value that splits the distribution exactly in half, and the mean is the arithmetic average of the distribution. The mean is generally the most useful of the three measures. It is the most stable of the three, and it is the entry point for the calculation of more advanced statistics.

The range is a measure of the difference between the highest and lowest scores in the distribution. It is minimally useful because only the two extreme scores in the distribution are used in its calculation. Although the IQR is something of an improvement over the range, it also utilizes only two scores in its calculation. The sum of squares is the most basic of the measures of dispersion away from the mean. It is the sum of the squared differences between each score or observation and the mean. The variance is the sum of squares divided by N for populations and $n - 1$ for samples. We use $n - 1$ for samples to correct for the fact that there is more variance in populations than in samples (referred to as error). The standard deviation is the square root of the variance. The standard deviation plays a key role in many of the statistics we will be discussing in the following chapters. Much of what we have covered has been heavy on the math and fairly light on the interpretation; what these statistics mean exactly, and how they are put to work in statistics, will become clearer the further we go.

Journal Table 3-1 shows descriptive statistics from the article "Social disorganization and crime in rural communities" by Kaplan and Pridemore (2013) and reports variable ranges and means. For this study, the authors used three dependent variables in their analysis, including property crime, violent crime, and total crime victimization rates, to determine the effects of social structural antecedents of social disorganization on crime rates in rural communities. Each variable was then standardized by dividing frequencies of victimization by the number of respondents in each sector that was included in the analysis. As shown in Journal Table 3-1, the researchers included explanatory variables to measure social structure and social disorganization. Social structural variables in the analysis include socioeconomic status, residential stability, ethnic heterogeneity, and family disruption. Density of local friendship networks, problematic teenage groups, and participation in organizations were included as social disorganization variables. According to this model, there is a lot of variation between the theoretical constructs. For example, there is

JOURNAL TABLE 3-1. *Descriptive Statistics (n = 318)*

	MINIMUM	MAXIMUM	MEAN	SD
Socioeconomic status	−4.74	8.64	0	2.55
Ethnic heterogeneity	0	0.76	0.1	0.15
Residential stability	0.27	0.93	0.62	0.12
Family disruption	−2.54	6.92	0	1.68
Local friendship network	2	3.82	2.69	0.35
Problematic teenage groups	0	0.39	0.07	0.07
Organizational participation	0	0.3	0.08	0.06
Property crime	0.04	1.96	0.77	0.4
Violent crime	0	0.83	0.16	0.15
Total crime	0.11	1.5	0.72	0.27

quite a difference in the means of local friendship networks (2.69) and socioeconomic status and family disruption (0). Based on the information listed in the table, readers can determine that respondents who reported that the presence of teenage peer groups was problematic ranged from 0 to 40 percent. Moreover, the proportion of respondents who reported organizational participation ranged from 0 to 30 percent. Recall that the standard deviation helps us get a handle on how often things depart from the mean. So for socioeconomic status, we know that about 68 percent (that is, plus and minus 1 standard deviation) of all respondents are somewhere between −2.55 and +2.55 on the socioeconomic status scale and that for property crime, 68 percent of neighborhood rates are somewhere between 0.37 and 1.17 per capita.

REFERENCE

Kaplan, M. T., & Pridemore, W. A. (2013). Social disorganization and crime in rural communities. *British Journal of Criminology* 53, 905–923.

CHAPTER 4

Probability and the Normal Curve

LEARNING OBJECTIVES:

After reading this chapter, the student will understand the following concepts:

- The basic theoretical underpinnings of "probability" and how to calculate probability for both classical and empirical outcomes
- How to calculate and interpret the multiplicative and additive properties of probability, as well as probability for combinations of events
- The relationship between probability and the normal curve and how the normal curve is used to compare what we expect to happen with what actually does happen
- How to calculate, interpret, and use the z score

PROBABILITY

In the last chapter, you learned about two of the most fundamental building blocks for statistics: measures of centrality and measures of dispersion. In this chapter, you'll learn about two other essential building blocks to statistics: probability and the normal curve. As in the last chapter, some things will become clear quickly, whereas other things may remain a bit murky. Don't worry: we promise that when we put everything together later in the book, everything will be clear. For now, hang in there, and try to absorb as much as you can about these concepts.

The mathematical underpinning of statistical analysis is the idea of probability, which provides a framework for making predictions that are based on more than just "guessing." Briefly described, probability is the mathematical likelihood of something occurring. This means that probability is *not* deterministic. Because statistics are based on probability, anything we learn from our statistics is also not deterministic. We do not say that given *A*, *B* will occur. This is a deterministic statement. Rather, we might make a statement such as, "Given *A*, *B* has a higher likelihood of occurring" or, more appropriately, "*B* has a 0.33 probability of occurring." We are all familiar with probability statements such as "The chances of rolling a 6 in one throw of a fair die are 1 in 6, or 0.16," "There is a 60 percent chance of rain through tomorrow morning," or "The chances of a cancer patient surviving for five years after diagnosis are 75 percent."

The first probability statement, regarding a throw of a die, is an example of classical probability; the second two statements are examples of empirical probability. **Classical probability** is probability based on *a priori* knowledge of all possible numerical values. Each throw of a fair die is a random event, with any one of six die values being equally probable for any toss. The variables (die, cards, coins, etc.) on which classical probability is based are called random variables because, assuming fairness, each has an *equal numerical chance of occurring*—and we know exactly how many "options" there are. That is, each of the six values of a die has a 1/6 probability of coming up, each card in a shuffled deck has a 1/52 chance of being drawn, and a head or a tail is equally likely each time a coin is tossed—1 in 2. This is not to say that it is impossible to get four heads in four tosses of a coin; rather, such an outcome is not likely—it is, in fact, improbable. Even if this sequence of events were to occur, we would not rule out that, in the long run, our coin would land on heads 50 percent of the time and tails the other 50 percent. (Incidentally, this is referred to as the law of large numbers, and it is a primary assumption of probabilistic statistics.)

Empirical probability is based on observation rather than known quantities. When meteorologists talk about a 60 percent chance of rain, they mean that based on previous occasions when weather patterns were similar, it rained about 60 times of 100. Probability in the real world is empirical probability. In other words, outcomes do not rest on pure chance in the same way as does the fall of a fair coin—there are too many options, too many unexplained variables, and too many opportunities for "real life" to muck things up. Although the statistics in the rest of this book result from empirical observations, classical probability is useful for the demonstration of some basic principles of probability.

As you can probably glean from the preceding two paragraphs, the probability of an event occurring is determined with a simple mathematical formula: we take the number of events we *want* to occur and divide this number by the total number of events *possible* (including the event we want to see happen). Thus, if we want to roll a 20 on a 20-sided die, our probability would be 1 (there is only a single 20 on a 20-sided die) over 20 (the total number of all possibilities), or $1/20 = 0.05$, or a 5 percent chance. We can use the same formula if we are interested in several events occurring. For example, let's say that we want to roll a 15 or higher on our 20-sided die. That means we would want to have any of the following results: 15, 16, 17, 18, 19, or 20; this is six results, so our numerator becomes 6, or $6/20 = 0.30$, or a 30 percent chance of success. This, of course, is classical probability; empirical probability is based on the same formula, it simply determines the number of possible outcomes by what has previously been observed. This formula is traditionally noted simply as P, where the probability of event A occurring is given as $P(A)$—as formally outlined in formula 4-1 below:

4-1

$$P(A) = \frac{\text{number of ways the event can occur}}{\text{total number of possible outcomes}}$$

It should be noted that the probability of event A *not* occurring is $1 - P(A)$. This is because our formula (P) will *always* be less than or equal to 1. We know this is true because the resulting quotient from P is calculated from a numerator that, by necessity, is equal to or less than its denominator. For example, in our example of a 20-sided die, because there are only 20 options, it's impossible to have more than 20 possible successes. Any division problem where the numerator is less than the denominator will mathematically equal less than 1. Because of this math, we can easily ascertain the probability of an event *not* occurring by simply subtracting its probability *of* occurring from 1. This saves us the time of figuring the probability of all other events occurring. For example, if we want to roll at least a 15 on our 20-sided die, we already know our probability to be 0.30. We can now easily calculate the probability of its *not* occurring as $1 - 0.30 = 0.70$. This is easier than dividing 14 by 20 (which, of course, also equals 0.70).

From this simple formula (P), we can learn two important properties of probability that will help us do more advanced statistics: the multiplication rule and the addition rule (see Box 4-1).

The Multiplication Rule

Suppose we want to determine the probability of getting two heads on two tosses of a fair coin. For each toss of the coin the probability of getting a head is equal to one-half, or 0.50. Each successive toss is independent of the outcomes of previous tosses. That is, what happens on the first toss does not in any way influence what happens on the second. The probability of getting a head (or tail) remains 0.50 regardless of how many times you toss the coin. If you want to determine the probability of two *independent* events occurring, such as two heads in two tosses of a fair coin, you must *multiply* the two independent probabilities. This is known as the **multiplication rule**, which has two forms (this rule is sometimes called the *multiplicative rule*). One is based on mutually exclusive (independent) outcomes and the other on nonindependent (conditional) outcomes. For independent outcomes, the multiplication rule is straightforward:

MULTIPLICATION RULE. The probability of two *independent* events (A and B) occurring is equal to the product of their respective probabilities (formula 4-2):

4-2

$$P(AB) = P(A) \times P(B)$$

Where A and B are independent events.

So, from our example above, if we note that the probability of flipping a coin and it landing on heads as P(heads), and we are interested in two independent head flips, then:

STEP 1: Calculate the probability of each event in which we are interested:

$$P(\text{heads}) = 1/2 = 0.50$$

Since we are only interested in flipping onto heads, we do not need to calculate this same probability.

STEP 2: Multiply the two probabilities together:

$$P(\text{heads on two separate flips}) = P(\text{heads}) \times P(\text{heads})$$

$$P(\text{heads on two separate flips}) = 0.5 \times 0.5 = 0.25$$

STEP 3: Interpret our result: the probability of flipping heads twice in a row, on two independent coin flips, is 0.25, or 25 percent.

We can easily extend this process: P(heads on three separate flips) $= 0.5 \times 0.5 \times 0.5 =$ 0.125, or 12.5 percent. You can see how this works: the more results we want, the lower the probability is. We can do the same thing with two die rolls. Imagine that you have two six-sided die, and on both you need to roll at least a 4. If you're really quick, you'll realize that this is the exact same thing as flipping two coins and having them land on heads (0.25), because P(rolling at least a 4) $= 0.5$. So let's pick a different number: you want one die to roll a 6 and the other die to roll at least a 5. Thus:

STEP 1: P(rolling a 6) $= 1/6$ or 0.16; P(rolling a 5 or 6) $= 2/6$ or 0.30
STEP 2: P(rolling a 6 AND at least a 5) $= 0.16 \times 0.30 = 0.048$
STEP 3: Practically, what this means is that, if you roll two six-sided die together, you can expect to roll a 5 or higher on one die and a 6 on the other die 4.8 percent of the time.

If outcomes A and B are *not* independent of one another, the multiplication rule changes: the probability of two *dependent* events occurring together is the product of the probability of A and the probability of B *given* A, written as formula 4-3:

4-3

$$P(AB) = P(A) \times P(B|A)$$

Where $P(B|A)$ is the probability of B, given A has already occurred.

Let's take an example from criminology to see how this works. Social scientists often want to know the probability of joint occurrences far more complex than the simple coin-tossing experiment or even the die-rolling example. For example, suppose we have a random sample of 200 men divided according to race and attitude about the death penalty as shown in Table 4-1. Of the men in the table, 120 are white and 70 of them are in favor of the death penalty. The other 80 men are black and 20 of them are

TABLE 4-1. *Race and the Death Penalty*

	White	Black	Total
Favor	70	20	90
Oppose	50	60	110
Total	120	80	200

in favor of the death penalty. We select an individual at random from the sample: what is the probability that a person is white and in favor of the death penalty?

STEP 1: Figure out P(white). The probability of being white is 120/200 = 0.6. This is taken from the total of the white column.

STEP 2: Figure out the probability of being in favor of the death penalty—P(favors the death penalty), given being white, or P(favors the death penalty|white). 70/120 = 0.5833. This was found by looking at the intersecting cell of favor and white and using the total white amount.

STEP 3: Multiply these probabilities together:

$$P(\text{white}) \times P(\text{favors the death penalty}|\text{white}) = 0.6 \times 0.5833 = 0.35$$

STEP 4: We can now interpret our probability: the chances that a person from our sample is white and in favor of the death penalty is 0.35, or 35 percent.

This is an example to demonstrate the process of figuring out the probability of co-occurring, dependent events. We also could have figured this out by simply taking the total number of white respondents who favor the death penalty and dividing it by the entire sample, or 70/200. This gives us the same answer as the exercise above (0.35). As easy as that was, it is vital to see exactly *what* is happening when we are dealing with probability properties. Understanding the underlying math will make future interpretations more clear and accessible.

The Addition Rule

Another probability rule you should be familiar with is the **addition rule.** Whereas the multiplication rule is invoked whenever we want to figure out the probability of two events co-occurring, the addition rule is used to figure out the probability of one of several events occurring. As the name implies, figuring this sort of probability out will take some addition. And as with the multiplication rule, we have two versions: one for independent and one for dependent events. Take a simple example: above, we figured out the probability of rolling a 15 or higher on a 20-sided die—it was 0.30. The formula we used was 6/20. This is an abbreviated form of what was going on behind the scenes: we were simply adding the individual probabilities of rolling a 15, 16, 17, 18, 19, *or* 20 on a single 20-sided die:

$$1/20 + 1/20 + 1/20 + 1/20 + 1/20 + 1/20 = 6/20 = 0.30$$

Box 4-1
When to Multiply or Add Probabilities?

Formally, the choice between the multiplicative rule and the additive rule is focused on the outcome of interest: do you want *all* the events to occur or *any* of the events to occur? To put a concrete example to this, take two six-sided die. Do you want each die to land on 6 when you roll them together, or do you only want at least *one* of the die to roll a 6? If the former, you invoke the multiplication rule; if the latter, the additive rule.

The results differ to a great degree. If you are interested in rolling a 6 on both die when you roll them together, the probability is $0.16 \times 0.16 \times 0.0256$. However, if you only need to roll a 6 on one of the die, the probability is $0.16 + 0.16 = 0.32$—substantially better odds!

Informally, you can usually figure out whether to use the multiplicative rule over the additive rule based on the following question sequence:

- *Am I using the word "and" to describe my desired outcome?* If you answer *yes* to this question, then you'll *multiply* probabilities together.
- *Am I using the word "or" to describe my desired outcome?* If the answer is *yes* to this question, then you'll *add* probabilities together.

Let's use this question sequence with the examples here. First, we want *each* die to roll a 6. In other words, we want the first die to land on a 6 *and* we want the second die to land on a 6. Thus, we invoke the multiplication rule. Second, we want either die to land on a 6. In other words, we want either the first die to land on 6 *or* the second die to land on 6. Thus, we invoke the additive rule.

We are able to add these probabilities together because there are only 20 possible mutually exclusive outcomes, and each face of a die has an equal chance of coming up (in this case, 1/20). The addition rule for two independent outcomes occurring is thus formula 4-4:

4-4

$$P(A \text{ or } B) = P(A) + P(B)$$

This example assumes that all outcomes are *independent* of each other. As with the multiplication rule, so too with the addition rule: this is rarely the case. Therefore, we rely on a different equation whenever our outcomes depend on each other. To go back to our death penalty example, what if we wanted to determine the probability that a respondent selected at random from the sample is white *or* in favor of the death penalty? We know that the probability is 0.6 that an individual in our sample is white. The probability of being in favor of the death penalty 90/200 = 0.45. If we simply sum these two probabilities, we get 1.05. This would be the same as summing the number of whites (120) and the number of men in favor of the death penalty (90) and dividing by the total sample *n* (210/200 = 1.05).

Such an outcome is a logical impossibility because the probability of anything cannot exceed 1, as we discussed earlier. We have exceeded 1 because there is an overlapping of occurrences of outcomes (i.e., they are not mutually exclusive outcomes). If we roll a 3 on a die, all other numbers are automatically excluded for that roll, but being white does not automatically tell us whether a respondent is in favor of or opposed to the death penalty. In fact, we have counted something twice. Specifically, 70 of the 90 respondents in favor of the death penalty are white, and we have already accounted for all whites when we broke the sample down by race. We cannot count them again when we break the sample down by "favors the death penalty." To eliminate this overlap of probabilities, we must add the individual probabilities and subtract the probability of their joint occurrence, which we know from the previous example to be 0.35. This is known as the addition rule for non–mutually exclusive occurrences and is noted in formula 4-5.

4-5

$$P(A \text{ or } B) = P(A) + P(B) - P(A \text{ and } B|A)$$

This equation assumes, of course, that $P(A)$ and $P(B)$ are dependent. Thus, the probability of selecting a white male *or* someone in favor of the death penalty is as follows:

STEP 1: Calculate all necessary probabilities. In this case, $P(\text{white})$ and $P(\text{favors the death penalty})$:

$$P(\text{white}) = 0.60$$

$$P(\text{favors the death penalty}) = 0.45$$

$$P(\text{white and favors the death penalty}) = 0.35 \text{ (from formula 4-3)}$$

STEP 2: Plug these probabilities into our equation 4-5:

$$P(A \text{ or } B) = P(A) + P(B) - P(A \text{ and } B|A)$$

$$P(A \text{ or } B) = (0.6) + (0.45) - (0.35) = 1.05 - 0.35 = 0.70$$

STEP 3: Interpret our findings: the probability of either being white *or* being in favor of the death penalty is 0.70.

To make it more intuitively clear, look back at Table 4-1. The only value that does not satisfy our criteria of being white or in favor of the death penalty is the 60 blacks in the lower right of the table (that is, they are neither white nor in favor of the death penalty). So we count $70 + 50 + 20 = 140$ and then divide the sum by the total number of males: $140/200 = 0.70$.

A Research Example

Let us illustrate the two rules of probability for independent outcomes with a sociological example. It has been estimated that in 1980 less than 1 percent of marriages in the United States were interracial (Reiss and Lee, 1988, p. 297). What if there were no cultural, economic, or psychological barriers to interracial marriage? How many interracial marriages might we expect if marriages were determined simply by chance? In other words, what if marriages were arranged completely by chance? Let us assume that the racial groups in the United States broke down in 1980 according to the following proportions: white = 76 percent, black = 14 percent, and other racial groups = 10 percent. Let us also assume an equal number of men and women in each race, who are free and able to marry, such that 76 percent of men are white and 76 percent of women are also white, etc. Under these conditions the probabilities of inter- and intraracial marriages would be as shown in Table 4-2. The multiplication rule is illustrated by the probabilities of marrying by specific racial groups—for example, the probability of a white man marrying a white woman would be $0.76 \times 0.76 = 0.5776$. The 0.76 is derived from the total percentage of the population that group composes—in other words, the probability of that person being from the group (76/100). These probabilities represent the chance that a marriage is composed of a person of one race *and* of another (perhaps including but not limited to the same) race and that in theory these marriages omit same-sex pairings.

The addition rule for mutually exclusive events is illustrated in the summation of the proportion of inter- and intraracial marriages expected under the assumed conditions (marrying a person of one race automatically excludes marrying a person of

TABLE 4-2. *Probabilities of Inter- and Intraracial Marriage under Assumed Conditions*

White/white	=	(0.76)(0.76)	=	0.5776
White/black	=	(0.76)(0.14)	=	0.1064
White/other	=	(0.76)(0.10)	=	0.076
Black/black	=	(0.14)(0.14)	=	0.0196
Black/white	=	(0.14)(0.76)	=	0.1064
Black/other	=	(0.14)(0.10)	=	0.014
Other/other	=	(0.10)(0.10)	=	0.01
Other/white	=	(0.10)(0.76)	=	0.076
Other/black	=	(0.10)(0.14)	=	0.014
Sum of probabilities = 1.000				

Proportion of intraracial marriages			**Proportion of interracial marriages**		
White/white	=	0.5776	White/black	=	0.1064
Black/black	=	0.0196	White/other	=	0.076
Other/other	=	0.01	Black/white	=	0.1064
Sum = 0.6072			Black/other =	=	0.014
			Other/white	=	0.076
			Other/black	=	0.014
			Sum = 0.3928		

Total marriages probabilities = 0.6072 + 0.3928 = 1.00

another, at least at the same time). Since they are mutually exclusive events, we can simply sum the individual probabilities. In other words, the probability of marrying someone of one's *own* race would be the sum of the probabilities of all intraracial categories: 0.5776 for white/white, 0.0196 for black/black, and 0.0100 for other/other:

$$0.5776 + 0.0196 + 0.0100 = 0.6072$$

Similarly, the probability of marrying someone of a different racial group—whatever the dyad—is 0.3928, which is very much less than the probability of marrying within one's group. These are what we call *expected* probabilities, and we will revisit them again when we compare them with *observed* probabilities. Expected probabilities are just that: the probabilities we expect to occur given only chance. Observed probabilities, on the other hand, are the probabilities we can calculate given what *actually* occurs. You might think of the difference between observed probabilities and expected probabilities as the difference between empirical probability and classic probability. We will revisit this topic again when we discuss certain statistical models that rely on the magnitude of difference between the expected and observed probability of an event.

THEORETICAL PROBABILITY DISTRIBUTIONS

One of the reasons for talking so much about probability is that we can use classical probability to create theoretical distributions. A **distribution** is a way to arrange data by frequency. For example, if we have 100 police officers and are interested in their height (for whatever reason), we can categorize individual officers into discrete categories, such as 5 feet 5 inches, 5 feet 6 inches, 5 feet 7 inches, etc., until 6 feet 5 inches. Imagine that, among our 100 respondents, we created the following table (Table 4-3). This table indicates that there were 25 respondents who were

TABLE 4-3. *Frequency Distribution*

	Number of Officers
5'5"	3
5'6"	4
5'7"	5
5'8"	9
5'9"	14
5'10"	25
5'11"	15
6'	10
6'1"	5
6'2"	4
6'3"	3
6'4"	2
6'5"	1

FIGURE 4-1

Distribution of police
officer heights

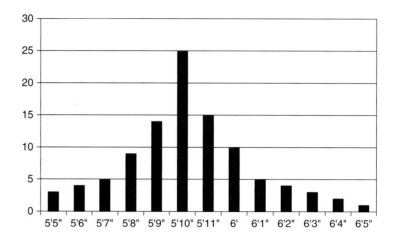

5 feet 10 inches and 14 who were 5 feet 9 inches. This is a tabular frequency distribution: it tells us how the data are distributed according to how we measured things (in this case, by height per inches). We can create a bar chart with these frequencies, which would look something like Figure 4-1. Because we have fudged the numbers, you'll note that this is an essentially perfect normal curve, as we discussed in chapter 3. In Figure 4-1, our curve is created with "real" (albeit imaginary) data. But the normal curve, you'll recall, is hypothetical. How did we come up with it?

To demonstrate how the normal curve is created, let's consider another kind of distribution, called a **binomial distribution**. A binomial distribution, as the name implies, is created by considering the frequency of the probabilities of two potential outcomes. Before we can do this, we need some preliminary formulas. We'll use coins—a coin is something we know has a probability of 0.5 of landing on either heads or tails. Let's go over the probabilities of tossing three fair coins. If we toss three fair coins, there are eight possible outcomes (**H** = heads and **T** = tails): **HHH, HHT, HTH, THH, TTH, THT, HTT, TTT**. Suppose we want to determine the probability of getting *just* two heads (no more, no less) in three tosses. Checking our eight possibilities, we see that three of them had just two heads (HHT, HTH, and THH). As already indicated, for discrete events the probability of any random event occurring is the ratio of the number of ways the event can occur to the total number of possible outcomes. We have determined that just two heads can occur three ways and that the total number of possible outcomes in three tosses is eight. Therefore, the probability of two heads in three tosses = 3/8 = 0.375.

Now, this example was fairly easy to compute without resorting to a mathematical formula. But what if instead of 3 tosses we toss the coin 10 times, or even 100 times? Determining the possible number of unique outcomes by listing them as we did with 3 tosses would be a formidable task. Luckily, there is a simple formula for determining the number of possible outcomes, formula 4-6.

4-6

$$_nC_r = \frac{N!}{r! \, (N - r)!}$$

Where:
C = number of combinations
N = number of trials
r = number of successes
! = factorial (the product of all positive integers from N to 1)

A factorial is calculated by multiplying all the positive integers between 1 and the number we write down. So $5! = 1 \times 2 \times 3 \times 4 \times 5 = 120$. For purposes of illustration, let us apply the formula to the three-toss example. We have three trials, so $N = 3$. We want to determine the number of ways we can get two heads, so $r = 2$. The factorial (!) means that we start at N (3) and determine the product of all positive integers from 1 to 3 ($1 \times 2 \times 3$). The complete calculation is

$$\frac{3!}{2! \, (3 - 2)!} = \frac{6}{2} = 3$$

So this gives us the total number of possible combinations when flipping three coins. The next step is to determine the probability of observing two heads in three tosses using formula 4-7. You'll see that formula 4-2 explicitly integrates formula 4-6.

Box 4-2
What to Do with 0!

Mathematically, 0! always equals 1. Always. Thus, if called upon to figure out 0!:

$$0! = 1$$

4-7

$$_{n}P_{r} = \frac{N!}{r!(N-r)!}p^{r}q^{n-r}$$

Where:

p = probability

$q = 1 - p$

For this formula, p is the probability of success on one toss, which we know to be 1/2 or 0.5. Q is therefore $1 - p$, or $1 - 0.5 = 0.5$. These are things we learned previously. The formula applied to the problem of the probability of getting two heads in three tosses then becomes (plugging in our answer above from formula 4-6):

$$_{n}P_{r} = \frac{3!}{2!(3-2)!}p^{2}q^{3-2} = \frac{3 \times 2 \times 1}{2 \times (1 \times 1)} = (0.5^{2})(0.5^{1})$$

$$= 3(0.25)(0.5) = 3(0.125) = 0.375$$

If we were calculating the probability of getting four heads from 10 tosses, the calculations would be as follows. Note that p^{4} means that the probability of a single success (0.5) is multiplied by itself four times.

$$_{n}P_{r} = \frac{10!}{4!(10-4)!}p^{4}q^{10-4}$$

$$\frac{10 \times 9 \times 8 \times 7 \times 6 \times 5 \times 4 \times 3 \times 2 \times 1 \ (0.5^{4}) \ (0.5^{6})}{(4 \times 3 \times 2 \times 1)(6 \times 5 \times 4 \times 3 \times 2 \times 1)}$$

This will all boil down to $P = (210)(0.000976562) = 0.2051$. So the probability of flipping two heads with three coins across 10 tosses is 20.51 percent.

We are now ready to construct a binomial distribution by the simple operation of tossing *one* fair coin 10 times—something with only two possible outcomes, that is, something is binary or binomial. Table 4-4 does this for us. The first column lays out all possible outcomes if you flip a coin 10 times. For example, it's possible to only get 1 head; it is also possible to get 10 heads. The second column ($_{n}C_{r}$) indicates just how *probable* these outcomes are, using formula 4-6. For example, for 1 head,

$$_{n}C_{r} = \frac{10!}{1! \ (10-1)!} = \frac{3,628,800}{362,880} = 10$$

TABLE 4-4. *Binomial Distribution with Coin Tosses*

0 heads	1	$(1/2)0$	$(1/2)10$	$=$	$1/1024$	$1/1024$	$=$	0.0009765
1 heads	10	$(1/2)1$	$(1/2)9$	$=$	$1/1024$	$10/1024$	$=$	0.0097650
2 heads	45	$(1/2)2$	$(1/2)8$	$=$	$1/1024$	$45/1024$	$=$	0.0439453
3 heads	120	$(1/2)3$	$(1/2)7$	$=$	$1/1024$	$120/1024$	$=$	0.1171875
4 heads	210	$(1/2)4$	$(1/2)6$	$=$	$1/1024$	$210/1024$	$=$	0.2050781
5 heads	252	$(1/2)5$	$(1/2)5$	$=$	$1/1024$	$252/1024$	$=$	0.2460937
6 heads	210	$(1/2)6$	$(1/2)4$	$=$	$1/1024$	$210/1024$	$=$	0.2050781
7 heads	120	$(1/2)7$	$(1/2)3$	$=$	$1/1024$	$120/1024$	$=$	0.1171875
8 heads	45	$(1/2)8$	$(1/2)2$	$=$	$1/1024$	$45/1024$	$=$	0.0439453
9 heads	10	$(1/2)9$	$(1/2)8$	$=$	$1/1024$	$10/1024$	$=$	0.00097650
10 heads	1	$(1/2)0$	$(1/2)10$	$=$	$1/1024*$	$1/1024$	$=$	0.00009765

The third column, then, is the second part of formula 4-7: $(p^r)(q^{n-r})$. Recall that p is the probability of our outcome, and q is the probability of our desired outcome *not* occurring, or simply $1 - p$. Our final column is therefore the probability of each potential combination. You can verify this by summing all the probabilities: they do, in fact, equal 1. What's also important to note here is the distribution of outcomes: if we plot them on a bar chart, such as Figure 4-2, you'll see that this looks like a perfectly symmetrical normal curve (at this point, it is important to point out that bar charts created from frequency distributions such as this are also called histograms, as we discussed in chapter 2).

Because this probability curve is so easily created and based on classical probability, it can serve as a standard by which we can judge empirical, or real-life, outcomes. If we wanted to test the fairness of a suspect coin, for instance, we could actually toss it in the air 10 times and compare the observed outcome to the theoretically expected outcome. If the empirical outcome departs significantly (we have ways of quantifying what we mean by *significantly*, but that discussion comes in chapter 6) from the theoretically expected outcome, we reject the notion that the coin is a fair one and assume it is a trick coin (or a loaded die, etc.). As we have previously indicated, inferential statistics are built around comparisons of observed and theoretically expected outcomes. In probabilistic statistics, our expected statistics are gleaned from probability distributions. If we only have two potential outcomes, as we do with a coin, we would use a binomial distribution such as the one we created here.

FIGURE 4-2

Binomial distribution of coin tosses

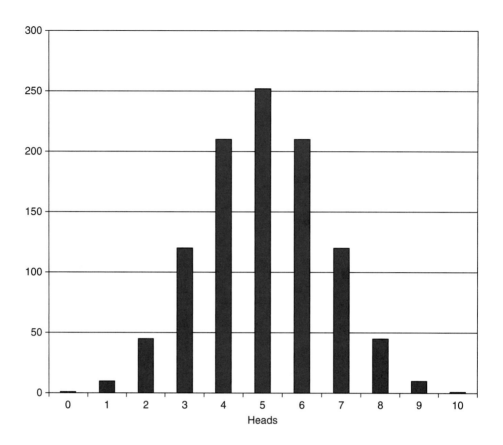

If we were to make 1,000 tosses of a fair coin rather than 10, we would have 1,001 possible values rather than 11. The bars for a histogram for this number of possibilities would be so close together that they would almost describe a smooth, curved line. But it would otherwise look just like Figure 4-2. As the number of possible probability outcomes gets larger and larger, the histogram becomes smoother and smoother (recall Galton's Quincunx in chapter 1).

The Normal Curve

The binomial distribution works well for when we only have two outcomes. But what if we have continuous outcomes—that is, infinite outcomes? Such a distribution is what the normal curve, briefly discussed in the last chapter, provides for us. To create such a hypothetical normal curve, we will make use of the mean and standard deviation. From the last chapter, recall that about two-thirds of all observations are found within 1 standard deviation (plus *and* minus) of the mean. Knowing this will help you understand the process underlying the math used to create a normal curve. We will only briefly cover this math because it is too advanced for an introductory course.

To be clear: the normal curve is a probability distribution for continuous random variables that is entirely specified by two parameters, its mean (μ) and its standard deviation (σ). (Note we are using the Greek letters here because a normal curve is drawn from a hypothetical population, not a sample.) By normal we don't mean that it is the typical or most often observed distribution, although we do find rough approximations with fair regularity in large samples. *Normal* is used in the sense that the curve is a norm, or idealized version, of a distribution against which we can compare the distributions we obtain in our research—such as above with the binomial distribution and a trick coin. It is a completely hypothetical curve, with three special attributes. First, it is perfectly symmetrical and smooth. Second, its mean, median, and mode are all centered (it is not skewed). Third, we say that the normal curve is *asymptotic* to the *x*-axis or simply that the tails of the curve never touch the horizontal axis. This property reflects the assumption that any score, value, or outcome is theoretically possible, although extreme values are highly unlikely.

When we say that the normal curve is perfectly symmetrical we mean that each side of a curve (split in the middle by its mean, median, and mode) occupies exactly one-half of its total area. This means also that precisely 50 percent of the observations are on one side of its center and 50 percent are on the other side. Further, exactly 68.26 percent of the total area of the curve falls between plus and minus 1 standard deviation, exactly 95.44 percent of the area falls between plus and minus 2 standard deviations, and exactly 99.74 percent of the area falls between plus and minus 3 standard deviations (see Figure 4-3). Summing these proportions under the curve, you will note that you get 0.9974 rather than 1.00 (what we call unity). Normally, you'd expect this to be 1, or 100 percent. This result reflects the fact that scores that deviate from the mean further than plus or minus 3 standard deviations are possible. Such highly unlikely scores account for the remainder of the area (0.0026). This amount would be, of course, split evenly on either side of the mean because of the symmetrical nature of the normal curve. For example, in a sample of 10,000 we would expect only 13 cases more than 3 standard deviations below the mean and 13 cases more than 3 standard deviations above the mean.

This is our idealized, normal curve composed of the probabilities we expect on any properly collected ratio-level data (and it usually works out for interval-level data, too). In the more advanced statistics we'll be doing in later chapters, we'll compare our outcomes—our observed results—against the backdrop of our normal

FIGURE 4-3
Standard normal curve

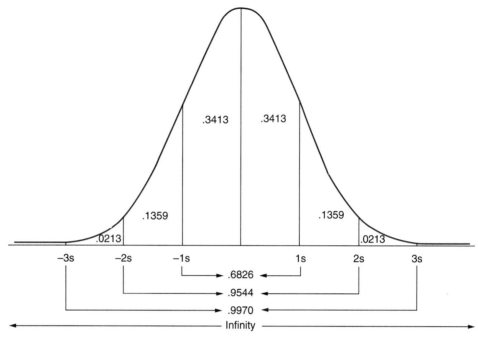

curve—our expected results. To the degree that the two results *disagree*, we can rule out chance in our observed outcome. But first, we must go over some more information on the normal curve.

It might help you to better understand the normal curve if we conceptualized these proportions or percentages of the area under the normal curve as numbers of observations in a sample. Suppose that we had a random sample of 1,000 observations of male heights (a variable that is roughly normally distributed). In such a sample we should find about 683 cases within plus or minus 1 standard deviation of the mean, about 954 between plus or minus 2 standard deviations, and about 997 within 3 standard deviations. We calculated these numbers using the percentages above: if roughly 68.3 percent of all observations are found within a standard deviation (plus or minus) of the mean, then of 1,000 cases, about 683 should be found within a standard deviation of our mean. If our mean is 5 feet 10 inches and our standard deviation is 3 inches, we would observe that 683 cases were between 5 feet 7 inches and 6 feet 1 inch—or 5 feet 10 inches ± 3 inches. We can extend this further and find that about 341 cases are between 5 feet 10 inches and 6 feet 1 inch. If we did *not* find this to be the case, then there would be something unique going on with our sample of 1,000 persons because they no longer fit what *probably* should be happening.

The smoothness of the curve is based on the theoretical assumption of an infinite number of observations. Since the normal curve is a distribution of probabilities rather than empirical frequencies, we observe no peaks, valleys, or gaps in the normal distribution as we did in the empirical distributions in chapters 2 and 3. This fact has an important implication for research in that it suggests that the larger the sample size, the more the distribution of scores will approximate the normal curve if the underlying population is normally distributed. Again: bigger samples are better.

The formidable-looking equation for a normal curve is the following (formula 4-8):

4-8

$$Y = \frac{1}{\sigma\sqrt{2\pi}}e^{-(x-\mu)^2/2\sigma^2}$$

Where $\pi = 3.14$ and $e = 2.72$. Both of these are mathematical constants and irrational numbers. Fortunately, you will never have to construct a normal curve for yourself, but the formula should convince you that curves can differ infinitely according to their means and standard deviations. When we talk about differentiations in these curves regarding flatness/peakedness, as opposed to skewness (when the mean, median, and mode all differ), we are referring to kurtosis. Distributional curves may be tall and thin relative to the theoretical normal curve, indicating a small amount of variation around the mean. Such a curve is called **leptokurtic** (from the Greek term *lepto*, meaning *thin*), as the top curve in Figure 4-4. A curve that is wide and flat relative to the theoretical normal curve, indicating a great deal of variation around the mean, is called **platykurtic** (*flat*), as in the bottom curve. A **mesokurtic** (*middle*) curve is a curve with a normal scatter of observations about its mean, as is the theoretical normal curve shown in Figure 4-3. Note that the curves in Figure 4-4 have the same mean but different standard deviations. The reason why these curves differ in height is that the area under the curve is unity (100 percent). Therefore, it follows that as the base of the curve expands or shrinks, the height must decrease or increase accordingly to keep the area constant.

The Standard Normal Curve

The **standard normal curve** is a special case of the normal distribution curve in that it has a mean of zero and a standard deviation of 1. The utility of the standard normal curve is that any normally distributed variable can be transformed into a standardized

FIGURE 4-4

Normal curves with the
same mean but
different peakedness

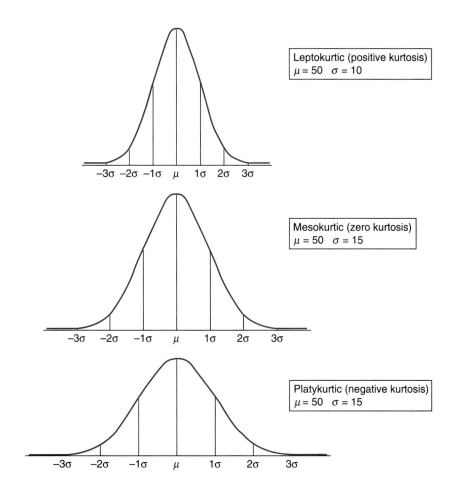

Leptokurtic (positive kurtosis)
$\mu = 50$ $\sigma = 10$

Mesokurtic (zero kurtosis)
$\mu = 50$ $\sigma = 15$

Platykurtic (negative kurtosis)
$\mu = 50$ $\sigma = 15$

distribution, allowing a single reference distribution for comparing otherwise noncomparable values. In other words, regardless of how a variable is distributed, we can mathematically transform it to be normally distributed. The utility of doing so is that we can compare any continuously distributed variable against the expected frequencies of the normal curve. And this, as we've been pointing out, is the very nature and purpose of probabilistic statistics: compare observed frequencies with expected frequencies.

For instance, if we wished to compare the IQ of one of our juvenile delinquents with the IQ of one of our adult criminals, it would be difficult because the two different distributions have different means and standard deviations. Standardizing both distributions to a mean of zero and a standard deviation of 1 renders such comparisons meaningful. To do so we will compute what are called z scores. But first we will look at the distribution of IQ scores reported in some hypothetical offender data. Since we have $n = 376$ cases for which we have IQ data, we can expect a good

TABLE 4-5. *IQs of Offenders*

N	376	Sum	31,179
Mean	93.561	Variance	148.359
Standard deviation	12.180	Kurtosis	0.743
Skewness	0.182	Range	80
Mode	94	Median	94

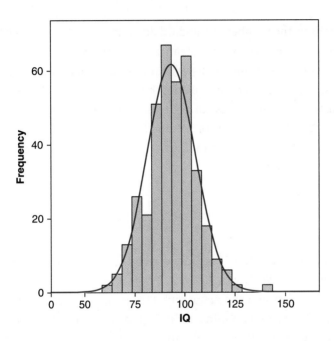

FIGURE 4-5
Distribution of IQs among offenders

approximation of the normal curve. The distribution of IQ scores for the offender data is presented in Table 4-5 and graphically presented in Figure 4-5.

A visual inspection of the graph suggests that this distribution is close to normal. If we rounded the mean to the nearest whole number, the mean, median, and mode would all be 94, and the skewness and kurtosis statistics values are quite small.

z SCORES

z scores are a way of tying the theoretical probability distribution to empirical raw scores. When we convert raw scores into *z* scores the distribution of scores is standardized to the theoretical normal curve. This allows us, essentially, to compare the expected with the observed. The formula for converting raw scores to z scores is simple: we subtract the sample mean from an individual score and divide the difference by the sample standard deviation as follows:

4-9

$$z = \frac{x - \bar{x}}{s}$$

A z score tells us the number of standard deviations a score lies above or below its mean. A positive z score is above the mean, and a negative z score is below the mean. In essence, z scores are synonymous with standard deviation units. For all intents and purposes, z scores *are* standard deviations.

To demonstrate the usefulness of z scores, let us take a hypothetical individual from our offender data with an IQ of 106 and transform this raw score into a z score. We have rounded the mean and standard deviation to their nearest whole numbers: 94 and 12, respectively.

$$z = \frac{x - \bar{x}}{s} = \frac{106 - 94}{12} = \frac{12}{12} = 1.00$$

A z score of 1.00 means that this individual has a score that lies 1 standard deviation above the mean. We saw in Figure 4-3 that 0.3413 of the total area under the normal curve lies between the mean and +1 standard deviation. Below the mean lies 0.50 (or 50%) of the remaining area. To find the total area of the curve corresponding to a z score of 1.0 we simply sum those two proportions to get 0.8413 (or 84.13%). This strategy is demonstrated graphically in Figure 4-6. What this means in substantive terms is that an offender with an IQ score of 106 has an IQ higher than 84.13 percent of the offenders in the sample. Conversely, their IQ score is lower than 15.85 percent of the sample. Applying these to our total sample of about 376 inmates, he or she scores higher than about 316 of the other subjects in the sample and lower than about 60.

Let us now take an individual from a hypothetical sample of juvenile delinquents who also has an IQ of 106 and compute their z scores. The mean IQ for the sample of juvenile delinquents is 92.2 and the standard deviation is 10.5. We will not round our figures this time.

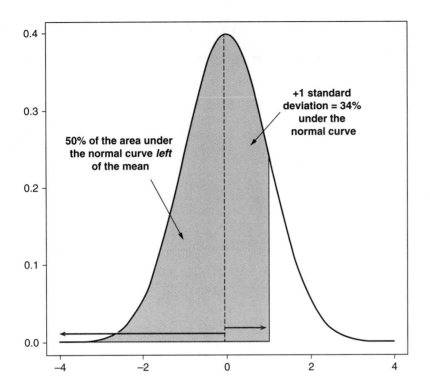

FIGURE 4-6

Calculating the area under the normal curve using z scores

$$z = \frac{x - \bar{x}}{s} = \frac{106 - 92.2}{10.5} = \frac{13.8}{10.5} = 1.31$$

A z score of 1.31 is not readily converted to an area under the curve by visual inspection. That is, we're not certain what percentage of the normal curve is found between the mean and a z score of 1.31. We only know that the area below the mean is 0.50 and that the total area above the mean with a z of 1.31 (which is also a standard deviation) is greater than 0.3413 (or 1 standard deviation). Luckily, there is a table in which the areas under the curve for any z score have been precisely determined. This z score and areas under the normal curve table are presented in the z distribution table (see p. 343). Table 4-6 reproduces a small portion of this table for our present use.

The four-digit numbers in the body of the table represent areas of the curve falling between a given z score and the mean. The numbers in the column at the far left are the first two digits of the z score, and the numbers in the top row correspond to

TABLE 4-6. *Section of z Distribution Table (See p. 343): Section of the Area under the Normal Curve*

z/SD	0.00	0.01	0.02	0.03	0.04	0.05	0.06
1	0.3413	0.3438	0.3461	0.3485	0.3508	0.3531	0.3554
1.1	0.3643	0.3665	0.3686	0.3718	0.3729	0.3749	0.3770
1.2	0.3849	0.3869	0.3888	0.3907	0.3925	0.3944	0.3962
1.3	0.4032	0.4049	0.4066	0.4083	0.4099	0.4115	0.4131
1.4	0.4192	0.4207	0.4222	0.4236	0.4251	0.4265	0.4279
1.5	0.4332	0.4345	0.4357	0.4370	0.4382	0.4394	0.4406
1.6	0.4452	0.4463	0.4474	0.4485	0.4495	0.4505	0.4515

the third digit of the z score. A z score of 1.0, for instance, is located at the top left-hand corner of the table (0.3413). To find the area corresponding to our computed z score of 1.31, go down the column until you reach the value of 1.3. Then go across that row until you come to the third digit of 1.31, which is 0.01. The value you find there is 4049. You can read this as either a proportion (0.4049) or a percentage (40.49%) of the area under the normal curve from the mean. The total area under the curve corresponding to a z score of 1.31 is this value plus the area below the mean (0.5000 + 0.4049 = 0.9049). Our juvenile delinquent with an IQ of 106 has a score that exceeds 90.49 percent of all the other scores in the sample. An important point for you to remember is that the probability of finding a juvenile delinquent with an IQ score of 106 or higher is only about 10 percent (only about 10 percent of the area of the curve contains scores that high or higher).

We now have a basis for comparing similar IQs across two different samples. Although both the juvenile and the adult had an IQ of 106, the juvenile scores better relative to his peers in the sample. We could also compare scores of an individual on different attributes using z scores. What if an adult offender scored 79 on an IQ test? How many of his peers would score higher or lower than he did? His z score would be (79 − 94)/12 = −1.25. Ignoring the negative sign for the moment, we see that the area corresponding with a z score of 1.25 is 0.3944. Since the sign is negative, this figure corresponds with 39.44 percent of the area *below* the mean. Note that in the negative case the z score area is subtracted from 0.5000 rather than added to it. An offender with an IQ of 79 scores higher than only about 10 percent of his peers in the sample and lower than about 90 percent (0.5000 − 0.3944 = 0.1056 or 10.56%).

On occasion you may wish to determine the area under the curve between two scores rather than simply the area above or below the mean. For example, suppose that we wanted to determine what proportion or percentage of our adult offenders had IQ scores considered in the normal range, between 90 and 110. The first thing you would do is convert these two raw scores (90 and 110) into z scores.

$$\text{Raw score } 90 : z = \frac{90-94}{12} = \frac{-4}{12} = -0.33$$

$$\text{Raw score } 110 : z = \frac{110-94}{12} = \frac{16}{12} = 1.33$$

Since we have not included z scores as low as −0.33 in Table 4-6, you will have to turn to the z distribution table (see p. 343) to complete this exercise. The first two digits are 0.3. Tracing along this row until you reach the final digit (0.03), you will find an area of 0.1293, which corresponds to the area below the mean. For our second z score of 1.33, the area is 0.4082, which corresponds to the area above the mean. To find the total proportion of the area corresponding to IQ scores of 90 and 110, you simply sum the two areas (0.1293 + 0.4082 = 0.5375). Thus, 53.75 percent of our offenders had IQs in the normal range.

If you wanted to find the area between two positive z scores, say 0.50 and 1.55, you would first find the areas lying between the mean and 0.50 (0.1915) and 1.55 (0.4394). Next, you would simply subtract the smaller area from the larger (0.4394 − 0.1915 = 0.2479). The area of the curve between z scores of 0.50 and 1.55 is 24.79 percent. A similar strategy would be followed if both z scores were negative.

In our examples so far we have started with a known score, computed z, and then found the corresponding area of the curve. We will now illustrate the reverse process. Suppose, for instance, we wish to know between what two IQ scores in our hypothetical adult offender data the middle 50 percent of the cases fall. If we start from the mean, a figure of 50 percent means that 25 percent of the cases will be below the mean and 25 percent will be above the mean. We turn to page 343 to find what z score is associated with an area of 0.2500. The closest value in the table is 0.2486, which is associated with a z score of 0.67. A z score of 0.67 is 67 percent of 1 standard deviation. How do we get this back to raw numbers? We multiply our z score by the actual standard deviation. Remember, the z score is associated with the perfect normal curve, where z = s = 1; the standard deviation of our example sample is 12. We therefore multiply the z score (0.67) and value of our sample standard deviation (12): 0.67 × 12 = 8.04. Adding and subtracting 8 (rounded) from the mean, we find that the middle 50 percent of the cases fall between IQ values of

86 and 102. Therefore, if we know a person's z score we can convert it into a raw score using this formula:

4-10

$$x = (z)(s)$$

SUMMARY

Probability is a ratio of an event or outcome to the total number of possible events or outcomes. Probability is a vital concept to the understanding of statistics. We have discussed some basic ideas of probability, such as computing probabilities using the addition and multiplication rules for independent and dependent events. We will discuss these concepts again as the need arises. We also showed how a theoretical binomial probability distribution curve is generated.

The normal curve is a useful tool in statistical analysis. There are many different normal curves, the shapes of which are determined by their means and standard deviations. Curves with small standard deviations are leptokurtic, and curves with large standard deviations are platykurtic. Normal curves are perfectly symmetrical, with 50 percent of the area falling on one side of the mean and 50 percent falling on the other side of the mean. One standard deviation on either side of the mean contains 68.26 percent of the area, 2 standard deviations on either side contain 95.4 percent, and 3 standard deviations on either side contain 99.74 percent.

A standardized normal curve is one that has been standardized to a mean of zero and a standard deviation of 1. It is a model by which we compare chance events in an empirical distribution using z scores, which give us the proportion of the normal curve corresponding to a given raw score. The larger the value of the computed z score (either positive or negative), the rarer is the value of the raw score. We find the area corresponding to a z score in the table of z scores on page 343. This is an important use of the normal curve and z scores because inferential statistics is concerned with estimating the probabilities of events.

REFERENCE

Reiss, I. L., & Lee, G. R. (1988). *Family systems in America* (4th ed.). New York: Holt, Rinehart & Winston.

PRACTICE APPLICATION: THE NORMAL CURVE AND z SCORES

Suppose we have a population of police officers in which 50 percent are married. If we draw a random sample of 4 officers from this population and determine whether they are married, there are five possibilities: 0 married officers, 1 married officer, 2 married officers, 3 married officers, or 4 married officers. Construct a probability table of these outcomes (remember, the probability of a randomly selected officer's being married is 0.5.) We will start with the probability of getting 0 married officers in a randomly selected sample of 4 officers.

$$_nP_r = \frac{N!}{r!(N-r)!}p^r q^{n-r}$$

$$= \frac{4 \times 3 \times 2 \times 1}{0!(4 \times 3 \times 2 \times 1)}(0.5^0)(0.5^4) = -\frac{1}{1}(0.5^0)(0.5^4) = 1 \times 0.0625$$

Remember, $0! = 1$, and any number raised to the 0 power is also 1.
Now fill in the rest of the table.

Number

Married Officers	$_nP_r$	$p^r q^{n-r}$	Probability
0	1	$(0.5^0)(0.5^4) = 1/16$	$1/16 = 0.0625$
1			
2			
3			
4			
.	16		16/16 1.0000

Now, imagine that you have a random sample consisting of 80 men and 70 women police officers; 50 men and 25 women are smokers. What are the probabilities of the following:

A randomly selected officer being a man?   80/150 = 0.533
A randomly selected officer being a woman?   70/150 = 0.466
A randomly selected officer being a smoker?   75/150 = 0.500
A randomly selected officer being a man *and* a smoker?

$$P(A \text{ and } B) = P(A) \times P(B/A) = P(AB) = (0.533)(0.625) = 0.333$$

A randomly selected officer being a woman *or* a nonsmoker?

$$P(A \text{ or } B) = P(A) + P(B) - P(A \text{ and } B)$$
$$= (0.466 + 0.500) - 0.30$$
$$= 0.966 - 0.30 = 0.666$$

A psychologist in the process of assessing various juvenile delinquents for the courts wants to determine the relative standing of selected members on IQ from our sample of juvenile delinquents, for which the mean IQ is 92.2 with a standard deviation of 10.5.

Sam and Dean are particularly troublesome children. Sam's IQ score is 75 and Dean's is 120. Calculate their z scores.

$$\text{Sam } z = \frac{75 - 92.2}{10.5} = \frac{-17.2}{10.5} = -1.64$$
$$\text{Dean } z = \frac{120 - 92.2}{10.5} = \frac{27.8}{10.5} = 2.65$$

Pull out a piece of paper and graph their positions on the normal curve. What percentage of the juveniles scored higher and lower than Sam?

Higher: 0.4495 + 0.5000 = 0.9495 = 94.95%

Lower: 1 − 0.9495 = 0.0505 = 5.05%

Total: 1.000 = 100%

What percentage of the juveniles scored higher and lower than Dean?

Higher: $1 - 0.9956 = 0.0044 = 0.44\%$

Lower: $0.4956 + 0.5000 = 0.9956 = 99.56\%$

Total: $1.000 = 100.00\%$

What percentage of the cases fall between Sam's and Dean's scores?

$0.4495 + 0.4956 = 0.9451 = 94.51\%$

The Sampling Distribution and Estimation Procedures

LEARNING OBJECTIVES:

After reading this chapter, the student will understand the following concepts:

- The importance of random sampling to probability and inferential statistics
- How to interpret and calculate confidence intervals using z scores
- The relationship between z scores, alpha levels, and the area under the normal curve and how these things relate directly to probability
- How we can draw conclusions about the population parameters from our sampling statistics and the nature and type of statistical estimates

SAMPLING

In chapter 1 we noted that populations of interest to the social scientist are usually much too large to be studied as a whole. Social researchers have to study small subsets of the population, called samples, and from the information derived from these samples they draw conclusions about the population from which the samples were taken. In other words, we use statistics to estimate parameters or to make conclusions from a sample about everything or everybody. The present chapter extends this discussion. In the next chapter, we will complete our last piece of the puzzle that will allow us to move forward to calculating inferential statistics.

To start things off, assume that we have a defined population of 10,000 individuals and know that their mean (μ) income is $25,000. If we took a representative sample of 100 individuals from this population and calculated the mean ($\bar{x}$) income for this sample, what would you expect that value to be? You would expect it to be about $25,000. Now suppose you had such a defined population but did not know what their mean income was. Suppose that you drew a representative sample of 100 individuals from that population and calculated the mean income and found it to be $25,000; what would you expect the population income to be? You would also expect it to be about $25,000. Few people have problems with the first example (estimating $\bar{x}$ from μ), but considerably more have problems with the reverse (estimating μ from $\bar{x}$), although the logic is really no different.

To make inferences about population parameters from sample statistics we must make sure that our sample is representative of the population. This is easily accomplished in the physical sciences since one piece of tungsten, for instance, is probably fully representative of every other piece of tungsten in the universe. It is less easily accomplished in the social and behavioral sciences because, unlike inanimate substances, human beings and situations vary enormously. Because of this variability we cannot make general statements about the elements of interest unless we have a truly representative sample of the population of interest. It would be of no value to obtain the mean height of a college basketball team, just because its members were readily available, to estimate the height of all males at the college. Such a sample is obviously biased and would greatly overestimate the population's height, since basketball players are not physically representative of all males, and the researcher could not generalize beyond that sample.

But how do researchers know whether their sample is representative unless they already know what the population parameters are? And if the population parameters are known, why bother to sample? In a great many instances we can never know the population parameters, so however methodologically correct we are able to be, some degree of uncertainty will always remain. However, we can collect samples that are as representative as possible, which will allow us to cautiously generalize to the population of interest. An exhaustive discussion of sampling techniques more properly belongs in a research methods text. However, we will briefly discuss some of the more usual methods of sampling with special attention to their implications for probabilistic statistics.

SIMPLE RANDOM SAMPLING

Simple random sampling is the ideal method of achieving representativeness, although it does not guarantee it. Simple random sampling is the ideal method for achieving representativeness because it is based on *probability*. A probability sample is one in which the probability of selecting any case in the population is known or is ascertainable prior to selection. *Random* does not mean haphazard or coincidental sampling. Rather, random sampling relies on precise methods in which every member of a defined population has an equal chance of being included in the sample. Knowing the probability of being included in the sample helps us ascertain how representative our sample actually is. Imagine if there were 100,000 potential respondents of a survey about perceptions of crime. Of this 100,000, 1,000 were divorced women. This means that divorced women comprise 1 percent of the total population, with each divorced woman having an equal 1/100 chance of being chosen for a random sample. If our random sample of $n = 100$ respondents included 1 divorced woman, then it would be considered representative of the population. This would most likely be the case if we *randomly selected our sample*.

A random sample requires three things: (1) a defined population; (2) an exhaustive list of all members of the population; and (3) a selection process that assures that every case or group of cases in the population has an equal probability of being selected. The first two requirements constitute a **sampling frame**, that is, how we go about creating our list of things or people to be sampled. Ideally, the sampling frame and the target population should be identical, but this is rarely possible. No lists are ever completely exhaustive. For instance, if we wanted to poll the citizens of Waterloo, Iowa, probably the best list we could obtain would be the telephone directory. But because we know that some people do not have landlines, we would have to rely on an incomplete list to conduct our poll. In countries where a telephone is considered a luxury, such a sampling procedure would be useless because we would presumably be polling only the wealthy—hardly a representative sampling frame.

Assuming that a list of the population exists, the selection process can begin. The usual way of approaching case selection is to begin with a randomly selected number from a table of random numbers (a list of numbers without any pattern to them) or using some random number generator from a statistical software package (or, perhaps, random.org). The researcher then selects the case on the list that corresponds to the randomly selected number, repeating this process until the desired sample size is selected. If you are lucky enough to have a sampling frame stored in a computer, you can have the computer generate a random sample for you. However, we are not assured of complete representativeness even with this procedure because although our procedure may select a subject, that subject may well decide not to participate in the research. Even the most assiduous attempts to select a truly random sample are not free of research design and sampling problems that are beyond the power of the researcher to control. It is for this reason that statistics are so important: they will provide you with the probability that your sample is representative of the population (you can also think of this as how likely what you observe is similar to what you might expect if you could look at the population). The hallmark of simple random sampling is that each subject in the sampling frame has an equal probability of being chosen. By the nature of large numbers and probability, such a method results in a sample relatively representative of the population.

Unfortunately, examples of nonrandom sampling abound. Websites often invite their readers to send in their answers to quizzes and polls. These requests often result in much larger samples than the typical social science researcher is able to collect. Samples of more than 100,000 are not uncommon. Such a tradition is not new to the age of the Internet. Take, for instance, *Redbook*'s survey of female sexuality and the now famous Ann Landers question asking whether women would rather cuddle or have sex. Despite the numerically overwhelming responses to these requests, the results are extremely unreliable because respondents were self-selected and thus perhaps captured only those respondents who have a certain grievance or who are particularly interested in the topic. For instance, 10,000 women responded to Ann Landers's request, with 70 percent of the respondents saying they would rather cuddle. Do you think this is representative of all American women? The readers of *Redbook* and the Ann Landers column constitute special populations that we cannot assume to be representative of all American females. Furthermore, those readers who are willing to talk about their sex lives are a subset of even these unique populations. This is not to say that the results were inherently uninteresting or even inaccurate, but they cannot be generalized beyond their respective samples, and so we are unable to comment on their accuracy.

STRATIFIED RANDOM SAMPLING

The second kind of probability sampling is **stratified random sampling.** These designs subdivide a heterogeneous population into homogeneous subsets (strata) and randomly select cases from each subset as in simple random sampling.

Suppose you are interested in determining the average (or mean) crime rate in your city of each of four racial groups based on a sample of 400 cases. Further suppose that Asians make up only 5 percent of the population. If you want proportional representation in your sample, you would have to select the sample in such a way as to ensure that Asians constitute 5 percent. So with your proposed sample of 400 cases you would randomly select 20 cases from the Asian population of your city. This is known as proportional stratified sampling.

Another type of stratified sampling is disproportionate stratified sampling, used when the researcher wishes to get an equal number of *cases* from each list regardless of the proportion of cases in each sublist. For instance, the 20 Asian cases in the preceding example may not be adequate for interstratum comparisons of income (remember: larger numbers are better for running statistics), and you might find it necessary to select disproportionately more Asians to make such comparisons. As long as disproportionate substrata are analyzed comparatively, the disproportionate sampling method can be effective. However, if the subgroups are to be combined and then analyzed to obtain an income picture of the entire city, we must take the sampling method into consideration. We would have to adjust for the disproportionate number of Asians by a process known as weighting. This process is simple and is found in texts on sampling and research methods.

There are many other ways of selecting a sample that we have no room to discuss here. All of them in one way or another are attempts to compensate for the inability to select a truly representative sample. As the population to which we want to generalize becomes larger and more diverse, the difficulties of selecting a representative sample increase. We could easily select a truly random sample from the population of female college students. But if the population to which we wanted to generalize was "American women," our sampling task would be monumental since every woman in America would have to have an equal probability of being selected. Such a sample would require a sampling technique known as multistage cluster sampling, whereby the researcher would sample clusters, or subpopulations, of women living in various areas in the United States—and, like weighting, is a topic for a different textbook.

Whatever the sampling design, whether relatively simple or complex, the basic steps of listing and randomly sampling are always the same. The main obstacle to truly random sampling is the unavailability in many instances of the exhaustive lists we mentioned. In many cases such lists simply don't exist, and if they do exist they may not be freely supplied to researchers. Even if lists exist and are available, we still must confront the problem of nonresponse. We have to be careful not to make generalities beyond those warranted by the data. There is an important lesson here: as powerful a tool as statistics are, they are no replacement or cure-all for poorly gathered data.

THE SAMPLING DISTRIBUTION

How is it that we are justified in making inferences about the population from the information in a random sample? In chapter 3 we saw that the mean IQ of our adult felony offenders was 93.561. If we want to estimate the population parameter (the population mean IQ), this would be our best estimate. But, what if we took another sample and found the mean to be 95.5 or took a number of samples and found that the mean differed each time? We would almost certainly find different means with each sample, since means vary across samples just as scores within them vary from their mean. In fact, we actually did take 60 different random samples of 30 cases each from the IQ data and not once did we find exactly the same mean. How then do we know that our single sample mean is our best estimate?

This apparent dilemma is solved by a theoretical probability distribution known as the **sampling distribution of means.** The sampling distribution of means is a frequency distribution (like we discussed in chapter 4) of all possible unique sample means of a constant sample size that we could draw from the same population. In other words, imagine we have a population of 100,000 inmates. If we took 100 samples of 1,000 inmates each, the sampling distribution of means would be the frequency distribution of the means of each of our 100 samples.

To determine the number of possible unique samples of size n from a population of size N we use the combinations formula we used in chapter 4, with a few tweaks to the notation:

5-1

$$C = \frac{N!}{n! \, (N - n)!}$$

Where N = the size of population; n = the size of the sample.

You can see that the possible number of samples from a population of any decent size would soon become huge. If we take a population of only 100 units and draw small samples of size 5, the number of possible samples is 75,287,520! (We'll save the math for your calculator. Good luck!)

If we were able to take *all* possible sample means, sum them, and divide by the number of samples (that is, take the average of all of these means), we would have the exact value of the population mean. As with all distributions, the distribution of sample means has a mean, which we call a **mean of means**, symbolized as $\mu_{\bar{x}}$ (read "*mu sub-X bar*"). The sampling distribution of sample means is a purely theoretical mathematical construct, not something to be calculated as we can calculate the normal curve by defining its mean and standard deviation. What this theoretical distribution tells us is that we are justified in using sample statistics to estimate parameters. An example will help clarify this last statement.

Suppose we have a population of five men (Allan, Bill, Carl, Dennis, and Edward), with height being the element of interest. Instead of simply adding their heights together and dividing by 5 (as sane people would do), we decide to do it the hard way and select all possible samples of size 3 from this population of five men. The data for this exercise are presented in Table 5-1. Using the combinations formula we find that we can form 10 unique samples of size 3 from a population of 5:

$$C = \frac{5!}{3!(5-3)!} = \frac{120}{12} = 10$$

The mean height for the population is 70 inches with a population standard deviation of 1.4 inches. The 10 unique samples of size 3 that can be formed by these five men are then presented in Table 5-1. The sum of these sample means is 700 and when divided by the number of samples (10), we have a *mean of means* ($\mu_{\bar{x}}$), which is the same as the population mean (70). We then calculate the standard deviation of the distribution of sample means and find it to be 0.578. How can the standard deviations be so different (1.41 versus 0.578) when $\mu_{\bar{x}}$ is the same as μ? Look at the range of individual heights in the population (72 − 68 = 4 inches). Compare this with the range of the sample means (71 − 69 = 2 inches). This illustrates an important point: the sampling distribution is always less variable than the population from which the samples were taken because it is a distribution of means, and by definition, means "pull" variation into the center—remember, a mean is a measurement of what makes a distribution *similar*. By shear mathematical force, the average deviation scores between the sampling means and the mean of means will be substantially less than the entire population's standard deviation. The special symbol for the standard deviation of the sampling distribution is $\sigma_{\bar{x}}$, which is also called the standard error of the sampling distribution.

Figure 5-1 is a distribution of sample means consisting of 60 computer-selected random samples of size 30 taken from our adult offender IQ data. Random selection means that every unit or case has an equal probability of being selected in each of our 60 samples of 30 cases.

There are 376 cases with IQ data, so each case has a 30/376 = 0.08 probability of being included. We are treating the sample distribution of offender IQs as a population distribution for the purpose of making our point, but you should realize that the population mean is generally unknown and probably unknowable. The "population" mean IQ has been rounded to 94 (it is, in fact 93.561), and each mean was rounded to the nearest whole number for ease of diagraming.

As we see from Figure 5-1, the distribution of sample means clusters around the known population mean. The mean of these means (calculated prior to rounding) is 93.983,

TABLE 5-1. *Illustrating That* $\mu_{\bar{x}} = \mu$

Population	Height (inches)	Name and height				$\overline{X}$	$(\bar{x} - \mu_{\bar{x}})^2$
Allan	68	Sample 1	Allan	Bill	Carl		
Bill	69		68	69	72	69.70	0.09
Carl	72	Sample 2	Allan	Bill	Dennis		
Dennis	71		68	69	71	69.30	0.49
Edward	70	Sample 3	Allan	Bill	Edward		
$\mu = 70$			68	69	70	69.00	1.00
$\sigma = 1.4$		Sample 4	Allan	Carl	Dennis		
			68	72	71	70.30	0.09
		Sample 5	Allan	Carl	Edward		
			68	72	70	70.00	0.00
		Sample 6	Allan	Dennis	Edward		
			68	71	70	69.70	0.09
		Sample 7	Bill	Carl	Dennis		
			69	72	71	70.70	0.49
		Sample 8	Bill	Carl	Edward		
			69	72	70	70.30	0.09
		Sample 9	Bill	Dennis	Edward		
			69	70	71	70.00	0.00
		Sample 10	Carl	Dennis	Edward		
			72	71	70	71.00	1.00
					Sum	700.00	3.34

$$\mu_{\bar{x}} = \frac{\Sigma \overline{X}}{N} = \frac{700}{70} = 70$$

$$\sigma_x = \sqrt{\frac{\Sigma(\overline{X} - \mu_{\bar{x}})^2}{N}} = \sqrt{\frac{3.34}{10}} = 0.578$$

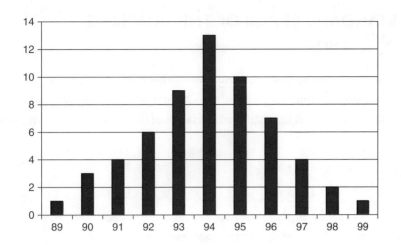

FIGURE 5-1
Distribution of 60
sample means (*n* = 30)
of offender IQ
population

which only differs from the unrounded population mean by 93.983 − 93.561 = 0. If we took more random samples we would come even closer to the true population mean. Realistically, we can only approximate the sampling distribution since it is a purely theoretical distribution based on all possible unique samples of size *N* from the population. The beauty and elegance of the sampling distribution is such that even if the population, and hence the samples drawn from it, do not create a normal curve when plotted as a histogram (we call this being normally distributed), repeated representative samples will generate means that are approximately normally distributed.

We rarely take more than one sample to estimate population parameters, which means that we will almost certainly be in error in making our estimations. The difference between a sample statistic and its corresponding population parameter is known as **sampling error.** Each mean in Figure 5-1 whose value is not 93.561 is in error. Fortunately, because of simple random sampling, we are able to consider the error random because of the variability that occurs from random sample to random sample. Nevertheless, if we use the sample mean as an estimate of the population mean, we will make an error of less magnitude than if we use any other value (such as the value of any given case). Just as there are fewer and fewer raw scores in a frequency distribution as we move away from the mean toward the tails of the distribution, Figure 5-1 demonstrates that fewer and fewer samples have means that are much larger or much smaller than the population mean in the sampling distribution. The means are clustered around the population mean and have peaked at these values. Some sample means missed the mark, but the frequency of the misses became less and less as the magnitude of the difference became larger and larger. Thus, we can say that our sample means are *probably* reflective of the population mean.

THE STANDARD ERROR OF THE SAMPLING DISTRIBUTION

As with all distributions, the sampling distribution has a standard deviation. As we have already pointed out, the mean of the sampling distribution will be the same as the population mean, but the standard deviation of the sampling distribution will be

---

Box 5-1
The Central Limit Theorem

We can summarize much of what we have discussed so far in this chapter by an important statistical concept known as the **central limit theorem**:

> *If repeated random samples of size* n *are drawn from a population having a mean* μ *and a standard deviation* σ, *as* n *becomes large, the sampling distribution of sample means will approach normality with a mean* μ *and a standard deviation (standard error) of* $\sigma_{\bar{x}} = \dfrac{s}{\sqrt{n}}$

That is a lot to take in. In a nutshell, here's what the central limit is telling us: as long as our samples are random, our sample mean will equal our population mean. The central limit theorem tells us that this is "more true" the larger our sample becomes. In addition, it lays out the formula for figuring out our standard error, or sampling deviation: we take the sample standard deviation and divide it by the square root of *n*. If our sampling mean approximates our population mean as the sample becomes larger, why can we not say the same thing for our sample and population standard deviations? Recall from our examples above that although our mean of means did equate our population mean, our standard deviations did not—this is our standard error and is discussed below.

The ramifications of the central limit theorem are profound. The central limit theorem is the most important concept in probabilistic statistical theory. It tells us that we can make inferences from samples to populations regardless of the shape of their distributions and regardless of whether the population values are discrete or continuous. Further, it tells us that we can do so with relatively small samples, providing they are randomly selected. The theorem states "as *n* becomes large," but "large" is usually considered any number greater than 30, although this is a somewhat arbitrary rule of thumb that is sometimes distinguished from the central limit theorem as the *law of large numbers* (see chapter 1). It should be intuitively reasonable that as sample sizes become larger the data will come closer to the true population values.

smaller than the population standard deviation. As we have seen, the standard deviation of the sampling distribution has a special name: the **standard error**, or sometimes the *standard error of the mean*. The standard error is so called because it represents error caused by sampling variation and is equal to the sample standard deviation divided by the square root of the sample size (see Box 5-1 and formula 5-2 below). *The smaller the standard error, the more confident we can be that the sample mean is close to the population mean.*

5-2

$$\sigma_{\overline{X}} = \frac{s}{\sqrt{N}}$$

From formula 5-2 we note that the standard error of the sampling distribution is a function of sample size. As mentioned in our discussion of the standard deviation in chapter 3 and in our discussion of the sampling distribution earlier in this chapter, there is less variability in a sample than there is in the parent population since the population, by definition, includes all extreme scores. The smaller the sample, the less likely it is to include extreme scores because they are rare relative to scores closer to the mean. And as we have repeatedly said, the more cases in a sample, the more representative of the population the sample is.

The standard error is an important part of understanding the relationship between estimates and parameters—that is, between our statistics and the actual population values. The former are always known, whereas the latter are rarely known. Before we see how the standard error is used in estimating parameters, it is a good idea to summarize the distinctions between the symbols used for the different types of distributions (populations, samples, and sampling) we have so far discussed in this book (see Table 5-2).

TABLE 5-2. *Symbols for Different Distributions*

Distribution	Mean	Standard deviation
Population	μ	σ
Sample	$\overline{x}$	s
Sampling	$\mu_{\overline{x}}$	$\sigma_{\overline{x}}$

Box 5-2
Types of Estimates

There are two kinds of estimates of population parameters from sample statistics: point estimates and interval estimates. A **point estimate** is a single value and an **interval estimate** is a range of values. When we say that the mean IQ of our offenders is 93.561, this is a point estimate of the population parameter, the mean IQ of all criminal offenders. When a pollster says that 60 percent of the American population is pro-choice on the issue of abortion, this is a point estimate of the percentage of people in the population who are so inclined. An interval estimate would be of this kind: "The mean IQ of criminal defendants is between 90.5 and 95.5" or "Between 57 percent and 63 percent of the American population is pro-choice on the issue of abortion."

A statistic used to estimate a parameter should be unbiased, consistent, and efficient. For instance, a sample mean is an **unbiased estimate** of the population mean if the mean of the sampling distribution (the mean of means) is equal to the population mean. We know from our discussion of the central limit theorem that sample means are unbiased estimates of population means if the sample is randomly selected. However, the sample standard deviation (s) is a biased estimator of the population standard deviation σ. We also saw that the sample s is considered an unbiased estimator of σ if $n - 1$ is used rather than n to calculate it. Unbiasedness only means that *over the long run* the average sampling error is zero.

A consistent estimate is one in which there is agreement between the value of the sample statistic and its parameter. The larger the sample size, the greater the consistency of these values. As sample size increases the standard error decreases, meaning that the potential for sampling error decreases. If two random samples ($n = 50$ and $n = 500$) are drawn from the same population, there will be greater consistency in the larger sample.

The efficiency of a statistic refers to its relative superiority as a point estimate compared to alternative estimates. The mean, for instance, is a more **efficient estimate** of central tendency than is the median or the mode because of its greater stability in a normally distributed population.

CONFIDENCE INTERVALS AND ALPHA LEVELS

As discussed in Box 5-2, we can talk about estimates in terms of point or interval estimates. To establish the range of interval estimates we use the standard error. We establish the interval range for the population mean of offenders using our sample mean (an unbiased estimate). Now we calculate the standard error. We know that the sample mean IQ is 93.561 and that $n = 376$. Since we do not know the population standard deviation, we estimate it with the sample standard deviation, which we know from chapter 4 to be 12.18. Putting these numbers into the formula for the standard error (5-2), we get

$$\sigma_{\bar{x}} = \frac{s}{\sqrt{n}} = \frac{12.18}{\sqrt{376}} = \frac{12.18}{19.39} = 0.628$$

We know that the sampling distribution performs the same function for samples that the normal distribution performs for raw scores. With a distribution of raw scores, approximately 68 percent of all scores lie between plus and minus 1 standard deviation, approximately 95 percent lie within plus and minus 2 standard deviations, and approximately 99 percent lie within plus and minus 3 standard deviations. Similarly, the same percentages of sample means lie within the respective standard errors. That is, if an infinite number of sample means were calculated, 68 percent of them will be between plus and minus 1 standard error of the population mean. Assuming our sample IQ mean is the population mean once again, 68 percent of all sample means from this population will be within plus and minus 0.628 of 93.561. So, 68 percent of the sample means in the sampling distribution will fall within the range 92.933 to 94.189. Ninety-five percent of sampling means in the sampling distribution will fall within plus and minus 2 standard errors of the mean ($\pm 0.628 \times 2 = 1.256$), and 99 percent within $0.628 \times 3 = 1.884$ on either side of the mean. This range of values constructed around the point estimate is known as the **confidence interval** (or CI). Thus, we are 99 percent confident that the population parameter (μ_{IQ}) lies within the range of 3 standard errors on either side of our point estimate ($\bar{x}_{IQ}$).

An interval estimate is wrong if it does not contain the population parameter. How do we know whether it does or does not? We never do, although we can state that the interval estimates contain the parameter with a given level of confidence— that is, a range of probability. Confidence levels correspond to probabilities, which are conventionally set at 0.95, 0.99, and 0.999. These values represent researchers' confidence that the interval estimates contain the population parameter. A value called an **alpha level** (symbolized as α) represents the probability that the confidence interval does not contain the parameter ($1 - CI = \alpha$). Researchers select their alpha levels depending on how confident they wish to be that their confidence interval contains the population parameter. By selecting an alpha level of 0.05 ($1 - 0.95$), for instance, the researcher is saying that he or she is willing to run the risk of being wrong (concluding that the confidence interval contains the parameter when it does not) 5 times of 100. At the 0.01 ($1 - 0.99$) level the risk of being wrong is 1 time out of 100. Estimating the

TABLE 5-3. *To CI = α = z*

CI (%)	α	z	Area under Curve
95	0.050	1.96	0.4750
99	0.010	2.58	0.4950
99.90	0.001	3.30	0.4995

standard error using the sample mean allows us to state the probability that what we are looking at (that is, observing) differs from what we expect to see—and we can manipulate that probability in the sense that we can be more confident ($\alpha = 0.1$) or less (but still acceptably) confident ($\alpha = 0.5$) that our sample estimate reflects the population parameter.

In the z distribution table (see p. 343), we note that the area under the normal curve that corresponds to the 95 percent confidence level has a z value of 1.96. To refresh your memory, turn to the z table and locate the area of the curve above a z score of 1.96. We find this value to be 0.4750. Doubling this value to take in both sides of the curve, we get 0.95, or 95 percent. The area beyond this value ($1 - 0.95 = 0.05$) is the alpha level. Table 5-3 presents the areas under the curve and the corresponding alpha levels and z scores for three different confidence levels. Note that the alpha level corresponds to the area beyond the z score—the rare events. We boil this down to CI = α = z.

CALCULATING CONFIDENCE INTERVALS

We are now in a position to calculate confidence intervals for our population mean. This relies on the assumption that our sample mean is within 1.96 standard deviations of the population mean 95 percent of the time (consult Table 5-3). We determine the risk we are willing to take that we are wrong by specifying the z score corresponding to a given alpha level in the following formula 5-3:

5-3

$$CI = \bar{x} \pm z\left(\frac{s}{\sqrt{n}}\right)$$

Where:
CI = confidence interval
$\bar{x}$ = the sample mean
s = sample standard deviation
z = a z score (usually 1.96)

We know that the sample mean and standard deviation for our offender data in chapter 4 are 93.561 and 12.18, respectively. All that remains is to select a level of confidence. We choose the 95 percent level ($z = 1.96$). Therefore, the confidence intervals for the population mean are

$$CI = 93.531 \pm 1.96 \left(\frac{12.18}{\sqrt{376}} \right)$$

Working through the math gives us CI = 93.561 ± 1.231. Our lower confidence interval is found by subtracting 1.231 from the mean (93.561), which equals 92.330. Similarly, our upper confidence interval is calculated by adding 1.96 to the mean, which equals 94.792. From this, we are 95 percent confident that the population mean is somewhere between 92.33 and 94.792. More precisely, if we took an infinite number of random samples from the same population and constructed confidence intervals for each one, the confidence interval would contain μ 95 of every 100 samples. If we want more confidence, we substitute the z value for the desired level. If we want to be 99.9 percent confident, meaning we wish only to run the risk of being wrong 1 time in every 1,000, we set z at 3.3. Running the numbers through formula 5-3 gives us a lower confidence interval of 93.561 − 2.072 = 91.489 and an upper confidence interval of 93.561 + 2.072 = 95.633.

Confidence and Precision

Note that as confidence that our sample mean includes the population mean increases, the confidential intervals widen. There is a constant trade-off in statistics between confidence and precision of estimates. You could be absolutely sure, for instance, if you estimated the population mean IQ of offenders to be between 80 and 120, but it wouldn't be very useful. Conversely, the narrower the confidence intervals, the less confident we are that they include the population mean. One way to narrow the range of the interval estimates without sacrificing confidence or precision is to increase sample size. As we have seen, the larger the sample, the smaller the standard error.

Some of you may have looked at Figure 5-1 after our discussion of confidence intervals and wondered how many of the computer-generated samples actually fell outside 1.96 standard errors of the mean. We hope that you realize by now that it should be about 5 percent, since a z of 1.96 is the same as 95 percent of the area under the curve, which is equal to $\alpha = 0.05$. Since 5 percent of 60 is 3, that's about how many samples should theoretically have means falling outside plus and minus 1.96 standard errors. The standard error for each sample is identical because the known population standard deviation is the numerator and the square root of 30, which is the constant sample n, is the denominator in *each* case. We can use formula 5-3 and Table 5-3 to figure this out. The standard error is $12.18/\sqrt{30} = 2.224$, and 1.96 times this $= 4.395$. The lower and upper confidence intervals are therefore $94 - 4.395 = 89.6$ and $94 + 4.359 = 98.359$. Only one mean (99) fell 1.96 standard errors above the mean of means, and none fell 1 standard error below.

SAMPLING AND CONFIDENCE INTERVALS

Could we use this sample mean of 93.561 IQ points to estimate the mean IQ of the general American population? (Not that we would want to because IQ is one of the few population parameters actually known—IQ has $\mu = 100$ and $\sigma = 15$). Your first guess is that we probably could not, because even with z set at 3.3, we saw that the upper confidence level is only 95.633, which is a long way from 100. Thus we know that it would require a z much larger than 3.3 to encompass the population mean. We know that the difference between the mean population IQ (100) and the mean IQ of our sample of offenders (93.561) is about 6.44 IQ points. This is the *known interval* (CI) between $\bar{x}$ and μ. We can rearrange formula 5-3 to find out how large a z would be required to encompass this difference. In this case, z is the unknown and the interval between $\bar{x}$ and μ is known (6.44). Rearranging the confidence interval formula 5-3 to find z, we get

$$z = \frac{CI}{\left(\dfrac{s}{\sqrt{n}}\right)}$$

Since we know the population standard deviation is 15, we no longer have to estimate it with our sample standard deviation. Putting the numbers in we get

$$z = \frac{6.44}{\left(\dfrac{15}{\sqrt{376}}\right)} = \frac{6.44}{\left(\dfrac{15}{19.39}\right)} = \frac{6.44}{0.744} = 8.32$$

Thus, it would require us to choose a z of 8.32 to calculate a confidence interval large enough to include the population parameter. Since z scores correspond with areas under the normal curve and since area corresponds with probabilities (refer to

Table 5-3), our calculated z tells us that it is extremely improbable that criminal offenders and the general population are from the same IQ population.

ESTIMATING SAMPLE SIZE

We have spent considerable time reiterating that the bigger the sample, the better for probabilistic statistics. This begs an important question: just how big should our sample be? The answer to the question "How big should my sample be?" depends on three things: (1) the degree of precision desired in estimating the parameter, (2) the desired level of confidence, and (3) a general idea of the parameter's standard deviation. The first two requirements are easily met because they are determined by the researcher, typically by referring to previous research or their study's methodology. The last requirement is problematic, because if we knew the population standard deviation we would also know the mean, and sampling the population to get a value we already know would be a redundant exercise found in a statistical textbook. What we do is to make an *enlightened guess* about the unknown population standard deviation.

For example, suppose that we wish to estimate the mean IQ for offenders and do so with 95 percent confidence. Further imagine that we want to be wrong by only *1* IQ point on either side of the population mean. An enlightened guess would have to be derived from previous studies or a pilot study (a pilot study is a small-scale study done to provide a larger study with guidelines). Assume that our offender study was a pilot study. In that case we can use the standard deviation derived from it (12.18) to estimate the population standard deviation. Under these conditions we can determine the required sample size by the following formula 5-4:

5-4

$$n = \left[\frac{(z)(\sigma)}{e} \right]^2$$

Where:
z = desired level of confidence
σ = population standard deviation estimated from sample s
e = desired accuracy, as measured by the amount of error we are willing to accept

Formula 5-4 is based on the standard error being an estimate of how much our sample mean will differ from our population mean—in this case, as measured by e.

(Incidentally, we could write e, with the 95 confidence level, as $e = (1.96)\,(s/\sqrt{N})$. This is simply a rearrangement of formula 5-4 to solve for e.) To obtain an estimation of the desired sample size that would allow us to say that our sample mean accurately estimates the population mean plus or minus 1 IQ point, we substitute our tolerable error (1) for e in formula 5-4 and solve for sample size. Remember that our z will be 1.96 (95%), and our estimated σ will be 12.18 (from our "pilot study"). Thus:

$$n = \left[\frac{(z)(\sigma)}{e}\right]^2 = \left[\frac{(1.96)(12.18)}{1}\right]^2 \left[\frac{23.8728}{1}\right]^2 = 23.8728^2 \approx 570$$

We would need a sample of about 570 cases if we wanted to have an error of 1 IQ point on either side of the population mean with a confidence level of 95 percent. If, therefore, we were willing to tolerate an estimation error of no more than 1 IQ point, we know then that a sample size of 376 is inadequate. We can verify that if we are willing to be wrong by 2 IQ points with the same level of confidence, our sample size of 376 is more than adequate:

$$n = \left[\frac{(1.96)(12.18)}{2}\right]^2 = \left[\frac{23.8728}{2}\right]^2 = 11.9364^2 \approx 143$$

SUMMARY

When we estimate population parameters from sample statistics we assume that the sample is representative of the population. A simple random sample is one in which every element in the population has an equal chance of being included. There are other types of samples such as proportionate and nonproportionate stratified samples. Although our statistical tests assume representative samples, you should be aware of the difficulties of collecting such samples in social science.

When making inferences from samples to populations we are actually dealing with three kinds of distributions—sample, population, and sampling distributions. The sampling distribution is a theoretical distribution of an infinite number of sample means of equal size taken from a population. This distribution of sample means has a mean, and we take this *mean of means* to be the mean of the population from which the infinite samples were selected. An interesting observation of the sampling distribution is that even if the underlying distribution of some characteristic is not normally distributed, repeated sampling from this population will result in a sampling distribution of means that is approximately normally distributed. As with any other distribution, the sampling distribution has a standard deviation. We call the standard deviation of a sampling distribution the standard error. The smaller the standard error the more confident we can be that the sample mean is a good estimate of the population mean. The central limit theorem is a pivotal concept in inferential statistics that allows us to make interferences from our sample to the population using these distributions. It states that if repeated random samples of size n are drawn from a population, the sampling distribution of sample means will approach normality as n becomes large.

We can estimate two types of parameters from statistics, point and interval estimates. A point estimate is a single value, and an interval estimate is a range of values. We use sample statistics and the standard error to place confidence intervals around interval estimates. We have shown in this chapter how confidence intervals are placed around means and proportions. Confidence intervals become smaller, and therefore more precise, as sample size increases because the larger the sample, the smaller the standard error. We discussed techniques for estimating required sample sizes for given confidence levels and amount of error the researcher is willing to tolerate.

PRACTICE APPLICATION: THE SAMPLING DISTRIBUTION AND ESTIMATION

A police chief collects information on the annual salaries of all supervisors in her department and obtains the following list of 30 salaries rounded to the nearest thousand dollars and computes the mean, standard deviation, standard error, and range. Since she has included all supervisors in the company, she has a population, not a sample.

Annual Salary in Thousands of Dollars for Supervisors

16	18	25	28	32
18	20	26	29	32
19	24	26	30	35
20	24	27	30	36
23	25	27	31	40
24	25	28	32	40
$\overline{X} = 27.00$	$s = 6.159$	SE = 1.124	Range = 24	

From this population, take 10 random samples of various sizes and compute means, standard deviations, and ranges.

Sample	N	Mean	s	Range	Sample	N	Mean	s	Range
a	8	30.37	2.56	8	f	8	25.50	5.88	16
b	7	27.71	5.22	16	g	9	28.89	4.86	16
c	10	28.70	4.99	16	h	13	25.92	4.17	22
d	4	24.75	6.18	14	i	8	25.62	6.45	14
e	9	24.56	5.43	16	j	7	27.57	6.83	21

The ranges of the samples are smaller than the range in the population. The population range is 24, the smallest sample range is 8, and the largest is 22.

Compute the mean of means.

$$\bar{X}_1 + \bar{X}_2 + \ldots \bar{X}_{10}/\bar{N} = (30.37 + 27.71 + \ldots 27.57)/10 = 26.959$$

The mean of means only differs from the population mean by 0.041. The mean of means will equal the population mean in the long run.

Compute 95 percent confidence intervals for sample mean a.

$$CI = X \pm z(s/\sqrt{N}) = (1.96)2.56/\sqrt{8} = (1.96)(2.56/2.828) = (1.96)(0.905) = 1.774$$

$$LCI = 30.37 - 1.774 = 28.596 \qquad UCI = 30.37 + 1.774 = 32.144$$

Mean a misses the population mean at the 95 percent confidence interval. Only means i, h, j, and b fall within 2 standard errors of the mean. Sample sizes are too small to adequately estimate the population mean.

Imagine that our population of supervisors is a random sample of supervisors from all municipal departments in the state. How big should our sample be if we are willing to tolerate an error of plus or minus $500 in estimating the population mean with 95 percent confidence?

$$N = \frac{(z)(\sigma)^2}{E} = \frac{(1.96)(6.159)^2}{0.5} = \frac{(0.071612)^2}{0.5} = (24.1433)^2 = 583$$

CHAPTER 6

Hypothesis Testing: Interval/Ratio Data

LEARNING OBJECTIVES

After reading this chapter, the student will understand the following concepts:

- The logic and process of hypothesis testing and potential errors (types I and II) in hypothesis testing
- How to calculate and interpret z tests
- How to calculate and interpret t tests for independent and dependent means and for unequal and equal variances
- The difference between statistical significance and substantive significance and how effect sizes can help distinguish between the two

INTRODUCTION

Chapters 4 and 5 discussed probability and how we can use probability to understand whether what we observe is what we'd expect. If what we observe *is* what we'd expect, then there is nothing special involved: our observations are by chance. If, however, what we observe differs from what we expect, then we're onto something interesting. We also talked a lot about means, standard deviations, and z scores and how we use sample statistics to estimate population parameters. We have been, and will remain for most of the rest of the book, heavily dependent on the normal curve, in which the bulk of observations cluster around their mean and become rarer and rarer as we approach the tails of the curve. We build on this knowledge in this and subsequent chapters to help us make decisions about how well sample statistics accurately reflect population parameters. Sample statistics either do or do not reflect their respective population parameters. Fortunately, we have a system to help us to decide which of these two alternatives is probably correct. This system is called **hypothesis testing**. Recall from chapter 1 that *hypotheses* are testable statements that researchers make about relationships between or among variables based on theory.

THE LOGIC OF HYPOTHESIS TESTING

Suppose a Michigan state politician argues for the passage of a gun control bill because 56 percent of Michiganders say they support such a bill. We decide to check this claim out by conducting a telephone survey of 500 randomly selected Michigan homes and find that only 48 percent support the bill. What do we conclude? We do not know how the politician arrived at her figure, but we know how we arrived at ours. There are two possible explanations for the difference between the politician's claim and our survey results (excluding fibbing, which we know we're not doing and which we know politicians *never* do):

1. Sampling error caused us to underestimate the true magnitude of the support for the gun control bill in Michigan, which really is 56 percent. Recall that sampling error is the degree to which our sample does not reflect the population from which it is drawn.
2. Our survey accurately reflects the state's sentiments regarding gun control, and thus the true magnitude of support for the bill is not 56 percent.

The process of hypothesis testing involves testing the first of these competing explanations—that there is *no difference* between what Michiganders said and what the politician suggested they said. The test of *no difference* is referred to as the **null hypothesis,** symbolized as H_0. The researcher states the null hypothesis and subjects it to rigorous testing procedures. These procedures test to see whether the relationship we *observe* is the result of *chance* or if it is, indeed, real. Stated otherwise, hypothesis testing tells us the probability that we can recreate the relationships we observe by mere chance. If we are able to recreate these relationships within a certain threshold of probability (typically more than 5% of the time—recall Table 5-3), then we assert that the relationship we observe is not indicative of the population; rather, it is a result of sampling error insofar as there is something unique about our sample driving this relationship, rather than something endemic to the population as a whole.

Typically, we are not really *interested* in the null hypothesis. We usually want to find out whether any differences or relationships we observe are, in fact, real, rather than simply chance. So why do we test such a weird idea as *no difference* when we clearly don't believe it or at the very least are not that interested in it? The answer is that we wish to be cautious. Testing the null hypothesis is similar to the logic of the criminal trial process in the Anglo-American common law tradition. The police and the prosecutor have educated guesses concerning the relationship between the crime committed and the accused, namely, that he or she is guilty. The jury is analogous to the scientist's sample in that it is supposed to be representative of the population. The assumption that the accused is not guilty is identical to the null hypothesis. The alternative assumption (the accused is guilty) is put to a stringent test in that his or her guilt must be *proved beyond a reasonable doubt*. If the null hypothesis of *not guilty* cannot be rejected, the accused is set free. Science, by design, aims to *falsify* rather than *confirm*; this is reflected in statistical analysis.

Prosecutors are not really interested in a *not guilty* verdict. If they did not have good reasons for believing in the accused person's legal guilt they would not have bothered with the indictment in the first place. The assumption of innocence is a cautionary mechanism to maximize the probability that a person who is innocent will not be unjustly punished. Nevertheless, prosecutors believe that the truth is contradictory to the assumption of innocence. Likewise, researchers are really interested in the opposite of the null hypothesis, which is called the **alternative** or **research hypothesis.** If the sample results can be shown not to be a function of sampling error, we can reject the null hypothesis just as a jury, after examining the evidence, may reject the assumption of the accused's innocence. In both cases, however, the operating assumptions are considered true until the evidence suggests otherwise. This process will become clear as we discuss it throughout the chapter.

In a court of law the accused is found guilty because the evidence supposedly points to the conclusion that he or she committed the crime *beyond a reasonable doubt*. This does not mean beyond all possible doubt, only beyond *reasonable* doubt. What constitutes *beyond reasonable doubt* for the researcher that will allow him or her to reject the null hypothesis? In chapters 4 and 5 it was shown that by marking off standard units of distance under the normal curve we were able to determine the percentage of the area that was within and beyond those points. The measures used to mark off the units are z scores. We saw that a z score of plus or minus 1.96 marks an area of the normal curve beyond which 5 percent of the area lies (2.5% on each side). For statistics, this 0.05 (typically) demarks our benchmark for "beyond a reasonable doubt."

ERRORS IN HYPOTHESIS TESTING

It must be understood that it remains possible that our decision to reject a null hypothesis could be wrong. This is what we mean by probabilistic statistics. Just as innocent people are sometimes found guilty, true null hypotheses are sometimes rejected. Wrongly rejecting a true null hypothesis is called a **type I,** or alpha (α), **error.** We never really know whether we have committed a type I error, but we can guard against the likelihood by requiring more stringent rules of evidence before making our decision. In science we do this by setting alpha at a lower level (that is, lower than 0.05, such as 0.01 or even 0.001), thus moving the critical region farther toward the tails of the normal curve. That is, a more conservative test of the null is to set the alpha level at 0.01 or even lower. When we select an alpha level, we are defining *unlikely* as being the selected probability level.

There is a problem with selecting lower alpha levels that should be obvious: as the critical region becomes smaller, the noncritical region necessarily becomes larger. This presents us with a problem parallel with the problem of choosing between confidence and precision that we confronted in chapter 5. That is, as we minimize the risk of rejecting a true null, we increase the probability of failing to reject a null hypothesis that is in fact false. Failing to reject a false null hypothesis is known as a **type II,** or beta (β), **error.** Which do we chose to minimize? A type II error is analogous to setting free an accused person who is in fact guilty and a type I error is analogous to imprisoning an accused person who is in fact innocent. In principle, the law would rather let the truly guilty free than imprison the truly innocent, and science would rather fail to record a result that (unknown to us) is in fact true than to claim a result that (also unknown to us) is illusory. In other words, we err on the side of type I errors to the expense of type II errors. Table 6-1 summarizes types I and II errors.

TABLE 6-1. *Type I and II Errors*

Hypothesis testing			Jury trial		
Null hypothesis is actually			**Defendant is actually**		
Your decision	False	True	Verdict	Guilty	Not guilty
Reject H_0	Correct decision	Type I error	Guilty	Justice done	Justice not done
Fail to reject H_0	Type II error	Correct decision	Not guilty	Justice not done	Justice done

Knowing the probability of a type I error is straightforward: it is our alpha level. The probability of making a type II error, however, is not simply $1 - \text{alpha}$, as you might expect. The two types of errors are only roughly inversely related to one another. The reason that this is so is a subject for a more advanced statistics course. Suffice to say that as the probability of one type of error decreases, the probability of committing the other increases, and it is impossible to minimize the risk of committing both types of errors simultaneously, with the following caveat: to minimize the probability of a type I error without increasing the probability of a type II error we must increase sample size. As we have seen, sampling error is inversely related to sample size, so increased sample size will lower the probability of making either type of error.

ONE-SAMPLE *z* TEST

In chapter 4 we saw that we could translate a raw score in a distribution into a *z* score. We can also do so for a group of cases. We can then use this test to determine the probability that a sample mean differs from the population mean. This is seen in formula 6-1:

4-9

$$z = \frac{x - \bar{x}}{s} \text{ for a single score becomes}$$

6-1

$$z = \frac{\bar{x} - \mu}{\sigma/\sqrt{n}} \text{ for groups of scores}$$

Where:
$\bar{x}$ = sample mean
μ = population mean
$\sigma / \sqrt{n}$ = the standard error

We can illustrate how to use this formula to test a hypothesis $\bar{x} = \mu$ by comparing the mean graduate record exam (GRE) of a sample of 400 college students at a state school who took a preparatory course ($\bar{x} = 632$, $s = 47$) with the known national mean score ($\mu = 614$, $\sigma = 52$). Since we know the population σ we do not have to estimate it with s. We begin the process conservatively by assuming that the sample mean is equal to the population mean (the null hypothesis) $\bar{x} = \mu$. The opposite assumption is that the observed difference is real and not chance (the research hypothesis), or $\bar{x} \neq \mu$.

We know that there is a difference of 18 GRE points ($632 - 614 = 18$) between the students who took a preparatory course and the population mean, but we also know that this difference could have been caused by sampling error rather than the preparatory course (the independent variable). Formula 6-1 will help us figure this out:

STEP 1: We have all the pieces to this puzzle; we just need to plug them into the formula:

$$\bar{x} = 632$$
$$\mu = 614$$
$$\sigma = 52$$
$$n = 400$$

and then solve for z:

$$z = \frac{\bar{x} - \mu}{\sigma / \sqrt{n}} = \frac{632 - 614}{52 / \sqrt{400}} = \frac{18}{52 / 20} = \frac{18}{2.6} = 6.92$$

STEP 2: The question remains, what do we do with this number? Recall Table 5-3—we have just solved for a z score, which means we also have an alpha level and the percentage of area below the normal curve. If an alpha of 0.05 is the same thing as a z of 1.65, what does calculating a z score of 6.92 mean? That is, which do we conclude, that $\bar{x} = \mu$ or that $\bar{x} \neq \mu$?

To make this decision, we first would have had to establish a cutoff point to separate sample results leading to a decision to accept H_0 ($\bar{x} = \mu$) from sample results leading to a decision to reject it ($\bar{x} \neq \mu$). This cutoff point is known as the **critical value** and is the same thing as our alpha level. The decision rule is that we can reject H_0 if our calculated z is *equal to or greater than plus or minus a specific number*. For

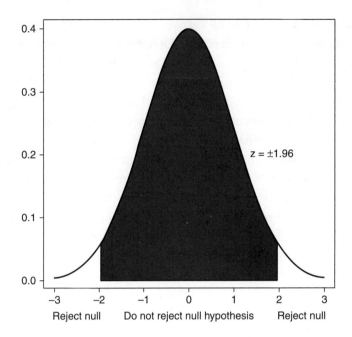

FIGURE 6-1
Areas under the normal curve and z values necessary to reject the null hypothesis at the 0.05 level of significance

social scientists, that number is typically 1.96, because in such a case there is only a 5 percent (or lower) probability that an observed difference is the result of sampling error. Why not 1.65? Well, because the normal curve has two sides to it—the side above the mean and the side below the mean. With a z of 1.65, we are only considering one side (think back to chapter 5). If we are interested in a 5 percent probability of failing to reject the null hypothesis when we should do so, we must consider the entire curve. This cuts our 0.05 in half to 0.025 (see Figure 6-1). When we consult the z table (see p. 343), we see that this is equal to $z = \pm 1.96$. Therefore, if we are interested in a 5 percent probability that our sample is different than the population sample, we want our formula 6-1 to be equal to or greater than ±1.96.

Prior to testing our hypotheses we must specify our alpha level (probability of being wrong). These cutoff points should be formulated prior to data collection to keep us honest. So in practice, STEP 1 should have looked something like this:

Decision rule: chosen alpha level = 0.05. Reject H_0 if calculated $z \geq \pm 1.96$
Null hypothesis: $H_0 : \mu_1 = \mu_2$ (GRE scores in both populations are equal)
Research hypothesis: $H_1 : \mu_1 \neq \mu_2$ (GRE scores in both populations are not equal)

We would then calculate z as in STEP 1 above and then consider our calculated z score: our computed z of 6.92 greatly exceeds 1.96. It is therefore extremely unlikely that the observed difference between the sample and population means is a result of chance (sampling error). That is, what we observe is different from what we'd expect if things were left only to probability. We would write this in the following way: $z = 6.92$, $p < 0.05$. The notation following the z value is shorthand for saying "probability (p) is less than (<) the selected alpha level (0.05)." If we had attained a z value of less than 1.96, the notation would have been $p > 0.05$ (greater than 0.05) or not significant.

It must be kept in mind that any conclusion the researcher makes must be based on a random sample that is representative of the population. It is also important that you remember that although we have rejected the null hypothesis, we have *not* proven the research hypothesis. We have simply made a decision based on probability that the null hypothesis is untenable. As with the trial, guilt is never fully ascertained—only beyond a reasonable doubt.

THE *t* TEST

What happens when we don't know any information about our population? Or when we're interested in comparing the difference between two sample means? When we have small samples, we can no longer assume that sample variances are close approximations of their population variances. We saw in chapter 5 that the smaller the sample, the larger the standard error tends to be. For these reasons, the use of the normal curve, and hence the z test based on it, would be inappropriate. In addition, formula 6-1 clearly requires knowledge of the population. Fortunately, there is a test we can use when we have small samples or when we want to compare means from different samples: the t test.

The t test uses its own distribution called the t distribution. The reason why the t test works for small samples is that the t distribution only approximates the normal curve, being more platykurtic (flatter) than the normal curve. As sample size increases, however, the t distribution begins to look similar to a standard normal curve until at a certain point they are identical. To understand this we must briefly discuss the concept of **degrees of freedom (*df*)**, which is involved in many of the statistics we will be learning. Degrees of freedom basically represent restrictions placed on the data. For example, suppose that we have to select five numbers that must sum to 30. We can choose any five as long as their sum is 30, but only our first four choices are free choices since the fifth number is entirely determined by our previous choices. If we select numbers 9, 6, 5, and 4, for example, our fifth number is restricted to 6.

Degrees of freedom in the context of the *t* test refers to the size of the sample(s) minus the number of parameters being estimated. In testing the difference between two means based on samples, one sample having an *n* of 50 and the other an *n* of 40, the degrees of freedom would be 49 and 39, respectively, for a total of 88 *df*. Degrees of freedom are the number of ways that the data can vary—since we are interested in the mean (the statistic estimating the parameter), which we know, we cannot change that for each sample. Hence, *df* = 88, or 90 (the sum of the two *n*'s) minus 2 (the number of parameters to estimate, or two means). We will return to degrees of freedom where necessary throughout this book. If you don't understand the concept quite yet, don't worry: it takes some time and work to sink in (and mathematical proofs beyond this textbook to fully explicate).

For all practical purposes, when *df* > 120, the *t* distribution is identical with the normal curve. The *t* distribution is a continuous distribution, like the normal curve, but unlike the normal curve, the shape of *t* is the number of *df*. It is easy to see that as the sample size changes, the shape of the curve also changes. Unlike the normal curve, for every value of *df* we generate a unique *t* distribution. As sample sizes become larger and larger, the shape of the curve approaches that of the normal curve.

Figure 6-2 illustrates the *t* distribution with 20 *df*, 4 *df*, and 1 *df* superimposed on the normal curve. Because the *t* distribution is flatter, its tails appear to contain more

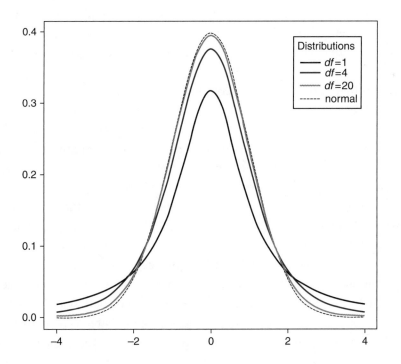

FIGURE 6-2
t distributions with 20, 4, 1, and infinite *df*

area in the critical region than the tails of the normal curve, but in actuality the area is the same. However, we must obtain higher t values to reject the null than we do for z at the same alpha level, *according to the degrees of freedom* (more on this below). The smaller the sample, the more platykurtic the t distribution and the larger the t value required to claim significance. For instance, with two samples having a combined N of 22 ($df = N - 2 = 20$), the 0.05 rejection region is 2.086 rather than the 1.96 required by z. With $df = 4$, a value of 2.776 or higher is required to reject the null at the 0.05 level of significance. You can see this in the t table (p. 344). Turning to this table, you will also note, with degrees of freedom greater than 120, that the critical region for rejection of the null hypothesis is exactly the same (1.96) as it is for z.

Directional Hypotheses: One- and Two-Tailed Tests

Before we learn how to calculate the t test, there are a few more things we should go over. First, if researchers have no theoretical reason to believe one group should have a mean greater or lesser than the other, they would conduct what is called a **two-tailed** or a **nondirectional** test of the hypothesis. In a nondirectional hypothesis test we might find a significant difference at either side of the distribution curve. We refer to a nondirectional test as two-tailed because we can reject the null (assuming we have chosen the 0.05 level of significance) only if our computed statistic corresponds with an area of the normal curve that contains 2.5 percent of the probabilities on either tail ($z \geq 1.96$)—as above. If our computed statistic corresponds with an area under the normal curve that contains 95 percent of the probabilities ($z \leq 1.96$), we cannot reject the null.

If, on the other hand, there are theoretical reasons for expecting a difference in a particular direction, researchers may conduct a **one-tailed** or **directional** test. In such cases researchers are concerned only with sample outcomes in one of the tails of the curve. In a one-tailed test the rejection region is plus or minus 1.65 z rather than 1.96 z. To convince yourself of this, turn to the z table (see p. 343), which contains areas under the normal curve, and you will find that a z of 1.65 corresponds to 0.4505. When we add the side we are *not* interested in (that is, the other 50% of the normal curve), we arrive at $0.5000 + 0.4505 = 0.9505\%$, or an alpha of 0.05. There are now only about 5 percent of outcomes beyond this single-tailed range, so we can reject the null if our calculated value falls in this region.

When we determine whether we are conducting a two-tailed or a one-tailed test, we are actually deciding *where* our alpha is to be: either on both sides (two-tailed) or on one side (one-tailed). In a two-tailed test, our critical area is on both sides. We therefore must split the 5 percent between both above and below the mean. We do

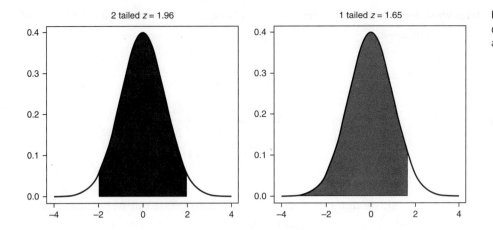

FIGURE 6-3

Critical regions for one- and two-tailed tests

not do this for a one-tailed test. The net effect is that two-tailed tests are more difficult to reject (we would say more conservative)—a z (or t) of 1.96 is always more difficult to meet or beat than a lesser z (or t) of 1.65. A one-tailed test thereby increases the probability of rejecting the null. But beware. One-tailed tests should be used only when the direction of the outcome can be theoretically justified *prior* to conducting the test. It should not be used in exploratory research or in research that has previously produced mixed results, and it should never be used simply to increase the probability of rejecting the null hypothesis. Figure 6-3 illustrates the differences in rejection regions for two-tailed and one-tailed tests.

Computing *t*

To illustrate the computation of *t* we will use a simple example. Suppose researchers are interested in comparing the mean alienation scores of guards from one correctional facility and guards at another correctional facility. They take a random sample of 12 guards$_1$ and 13 guards$_2$ and find that the guards$_1$ have a mean score of 50 and a standard deviation of 19.54, and the guards$_2$ have a mean of 57.69 and a standard deviation of 14.23. Implicit in the research is the assumption that one's occupational setting will affect one's alienation score. Put otherwise, the researchers believe that they can predict the level of alienation on the basis of job location. Thus, the alienation level is viewed as being dependent on one's employer. Recall that a variable considered dependent on some other variable is called a *dependent variable,* and a variable that is thought to influence or predict the values of the dependent variable is called an *independent variable.* In the present case, the independent variable, correctional facility, is assumed to affect variation in alienation scores of the guards who work there—the dependent variable. Let us proceed with the calculation of t using formula 6-2.

6-2

$$t = \frac{\bar{x}_1 - \bar{x}_2}{\sqrt{\frac{(N_1 - 1)S_1^2 + (N_2 - 1)S_2^2}{(N_1 - 1)(N_2 - 1)}}\sqrt{\frac{N_1 + N_2}{(N_1)(N_2)}}}$$

STEP 1: First, we determine our alpha level and state our hypotheses. We choose a two-tailed test because we have no apparent theoretical reason to believe that guards in the first institute should have a lower or higher level of alienation than guards in the second institute, regardless of what the numbers suggest. Remember: we are testing our observations against what we expect. You can certainly think of theoretical reasons why the scores may differ in one direction or the other, but for our example, we are assuming a theoretical *tabula rasa* (blank slate).

$$\alpha = 0.05, \text{ two-tailed test}$$
$$H_0 = \bar{x}_{\text{guards}_1} = \bar{x}_{\text{guards}_2}$$
$$H_1 = \bar{x}_{\text{guards}_1} \neq \bar{x}_{\text{guards}_2}$$
$$df_1 = 11, df_2 = 12, \text{ total } df = 23$$

STEP 2: We use our numbers to solve for t using formula 6-3.

$$t = \frac{50 - 57.69}{\sqrt{\frac{(11)(19.54)^2 + (12)(14.23)^2}{12 + 13 - 2}}\sqrt{\frac{12 + 13}{(12)(13)}}}$$

$$t = \frac{-7.69}{\sqrt{\frac{(11)(381.8) + (12)(202.49)}{25 - 2}}\sqrt{\frac{25}{156}}}$$

$$t = \frac{-7.69}{\sqrt{\frac{4199.8 + 2429.88}{23}}\sqrt{0.1603}}$$

$$t = \frac{-7.69}{\sqrt{288.24}(0.40)} = \frac{-7.69}{(16.98)(0.40)}$$

$$t = -\frac{7.69}{6.79} = -1.132$$

STEP 3: Determine statistical significance. Our calculated t value is -1.132. To determine whether this value is statistically significant (whether it is sufficiently large to allow us to reject the null), we turn to the table of t values (see p. 344). Since we have no theoretical reasons to assume that either group would have higher alienation scores, we use a two-tailed test. We have selected an alpha of 0.05, so we use the 0.05 column and read down the extreme left-hand column until we get to the number 23, which is our number of degrees of freedom. Where these two values intersect in the body of the table we find the number 2.069. *This means that to claim a significant difference between the means with alpha set at 0.05, the difference between the means must be equal or greater than 2.069.* Our calculated t value is only -1.132, which is less than 2.069 (the negative sign is ignored in reading the t table, as it is when reading areas under the normal curve—remember, the normal curve is symmetrical; the negative sign is really the mathematical artifact of which mean we subtracted from which), and thus we conclude that there is no significant difference between the means of these two populations with regard to their alienation scores. In other words, t calculated did not equal or exceed t critical (the tabled value needed to reject the null), and therefore correctional facility does not predict alienation level. (The possibility remains, however, that we could have made a type II error given the small sizes of our samples.)

STEP 4: We interpret our results:

t calculated $= -1.132$, t critical $= 2.069$, $\alpha = 0.05$, two-tailed.
Conclusion: t calculated is not equal or greater than t critical at $\alpha = 0.05$
Decision: Do not reject the null. Guards from one correctional facility and guards from another correctional facility do not differ in their alienation scores.

Looking carefully at the t test formula (6-3), you can see that it actually resembles a z test (which itself resembles closely the formula for standard deviation): you are looking at the difference between two means and then standardizing this difference by the standard error, in this case, the combined standard error of two samples. *Whenever we divide a difference score by a standard error, we standardize the score to the normal curve.* And when we can place things on the normal curve, we can determine whether they occur by chance or something different (and this something different must, of course, be informed by theory).

The Effects of Increasing Sample Size

We have talked a lot about how sample size affects our ability to discover the "true" situation in a population from a sample drawn from it. Samples of 12 guards$_1$ and 13 guards$_2$ at two different correctional facilities are hardly large enough to discover much meaningful about them because the sample is so small; when samples are small, our error in prediction increases. That is, the chances that our sample does not represent our population increase. Let us see what would happen if we quadrupled both sample sizes but retained the same means and standard deviations. The new data and calculation are presented below.

$$t = \frac{\overline{X}_1 - \overline{X}_2}{\sqrt{\frac{(N_1-1)S_1^2 + (N_2-1)S_2^2}{(N_1-1)(N_2-1)}} \sqrt{\frac{N_1+N_2}{(N_1)(N_2)}}}$$

$$t = \frac{50 - 57.69}{\sqrt{\frac{(47)(19.54)^2 + (51)(14.23)^2}{48+52-2}} \sqrt{\frac{48+52}{(48)(52)}}}$$

$$t = \frac{-7.69}{\sqrt{\frac{(47)(381.8) + (51)(202.49)}{100-2}} \sqrt{\frac{100}{2496}}}$$

$$t = \frac{-7.69}{\sqrt{\frac{17944.6 + 10326.99}{98}} \sqrt{0.04}}$$

$$t = \frac{-7.69}{\sqrt{10424.99}(0.20)} = \frac{-7.69}{(16.98.)(0.20)}$$

$$t = \frac{-7.69}{3.40} = -2.26$$

Our calculated t is -2.26. Turning to the table of critical t values with 98 degrees of freedom, we find that there is no value associated with 98 df. This is because there are only small differences in probability values after we get past 60 df. However, we always want to load the die in favor of accepting the null; thus we always go to the value below our actual df, which is 60 df, rather than the closest df, which is 120 df. Thus, the value we need to reject the null this time is 2.00. (Remember, the calculated t is negative simply because we subtracted the $guards_2$ mean from the $guards_1$ mean. We could have done exactly the opposite because which group comes first in the numerator is entirely arbitrary.) Thus, t calculated (-2.26) beats t critical (2.00) so we can reject the null hypothesis. Sample size does matter.

Placing Confidence Intervals around t

It is recommended that you always put confidence intervals around the mean difference estimate. You actually know how to do this from the previous chapter: the confidence interval is obtained by multiplying the relevant critical t value for the number of degrees of freedom by the standard error of the difference. In our example, t critical is 2.00, and the standard error of the mean difference is 3.40 (this is the denominator). The confidence interval is thus

$$-7.69 \pm (2.00)(3.40) = -7.69 \pm 6.8$$

$$\text{Lower confidence interval} = -7.69 - 6.8 = -14.49$$

$$\text{Upper confidence interval} = -7.69 + 6.8 = -0.89$$

The fact that zero (the null assumption of no difference between the means) is outside and *not between* the lower and upper confidence intervals gives us further confidence that our finding is a fairly accurate representation of the situation in the populations from which the data came. If we were to place confidence intervals around the first example (t calculated $= -1.132$, t critical $= 2.069$, standard error of difference $= 6.79$) the intervals would contain zero, meaning that population mean difference could be equal to zero.

t Test for Correlated (Dependent) Means

The t test formulas discussed so far have assumed random samples from independent groups; that is, there was not any connection between cases in each sample or subsample. However, we sometimes have occasion to test differences between means from nonindependent groups, such as means obtained from matched pairs of subjects or from the same individuals tested twice. If we match individuals on IQ scores obtained from one test, for instance, and then compare group IQ means from a second test, we are not likely to see a large difference between the means. Similarly, if we test individuals at time 1 and time 2, an individual who scored high at time 1 is likely also to score high at time 2. In other words, the two means being compared have a built-in connection (what we'll later learn as *correlation*). The correlated *t* test, also known as the *t* test for dependent means, provides a basis for testing correlated groups because it has a factor in its formula that corrects for the built-in correlation.

Suppose we ask 10 probation officers on July 20 (time 1) to rate a hypothetical probationer's need for intensive supervision. The ratings are based on a scale of zero (no need) to 20 (extreme need). We then go back to the same probation officers on December 20 (time 2) and present them with the same case. Since December 20 is close to Christmas, we expect them to be more charitable this time around. What we want to find out, then, is how susceptible the assessment instrument is to subjective judgment. If the mean at time 2 is significantly greater than the mean at time 1 at $p < 0.05$, we conclude that the assessment instrument is subject to subjective bias. The data for the two testing times and the statistical procedure for testing our assumption are presented in Table 6-2.

We can use this information to complete formula 6-3:

6-3

$$t = \frac{\bar{x}_1 - \bar{x}_2}{\sqrt{\dfrac{\sum D^2 - \dfrac{(\sum D)^2}{n}}{n(n-1)}}}$$

STEP 1: We state our alpha level as being 0.05. We also figure out our degrees of freedom, in this case, 9 ($n - 1$, because we are only looking at one group).

STEP 2: Next, we would array the probation officers' scores according to time 1 and time 2 and then find the difference between them (D). We would then square each of these differences (D^2). Consulting formula 6-3, we see that we'll also need the sum of the squared differences ($\sum D^2$), and the sum of the differences ($\sum D$), which will be squared. Formula 6-3 also

TABLE 6-2. *Data and Procedures for a Dependent t Test*

Probation officer	Time 1	Time 2	Difference (D)	Difference squared (D²)
1	17	19	2	4
2	16	17	1	1
3	14	15	1	1
4	13	16	3	9
5	12	15	3	9
6	17	19	2	4
7	16	16	0	0
8	9	11	2	4
9	9	10	1	1
10	13	14	1	1
$N = 10$	$\Sigma X_1 = 136$	$\Sigma X_2 = 152$	$\Sigma D = 16$	$\Sigma D^2 = 34$
	$\overline{X}$ time 1 $= 13.6$	$\overline{X}$ time 2 $= 15.2$		

indicates that we need to use the means from time 1 and time 2. It is important to note that n is 10, not 20, because we are working with one group at two times.

STEP 3: We plug these numbers into formula 6-3:

$$t = \frac{\overline{x}_1 - \overline{x}_2}{\sqrt{\dfrac{\Sigma D^2 - \dfrac{(\Sigma D)^2}{n}}{n(n-1)}}} = \frac{13.6 - 15.2}{\sqrt{\dfrac{34 - \dfrac{256}{10}}{10(9)}}} = \frac{-1.6}{\sqrt{\dfrac{34 - 25.6}{90}}} = \frac{-1.6}{\sqrt{0.0933}} = \frac{-1.6}{0.3055} = -5.24$$

STEP 4: We can now interpret our t score: the computed t (t calculated) $=$ -5.24. Consulting the t distribution table, with 9 df, and $\alpha = 0.05$, the t value required to reject the null (t critical) $= 2.262$.

Decision: reject the null; the mean at time 2 *is* significantly greater than the mean at time 1. On your own, interpret what this means for our subjective hypothesis above.

If we had used the *t* test for independent samples with these data do you think we would have found a significant difference between the means? Your emerging statistical intuition will tell you that with a difference of only 1.6 rating points between the mean at time 1 and the mean at time 2, you would not be likely to reject the null using formula 6-2 because it does not account for the relationship between a person at time 1 and the same person at time 2. The correction factor built into formula 6-3 assures that you are more likely to pick up a difference, if one exists. Hence you are less likely to make a type II error.

Calculating *t* with Unequal Variances

Formula 6-2 assumes that the variances of the two means are the same. Sometimes this is true, and other times, it is not. When it is true, we can use formula 6-3 and pool the variances together. When variances are not the same, we have to use a less parsimonious formula (6-4):

6-4

$$t = \frac{\overline{X}_1 - \overline{X}_2}{\sqrt{\dfrac{s_1^2}{N_1 - 1} + \dfrac{s_2^2}{N_2 - 1}}}$$

The formula used to accomplish this computation is formidable, and it is not really necessary for you to know at this stage in your statistical education. We will revisit this *t* test shortly in the computer example, below.

STATISTICAL VERSUS SUBSTANTIVE SIGNIFICANCE AND STRENGTH OF ASSOCIATION

The point should be strongly made that statistical significance is not necessarily the same as substantive or theoretical significance, although, of course, it may be. Statistical significance tells us when some difference is large enough to be consistently and reliably found, not whether the difference is theoretically important. With a large enough sample even small differences will be found if they exist in the population. A particular research finding may be like an old penny on the floor. You may be able to find it but be unwilling to pick it up.

One strategy to determine whether a statistically significant finding is worth picking up is to compute a **measure of association** or **effect size** in conjunction with every test of significance. We will more fully discuss the concept of association in chapter 9. It is enough to say now that a measure of association quantifies the degree to which two variables are related, linked, or associated. These measures range within fixed limits between −1.0 and +1.0, or sometimes between 0.0 and 1.0. The closer the value to −1.0 or +1.0, the closer the two variables are related to one another, or the greater the effect that one has on the other. The logic is similar to computing percentages or rates, which enables us to compare samples and populations that differ in size.

The first effect size for differences between means is simply the raw difference between the means. In our example above, the mean at time 1 for probation officers was 13.6 compared to 15.2, with a mean difference of 15.2 − 13.6 = 1.6. Is this really that big of a deal? With a scale of 0 to 20, perhaps. One would have to have both theoretical and substantive knowledge in the area under study to adequately answer that question. A more standardized approach best suited to difference between means tests is eta squared (η^2), the simple formula for which is given in formula 6-5:

6-5

$$\eta^2 = \frac{t^2}{t^2 + df}$$

Where $t^2 = t$ calculated squared
$df =$ the degrees of freedom associated with the t test
Applying this to our probation officer example, we use −5.24:

$$\eta^2 = -\frac{-5.24^2}{-5.24^2 + 9} = \frac{27.46}{27.46 + 9} = \frac{27.46}{36.46} = 0.753$$

What this tells us is that 75.3 percent (0.753×100) of the variance in probation officer decision making regarding the need for intensive supervision is somewhat dependent on subjective assessment. The variance represents 100 percent of the variability in our sample. Certain factors *account for* or *explain* portions of that variance. The more variance we can account for, the more accurate are our predictions or explanations. In the present example, the *time* variable accounts for 75.3 percent of that variance, leaving just 24.7 percent to be accounted for by other variables. If we were looking at two independent groups, this variance would be explained by the grouping variable, rather than by time. The effect size, however, would be calculated the same.

Although significance testing is a valuable tool, you should constantly be aware of the shortcomings of your sampling procedures, of the distinction between statistical and theoretical significance, and of the need to compute a measure of association with each test. Do not generalize beyond the population from which the sample was drawn. Methods, research design, and the nature of your data will always influence the outcome of your statistics.

LARGE SAMPLE *t* TEST: A COMPUTER EXAMPLE

Now that you understand the logic underlying the two-sample *t* test, we can present a real-life example from sex offender data. Suppose that we want to find out whether sex offenders or non–sex offenders are punished more severely in this jurisdiction. Sentence severity is rendered in terms of days in prison. Thus, each offender group has a mean number of days of imprisonment. Our null hypothesis states that there is no significant difference between the sentence severity means of the two groups (see Table 6-3).

Our research hypothesis states that sex offenders receive significantly harsher penalties than do non–sex offenders. Offender type is our independent variable with two attributes (sex offender versus non–sex offender), and sentence severity is the dependent variable. The assumption is that sentence severity will change as we move from one attribute of the independent variable to the other. We could find this out by calculating formula 6-2 by hand. But with $n = 206$ and $n = 431$, this would not be reasonable. So for this example, we use a generic computer printout. Although they differ to some degree, most statistical packages will provide you with a table such as this one for interpretation.

Note that the first thing the table tells you is the dependent variable: SENSEV or "subjects sentence severity score." Below this, you'll see our two grouping variables: non–sex offenders and sex offenders. Each group has its own n, mean, standard deviation, and standard error. Since we are interested in the difference between the means, our attention is immediately drawn to this: $572.264 - 324.136 = 248.128$. That is a pretty large difference. The bottom half of the table will tell us whether this difference is significant.

At this point we must make a decision about which of these two tests we are going to use—equal or unequal variances. All statistical packages use some variation of an *F* test to help us with this decision. We will discuss the *F* test in greater detail in the

TABLE 6-3. *Computer Printout for a* t *Test of Independent Means* (n = 637)

VARIABLE: SENSEV = **SUBJECTS SENTENCE SEVERITY SCORE**

Group	N	Mean	Std dev	Std error
1. (Non–sex offender)	206	324.136	569.997	39.714
2. (Sex offender)	431	572.264	779.570	37.550

Variances	t	df	Probability
Unequal	−4.5399	532.5	0.0001
Equal	−4.0764	635.0	0.0001
Test for equality of variances			*F* = 1.87 with 430 and 205 *df* Prob < 0.0001

next chapter, but for now just think of it as simply another test of the significance. In this case it is a test of the significance of difference between sample variances— are the variances different or essentially the same? The part of the table that addresses the issue of whether the two group variances differ indicates that the test for equality of variances is $F = 1.87$, with 430 and 205 *df* (that is, $n - 1$ for both samples), and $p < 0.0001$. This means that under the null hypothesis that the variances are equal, *F* with 430 and 205 degrees of freedom was calculated to be 1.87, and the probability that the variances are equal is 0.0001, or 1 chance in 10,000. That is a very low probability—chances are they are unequal. What this statement means practically is that when the *F* value falls below 0.05 we must use the unequal variance test to determine whether *t* is significant.

Since our *F* value is significant, we have unequal variances and must use the *t* value based on unequal variance. This *t* value is given as −4.5399, which is significant at the 0.0001 level. The nice thing about the table is that it gives us the exact probability of the *t* test and we do not have to use the table in the back of the book. We conclude that there is a significant difference between the sentence severity score of sex offenders and non–sex offenders. We accept our directional hypothesis: sex offenders receive significantly more severe sentences (on average approximately 248 days more—the difference between our mean). It is always important to interpret our results in terms of what we are originally measuring.

We should point out that most computer printouts give us the two-tailed level of significance. If we are conducting a directional hypothesis we would simply divide the given probability value by 2. It makes no difference in the present example, but if the probability level was, say, 0.0650 under a two-tailed test, knowing this rule would prevent you from correctly rejecting a false null since 0.0650/2 = 0.0325 for a one-tailed test.

Journal Table 6-1: Hypothesis Testing

Journal Table 6-1 provides a good example of hypothesis testing using interval-ratio level data. This table shows the differences in offending before and after marriage in terms of age difference between men and their wives. It comes from the article "Why do crime-reducing effects of marriage vary with age?" by Theobold and Farrington (2011). For this analysis, which was based on convicted men, the researchers hypothesized that younger women would have less control over their husbands' behavior. Therefore, the researchers examined whether those who married late and married relatively younger women were less likely to reduce their offending behaviors. Participants were assigned to two groups: group 1 included women who were 11 years and 4 months older to 2 years younger than their spouse ($n = 53$), and group 2 included women who were 2 years and 2 months younger to 12 years and 5 months younger than their spouse ($n = 54$). According to this table, 30 percent of later-married men ($n = 9$) who married women in group 1 had

JOURNAL TABLE 6-1. *Differences in Offending from before to after Marriage versus Age Difference between the Man and His Wife*

	Count period	Mean no. convictions (SD)	Percent change	Comparison	t	p	Effect size
1							
Early	5 yrs pre "early"	1.25 (1.57)	−65.6	5 pre–5 post	−2.6	0.008	0.47
$n = 44$ (575)	5 yrs post "early"	0.43 (0.95)					
Late	5 yrs pre "late"	0.22 (0.44)	50				
$n = 9$ (30%)	5 yrs post "late"	0.33 (0.71)					
2							
Early	5 yrs pre "early"	1.79 (2.63)	−74.3	5 pre–5 post	−2.74	0.005	0.39
$n = 33$ (43%)	5 yrs post "early"	0.46 (0.79)					
Late	5 yrs pre "late"	0.33 (0.80)	−57.6				
$n = 21$ (70%)	5 yrs post "late"	0.14 (0.48)					

a 50 percent increase in the mean number of convictions from the period five years before to five years after the marriage. Of the early-married men, 57 percent ($n = 44$) who had married women in group 1 had a decreased number of convictions in the same period (mean $= -65.6$). The authors found a statistically significant difference between early- and late-married men in the change in the number of convictions from five years before to five years after married using t tests. Based on these findings, Theobold and Farrington (2011) suggested that women who were in group 1 were less likely to have an effect on the behavior of the later-married men. The results displayed in the table also indicate that in group 2, the offending of both the early- and the later-married men decreased from five years before to five years after. Despite this finding, a significant difference was found between men in the late-married group (57.6%) and the early-married group (74.3%) (Theobold and Farrington, 2011).

Again using the table provided by Theobold and Farrington (2011) to interpret the difference in means between early- and later-married participants in group 1 and group 2, we can refer to the t distribution table (see p. 344). For group 1, with a *degree of freedom* of 51 at a p level of 0.05 on the t distribution table, one will note that the t score for group 1 (-2.60) is a higher value than the two t values listed between 40 and 60 (2.021 and 2.000). Because we can claim a significant difference between the means with the alpha set at 0.05 if the difference between the means must be equal or greater than 2.069, it is assumed that the difference in means between participants in group 1 is statistically significant ($t = -2.60$). In regard to the early- and later-married participants in group 2, there is also a statistically significant difference between the means ($df = 52, t = -2.74$). The effect size for group 1 (0.47) and group 2 (0.39) provides us with an indication of the magnitude of the differences between the groups. In turn, the researchers determined that contrary to their hypothesis, older wives were found to have had less effect on their husband's offending behavior than younger wives (Theobold and Farrington, 2011).

SUMMARY

Hypothesis testing is a process of testing propositions derived from theory according to rigorous rules. We begin with a hypothesis about parameters in one or more populations and test it with sample statistics. The hypothesis to be tested is the null hypothesis of equality, or *no difference*. We reject the null hypothesis only if our computed statistics achieve a given level of significance. A level of statistical significance is known as an alpha level, conventional alpha levels being 0.05 and often 0.01.

These levels correspond with areas under the standard normal curve known as critical regions.

Two types of errors, type I (alpha) and type II (beta), were identified. A type I error is the wrongful rejection of a true null hypothesis, and a type II error is the failure to reject a false null hypothesis. The two errors are roughly inversely related, although the probability of β is not simply $1 - \alpha$. Scientists try to minimize the probability of a type I error by moving the rejection region closer to the tail of the normal curve, a strategy that simultaneously increases the risk of a type II error. Increasing sample size is one method of decreasing the probability of making either type of error.

We use the z distribution to test the hypothesis that some population mean estimated by a sample mean is equal to some constant (a known mean) or that two population means estimated from sample means are equal. When sample n's are 121 or fewer, we use the t distribution. The t distribution is more platykurtic than the normal curve, but it is identical to it when df are greater than 120.

Tests of hypotheses can be either nondirectional or directional. A nondirectional hypothesis is one in which the direction of any difference between means is not predicted from prior theoretical knowledge and in which the researcher is equally interested in outcomes in either tail of the distribution. This type of test is also known as a two-tailed test. A directional, or one-tailed test, is conducted when there are good theoretical reasons for expecting differences to occur only in one tail of the distribution. The effect of a one-tailed test is to move the rejection region closer to the mean. At the 0.05 level a one-tailed test will reject the hypothesis at z (or t if df are greater than 120) = 1.65, rather than the 1.96 required for a two-tailed test.

Depending on whether there are equal variances in the two groups, t tests are computed differently. Equality of variance is computed by obtaining the ratio of the larger variance to the smaller variance. If the variances are determined to be equal with the F ratio, t is computed by pooling the variances. If the variances are not equal, t is computed by the separate variance formula. Computer statistical packages have rendered these decisions and calculations secondhand—it remains important, however, to understand the processes underlying what the computer is doing, particularly the relationship between the mean and the standard deviation.

Statistical significance and substantive significance are not necessarily the same thing. One way to assess the substantive significance of an independent variable is to compute a measure of association directly from the computed value of the significance test. The measure typically computed in conjunction with the t test is *eta squared*, a measure that ranges between 0.0 and 1.0 and that standardizes a calculated t by dividing it by the maximum possible t for a given sample size.

REFERENCE

Theobold, D., & Farrington, D. P. (2011). Why do crime-reducing effects of marriage vary with age? *British Journal of Criminology* 51, 136–159.

PRACTICE APPLICATION: t TEST

Researchers are interested in determining whether differential socialization of males and females leads to a differential acceptance of sexual assault. They present 125 females and 85 males with a 5-point scale ranging from 0 for "sexual assault is never the girl's fault" to 5 for "sexual assault is sometimes the girl's fault." The null hypothesis is that there is no difference between males and females in acceptance of sexual assault. The researcher obtains the following data:

Female: $N = 125$, $\overline{X} = 2.75$, $s = 1.40$
Male: $N = 85$, $\overline{X} = 1.50$, $s = 1.30$

Use the t test formula for equal variances and set alpha at 0.05.

$$t = \frac{\overline{X}_1 - \overline{X}_2}{\sqrt{\dfrac{(N_1 - 1)S_1{}^2 + (N_2 - 1)S_2{}^2}{(N_1 - 1)(N_2 - 1)}} \sqrt{\dfrac{N_1 + N_2}{(N_1)(N_2)}}}$$

$$= \frac{2.75 - 1.5}{\sqrt{\dfrac{(124)(1.96) + (84)(1.69)}{125 + 85 - 2}} \sqrt{\dfrac{125 + 85}{(125)(85)}}} \qquad = \frac{1.25}{\sqrt{\dfrac{243 + 141.96}{208}} \sqrt{\dfrac{210}{10,625}}}$$

$$= \frac{1.25}{\sqrt{1.8508} \sqrt{0.01976}} = \frac{1.25}{(1.3604)(0.1406)} = \frac{1.25}{0.1913} = 6.53$$

The critical value of t with df above 120 (at infinity) at the 0.05 critical value is 1.96. Thus if our computed t is equal to or larger than 1.96, we reject the null hypothesis and accept the research hypothesis. Since 6.53 is larger than 1.96, we reject the null. Males are more accepting of sexual assault than females.

Compute eta squared:

$$\eta^2 = \frac{t^2}{t^2 + df} = \frac{6.53^2}{6.53^2 + 208} = \frac{42.64}{250.64} = 0.1701$$

Gender accounts for 17 percent of the variance in acceptance of sexual assault, leaving 83 percent of the variance accounted for by other factors. What do you think the other factors might be?

Part 2

Hypothesis Testing with Probabilistic Statistics

CHAPTER 7

Analysis of Variance

LEARNING OBJECTIVES:

After reading this chapter, the student will understand the following concepts:

- The logic and nature of analysis of variance, including its computation
- How to discuss effect sizes from an ANOVA model
- The difference between one-way and two-way ANOVA
- The relationship between sums of square and the mean square

INTRODUCTION

The z and t tests allow us to compare differences between two group means. But what happens when we have more than two groups? **Analysis of variance (ANOVA)** allows us to compare more than two group means for significant differences simultaneously. There are many forms of ANOVA, ranging from the relatively simple to the complex. In this chapter we will examine the most basic form of ANOVA, one-way analysis of variance, and then briefly discuss two-way ANOVA. In one-way ANOVA we are interested in the mean values of an interval- or ratio-level dependent variable among three or more groups. The math underlying ANOVA is not precisely complex, but it is meaty. We will therefore also consider a generic computer example. ANOVA and its associated F test are the benchmark for nearly all probabilistic statistics under what we call the general linear model. Master ANOVA and all other advanced general linear models (and even generalized linear model statistics—more on this in Appendix A) will come together.

A typical null hypothesis for an ANOVA model would look like this:

$$H_0 : \mu_1 = \mu_2 = \mu_3$$

What this is telling us is that, if chance is involved, we'd expect that most of the time our means would be equal. The research hypothesis would be that at least two of the means differ, for example:

$$H_1 : \mu_1 \neq \mu_2 \neq \mu_3$$

By itself, ANOVA will not tell us *which* means differ (although we can usually get a pretty good idea by just looking at the mean differences between the groups). For example, if we are interested in the difference in job satisfaction scores among black, white, and Latino police officers, we would run an ANOVA on the mean job satisfaction scores of each group. The result might indicate that there *is* a difference between the means of job satisfaction according to race/ethnicity. What it would not tell us is whether that difference was between black and white officers, white and Latino officers, or black and Latino officers or among all three. We have several tests to choose from when we want to figure out which mean differs from which, and we go over one of them in this chapter. ANOVA, by itself, simply tells us whether there is a difference somewhere between our means.

ASSUMPTIONS OF ANALYSIS OF VARIANCE

ANOVA carries with it a suite of assumptions. Assumptions in this context are things that we hold true about our data if we want to proceed with the statistic. The assumptions for ANOVA are the hallmark of the general linear model and include the following (among others that we will discuss later):

- The samples are randomly selected from a population and are independent of each other.
- Similarly, within a sample, the subjects are independent of each other. That is, this is not a matched sample or dependent *t* test situation (there are other ANOVA models for that).
- The data are at the continuous (interval or ratio) level of measurement.
- The distribution of all cases creates a normal curve that approximates the standardized normal curve.

If these assumptions are not met, our results may not be trustworthy—and we may never know. This may not make sense right away, but it's imperative to internalize these assumptions. If there is one thing you should be learning from this book, it's that statistics do not solve problems that start with the research design and data collection: those problems will manifest themselves in incorrect statistical output.

THE BASIC LOGIC OF ANOVA

Like almost all probabilistic statistics, ANOVA is trying to explain the amount of variance in the dependent variable that can be accounted for by the independent variable. In our job satisfaction example above, the dependent variable is job satisfaction, and the independent variable is (as it always is for ANOVA) the group variable, in this case, *race/ethnicity*. The research question being tested is *does one's race/ethnicity have an impact on one's job satisfaction as a police officer?* ANOVA gets at the answer by comparing not one, but two sources of variance: the variance *between* the groups and the variance found *within* each group. The **between-group variance** is often referred to as the *explained* variance because it is accounted for by the grouped or categorized independent variable—differences in the value of the dependent variable can be explained by the group in which a subject is located. The **within-group variance** is referred to as the *unexplained* variance because it is the proportion of the variance that cannot be accounted for by one's group—that is, the variance that exists *within* a group is independent of any influence *outside* of that group (such as the existence of other groups) and is therefore considered *random* (or, as we've put it here, unexplained). Its source of variability is the result of differences among the individual observations within the groups.

ANOVA is, conceptually, doing what all the other statistics we've talked about do: compare what we *observe* with what we *expect* (that is, what is random). If what we observe is close enough to what we expect, we assume that our observations are by chance and not the result of any special relationship. But if what we observe is significantly different (statistically speaking) from what we expect by chance, then we have a real relationship that we can theoretically explore. Recall that the *random* variance is coming from *within* groups, whereas the *explained* variance we are interested in is coming from *between* groups. The null hypothesis testing the equivalence of these two sources of variance is tested with the *F* distribution (*F* is capitalized because it is named after its originator, the British statistician Ronald Fisher). The logic of ANOVA is that if the variance between groups is significantly greater than the variance within the groups, the populations from which the groups came can also be considered different with regard to the dependent variable.

In a *t* test, the difference between two group means constitutes the numerator, and the denominator is the standard error of the difference of means, which is a measure of the differences within the two groups being compared. The larger the *t* ratio, the greater the probability of rejecting the null hypothesis. The logic of ANOVA is analogous (although the two tests are not the same), and with only two groups to compare, ANOVA provides the same answer as the *t* test. The difference is that *t* focuses on means whereas ANOVA focuses on variances (although, of course, means and variances are used in the calculation of both statistics), specifically the total variance *between* groups over the total variance within groups. More on this in a moment. First, let's revisit variance.

THE IDEA OF VARIANCE REVISITED

As we indicated in chapter 3, *variance* refers to the extent to which values on some attribute for individuals or objects differ from their mean. The objective of science is to determine the source of this variability. We ask questions like, "What is it that 'causes' or accounts for the observed differences between this group of people and that group of people?" The hypothetical distributions in Table 7-1 can help shed light on what we mean by *accounting for variance*. In Table 7-1, we have two samples, both of which are composed of three different groups divided according to the social class of their members. The numbers represent individual scores on some sort of standardized test. There is considerable variation in both samples, with individual scores ranging from 30 to 54 in sample A and from 12 to 70 in sample B, although their **grand means** (which is simply the mean of the means of the groups—see Box 7-1 for details) are identical at 42. Group means in both samples are also identical at 52, 42, and 32, so the dispersion of group means (*between-group* variance) around their grand means will be identical in both samples.

Within-group variance refers to the extent to which observations vary *within* a group. Which of the two samples has greater within-group variance? Obviously, it is sample B. In sample A the maximum difference within any group (among individual group members) is 4, whereas in sample B the maximum difference is 43 ($55 - 12 = 43$). In sample A the variance attributable to social class (our between-group variance) is larger than the variance attributable to individual differences within those class categories (our within-group variance). In sample B we observe the opposite situation, in which

TABLE 7-1. *Understanding Between- and Within-Group Variance*

	SAMPLE A					SAMPLE B		
	Social Class					Social Class		
	← Between group variance →					← Between group variance →		
	High	**Middle**	**Low**			**High**	**Middle**	**Low**
	50	40	30			30	28	12
	51	41	31			40	32	18
	52	42	32			55	40	30
	53	43	33			65	50	45
	54	44	34			70	60	55
Group means:	52	42	32		Group means:	52	42	32
	Grand mean = 42					Grand mean = 42		

between-group variance, although identical with sample A, is less than the variance *within* social class groups.

We can actually calculate the variance to see whether our eyeball estimates are accurate. Recall from chapter 3 that we can derive the formula for variance from the standard deviation (formula 3-2):

$$\sigma^2 = \frac{(x - \bar{x})^2}{n - 1}$$

Using this formula for samples A and B we can create Table 7-2.

TABLE 7-2. *Between- and Within-Group Variances Continued*

	SAMPLE A	SAMPLE B
	Within-group variances	
High	2.5	282.5
Middle	2.5	172
Low	2.5	324.5
	Between-group variances	
	73.571	294

Box 7-1
The Grand Mean

The grand mean is the mean of all means in an ANOVA. It is calculated just as any other mean is, although we can play with the notation a bit:

$$\bar{X} = \frac{\Sigma \bar{x}}{n}$$

In this case, $\bar{X}$ is the grand mean, and $\Sigma \bar{x}$ is the sum of all means. Our n for this formula is simply the total number of samples. So referring to Sample A from Table 7-1:

$$\bar{x}_{high} = 52$$
$$\bar{x}_{middle} = 42$$
$$\bar{x}_{low} = 32$$
$$n = 3$$

Then

$$\bar{X} = \frac{52 + 42 + 32}{3} = \frac{126}{3} = 42$$

Note how much larger the between-group variance is for sample A than any of the three within-group variances. Substantively, we would conclude from sample A that variation in social class (between-group variation) appears more important in accounting for variation in test scores than variation in any individual attributes (within-group variation) members of the groups may possess. We would conclude the opposite from sample B: individual differences are more important in accounting for test scores than is one's social class category: the variation for lower-class cases is much greater than the between-group variance, which is comparable to the high class variance. Note, however, that middle-class variance is much smaller than the between-group variance. This is where ANOVA will help us ascertain what, exactly, is going on with these numbers.

ANOVA AND THE *F* DISTRIBUTION

Whereas the *t* test uses the *t* distribution to determine significance, the variance ratios in ANOVA are tested for significance with the **F distribution**. Like the *t* distribution, the *F* distribution will vary in shape according to the number of degrees of freedom used in calculation. The F distribution begins to look something like the normal curve as df increases, but it always remains *positively* skewed (we cannot have a negative F value—you'll understand why this is momentarily). Unlike other distributions, the F distribution is described by two types of df: the degrees of freedom between groups (df_b) and the degrees of freedom within groups (df_w). The former (df_b) are determined by $k - 1$, where $k =$ the number of groups or categories being compared. We had three social class categories in Table 7-1, so df_b would be $3 - 1 = 2$. Within-group degrees of freedom (df_w) are determined by $n - k$, where $n =$ the total number of cases in all groups. If we were examining four groups of 25 members each (for an $n = 100$), df_w would be $100 - 4 = 96$.

With this background, you are now ready to calculate ANOVA, using the F test to determine statistical significance. The formula for ANOVA F is straightforward (with some meaty math underneath):

7-1

$$F = \frac{MS_{\text{between}}}{MS_{\text{within}}}$$

MS refers to what we call the mean square, and its calculation is tied to degrees of freedom. Conceptually, what ANOVA is doing remains unchanged: we are comparing what we *observe* (between variance) to what we *expect* or that which is *random* (the within variance). To figure out what's going on in this formula, let's learn by doing.

CALCULATING ANOVA

Suppose a researcher wants to study the effects of levels of prison confinement on levels of general knowledge. She randomly selects six minimum-security, six medium-security, and six maximum-security inmates and administers a general knowledge test. H_0 is that the means of the three groups will not differ between each other:

$$H_0 : \bar{x}_{\text{min}} = \bar{x}_{\text{med}} = \bar{x}_{\text{max}}$$

The research hypothesis is that at least two group means will be significantly different, which we can represent in equation form:

$$H_1 : \bar{x}_{\text{min}} \neq \bar{x}_{\text{med}} \neq \bar{x}_{\text{max}}$$

The computation of ANOVA utilizes the sum of squares (*SS*), which we examined in chapter 3. Recall that *SS* is expressed as $\Sigma(\bar{x} - x)^2$. However, in ANOVA we have separate group means and a total or grand mean and thus separate sums of squares. The formula for **total sum of squares** is given in formula 7-2:

7-2

$$SS_{\text{total}} = \Sigma(x - \bar{x}_t)^2$$

Where $\bar{x}_t$ = the total or grand mean

As you will recall from chapter 3, the business of subtracting the mean from every score, squaring the difference, and then summing is a tedious and error-prone process. Worse yet, in ANOVA we have to calculate between- and within-group sums of squares as well as the total sum of squares. Happily, the computational formula for the standard deviation is applicable to ANOVA. The computational formula for SS_{total} is given by formula 7-3, which is exactly the same as the formula in chapter 3.

7-3

$$SS_{\text{total}} = \Sigma x_t^2 - \frac{(\Sigma x_t)^2}{n_t}$$

Where Σx_t^2 = the sum of the squared *x* scores totaled over all groups
$(\Sigma x_t)^2$ = the square of the sum of the *x* scores totaled over all groups

We will calculate SS_{total} with the data in Table 7-3. We will use this formula (7-3) to eventually arrive at formula 7-1. Stay with us as we walk you through this process step by step, starting with the following:

STEP 1. First, and as always, we state our hypotheses and set our alpha level: our null hypothesis is that there is no difference in general knowledge among inmates according to their level of confinement. Our research hypothesis is that inmates' general knowledge will differ according to where they are confined. We set our alpha level at the standard $\alpha = 0.05$ and assume a two-tailed test, because we have no theoretical reason (for the present example) to assume that one's confinement will affect one's general knowledge in one direction or another.

TABLE 7-3. *Values for ANOVA Computations (n = 18, 6 per Group with 3 Groups)*

	Min	Min²	Med	Med²	Max	Max²
	73	5329	72	5184	83	6889
	75	5625	78	6084	86	7396
	77	5929	74	5476	89	7921
	75	5625	80	6400	85	7225
	78	6084	83	6889	90	8100
	75	5625	80	6400	95	9025
Sum	453	34217	467	36433	528	46556
Mean	75.5		77.8333		88	

STEP 2. Using the data from Table 7-3, we prepare to calculate SS_{total} with formula 7-3:

$$SS_{total} = \Sigma x_t^2 - \frac{(\Sigma x_t)^2}{n_t}$$

Formula 7-3 indicates we need to figure out Σx_t^2 and $(\Sigma x_t)^2$. For the former sum, we consider the columns min², med², and max²:

$$\Sigma x_t^2 = 34{,}217 + 36{,}433 + 46{,}556 = 117{,}206$$

Next, we find $(\Sigma x_t)^2$, which is the sum of all x's across the groups, squared:

$$(\Sigma x_t)^2 = (453 + 467 + 528)^2 = 1{,}448^2 = 2{,}096{,}704$$

STEP 3. Armed with all our tools, we are ready to calculate SS_{total}:

$$SS_{total} = 117{,}206 - \frac{2{,}096{,}704}{18}$$

$$SS_{total} = 117{,}206 - 116{,}483.56$$

$$SS_{total} = 722.44$$

This step tells us that the total sum of squares across all three groups is 722.44. This is a really abstract number, so our next step is to start to standardize things (just as we do with the t and z tests) to make sense of them.

Refer back to formula 7-1—ignoring what we mean by mean sum of squares for the moment (although you can probably guess what that means by now), note that we are trying to get at the between and the within variance. Currently, we only have the total. The total variance is equal to the sum of the between and within variance. Remembering that variance is simply the sum of squares divided by $n - 1$, we can also say that the total sum of squares is equal to the sum of the between sum of squares and the within sum of squares, or:

7-4

$$SS_{total} = SS_{between} + SS_{within}$$

Our next step, then, is to separate our $SS_{between}$ from our SS_{within}, moving us one step closer to formula 7-1.

STEP 4. Partition SS_{total} into $SS_{between}$ and SS_{within}, starting with $SS_{between}$. The formula for computing $SS_{between}$ is formula 7-5.

7-5

$$SS_{between} = \Sigma \left[\frac{\left(\Sigma x_g\right)^2}{n_i} \right] - \frac{\left(\Sigma x_t\right)^2}{n_t}$$

Where $\dfrac{\Sigma\left(\Sigma x_g\right)^2}{n_i}$ = the square of the sum of the x scores in each group

n_i = the number of observations in each group

We are now looking at g and i precisely because we are calculating the *between* group scores—differences *between* each group. Using our data from Table 7-3 again:

$$SS_{between} = \left[\frac{453^2}{6} + \frac{467^2}{6} + \frac{528^2}{6} \right] - \frac{2,096,704}{18}$$

$$SS_{between} = (34,201.5 + 36,348.2 + 46,464) - 116,483.5$$

$$SS_{between} = 117,013.67 - 116,483.5$$

$$SS_{between} = 530.2$$

We now have our between sum of squares. To calculate our within sum of squares we can simply subtract $SS_{between}$ from SS_{total} (see Box 7-2).

STEP 5. Calculate SS_{within} by subtracting $SS_{between}$ from SS_{total}:

$$SS_{within} = SS_{total} - SS_{between}$$

$$SS_{within} = 722.44 - 530.2 = 192.24$$

Box 7-2
Calculating SS$_{within}$

Because $SS_{between}$ plus SS_{within} must equal SS_{total}, we can simply subtract $SS_{between}$ from SS_{total} to find SS_{within}. However, we can calculate SS_{within} as a check on our other computations made so far.

$$SS_{within} = \Sigma \left[\Sigma x_g^2 - \frac{\left(\Sigma x_g\right)^2}{n_i} \right]$$

$$SS_{within} = \left[34,217 - \frac{453^2}{6} \right] + \left[36,433 - \frac{467^2}{6} \right] + \left[46,556 - \frac{528^2}{6} \right]$$

eventually works out to

$$SS_{within} = 192.27$$

Reversing the process, we can find for SS_{total}:

$$SS_{total} = SS_{between} + SS_{within}$$

$$SS_{total} = 530.2 + 192.27$$

$$SS_{total} = 722.44$$

STEP 6. So far, we have the following information:

$$SS_{total} = 722.44$$

$$SS_{between} = 530.2$$

$$SS_{within} = 192.4$$

The next step is to calculate our variances. What we have at this point are sums of squares, but ANOVA is based on variance ratios. In chapter 3 we defined variance as the sum of squares divided by $n - 1$. We cannot do so here because we have partitioned the sums of squares—the SS_{within} and the $SS_{between}$ are parts of the SS_{total}, and thus their variances will also be a product of the total variance, rather than related directly back to the sample size. To arrive at the variances between and within, we divide each of the SSs by their respective degrees of freedom to arrive at a value called **mean square** (*MS*), which is the ANOVA term for variance. We previously defined the degrees of freedom for $SS_{between}$ as $k - 1$ and for SS_{within} as $n - k$. We have three categories of the dependent variable (k, min, med, and max) and 18 observations (n) across all three categories. The degrees of freedom for $SS_{between}$ are therefore $3 - 1 = 2$, and for SS_{within} df is $18 - 3 = 15$. The mean square values are calculated using formulas 7-6 and 7-7:

7-6

$$MS_{between} = \frac{SS_{between}}{df_{between}}$$

7-7

$$MS_{within} = \frac{SS_{within}}{df_{within}}$$

If we use our values from above with the newly calculated *df*s, we calculate the following:

$$MS_{between} = \frac{530.2}{2} = 265.1$$

$$MS_{within} = \frac{192.27}{15} = 12.82$$

STEP 7: The final step is to determine whether our finding is statistically significant. We are now in a position to test for significance with the F distribution. The **F ratio** is determined by the ratio of the mean square within to the mean square between, as in formula 7-8. If there are no differences among the groups, the between-group and within-group variances will be approximately equal, and the value of F will be about 1. The more the between-group variance exceeds the within-group variance, the greater the probability that the groups represent different populations (check back to Table 7-1 to see what we mean).

$$F = \frac{MS_{\text{between}}}{MS_{\text{within}}} = \frac{265.1}{12.82} = 20.68$$

This F value means that the between-group variance is 20.68 times larger than the within-group variance.

We now have to make our decision regarding H_0 by comparing our computed F (what we observe) with the critical F (what we expect by chance) found in the F distribution table (see pp. 345–346; see Box 7-3 for instructions on reading the F table), which, in this case, is 3.68 at the 0.05 level. Our computed F of 20.68 greatly exceeds this value. (As an exercise, use the 0.01 table to see whether it also exceeds that critical F value.) We may therefore reject the null hypothesis.

STEP 8: There is actually one more step involved: we must interpret our results. At this point, all we can say is that there is a statistical difference (at the 0.05 level) somewhere between the means in inmates' general knowledge according to levels of security: minimum, medium, and maximum.

Box 7-3
Reading the F Table

There are two sets of degrees of freedom in the F distribution corresponding to the denominators of the mean square formula (in the present example, $dfs = 2$ and 15). The F distribution table has separate tables for the 0.05 and 0.01 alpha levels. Note that df_{between} (the numerator) runs across the top of the table and that df_{within} (the denominator) runs down the side. To read this table, start at the top and find the degrees of freedom between (for our example, 2); then trace the column down until you come to degrees of freedom within (15). At the intersection of these two values is *the minimum value of F necessary to reject the null hypothesis.*

Box 7-4
Eta Squared

For effect size, we can use the raw mean differences and something called *eta squared*. Eta squared employs the SS_{total} that we previously calculated. Remember, we are interested in the amount of variance that we can explain. So eta squared is the percentage of variance that our between-group variance makes up of the total variance:

$$\eta^2 = \frac{SS_{between}}{SS_{total}}$$

If we plug in the numbers that we calculated for our inmate population, we arrive at

$$\eta^2 = \frac{530.2}{722.5} = 0.7338$$

As we noted in chapter 6, eta squared is interpreted as the amount of variance in the dependent variable explained by the independent variable. Statistically speaking, then, level of confinement accounts for about 73.4 percent of the variance in general knowledge. Note that this is not necessarily a causal statement: it is a statement of *association* or relationship.

What we are not in a position to say is *where* there is this difference. This is the topic of the next section: the **Scheffé test**. (For a brief discussion on a measurement of effect for ANOVA, see Box 7-4.)

Multiple Comparisons: The Scheffé Test

Since we have rejected the null hypothesis in our example above, we know that at least two means differ significantly, but we don't know which two or even if all three means differ from one another. There are a number of ways by which you can determine which means differ. We prefer the Scheffé multiple comparison method because it is both the most conservative and the most versatile method. It is the most conservative because it yields fewer significantly different pairs than other methods; it is the most versatile because it can be used with unbalanced designs (that is, ANOVA models where your groups are not of the same size—imagine, for example, if we still had our $N = 18$, but our groups were $n_{min} = 5$, $n_{med} = 7$, and $n_{max} = 6$).

The formula for the Scheffé test is given below as 7-8:

7-8

$$C = \left[\sqrt{(k-1)(F_{\text{critical}})}\right]\left[\sqrt{\frac{1}{n_1} + \frac{1}{n_2}}(MS_{\text{within}})\right]$$

Where k = the number of groups

n = the sample size of the contrasting groups (1 or 2)

From the formula you can see that the Scheffé test has to be computed for each unique pair being contrasted—but only *if* group sizes are unequal. This is so because that is the *only* variable that changes. In our case we need only compute it once since all groups are of equal size. Note that F critical in the formula is the F value required to reject the null—in our present case with 2 and 15 degrees of freedom. Substituting,

$$C = \sqrt{(3-1)(3.68)} \times \sqrt{\frac{1}{6} + \frac{1}{6}}(12.82)$$
$$C = 2.71 \times 1.487$$
$$C = 4.043$$

What this number means is that the minimum difference between a pair of means in our sample must be 4.043 or greater to claim significance. We can identify the significantly different group means in Table 7-4, which is a summary table of our results. This will let us complete our interpretation from step 8 above:

TABLE 7-4. *ANOVA Summary Table*

Source of variance	SS	df	Mean square	F	Sig
Between groups	530.2	2	265.1	20.66	<0.05
Within groups	192.3	15	12.82		
Total	722.5	17			

Scheffé multiple comparison
Minimum 75.5 − medium 77.83 = 2.33, ns
Minimum 75.5 − maximum 88.00 = 12.5, $p < 0.05$
Medium 77.83 − maximum 88.00 = 10.17, $p < 0.05$

> **Box 7-5**
> **The Advantage of ANOVA over Multiple Tests**
>
> You might wonder why we do not simply calculate separate t tests between all possible pairs of groups rather than bother with another—and rather involved—statistical model. The simple answer is that it would be both inefficient and misleading to do so. The number of possible pairwise group comparisons is determined by the formula $n(n-1)/2$. If we were comparing four group means we would have to run $(4)(3)/2 = 6$ separate t tests. With ANOVA we have to perform only one test. Further, if we run six separate t tests they would not all be independent comparisons and the resulting probabilities would overlap, thus increasing the probability of making a type I error. Remember, if we are looking for a difference that is statistically significant at the 0.05 level, we would falsely reject a true null hypothesis in the long run in 1 of every 20 comparisons. The more separate tests we conduct, the more likely it becomes that we will claim that some difference is real when it is actually by chance.

Running a single ANOVA versus several t tests may seem overly complicated; it is, in fact, more elegant and robust; see Box 7-5 for a discussion as to why this is so.

TWO-WAY ANALYSIS OF VARIANCE

We are often interested in understanding the impact of more than one independent variable on a dependent variable. Two-way ANOVA is a way to explore such questions. **Two-way** ANOVA examines the effects of two independent variables on the dependent variable. In experimental research the researcher randomly assigns subjects to experimental and control groups and then manipulates the independent variable (or variables). Since subjects are randomly assigned, the researcher is reasonably assured that any posttest difference in the dependent variable is accounted for by the independent variable(s). The random assignment of subjects into one of the groups essentially means that all potentially confounding additional variables are evenly distributed across all groups. In experimental research, a one-way ANOVA is sufficient to test the null hypothesis. In nonexperimental research, however, we cannot be confident that all subjects are similar in terms of other variables that may influence scores on the dependent variable. And sometimes it is scientifically interesting to see the impact of more than one variable on an outcome. This

TABLE 7-5. *General Knowledge Scores by Gender and Level of Supervision*

FACTOR 2: GENDER	FACTOR 1: LEVEL OF SUPERVISION				
	Min	**Med**	**Max**	**Totals**	**Means**
Male	73	72	83	228	76.00
	75	78	86	239	79.67
	77	74	89	240	80.00
Totals	225	224	258	707	
Means	75.00	74.67	86.00		
Group mean	78.56				
	Min	**Med**	**Max**	**Totals**	**Means**
Female	75	80	85	240	80
	78	83	90	251	83.6667
	75	80	95	250	83.3333
Totals	228	243	270	741	247
Means	76	81	90		
Group mean	82.3333				
	Min	**Med**	**Max**		
Column totals	453	467	528		
Column means	75.50	77.83	88.00		
Grand mean	80.44				

being the case, researchers must attempt to eliminate the influence of additional variables by statistical control. This is done by incorporating one or more additional independent variables that are theoretically meaningful into an ANOVA.

For example, suppose we add "gender" to "level of supervision" in our above example. We want to determine whether gender has any effect on levels of general knowledge and whether the effects of supervision levels on general knowledge are the same regardless of gender. With three levels of supervision (minimum, medium, and maximum) and two genders, we have $3 \times 2 = 6$ different combinations or conditions. Table 7-5 presents the raw data within each of the six conditions. We have calculated the cell, column, row, and grand means.

In a one-way ANOVA we partitioned SS_{total} into two parts: between- and within-group components. In a two-way ANOVA things get more complicated because we now have two classification schemes, level of supervision (*a*) and gender (*b*). Each individual is classified according to both of these variables. We will thus have two between-group contrasts to examine: between-group supervision (SS_a) and between-group gender (SS_b). Additionally, the effects of supervision on general knowledge may differ across categories of gender. That is, although unlikely, supervision may affect general knowledge differently for males and females. This means that we have yet another source of variance. In a two-way ANOVA, SS_{total} is partitioned *four* ways: SS_a, SS_b, SS_{ab}, and SS_{within}:

$$SS_{total} = SS_{between_a} + SS_{between_b} + SS_{interaction_{ab}} + SS_{within}$$

SS_a and SS_b are what we call the *main* effects. They represent the individual sums of squares for each separate grouping variable. SS_{ab} is what we call the *interaction effect* and represents the *joint* variance attributable to the co-occurrence of both groups.

Interaction effects are some of the most complicated results to understand and interpret in statistics. This difficulty can be mitigated if you draw on what you learned about probability in chapter 3. Remember that when we want to calculate the probability of any *of* two outcomes, we *add* their respective probabilities together. The resulting sum is our final probability. But in interaction effects, we are interested in the effect of two variables simultaneously: that is, the interaction of two (or sometimes more) things *co-occurring*. Whenever we are interested in the joint probability of outcomes, we invoke the *multiplicative rule*, which instructs us to multiply the probabilities of our desired outcomes together. The resulting product is our probability. Interaction effects work similarly (and for similar reasons). You will see below that to get at the variance attributable to the interaction term (SS_{ab}), we will be using some multiplication.

    STEP 1: State our hypotheses and set our alpha level. Our null hypothesis is that there will be no main or interaction effects on the dependent variable, stated substantively, that neither gender nor level of supervision will impact general knowledge. Our research hypothesis could be any number of options. Let's assume that we are not really interested in gender, but because of some methodological flaw in our research design, we were unable to randomly control for it. Our research hypothesis could therefore be something like this: net of gender, level of supervision will impact an inmate's general knowledge. The phrase, "net of . . ." means "controlling for" or "taking gender into account." Note also that we are not providing a direction for our hypothesis; therefore, we will be performing a two-tailed, two-way ANOVA at the $p < 0.05$ level.

STEP 2: Similar to what we did above, we must compute our total sum of squares. Since we are using the same data, our SS_{total} will not differ—it remains 722.44. We now need to calculate our $SS_{between}$.

STEP 3: Unlike our SS_{total}, our $SS_{between}$ will change, because we are now breaking it down into three components: $SS_{supervision}$ (for level of supervision, which includes minimum, medium, and maximum), SS_{gender} (which includes male and female), and $SS_{supervision \times gender}$. The "supervision × gender" represents the interaction term and is often read as either "the interaction of supervision and gender" or "supervision by gender." Together, these three sources make up the $SS_{explained}$—the variance that is explained by the grouping variables. The formula for $SS_{explained}$ is the following:

7-9

$$SS_{explained} = \Sigma \left[\frac{(\Sigma x_a)^2}{n_c} \right] - \left[\frac{(\Sigma x_b)^2}{n_t} \right]$$

Where Σx_a is the sum of all the values *by group*
n_c is the number of cases in each group
Σx_b is the sum of all values *across the groups*
n_t is the total sample size of all cases

Plugging in the numbers from Table 7-5:

$$SS_{explained} = \left[\frac{225^2}{3} + \frac{224^2}{3} + \frac{258^2}{3} + \frac{228^2}{3} + \frac{243^2}{3} + \frac{270^2}{3} \right] - \frac{1{,}448^2}{18}$$

$$SS_{explained} = 615.8$$

STEP 4: Now, we can partition $SS_{explained}$ (615.8) into its component parts. We will begin with $SS_{supervision}$. Note that this computation is essentially the same as computing $SS_{between}$ in the one-way ANOVA (formula 7-5).

$$SS_{supervsion} = \Sigma \left[\frac{(\Sigma x_a)^2}{n_a} \right] - \left[\frac{(\Sigma x_t)^2}{n_t} \right]$$

For this formula, n_a refers to just the supervision grouping (which is 6 for each group).

$$SS_{supervision} = \left[\frac{453^2}{6} + \frac{467^2}{6} + \frac{528^2}{6} \right] - \frac{1,448^2}{18}$$
$$SS_{supervision} = 530.2$$

We use the same formula for SS_{gender}. For this, n_a will be 9 because there are nine men and nine women.

$$SS_{gender} = \left[\frac{707^2}{9} + \frac{741^2}{9} \right] - \frac{1,448^2}{18}$$
$$SS_{gender} = 64.3$$

With these two values (530.2 and 64.3), we can compute the combined main effects:

$$SS_{main} = SS_{supervision} + SS_{gender}$$
$$SS_{main} = 530.2 + 64.3 = 594.5$$

We can also use these two values to compute our interaction effect. The main effects constitute the sum of squares jointly accounted for by the two factors in the model minus the interaction effects. Stated another way, the explained sum of squares (or simply what we called $SS_{between}$ in one-way ANOVA) combines $SS_{supervision}$, SS_{gender}, and the $SS_{supervision \times gender}$ interaction. Thus, $SS_{supervision \times gender}$ is obtained by subtracting SS_{main} from $SS_{explained}$:

$$SS_{interaction} = SS_{explained} - SS_{main}$$
$$SS_{interaction} = 615.8 - 594.5 = 21.3$$

STEP 5: We complete the portioning of SS_{total} by solving for SS_{within}. Since we already know SS_{total} and $SS_{explained}$, we can find SS_{within} by subtracting $SS_{explained}$ from SS_{total}:

$$SS_{within} = SS_{total} - SS_{explained}$$
$$SS_{within} = 722.5 - 615.7 = 106.7$$

STEP 6: We now have a lot of numbers to juggle:

$$SS_{total} = 722.5$$
$$SS_{explained} = 615.7$$
$$SS_{within} = 106.7$$
$$SS_{supervision} = 530.2$$
$$SS_{gender} = 64.3$$
$$SS_{main} = 594.5$$
$$SS_{interaction} = 21.3$$

Having partitioned the *SS* into their various components, we now have to determine whether the observed effects are significant. As we have seen, the *F* ratio is calculated by first dividing the sums of squares by their respective degrees of freedom to obtain the between and within mean squares and then dividing $MS_{between}$ by MS_{within}. We know that degrees of freedom in ANOVA are $n - 1$ for SS_{total} and $k - 1$ for a given condition. Determining the degrees of freedom for interaction effects is not quite so simple (of course). Calculating the mean square for interaction effects involves row and column means. As we know, degrees of freedom are the number of values free to vary. To determine the degrees of freedom, we ask ourselves how many cell means are free to vary, given the grand mean and all row and column means. Table 7-6 reproduces the grand mean and the row and column means for the present ANOVA problem. We have arbitrarily placed two cell means in the table: the male minimum security mean in cell A and the female maximum security mean in cell F. Any two cells not in the same column will do. Note that if we fill cell A, we need not fill the tied cell D since knowing the value of cell A and the column mean renders D no longer free to vary. Once any two cell means not in the same column in a 3 × 2 table are known, the values of the other cells are automatically determined (that is, not free to vary).

For example, if the mean is 75.5 in column 1 and cell A is 75, cell D *must* be 76:

TABLE 7-6. *Determining df for Interaction Effects*

	A	B	C	
	75			78.6
	D	E	F	82.3
			90	
Column means	75.5	77.8	88	80.4

$$75.5 = \frac{75 + x}{2}$$
$$75.5 \times 2 = 75 + x$$
$$151 - 75 = x$$
$$76 = x$$

We would then solve for cell *F*, which is also not free to vary—and neither are cells B or C. Therefore, the *df* for interaction effects are always determined by the number of rows minus 1 multiplied by the number of columns minus 1:

7-10

$$(r - 1)(c - 1)$$

In a 3 × 2 table such as ours it is $(2 - 1 = 1)(3 - 1 = 2)$, and $(1)(2) = 2$.

STEP 7: Armed with our eight values and our degrees of freedom (and a minor headache), we are now ready to calculate our mean squares and then discover our significance level. Each individual effect and the interaction term will have their own mean squares and *F* tests.

$$MS_{\text{supervision}} = \frac{SS_{\text{supervision}}}{df} = \frac{530.2}{2} = 265.1$$

$$MS_{\text{within}} = \frac{SS_{\text{within}}}{df} = \frac{106.7}{12} = 8.89$$

$$F_{\text{supervision}} = \frac{MS_{\text{between}}}{MS_{\text{within}}} = \frac{265.1}{8.89} = 29.82$$

Looking back to the F table, we find that this F ratio is significant at $p < 0.05$.

We now compute F for gender:

$$MS_{gender} = \frac{SS_{gender}}{df} = \frac{64.3}{1} = 64.3$$

MS_{within} remains the same (8.89).

$$F = \frac{MS_{gender}}{MS_{within}} = \frac{64.3}{8.89} = 7.23$$

Again, referring to the F table (see pp. 345–346), we find that this F ratio is significant at $p < 0.05$.

We now compute F for the interaction of supervision and gender:

$$MS_{interaction} = \frac{SS_{interaction}}{df} = \frac{21.3}{2} = 10.6$$

$$F = \frac{MS_{interaction}}{MS_{within}} = \frac{10.6}{8.89} = 1.20$$

The F ratios for both variables are statistically significant but the interaction effect was not. We now have to determine the F ratio for their combined effects, that is, the **main effect**. Remember that the sum of squares for the main effect is equal to the combined sums of squares for the grouping variables: $SS_{main} = 530.2 + 64.3 = 594.5$. SS_{main} is then divided by the degrees of freedom used in calculating both separate effects to obtain the mean square value. We used $df = 2$ for supervision and $df = 1$ for gender. Therefore, the df used to calculate the mean square for the main effects is $3 = 2 + 1$. The mean square is obtained by dividing the main effects by its associated df: $594.5/3 = 198.2$.

$$F = \frac{MS_{main}}{MS_{within}} = \frac{198.2}{8.89} = 22.29$$

Again, this indicates that the between-group variation is 22.29 times larger than the within-group variation. The critical region for rejecting the null hypothesis at the 0.05 level with 3 and 12 df is 3.49. Our computed F exceeds this value by a wide margin. Table 7-7 summarizes the partitioning of variance for each condition and gives their F ratios.

TABLE 7-7. *Two-Way ANOVA Summary Table*

Source of Variance	Sum of Squares	df	Mean Square	F	Sig	η^2
Main effects	594.5	3	198.2	22.29	0.001	0.823
Supervision	530.2	2	264.1	29.82	0.001	0.734
Gender	64.3	1	64.3	7.23	0.02	0.089
Interaction	21.3	2	10.6	1.2	ns	
Within group	106.7	12	8.9			
Total	722.5	17	42.5			

STEP 8: We are now ready to interpret our results. We've already calculated eta squared in Table 7-7, and this will aid in our interpretations. First, level of supervision and gender jointly account for 82.3 percent of the variance in general knowledge scores, with level of supervision being the most important variable of the two with an eta squared of 0.734 compared to 0.089. Eta squared is not computed for the interaction effect because it is not significant ($F = 1.20$, ns). Let us now look more closely at this concept of interaction.

Understanding Interaction

When we examine the effects of two or more independent variables on a dependent variable we must be aware of the possibility of interaction effects. Interaction occurs when the effects of an independent variable on the dependent variable differ significantly across different levels of a second independent variable. In our example we did not observe a significant interaction effect, which means that the effects of supervision levels on general knowledge were identical, within the bounds of random error, over both levels of the gender variable. If the interaction effect had been significant we could not interpret the main effects without first understanding the nature of this interaction.

Since the concept of interaction is somewhat difficult to grasp, a simple example in which there are no main effects but substantial interaction may help. Suppose we have 10 male inmates and 10 female inmates taking a test of cognitive ability. One section of the test favors verbal (VERBAL) abilities and the other favors visuospatial (VISPAT) abilities, but test results are rendered in terms of a composite (VERBAL + VISPAT). However, since we have a test representing two kinds of abilities, we would like to know whether

\n\n\n\n\n\n\n\n\n\n

TABLE 7-8. *Demonstrating Two-Way ANOVA with No Main Effects and Significant Interaction*

	VERBAL		VISPAT	
	x	x^2	x	x^2
Male inmates	84	7056	110	12100
	76	5776	102	10404
	85	7225	98	9604
	75	5625	90	8100
	80	6400	100	10000
Totals	400	32082	500	50208
Means	80		100	
Female inmates	105	11025	85	7225
	95	9025	75	5625
	100	10000	70	4900
	99	9801	90	8100
	101	10201	80	6400
Totals	500	50052	400	32250
Means	80		100	

Summary of means

	VERBAL	VISPAT	Row means
Male inmates	80	100	90
Female inmates	100	80	90
Column means	90	90	90

male and female inmates differ. To find out, we break down the scores by subtests and perform a two-way ANOVA. Table 7-8 provides hypothetical data for such a test.

It is obvious from the summary of means table within Table 7-8 that there are no main effects for gender on composite test scores. The mean test score is identical for both males and females at 90. Neither are there any main effects for test type averaged over tests; both tests resulted in an average score of 90. There is, however, substantial interaction. Females scored higher than males on the verbal test, and males scored higher on the VISPAT test. Although we cannot calculate any main effects (because we know there are none for the *composite test*), the interaction effects should tell us a lot about the effects of gender on the *subtests*. Using the formulas above provides us with the following numbers for the interaction effects:

$$SS_{total} = 2,592$$
$$SS_{within} = 592$$
$$SS_{interaction} = 2,000$$
$$MS_{within} = 37$$
$$MS_{interaction} = 2,000$$
$$F = \frac{2,000}{37} = 54.054, \; p < 0.05$$

We can conclude from the preceding discussion that although composite test scores did not differ by gender, the interaction between gender and subtest type was highly significant: male inmates showed greater visuospatial ability and female inmates showed greater verbal ability. Thus, the effect of gender on scores on the composite test depends on which level of the test (that is, which subtest) we examine.

A Research Example of a Significant Interaction Effect

The following serves as a further discussion of interaction effects and as a guide to interpreting two-way ANOVA computer output. You can imagine just how terrifying the math can get beyond having two or three groups composed of even six people. Suppose we wish to determine the effects of the relationship a convicted sex offender has with his victim on the sentencing recommendation of probation officers. We also want to find out whether probation officers' ideology affects their sentencing recommendations. The recommendations are given as number of days of incarceration. There are eight categories of victim/offender relationship in our data, which we collapsed into three more general categories: (1) family (relatives of the victim), (2) acquaintances (neighbors, ex-girlfriends, etc.), and (3) strangers. The probation officers were divided into two ideological groups according to scores on a questionnaire measuring liberalism and conservativism. The output produced is shown in Table 7-9.

Starting at the top of the table, we see that the grand mean recommendation for all 351 offenders is 520.99. This is followed by the mean recommendation scores for the family (311.30), acquaintance (410.27), and stranger (926.05) categories and

TABLE 7-9. *A Research Example of Two-Way ANOVA*

RECOMMENDATION OF PROBATION OFFICER AND RELATIONSHIP
OF SUBJECT TO VICTIM AND OFFICER IDEOLOGY

		VICTIM/OFFENDER RELATIONSHIP			PROBATION OFFICER IDEOLOGY	
	Total	**Family**	**Acquaintance**	**Stranger**	**Liberal**	**Conservative**
Means	520.99	311.3	410.27	926.05	362.98	735.21
Totals	351	92	166	93	202	149

	Ideology	
Relationship	**Liberal**	**Conservative**
Family	287.74	340.61
	51	41
Acquaintance	318.73	580.72
	108	58
Stranger	563.33	1238
	43	50

Source of Variation	Sum of Squares	df	Mean Square	F	Sig
Main effects	29858903.69	3	9952967.896	22.218	0
Relationship	977288.719	2	8988644.359	20.065	0
Ideology	8519771.725	1	8519771.725	19.019	0
Two-way interaction	4656985.602	2	2328492.801	5.198	0.006
Explained	34515889.29	5	6903177.858	15.41	0
Residual	154549331.7	345	447969.077		
Total	189065221	350	540186.346		

the mean recommendations for the liberal (362.98) and conservative (735.21) officers. This line is followed by six different categories listing the mean recommendations of liberal and conservative officers broken down by victim/offender relationship (for instance, liberal officers recommended an average of 318.73 days for offenders who were acquaintances of their victims. The numbers in parentheses are the category n's.

Turning to the ANOVA results, we note that the separate main effects of *relationship* and *ideology* are both significant. We also note that in this example, the sums of squares associated with each of the separate main effects do not sum to the value labeled *main effects* as they did in our computational example. This is because we have unequal group n's. Also, the term *residual* is used to denote SS_{within}. As we've stated elsewhere, it's important to be aware of small differences in usage and terminology like this because not all writers will talk about statistics in the same manner.

The interaction effect is significant ($F = 5.198$, $p = 0.006$), meaning that although the effects of both *relationship* and *ideology* are significant, we cannot get an accurate picture of their effects *unless* we explore the interaction effects further. A deeper understanding of the concept of interaction is facilitated by graphing the means. We have done this in Figure 7-1. Having plotted the means across categories of victim/offender relationships, we see that the lines drawn between the means for the liberal and conservative officers are not parallel. Although there is clearly a linear relationship between recommendation severity and victim/offender relationship for both sets of officers, the *severity* of the effects depends quite a lot on the probation officers' ideology.

FIGURE 7-1

Plot of sentence recommendation means for categories of victim/offender relationship by probation officer ideology

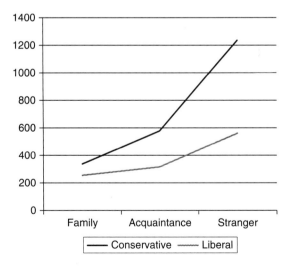

SUMMARY

ANOVA is a statistical technique used for comparing the significance of difference among multiple means. It is based on the comparison of two sources of variance: between- and within-group variance. Between-group variance is the variance attributed to categories of the independent variable, and within-group variance is attributable to individual differences. Within-group variance is also known as error or residual variance.

The statistical significance of ANOVA results is determined by the use of the F ratio, the ratio of the mean square within to the mean square between. *Mean square* is the ANOVA term for variance and is simply the sum of squares by their respective degrees of freedom. The F distribution table has two sets of dfs, one for between- and the other for within-group variance. Like the t distribution, the F distribution is defined by df, and there is a unique distribution for each pair of degrees of freedom.

ANOVA only tells us whether two or more means differ, not which ones. One of the ways to determine which pair or pairs of means differ is the Scheffé test, which is the most efficient and most conservative test for most analyses of variance. Effect sizes for ANOVA can be measured using eta squared, which is defined as the ratio of SS_{beween} to SS_{total}. Eta squared is a measure of the amount of variance in the dependent variable explained by the independent variable.

Two-way analysis of variance is an extension of one-way ANOVA to include the effects of a second independent variable through an interaction variable. Interaction is an important concept. If the effects of one independent variable differ significantly over levels of the second independent variable, we have interaction. Interaction renders the interpretation of the main effects problematic. If the interaction effects are significant, you must dig farther into the data to understand what is going on. One way to do so is to plot a graph of means and check for parallelism.

Journal Table 7-1 shows the mean scores for posttraumatic stress and alcohol use by frequency of reported physical violence and is from the article "Alcohol abuse, PTSD, and officer-committed domestic violence" by Oehme et al. (2012). For this study, the researchers used an ANOVA to assess the variability of alcohol use and posttraumatic stress symptomology by reported levels of violence. In this study, alcohol use was measured using the Alcohol Use Disorders Identification Test (AUDIT), a 10-question scale that was scored from zero to 4 (with a maximum score of 40). Domestic violence was measured by asking participants, certified law enforcement officers, single-item questions to determine their engagement in domestic violence following a training module on it. Responses were based on a 4-point Likert scale. Finally, the researchers measured posttraumatic stress disorder by screening

JOURNAL TABLE 7-1. *Mean Scores for Posttraumatic Stress and Alcohol Use by Reported Physical Violence*

Physical Violence	Posttraumatic Stress Mean (SD)	Alcohol Use Mean (SD)
Frequently	40.82 (17.75)	14.39 (11.87)
Occasionally	42.82 (15.18)	13.51 (10.18)
Rarely	41.69 (16.16)	12.44 (10.21)
Never	27.30 (12.86)	3.69 (5.65)
	$F(3,699) = 53.50,$	$F(3,736) = 87.15$
	$p < 0.001$	$p < 0.001$

officers with a posttraumatic stress disorder (PTSD) checklist, a 17-item self-report scale that is based on criteria listed in the Diagnostic and Statistical Manual of Mental Disorders (Oehme et al., 2012).

The authors used rates of self-reported domestic violence committed by law enforcement officers as a *dependent variable* and PTSD rates and alcohol abuse as *independent variables*. Referencing their table as an example, we can see that there are statistically significant differences found in posttraumatic stress ($p < 0.001$) and in alcohol use ($p < 0.001$). We know this because each p value is less than the predetermined threshold of 0.05. As noted earlier, the null hypothesis testing the equivalence of these two sources of variance is tested with the F distribution, and if the variance between groups is significantly greater than the variance within the groups, the populations from which the groups came can also be considered different with regard to the dependent variable. According to the F distribution table using a predetermined alpha of 0.05 for participants with posttraumatic stress, the between-group variance is 53.50 larger than the within-group variance. Similarly, also using an alpha level of 0.05 for participants who use alcohol, the mean score for alcohol use is 87.15 larger than the within-group variance. Based on this information, the researchers would know to reject their null hypothesis, since their computed F of 53.50 (posttraumatic stress) and 87.15 (alcohol use) greatly exceeds the values demonstrated on the F distribution table.

REFERENCE

Oehme, K., Donnelly, E.-A., and Martin, A. (2012). Alcohol abuse, PTSD, and officer-committed domestic violence. *Policing* 6(4), 418–430.

PRACTICE APPLICATION: ANOVA

A statistics instructor randomly divides her class of nine into three groups to test the hypothesis that a combination of instructional methods is a superior method of teaching statistics. Group 1 has lectures, a textbook, and a student workbook. Group 2 has lectures and a textbook, and group 3 has lectures only. After one month of instruction each group is given identical tests containing 10 questions. The following number of correct answers is obtained by each group. Are these differences statistically significant?

Group 1		Group 2		Group 3	
X_1	X^2	X_2	X^2	X_3	X^2
9	81	4	16	2	4
6	36	3	9	5	25
7	49	3	9	2	4
22	166	10	34	9	33

$\overline{X} = 7.33$ $\overline{X} = 3.33$ $\overline{X} = 3.0$ grand mean $\overline{X}_t = 41/9 = 4.55$

Compute ΣXt, ΣXt^2, and $(\Sigma Xt)^2$

$\Sigma Xt = 22 + 10 + 9 = 41$

$(\Sigma Xt)^2 = 41^2 = 1{,}681$

$\Sigma Xt^2 = 166 + 34 + 33 = 233$

Compute SS_{total}

$$SS_{\text{total}} = \Sigma X_t^2 - \frac{(\Sigma X)^2}{N_t} = 233 - \frac{1{,}681}{9} = 233 - 186.8 = 46.2$$

$$SS_{\text{total}} = 46.2$$

$$SS_{\text{between}} = \Sigma \left[\frac{(\Sigma X_g)^2}{N_i} \right] - \frac{(\Sigma X_t)}{N_t}$$

$$= \left[\frac{22^2}{3} + \frac{10^2}{3} + \frac{9^2}{3} \right] - \frac{1{,}681}{9}$$

$$= (161.33 + 33.33 + 27.0) - 186.8 = 221.66 - 186.8 = 34.86$$

$$SS_{\text{between}} = 34.86$$

Calculate SS_{within}:

$$SS_{within} = \Sigma\left[\Sigma X_g^2 - \frac{(\Sigma X_g)^2}{N_i}\right] = \left[166 - \frac{22^2}{3}\right] + \left[34 + \frac{10^2}{3}\right] + \left[33 + \frac{9^2}{3}\right]$$

$$= (166 - 161.33) + (34 - 33.33) + (33 - 27)$$

$$= 4.67 + 0.67 + 6.0 = 11.34$$

$$SS_{within} = 11.34$$

Check: Does $SS_{between} + SS_{within} = SS_{total}$? $34.86 + 11.34 = 46.2$
Compute mean squares

$$= \frac{SS_{between}}{df} = \frac{34.86}{2} = 17.43$$

Mean square between

$$= \frac{SS_{within}}{df} = \frac{11.34}{6} = 1.89$$

Mean square within

$$F = \frac{MS_{between}}{MS_{within}} = \frac{17.43}{1.89} = 9.22$$

With 2 and 6 df, the critical value at the 0.05 level is 5.14. The computed F exceeds this value; therefore, reject the null that there is no difference between the instructional methods.
Compute eta squared:

$$\eta^2 = \frac{SS_{between}}{SS_{total}} = \frac{34.86}{46.2} = 0.754$$

Compute the Scheffé test:

$$\text{Scheffé contrast} = \left[\sqrt{(K-1)(F_{crit})}\right] = \left[\sqrt{\frac{1}{N_1} + \frac{1}{N_2}(MS_{within})}\right]$$

$$= \left[\sqrt{(2)(5.14)} \right] \left[\sqrt{\frac{1}{3} + \frac{1}{3}(1.89)} \right]$$

$$= (3.21)(1.122) = 3.6$$

The minimum difference between group means for significance at 0.05 is 3.66. Group 1 ($\overline{X}$ = 7.33) differs from both group 2 ($\overline{X}$ = 3.33) and group 3 ($\overline{X}$ = 3.0) by at least this amount. Groups 2 and 3 do not differ significantly from each other.

CHAPTER 8

Hypothesis Testing with Categorical Data: Chi Square

LEARNING OBJECTIVES:

After reading this chapter, the student will understand the following concepts:

- The logic underlying chi square and how to calculate and interpret this goodness-of-fit test
- How to set up and interpret tabular data and prepare it for statistical analysis using chi square
- The relationship between phi and chi square
- How to apply hypothesis testing to nonparametric statistical models
- The continuing role of basic probability and its properties in statistical models

INTRODUCTION

So far, we have covered hypothesis testing using a continuous dependent variable and a categorical independent variable. Sometimes, we do not have the luxury of interval- or ratio-level data. In such cases, we must use a different statistical technique. A useful technique in social science research is cross tabulation using **chi square**, which is often represented by its Greek letter, χ^2. The **chi square test of independence** is a test of significance that is used for categorical data. Chi square is one of a number of tests of significance and measures of association known as *nonparametric* statistics. This terminology does not mean that the populations from which the data are gathered do not have parameters; the term simply means that unlike their parametric counterparts, such as z, t, and F, nonparametric statistics do not require any assumptions to be made regarding the underlying population. (For a refresher, go back to the beginning of chapter 7 and review some of the assumptions we covered regarding ANOVA). **Nonparametric tests** are therefore less restrictive than parametric tests. The trade-off for this characteristic is that they are less powerful than their parametric counterparts, which means that when using such tests we are less likely to reject a null hypothesis that *should* be rejected since they have a slightly larger probability of making a type II error. Nevertheless, if our data do not meet the demands of parametric tests, nonparametric tests are useful substitutes, as long as we keep these limitations in mind. This observation should not lead to dismissal of nonparametric tests as poor relatives of parametric tests; a popular science magazine (*Science 84*) listed the development of chi square as one of the 20 most important advances in science of the twentieth century (Hacking, 1984, p. 69)! And, like the F test, chi square is used in more advanced statistics (so advanced that they are beyond the purview of this textbook) to estimate a probability distribution for hypothesis testing (see Appendix A for examples).

Many of the variables in the social sciences have only two values: yes/no, agree/disagree, male/female, for/against, and so on. Further, two variables is the minimum number we can test for relatedness (after all, you can't really test to see whether something is related to itself). Cross tabulation analysis thus deals with the minimum number of variables that can be related (2), each of which has the minimum number of values that a variable can have (2), making a 2 × 2 cross tabulated table, or a contingency table, such as that shown in Table 8-1.

This is a minimum cross tabulation; we can have bigger tables, such as 3 × 6, as long as we are working with two variables. Chi square uses contingency tables to find whether the patterns we can see in such tables are the result of chance or are real. Stated otherwise, chi square helps us to understand whether the differences we observe in a cross tabulation table are the same as what we would expect if chance were involved. So we are going to do what we have been doing throughout the textbook: comparing what we *observe* to what we'd *expect* if only chance were involved. If we can essentially recreate what we'd expect with our observations (within a certain degree of risk—5%), then there is no significant pattern going on in our contingency table.

TABLE 8-1. *An Example of a Cross Tabulation Table*

Percentage of Inmates in Any Given State, by Race and Gender	White	Black
Male	w%	x%
Female	y%	z%

TABLE CONSTRUCTION

For the most part, constructing a contingency table is straightforward. How we set our table up is important enough, however, to merit some preliminary attention. Suppose we are interested in determining whether men and women differ in their stated willingness to vote for a woman for president of the United States regardless of the candidate's political party. We collect data from 116 men and 120 women asking them whether they would vote for a woman for president of the United States. This gives us one nominal-level variable called *gender* consisting of two attributes called *male* and *female* and another called *vote*, with two attributes called *yes* and *no*. The null hypothesis assumes that these two variables are independent of one another, meaning that willingness to vote for a female candidate and gender of voter are unrelated (i.e., men are just as likely as women to report that they would or would not vote for a female candidate). In other words, the classification of a case into a particular category of one variable (in this case, gender) does not affect the probability that the case will fall into a particular category of the other variable (willingness to vote for a woman). The data are distributed as shown in Table 8-2. We now have four mutually exclusive categories (or cells) informing us of the joint distribution of the two variables. For instance, in cell A we have 47 males who indicated their willingness to vote for a woman for president, and in cell D we have 39 females who indicated their unwillingness. The column and row marginals must both sum to *n*. Gender is the independent variable since being male or female can conceivably influence one's willingness to vote for a female, but willingness to vote for a female obviously cannot influence one's gender.

There are a few rules of thumb for constructing a table. Conventionally, the independent variable is placed at the top of the table and summed downward in the

TABLE 8-2. *Willingness to Vote for Woman by Gender*

TABLE 8-3. *Putting Percentages in the Table*

WOULD VOTE FOR WOMAN	GENDER		
	Male (%)	Female (%)	
Yes	**A** 47	**B** 81	128
	(40.5)	(67.5)	(54.2)
No	**C** 69	**D** 39	108
	(59.5)	(32.5)	(45.8)
Totals	116 (100)	120 (100)	236

columns, and the dependent variable is placed at the side and summed across the rows. The sums of each row and column are reported and placed in the marginals, and the total number of cases is also reported.

Putting Percentages in Tables

It is always useful to report percentages in the tables for ease of interpretation because percentages standardize the distribution of cases. In a sense, then, percentages are the effect size for chi square in the same way that *mean difference* is the effect size for t tests and ANOVA. When putting percentages in tables the basic rule is to compute percentages in the direction of the independent variable (down the columns). This rule is typically followed because we want to compare the distribution on the dependent variable within categories of the independent variable. In the present example, we see that 47 males and 81 females would vote for a female for president (the affirmative category of the dependent variable). Thus 47/116 = 40.5% of males and 81/120 = 67.5% of females indicated their willingness to vote for a female candidate, making a total of 128/236 = 54.2% of individuals (both genders) who would and 108/236 = 45.8% who would not. We percentage down and compare across, meaning that each column represents 100 percent of each category of the independent variable. This is all demonstrated in Table 8-3.

ASSUMPTIONS FOR THE USE OF CHI SQUARE

Now that we are on the same plane regarding how to create and read a contingency table, we can move on to how to set up, solve for, and interpret chi square. Like all statistics, chi square carries with it a suite of assumptions that should be met. These assumptions are less stringent than those for our parametric statistics, however:

1. We have independent random samples. This is similar, of course, to the assumptions associated with ANOVA.
2. The data are nominal or ordinal level. That is, they are categorical.
3. No expected cell frequency is less than 5. We actually have a few ways around this—see Box 8-1, for example. But for now, know that the traditional chi square formula that we will teach you requires expected cell frequencies of at least 5; otherwise the resulting significance test can be biased.

Returning to our voting example, we now want to determine whether this difference between the genders in their willingness to vote for a woman could have occurred by chance, that is, whether willingness to vote for a woman is *independent* of gender. There are two possibilities: (1) the observed difference in willingness to vote in our sample is also true in the population, or (2) there is no gender-based difference in willingness to vote in the general population. As always, we first state our hypotheses and set our alpha level:

STEP 1: We set our alpha level at the conventional 0.05. For this chi square, our null hypothesis is mathematically represented thus:

$$H_0 : P_m = P_f$$

Where P_m and P_f represent the probability of males and females, respectively, to vote for a female president. Our research hypothesis is therefore

$$H_1 : P_m \neq P_f$$

Chi square will test the hypothesis that the *observed* frequencies in the table equal the frequencies we would *expect* under conditions of random chance. To test the null hypothesis we compute chi square, the formula for which is given as formula 8-1:

8-1

$$\chi^2 = \sum \frac{(O - E)^2}{E}$$

Where O are the frequencies we observe in Table 8-3
E are the frequencies we would expect given only chance

STEP 2: We calculate the numbers we will need to solve for chi square. We already know the observed frequencies, which are the frequencies actually seen in each cell in Table 8-3: 47, 69, 81, and 39. When we ask *What is the expected frequency of cell A (males who are willing to vote for a female president)*, what we are actually asking is, "what is the probability of two independent events (the probability of being willing to vote for a female president, and the probability of being a male) occurring simultaneously?" As we saw in chapter 4, the probability of two *independent* events (A and B) co-occurring is equal to the product of their respective probabilities. Thus:

$$P(A \text{ and } B) = P(A) \times P(B)$$

$$P(\text{male}) = 116/236 = 0.491$$

$$P(\text{voting}) = 128/236 = 0.542$$

$$P(\text{male and voting}) = (0.491)(0.542) = 0.266$$

Did you see where we got those numbers from? There is a total $n = 236$—this is our denominator, because it represents all possible cases. For $P(\text{male})$, there are 116 males (the first column marginal in Table 8-2), and for $P(\text{voting})$, there were 128 individuals total who would vote for a female president. These two values provide us with our numerators. The probability of being male *and* being willing to vote for a woman is therefore $(0.542)(0.491) = 0.266$. This is our probability. To determine the expected *frequency* in cell A (which is what we need for chi square), we *multiply* this probability by the total number of cases: $(0.266)(236) = 62.9$.

We could go on calculating this way for each cell, but it is rather tedious. But now that we have given you an intuitive understanding based on what you already know, we will show you the easy way using formula 8-2.

8-2

$$E = \frac{(\text{Column marginal } n)(\text{Row marginal } n)}{\text{total } n}$$

This formula tells us that to get the expected frequency for each *cell* we multiply the relevant column marginal n by the relevant row marginal n and then divide the

TABLE 8-4. *Table of Expected Frequencies*

	GENDER		
Would Vote for Woman	**Male**	**Female**	
Yes	**A** 62.9	**B** 65.1	128
No	**C** 53.1	**D** 54.9	108
	116	120	236

product by the total number (n) of cases in the sample. Let us compute each expected cell frequency using formula 8-2 and place the results in a table of expected frequencies (Table 8-4).

Expected frequency for A = $(116 \times 128)/236 = 14{,}848/236 = 62.9$
Expected frequency for B = $(120 \times 128)/236 = 15{,}360/236 = 65.1$
Expected frequency for C = $(116 \times 108)/236 = 12{,}528/236 = 53.1$
Expected frequency for D = $(120 \times 108)/236 = 12{,}960/236 = 54.9$

STEP 3: Now that we have both the observed and the actual cell frequencies we can calculate chi square. A handy way to keep track of all the different calculations is to set up a table such as Table 8-5 with a column for each operation. This is similar to our standard deviation table from chapter 3. We must first subtract O from E, square the difference, and then divide by E (the sum of $O - E$ should always be zero; make sure you check that this is so before going on). When we have done this for each cell in the table, we sum $(O - E)^2/E$ to obtain our χ^2 value.

Our computed chi square is 17.27.

STEP 4: Armed with our chi square value, we now need to determine whether this value is statistically significant. To do so, we must determine the degrees of freedom. We defined degrees of freedom in chapter 6 as the number of values free to vary. In the case of tabular analysis, $df = (r - 1)(c - 1)$. The logic is identical with that discussed in chapter 7 for our two-way ANOVA degrees of freedom. For a 2×2 table, our df will always equal 1: $(2 - 1)(2 - 1) = 1$.

TABLE 8-5. *Calculating Chi Square*

Cell	O	E	O − E	$(O − E)^2$	$(O − E)^2/E$
A	47	62.9	−15.9	252.81	4.02
B	81	65.1	15.9	252.81	3.88
C	69	53.1	15.9	252.81	4.76
D	39	54.9	−15.9	252.81	4.60
Totals	236	236	0		17.27

We now use the chi square table (see pp. 347–349), looking for the value necessary to reject the null hypothesis at a 0.05 alpha level and a chi square value of 17.27. We look at the column labeled *df* to find the place where *df* = 1 (this is the first row). We then trace across the row until we get to the spot designated by 0.05, where you will find the critical value of chi square at the 0.05 alpha level (3.841). If our computed value exceeds 3.841, we can say that our chi square value is significant at the 0.05 level, and we can reject the null. Our computed chi square greatly exceeds this value, so we are fairly confident that our sample was not drawn from a population in which our two variables are unrelated.

STEP 5: We interpret our results. We are extremely confident that the relationship between gender and willingness to vote for a female found among the respondents in our sample is also true within the general population from which it was drawn. In other words, females are significantly more likely than males to report that they would vote for a female candidate. To round out our interpretation, we would draw on the actual cell observations: whereas less than half of all men (40.5%) were willing to vote for a female president, fully two-thirds (67.5%) of women were willing to vote for a female president.

THE CHI SQUARE DISTRIBUTION

As is the case with the *t* and *F* distributions, the shape of the **chi square distribution** is entirely determined by the degrees of freedom, and each *df* value describes a unique distribution. Figure 8-1 gives examples of the chi square distribution at 1, 4, and 8 degrees of freedom. Note that the chi square distribution is asymmetric and is skewed to the right. This does not mean that we are performing a one-tailed or directional test. Chi square testing yields only positive results because it is arrived at

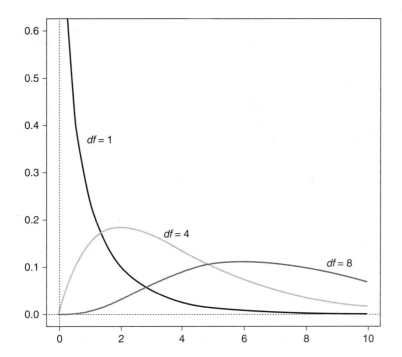

FIGURE 8-1

Chi square distributions with differing degrees of freedom

by *squaring* the differences between observed and expected frequencies. The chi square distribution becomes more and more symmetrical as the degrees of freedom increase, and it begins to look like the normal curve with *df* greater than 30. (For a discussion on the relationship between *z*, *t*, *F*, and chi square, see Box 8-2.)

CHI SQUARE WITH A 3 × 2 TABLE

The chi square distribution can be used whenever we have prior knowledge of expected values on categorical variables—such as knowing the total males, the total of persons willing to vote for a female president, etc. As we indicated above, it can be used for contingency tables that are larger than 2 × 2. For example, suppose we know that the racial composition of a given community is 88 percent white, 10 percent black, and 2 percent Hispanic, and we want to examine violent crime victimization in the community. Our *a priori* expectation is that in a sample of victims we would observe the racial/ethnic groups to be represented in proportion to their numbers in the population. That is, if race is irrelevant to victimization, we would expect 88 percent of the victims to be white, 10 percent to be black, and 2 percent to be Hispanic. However, if race is *not* independent of the probability of becoming a victim, we will observe some other percentage breakdown.

Box 8-1
Yates's Correction for Continuity

As indicated earlier, if there are fewer than five cases in any of the cells in a table of *expected frequencies* (not observed frequencies), we violate one of the assumptions of chi square. If such a condition exists we correct the chi square value by using **Yates's correction for continuity**, given by formula 8-3:

8-3

$$\chi^2_{corrected} = \Sigma \frac{\left(\left|O - E\right| - 0.5\right)^2}{E}$$

Yates's correction for continuity has the effect of reducing the value of chi-square since it reduces the *absolute value* of O – E for each cell by 0.5. This means that only the size, not the sign, of the difference is considered. For example: $(\left|2 - 6\right| - 0.5) = 4 - 0.5 = 3.5$, not, $2 - 6 = -4 - 0.5 = -4.5$. Some statisticians recommend using Yates's correction for any 2×2 table, whereas others believe that it overcorrects. The decision whether to use the correction for continuity with any 2×2 table depends on how conservative the researcher wishes to be when testing hypotheses. Computer printouts for 2×2 tables give both the corrected and the uncorrected chi square values. As is the case with all correction factors, this correction becomes less meaningful as the sample size becomes larger.

The research question is, therefore: "Is violent victimization in the community in proportion to racial composition in the community, or are people of different races significantly more likely to be victimized?" Stated more formally, "Does the proportion of victims of violent crime fit the racial composition of this jurisdiction?" The null hypothesis is that the observed ratio equals the 88:10:2 expected ratio. The dataset is presented in Table 8-6. Note that 322 whites (67.4%), 134 blacks (28.0%), and 22 Hispanics (4.6%) were victims of violent crimes in this community during the time period of data collection. This is different from the expected ratio, but is the difference "big enough" to be real or simply a function of chance? The first thing we have to do is calculate the expected frequency *if* the null hypothesis is true. This is simply accomplished by multiplying N (478) by the relevant population proportion of each of the racial/ethnic groups—this is also done for us in Table 8-6.

Box 8-2
The Relationship among z, t, F, and Chi Square

We saw earlier that the t distribution becomes identical in shape to the z distribution when $df > 120$. To give you a further appreciation of the symmetry of statistics, it is also true that the chi square critical value of 3.841, with $df = 1$, is equal to the square of the critical z value of 1.96. Put otherwise, z squared is equal to chi square under these conditions. Thus, our computed chi square of 17.26 is equivalent to a z value of 4.15 ($4.15^2 = 17.26$). In fact, all the distributions we have examined are related in the following fashion:

$$z = t_{df = \infty} = \sqrt{F_{df = 1, \infty}} = \sqrt{\chi^2_{df = 1}}$$

That can be read as $z = t$ with infinite df, which equals the square root of F with 1 and infinite df, which equals the square root of χ^2 with 1 df. Tuck this nugget of seeming trivia away for the future: it will save you quite a lot of time in calculating future statistics beyond this course.

TABLE 8-6. *Crime Victimization Data Set Up for Chi Square*

OBSERVED			
White	**Black**	**Hispanic**	**Total**
322 (67.4%)	134 (28.0%)	22 (4.6%)	478 (100%)

EXPECTED			
$478 \times 0.88 = 420.6$	$478 \times 0.10 = 47.8$	$478 \times 0.02 = 9.6$	$478 \times 1.00 = 100$

Group	O	E	O − E	$(O - E)^2$	$(O - E)^2/E$
White	322	420.6	−98.6	9721.96	23.11
Black	134	47.8	86.2	7430.44	155.45
Hispanic	22	9.6	12.4	153.76	16.02
Totals	478	478	0		194.58

$\chi2 = 194.58, df = 2, p < 0.01$

It is immediately obvious that whites are underrepresented among victims of violent crimes and that blacks and Hispanics are overrepresented. To determine whether these observed differences could be attributed to chance, we use the chi square distribution. We have 2 *df* because we have three categories that must sum to 478. Two of these categories can vary, but the size of the third is fixed (not free to vary) by the size of the other two. Thus, $(3 - 1)(2 - 1) = 2$.

We note from the chi square table that chi square critical at the 0.01 level with 2 *df* is 9.21. Our calculated chi square greatly exceeds this value, so we reject the null hypothesis at the conservative 0.01 level. The observed violent crime victimization does not fit the expected ratio based on knowledge of the racial composition of the community. Violent victimization therefore does depend on race. Blacks and Hispanics, particularly blacks, are victims of violent crime significantly more often than their proportions in the community would lead us to suspect.

CHI SQUARE-BASED MEASURES OF ASSOCIATION

If the chi square test of independence leads to the rejection of the null hypothesis, the two variables are not independent of one another and are therefore associated. But chi square does not reveal the strength of the relationship. As well as knowing whether there is a real difference between variables, we would also like to know how strongly they are related to one another. Although we will be discussing the concept of association more fully in the next chapter, it is appropriate to introduce chi square–based measures at this point. The measure based on a 2 × 2 chi square is *phi* and is analogous to eta squared. (Phi is a handy measurement to know for other reasons, too—see Box 8-3.) When computed directly from chi square, phi, like eta squared, is always positive, ranging between zero and +1.0. Phi is only applicable to data arrayed in a 2 × 2 table. The formula for computing phi directly from the chi square is formula 8-4:

8-4

$$\phi = \sqrt{\frac{\chi^2}{n}}$$

Applying phi to the gender and willingness to vote for a female example where $\chi^2 = 17.26$, we get

$$\phi = \sqrt{\frac{17.26}{236}} = 0.27$$

Box 8-3
More on Phi

Incidentally, if you only know phi and the sample size you can easily calculate chi square: square phi and multiply by the sample *n*. If

$$\phi = \sqrt{\frac{\chi 2}{n}}$$

then

$$\chi 2 = \phi^2 n$$

We have just seen in the willingness to vote for a female for president example that $\phi^2 =$ 0.073. Multiplying this by the sample size, we get (0.073)(236) = 17.228. With tolerance for all the rounding, it is the same as the chi square we obtained earlier.

We can interpret this value in variance-explained terms if we square it: $\phi^2 = 0.27^2 =$ 0.073. The proportion of variance in willingness to vote for a female for president accounted for by gender is 7.3 percent, leaving 92.7 percent accounted for by other variables. Phi is statistically significant because the chi square on which it is based is significant, but is it substantively significant? That depends on the context of the inquiry. If this were a real research finding, it may or may not be considered substantively significant, but interpreting the finding might prove difficult. Some may take it as indicative of male chauvinism because most males would not vote for a female presidential candidate. Since the question posed was whether the respondent would vote for a female candidate *regardless* of party affiliation, it might be that those who would vote this way are putting sexual politics above party politics. Statistics only inform us of the situation as it exists; the researcher must interpret them—and do so carefully.

To take the statistical versus substantive discussion a little further, suppose that we had found the same results using *liking for quiche* as the dependent variable and *gender* as the independent variable. We suspect that the substantive significance of such a finding would be profoundly uninteresting to you, as it would be to us. Even a perfect relationship would fail to excite us. On the other hand, if you were a caterer with a great deal of surplus quiche to get rid of, and if you were to be catering events at (1) the Ada County Gun Club and (2) the Boise Ladies Knitting Circle, where would you try to unload it? It may also be of some theoretical importance to the sex-role researcher if he or she is convinced that such a finding is a valid indicator of attempts on the part of males who believe that "real men don't eat quiche" (which was the title of a popular book in the 1980s) to emphasize their masculinity. Substantive significance, we emphasize, depends more on the *theoretical* context of the inquiry than on the magnitude and significance of the computed statistics.

Sample Size, Chi Square, and Phi

Another reason for computing a measure of association in conjunction with chi square is that just like the value of t, the value of chi square is sensitive to sample size. Chi square values are not directly comparable across different sample sizes, but phi values are. It is quite possible with large samples to attain a high level of significance when the variables are so weakly related that we are tempted to ask "so what?" The chi square–based measures of association help us to decide whether the significant difference is really worth attending to. To illustrate, let us compute three chi squares based on n's of 20, 200, and 2,000 while maintaining a constant 40/60 percentage difference across the cells. These are otherwise random numbers with no empirical value except for illustration. The results are found in Table 8-7.

Note that as the sample size is increased by a factor of 10, chi square is also increased by a factor of 10. However, phi remained constant at 0.20 because the percentage change across the cells remained constant. In effect, the phi measure of association standardizes the calculated chi square by the maximum attainable chi square. The maximum attainable chi square in a 2×2 table is equal to n (the sample size) and is only attained when *all cases fall in one of the diagonals*, as in Table 8-8 in which all A's are X's and all B's are Y's.

TABLE 8-7. *Hypothetical Chi Square Cross Tabulations with Differing n's*

$n = 20$			$n = 200$			$n = 2,000$		
4	6	10	40	60	100	400	600	1000
6	4	10	60	40	100	600	400	1000
10	10	20	100	100	200	1000	1000	2000
$\chi^2 = 0.8$, *ns*, $\phi = 0.20$			$\chi^2 = 8.0$, $p < 0.01$, $\phi = 0.20$			$\chi^2 = 80.0$, $p < 0.0001$, $\phi = 0.20$		

TABLE 8-8. *Demonstrating the Maximum Attainable Chi Square 2 × 2 Table*

	A	B	
X	50	0	50
Y	0	50	50
	50	50	100

The expected frequency for each cell is 25—you can verify this using the math above if you'd like (50 × 50)/100 = 25, but it should be intuitive that this is the case. Similarly, it should be intuitive that χ^2 = 100 and that therefore phi will equal 1.00. If this is not clear, use this as an opportunity to work through the math above and you'll see this to be the case. The take-home lesson from this exercise is that by dividing χ^2 by its maximum attainable value, we standardize it to a true range (between zero and 1) to render values based on different n's comparable—and this is exactly what phi does.

Other Measures of Association for Chi Square

Contingency Coefficient

Another chi square–based measure of association is the **contingency coefficient** (*C*), which is appropriate for nominal and ordinal variables having *more than two categories*. A problem with *C* is that its upper range depends on the size of the table—it is not necessarily bound by ±1. The upper limit of *C* is determined by the formula $\sqrt{(r-1)/r}$, where *r* equals the number of rows in the table. In a 3 × 3 table, for instance, the upper limit of *C* is $\sqrt{(3-1)/3}$ = 0.816. Even in a 10 × 10 table the upper limit is only 0.949. The interpretation of *C* does not go beyond that given by chi square, that is, the concept of deviation from independence, except to give us a *rough* idea of the magnitude of the relationship. We cannot square *C* as we did with phi to arrive at a variance-explained interpretation. The formula for *C* is formula 8-5.

8-5

$$C = \sqrt{\frac{\chi^2}{\chi^2 + n}}$$

Skipping ahead to the computer printout, Table 8-9, we obtain

$$C = \sqrt{\frac{25.073}{25.073 + 585}} = \sqrt{\frac{25.073}{610.073}} = \sqrt{0.0411} = 0.2027$$

This is a 3 × 2 table, which means that C's upper limit is $\sqrt{(3-1)/3} = 0.816$. So we can suggest that this is a fairly weak relationship—but given the flexible nature of C's upper limit, we cannot meaningfully compare this relationship to a different contingency table or firmly establish how much variance is explained by the independent variable.

Cramer's V

Cramer's V is yet another chi square–based measure given in Table 8-9. This statistic is a modification of the phi statistic that allows for the analysis of tables that are greater than 2 × 2. You will note from formula 8-6 that V is identical to phi except that n is multiplied by $k - 1$, where k is the lesser of either the number of rows or the number of columns. Note that in a 3 × 2 table, V turns out to be identical to phi. Cramer's V is superior to the contingency coefficient for tables greater than 2 × 2 because it can attain a value of 1.0.

8-6

$$V = \sqrt{\frac{\chi^2}{n(k-1)}}$$

Table 8-8 has 2 − 1 = 1 rows and 3 − 1 = 2 columns; thus we multiply n by 1:

$$V = \sqrt{\frac{25.073}{585 \times 1}} = \sqrt{\frac{25.073}{585}} = \sqrt{0.04286} = 0.207$$

Although similar in magnitude to C, knowing that V is bound by 1 helps us better suggest that this is indeed a weak relationship.

A COMPUTER EXAMPLE OF CHI SQUARE

We will now compute chi square from data arranged in a 3 × 2 table. From our juvenile delinquent data we generate the hypothesis that birth rank (first/middle/last

TABLE 8-9. A 3 × 2 Contingency Table Computer Example

Count	Birth Order			
Row %				
Col %				
Violence	**First**	**Middle**	**Last**	**Row Total**
No	101	82	56	239
	42.3	34.3	23.4	40.9
	54.3	30.8	42.1	
Yes	85	184	77	346
	24.6	53.2	22.3	59.1
	45.7	69.2	57.91	
Column	186	266	133	585
Total	31.8	45.5	22.7	100

	Chi Square		**df**	**Sig**
	25.0728		2	0.00001
	Cramer's V	0.20703		
	Contingency coefficient			0.20273

born) is associated with whether a juvenile has ever committed a violent offense (no/yes). We have asked the computer for chi square, the contingency coefficient, and Cramer's *V*. The results are presented in Table 8-9.

Note that the first row for each case ("No" and "Yes") is the count total, the next row is the percentages computed by row, and the final row for each case is the percentages computed by column. This information is given in a legend, of sorts, at the top of the table.

There is a significant relationship between birth order and the commission of a violent crime. It is highly unlikely that our data come from a population in which the probability of committing a violent crime is the same for each birth-order group. We see that 239 (40.9 percent) of our 585 juvenile delinquents had not been convicted of a violent crime and that 346 (59.1 percent) had. Firstborn children were the least likely to have committed a violent crime (45.7 percent), and middle-born children were the most likely (69.2 percent).

We can use this table to reinforce the discussion of probability in chapter 4. What is the probability that a delinquent drawn at random from the sample will be first-born *and* will have committed at least one violent crime? These two events (birth order and violent crime) are not independent events, as we have seen. We must use the multiplication rule for dependent events, which, you recall, is given as $P(A \text{ and } B) = P(A) \times P(B|A)$. The probability that a delinquent drawn from the sample at random will be firstborn is obtained by dividing the number of delinquents who are firstborn by the total number of delinquents in the sample. Therefore, $P(A) = 186/585 = 0.318$. The probability of having committed a violent crime given firstborn status is obtained by dividing the number of firstborns who have committed a violent crime by the total number of firstborns. Therefore, $P(B|A) = 85/186 = 0.457$. Multiplying the probability of A by the probability of B given A gives us $(0.318)(0.457) = 0.145$. As you know, there is a faster way to obtain this result. Simply divide the lower left-hand cell by the total sample size ($85/585 = 0.145$). This is simply the application of the general probability rule:

$$P = \frac{\text{Number of ways an event can occur}}{\text{Total number of possible outcomes}} = 85/585 = 0.145$$

In the same study previously discussed, Oehme and colleagues (2012) provide us with a good example of a chi square analysis. This table demonstrates cross tabulations on alcohol use, PTSD, and physical violence (see Journal Table 8-1). The researchers note that as the level of alcohol use increases, there is less of a difference in the rates of PTSD when examined by use of violence (χ^2 [1, $n = 473$] $= 32.17$). More specifically, 37.5 percent ($n = 21$) of participants who report PTSD and low-risk drinking also report using physical violence. Comparatively, about 10 percent ($n = 42$) of participants who reported low-risk drinking but no PTSD reported using physical violence. Based on the chi square analysis, Oehme and colleagues (2012) found that there is a statistically significant difference between the two groups at the $p < 0.001$ level ($p = 0.261$). Examining participants who report hazardous drinking, about 56 percent ($n = 41$) who reported no symptoms of PTSD reported using physical violence, whereas 71.8 percent ($n = 28$) who reported symptoms of PTSD also reported using physical violence. Accordingly, there is not a statistically significant difference in reported use of physical violence between those who do report PTSD and those who do not (χ^2 [1, $n = 112$] $= 2.62$, $p = 0.153$). Examining dependent drinkers, the researchers found that about 65 percent ($n = 15$) of those

JOURNAL TABLE 8-1. *Cross Tabulations on Alcohol Use, PTSD, and Physical Violence*

	NO VIOLENCE		PHYSICAL VIOLENCE	
	n = 466	**%**	**n = 175**	**%**
Low-risk drinking				
No PTSD	375	89.9	42	10.1
PTSD	35	62.5	21	37.5
	χ^2 (1, n = 473) = 32.17***, p = 0.261***			
Hazardous drinking				
No PTSD	32	43.8	41	56.2
PTSD	11	28.2	28	71.8
	χ^2 (1, n = 112) = 2.62, p = 0.153			
Dependent drinking				
No PTSD	8	34.8	15	65.2
PTSD	5	15.2	28	84.8
	χ^2 (1, n = 56) = 2.93, p = 0.229			

***$p < 0.001$.

with no PTSD symptoms reported use of physical violence, whereas about 84 percent ($n = 28$) with PTSD used physical violence. Based on this chi square analysis, there is not a statistically significant difference in reported use of physical violence between individuals with and without PTSD symptoms who reported that they were dependent drinkers ($\chi^2[1, n = 56] = 2.93, p = 0.229$). In sum, a majority of the officers who reported hazardous or dependent levels of alcohol use also reported PTSD and use of physical violence (Oehme et al., 2012).

SUMMARY

Chi square is a popular and much-used technique for testing statistical independence and goodness of fit with tabular data. A test for independence determines whether the distribution of scores on one attribute in a table is independent of the distribution on another attribute. In other words, we test whether the two attributes or variables are related in the population. We do so by examining and comparing the observed bivariate cell frequencies with the cell frequencies we would expect if the two variables were unrelated. A test of goodness of fit asks whether an observed distribution of scores fits a theoretically expected distribution. A significant chi square indicates a poor fit between theoretical expectations and empirical actuality. A nonsignificant chi square indicates a good fit.

The significance of the chi square statistic depends on the value of the computed statistic and its associated degrees of freedom. Since chi square is sensitive to sample size, the larger the sample, the more likely we are to observe a statistically significant difference if a difference actually exists in the population. Phi is a statistic suitable for 2×2 tables and measures the strength of association between two variables. When squared, phi gives the proportion of variance in the dependent variable accounted for by the independent variable. Phi standardizes chi square by dividing it by the maximum attainable chi square for a given sample, which is always n, the sample size. In the next chapter, we explore other nonparametric tests of association.

REFERENCES

Hacking, I. (1984). Trial by number. *Science*, 84(5), 69–70.

Oehme, K., Donnelly, E. A., and Martin, A. (2012). Alcohol abuse, PTSD, and officer-committed domestic violence. *Policing* 6(4), 418–430.

PRACTICE APPLICATION: CHI SQUARE

We ask a sample of 89 residents of an upper-middle-class apartment complex to identify themselves as being primarily either liberal or conservative in their political orientation. We also ask them their opinion on an issue raging on the university campus at present: "Do you think that the university should be allowed to fire a professor who advocates a communistic form of government for the United States?" The answer categories are no and yes. We place their answers into a 2×2 table and compute chi square and phi.

Should Be Allowed to Fire Professors	Ideology		
	Conservative	**Liberal**	
Yes	40	12	52
	(75.5%)	(33.3%)	(58.4%)
No	13	24	37
	(24.5%)	(66.7%)	(41.6%)
Totals	53 (100%)	36 (100%)	89

Compute χ^2

$$\chi^2 = \Sigma \frac{(O-E)^2}{E} \qquad \text{where } E = \frac{r \times c}{N}$$

expected A = 53 × 52/89 = 31.0
expected B = 36 × 52/89 = 21.0
expected C = 53 × 37/89 = 22.0
expected D = 36 × 37/89 = 15.0

Cell	Obs.	Exp.	(O − E)	(O − E)²	(O − E)²/E
A	40	31	9	81	2.61
B	12	21	−9	81	3.86
C	13	22	−9	81	3.68
D	24	15	9	81	5.40
	89	89	00.00		15.55

Chi square is significant at less than 0.001. We are confident that a person's opinion on this matter is not independent of his or her political orientation. We reject the null hypothesis.

Compute phi.

$$\phi = \sqrt{\frac{\chi^2}{N}}$$

$$= \sqrt{\frac{15.55}{89}} = \sqrt{0.175} = 0.418$$

Phi is moderately strong. Political orientation is moderately strongly associated with one's opinion about the university's right to fire professors who advocate a communistic form of government for the United States. The percentage of variance in a respondent's opinion accounted for by political orientation is 0.418 squared = 0.175, or 17.5 percent.

CHAPTER 9

Nonparametric Measures of Association

LEARNING OBJECTIVES:
After reading this chapter, the student will understand the following concepts:

- What association is, and what it is not, and how it can be established
- The concepts of *direction*, *strength*, and *proportional reduction in error*
- Measures of association, including their computation and interpretation
- The following measures of association: lambda, gamma, Somer's *d*, tau *b*, and Spearman's rho
- The difference between probability and odds and the usefulness of odds ratio and its relationship to Yule's *Q*

INTRODUCTION

Over the past few chapters, we introduced several measures of association, including eta squared, phi, Cramer's *V*, and the less impressive contingency coefficient. In this chapter, we more fully develop the idea of **association** in preparation for chapter 10, where we cover using tabular data to tease out causal relationships, and chapter 11, where we cover the Pearson's correlation coefficient. We will develop the idea of association in this chapter with nominal- and ordinal-level measures. Measures based on higher-level data are discussed elsewhere in the text. The statistical tests in this chapter are all nonparametric. Recall that this means that they do not require any assumptions about the population. Additionally, much of what we cover in this chapter is actually quite advanced. Take it slow and let it sink in; remember that learning statistics is a process that requires thinking in new terms. It can be quite daunting—don't let it be intimidating. Trust us: the more you read and the more you do, the better you'll understand what's going on with statistics.

In social science we ask questions such as "Why do less educated people tend to be more prejudiced than more educated people?", "Why do women make less money than men?", "Why are sex offenders punished more harshly than other kinds of offenders?" Each of these questions deals with the issue of how variables are connected, related, or associated. We are saying, for example, that the condition *being a woman* is related to *low income*, and we saw in chapter 6 that the condition *sex offender* was related to *harsher punishment*. Another way of phrasing this last sentence would be to say that income levels *depend* on gender and that harshness of punishment *depends* on type of crime. Thus, income and harshness of punishment are *dependent variables*, and gender and type of offense are *independent variables*. Three main questions arise in the assessment of association: (1) Does an association exist? (2) How strong is it? (3) What is its direction? This chapter will discuss each of these questions individually and then go over several measures of association designed to answer them.

ESTABLISHING ASSOCIATION

Does an Association Exist?

Before we can ask the *why* questions such as why women make less money than men, we first have to determine whether they actually do by subjecting the hypothesized relationship to a test of statistical significance. If income is found to be dependent on sex/gender, then we can say that the two variables are associated. An association exists if values of one variable vary systematically with variation in a second variable. Said with less derivatives of the Latin word *varius*, two things are associated if when one changes, so too does the other, in a predictable pattern. When we ask why women make less money than men, we take for granted that the value of the variable *income* changes as we move across conditions of the variable *gender*. As another example, we might expect that women and men commit differing levels of violent crime, thus *associating* gender with violent crime. We would have to see whether this were the case, however, prior to determining the strength of this association. If values of one variable do not change across conditions of another, there is no association between them.

In the previous chapter we noted that an association existed between gender and willingness to vote for a female for president of the United States and saw that as we moved from the male category of the independent variable to the female category that the percentage willing to vote for a female went from 40.5 percent to 67.5 percent. In other words, the distribution of frequencies of the variable *willing to vote* was conditioned by the distribution of frequencies of the second variable, *gender.* This is known as a **conditional distribution** and relates to the concept of proportional reduction in error, which we discuss below in more detail.

What Is the Strength of the Association?

Once we have evidence of a significant conditional distribution, the next step is to quantify the strength of the association. This is essentially a matter of examining the magnitude of change by moving from one condition to another. A crude yet meaningful measure of the strength of the association would be the simple percentage of change across cells. Table 9-1 presents a hypothetical conditional distribution of the relationship between whether a given individual was arrested and whether that person's father had also been arrested at some point in his life. We could compare the percentage of respondents who were arrested and whose fathers were also arrested ($95/115 \times 100 = 83\%$) with the percentage of respondents who were arrested but whose fathers were not arrested ($20/115 \times 100 = 17\%$), which is a difference of 66 percentage points. To simply rely on percentages, however, we would have to make multiple comparisons of the percentages from cell to cell. It would be much more efficient to have a single summary value of the strength of the association that varies within fixed, or normed, limits. When we discussed percentages, ratios, and proportions, we performed norming operations, or standardizing, of the raw data. All of the statistics of association we will look at involve ratios of one quantity to another. The statistics we will discuss in this chapter have the efficient properties of being single summary indices of the strength of the association and of

TABLE 9-1. *Hypothetical Conditional Distribution*

Arrested	Father Arrested		
Yes	**A**	**B**	Totals
	95	20	115
No	**C**	**D**	
	45	80	125
Totals	140	120	240

ranging within fixed limits. In addition, they have the property of indicating the direction of the relationship, something that becomes important when dealing with ordered and continuous variables.

What Is the Direction of the Association?

Relationships or associations between variables can be either positive or negative. There is a **positive association** when the values of one variable change in the same direction as another variable. For example, as low self-control increases in an individual, so too does that individual's offending behavior. There is **negative association** when we observe the opposite pattern; that is, as the values of one variable increase, the values of the other decrease. For example, crime rates go up in neighborhoods that have less collective efficacy. Another way of stating a negative relationship is to say that the variables are *inversely* related.

Table 9-2 illustrates positive and negative associations. In distribution A we see that crime varies positively with level of low self-control: high scores tend to go with high scores and low scores tend to go with low scores. In this distribution the highest category *n*'s are found on the main diagonal (top left-hand cell to bottom right-hand cell). In distribution B we have the opposite pattern, in which high scores on the education variable are negatively associated with low scores on TV watching, and low scores on education are associated with high scores on TV watching. In this distribution the higher category *n*'s are found in the secondary diagonal (top right-hand cell to bottom left-hand cell).

A normed measure of association generally ranges between −1.0 and +1.0 (although sometimes they are bound between zero and +1, in which case we cannot

TABLE 9-2. *Hypothetical Conditional Distributions Showing Positive (A) and Negative (B) Associations*

A					B			
Crime	Low Self-Control				TV Watching	Education		
	High	Medium	Low			High	Medium	Low
High	100	65	40		High	35	50	80
Medium	40	75	50		Medium	75	65	60
Low	30	55	100		Low	90	55	40
	Positive association					Negative association		

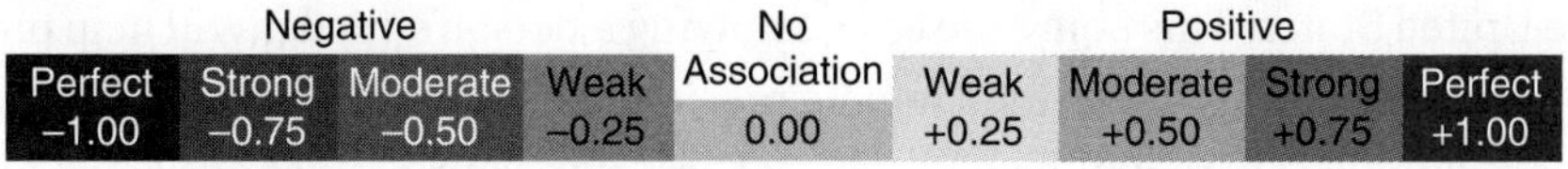

	Negative			No		Positive		
Perfect	Strong	Moderate	Weak	Association	Weak	Moderate	Strong	Perfect
−1.00	−0.75	−0.50	−0.25	0.00	+0.25	+0.50	+0.75	+1.00

FIGURE 9-1

Conventional rules of thumb for measurements of association

determine direction of association just from this number). An association of −1.0 is a perfect negative association, and a value of +1.0 is a perfect positive association. An association of zero means that there is no association between the two variables. Normed measures allow for the comparison of computed values across tables and across samples, something that could not be done if the measures were not restricted to defined ranges.

Unfortunately, there are no hard rules for interpreting the numerical values of the computed statistics *unless* they have a "variance explained interpretation," which most of the statistics discussed in this chapter do not. How strong does an association therefore have to be before it is considered worth our attention? And what do we mean by *strong*, anyway? The answer to these questions depends on the specific context of the research. In one context an association of 0.50 might produce nothing more than a shrug of the shoulders; in another it might set the heart pounding. Your unit of analysis has a lot to say about this, too: aggregate units of analysis typically have measures of association that are of larger magnitudes than individual units of analysis. The reason has less to do with the association itself and more to do with something called *measurement error*. We will revisit this topic later, but for now, know that in larger aggregates, there is more measurement error because we cannot control for as many contingencies as we can for an individual.

These qualifications aside, some conventional guidelines for interpreting the strength of association are presented in Figure 9-1. Be aware that it only makes sense to interpret a measure of association as weak, moderate, or strong *if* it is found to be statistically significant.

PROPORTIONAL REDUCTION IN ERROR

As you might have guessed, if two variables are associated we can use one of them to predict the other. This does not, however, necessarily mean that one *causes* the other (of course, it also does not necessarily mean that one does *not* cause the other—more on this in the next chapter). We saw in the last chapter that males and females differed significantly in their willingness to vote for a female for president of the United States. This being the case, knowing a person's gender will help predict his or her willingness to vote for a female president. Of course, your predictions will not be infallible. There will be a number of *errors* in your predictions since not all women indicated such willingness, and not all males indicated unwillingness. However, there will be fewer prediction errors armed with knowledge about the independent variable than without it. This is formally called the **proportional reduction in error (PRE),** which refers to the reduction of errors made as we move from predicting scores on the dependent variable *without* knowing the distribution of the independent variable to predicting scores on the dependent variable knowing how the independent variable is distributed. Stated otherwise, it's the extent to which we *improve* our predictions of any given variable when we know the value of another variable with which it is associated.

Lambda (λ) is a useful ratio for gaining a grasp of the concept of PRE because it uses the general formula for any PRE, which is found in formula 9-1:

9-1

$$PRE = \frac{\text{errors using rule 1} - \text{errors using rule 2}}{\text{errors using rule 1}}$$

We can denote "errors using rule 1" and "errors using rule 2" simply as E_1 and E_2. Therefore,

9-2

$$\lambda = \frac{E_1 - E_2}{E_1}$$

Rule 1 predicts the values of the dependent variable *without* knowledge of how the independent variable is distributed, and *rule 2* predicts the values of the dependent variable *with* knowledge of how the independent variable is distributed. If there is perfect association between the two variables, knowledge of the independent variable will reduce prediction errors to zero, and lambda will be 1.0. If there is no association, knowledge of the independent variable will be of no predictive value, and lambda will be zero. Lambda is an asymmetric measure of association (which means that it can produce different values according to which variable is considered dependent) with values ranging between 0.0 and 1.0, and it is best suited to distributions in which both variables are nominal level. Lambda is not a particularly popular statistic in actual research because it has a strange quirk, which will be discussed later,

TABLE 9-3. *Psychologists' Recommendations and Parole Board Decisions (Hypothetical)*

Parole Board's Decisions	Psychologists' Recommendations		
	Release	No release	Totals
Release	85	10	95
No release	25	75	100
Totals	110	85	195

but it is useful for illustrating the important concept of PRE. Let us compute lambda from the data in Table 9-3.

Suppose we want to determine the association between recommendations made by prison psychologists that prisoners be either released or not released and the parole board's actual release decision. From Table 9-3 we see that psychologists recommended release for 110 inmates, and the parole board released 85 of them, meaning that they disagreed with the psychologists in 25 cases. Psychologists recommended against releasing 85 inmates, and the parole board concurred in 75 instances. Altogether there are 195 inmates who went before the parole board, and the board agreed with the psychologists' recommendation in 160 cases. These data are set up in a 2 × 2 table (see Table 9-3).

What if we attempted to predict parole board decisions without knowledge of the psychologists' recommendations? Under conditions of ignorance about the independent variable, our best guess would be the *modal category of the dependent variable.* The modal category for the parole board's decision is the *no release* row ($N = 100$). We would make fewer errors if we predicted no release *for every inmate than if we predicted release for every inmate,* or half for release and half for no release. If we chose the modal category, there would be 95 errors (the number of inmates who were released). Therefore, $E_1 = 95$. E_1 is defined as $n -$ modal category of the dependent variable (in the present case, $195 - 100 = 95$).

Having found the number of prediction errors using rule 1, we now determine the number of errors using rule 2, which provides us with the knowledge that psychologists recommended releasing 110 inmates and not releasing 85. Knowing this we will make fewer errors if we predict that the board will release all 110 who were recommended for release and release none of those not recommended for release. Our errors are those cases in which the board disagreed with the recommendations. To determine the number of errors we will make with knowledge of the independent variable (rule 2), we simply subtract the modal cell frequency in each condition from its column total and sum the differences as follows:

$$\text{For release } 110 - 85 = 25$$

$$\text{For no release } 85 - 75 = 10$$

$$\text{Total } E_2 = 35$$

A total of 35 errors are made when taking the independent variable into account. To find the proportional reduction in error we substitute the values of E_1 and E_2 into the formula:

$$\lambda = \frac{E_1 - E_2}{E_1}$$

$$\lambda = \frac{95 - 35}{95} = 0.632$$

Thus, we have reduced our error in predicting inmate release with knowledge of the psychologists' recommendations by 63.2 percent. We will see the PRE again in all its variety; its basic formula is the hallmark for measures of association.

THE CONCEPT OF PAIRED CASES

Because the remaining statistics to be discussed in this chapter rely on comparisons of various types of **paired cases**, we should discuss this topic before proceeding. By *paired cases* we mean all possible pairs of cases that can be found in a given set of cases. Suppose we have the following small data set of 10 juveniles in detention who are categorized according to whether they scored high or low on the SAT and whether they began engaging in crime in their early or late teens (see Table 9-4).

The possible number of paired cases that could be made up from any data set is determined by formula 9-3:

9-3

$$\text{total pairs} = \frac{n(n-1)}{2}$$

N is our sample size, so for our juvenile data in Table 9-4 there are (10)(9)/2 = 45 possible pairs. Let us display the data in a bivariate table (Table 9-5).

TABLE 9-4. *Paired Cases Example*

Student	Age of Onset	SAT
Jim	Early	Low
Jean	Early	Low
Bill	Early	High
Frank	Late	High
Andre	Early	Low
Melissa	Late	High
Max	Late	Low
John	Early	Low
Jose	Late	High
Ann	Late	Low

TABLE 9-5. *Cross Tabulation of Age of Onset and SAT Scores*

Age of Onset	SAT	
	Low	**High**
Early teens	Jose	Bill
	Frank	
	Melissa	
Later teens	Max	Jean
	Ann	Andre
		John
		Jim

Clearly, we could predict a juvenile's age of onset by their SAT score from these data. A student who scores high on the SAT is likely to have a later age of onset. Similarly, a student who scores low on the SAT is likely to have started juvenile offending earlier. There are only three departures (Bill, Max, and Ann) from this general pattern compared to all possible 45 pairings. These three cases are discordant with our expectations. *It is the comparison of agreement to disagreement (similar to dissimilar pairs) in a data set that constitutes the basis for assessing the degree of association that exists between two nominal or ordinal variables.* As you can see, even measures of association follow our pattern of comparing what we expect with what we observe.

Box 9-1
Different Types of Pairs for Any Data Set

Let us now see the various kinds of pairs we could make from our data. *There are five possible pair combinations in any data set:*

1. Similar pairs, denoted by N_s in Table 9-6. These are pairs that are ranked in the same order on both variables. Jose, Frank, Melissa, Jean, Andre, John, and Jim constitute similar pairs (either high–late or low–early). The product of N_s in these categories ($3 \times 4 = 12$) constitutes similar pairs.

2. Dissimilar pairs, denoted by N_d. Bill (low–late) and Max and Ann (high–early) constitute dissimilar pairs. There are $1 \times 2 = 2$ dissimilar pairs.

3. Pairs tied on the independent variable (down the columns) but not on the dependent variable are denoted by T_x. Jose, Frank, Melissa, Max, and Ann are tied on the high category of the independent variable ($3 \times 2 = 6$ pairs), and Bill, Jean, Andre, John, and Jim are tied on the low category ($1 \times 4 = 4$ pairs). There are thus 10 T_x pairs.

4. Pairs tied on the dependent variable (across the rows), but not on the independent variable, are denoted by T_y. Jose, Frank, Melissa, and Bill are tied on the early category ($3 \times 1 = 3$ pairs) of the dependent variable, and the remaining six students are tied on the later category ($2 \times 4 = 8$ pairs). There are thus 11 T_y pairs.

5. Pairs tied on both the dependent and the independent variables are denoted by T_{xy}. These are the pairs that can be formed from the cases in the same cell. For instance, from the three cases in the later–high cell we could obtain $(3)(2)/2 = 3$ pairs and from the low–low cell we could obtain $(4)(3)/2 = 6$ pairs. Max and Ann form a single pair, and since Bill is all alone, we cannot form a pair in his cell. There are thus 10 T_{yx} pairs. These different pairs are presented in Table 9-6.

TABLE 9-6. *Possible Number of Pairs Example*

N_s	3×4	12
N_d	1×2	2
T_x	$(3 \times 2) + (1 \times 4)$	10
T_y	$(3 \times 1) + (2 \times 4)$	11
T_{xy}	$3 + 1 + 6$	10
Total pairs		45

A Computer Example

Computer programs for nominal- and ordinal-level variables supply a variety of statistics. The partial generic printout in Table 9-7 will serve to illustrate some of the ordinal-level measures of association we will discuss in this chapter. We have hypothesized that an association exists between the degree of social restrictiveness in prison and feelings of depression; that is, the more socially restricted an individual is in the prison, the more he or she will experience chronic depression. Our independent variable has three elements: (1) prisoners who are in the general population and share a cell with another inmate; (2) inmates who are in the general population,

TABLE 9-7. *Computer Printout for Social Restrictions and Depression among Prisoners*

	SOCIAL RESTRICTIONS			
Depression	**Low**	**Medium**	**High**	**Totals**
Low	**A** 20	**B** 14	**C** 8	42
Medium	**D** 14	**E** 23	**F** 14	51
High	**G** 4	**H** 24	**I** 14	42
Totals	38	61	36	135

Chi Square	**df**	**Sig**
15.10207	4	0.0045

Statistic	**Symmetric**	**With Depression**	**With Social Restrictions**
		as dependent	dependent
Lambda	0.08228	0.08333	0.08108
Somer's *d*	0.24979	0.25332	0.24636
Cramer's *V*	0.2365		
Contingency *C*	0.31719	**Sig**	
Kendall's tau *b*	0.24981	0.0006	
Gamma	0.37231	0.0006	

but who have their own cell; and (3) those that are in solitary confinement by themselves. We will call these three categories low, medium, and high, respectively. Our
measure of depression is a generic psychological scale that ranges from zero, indicating a complete lack of depression, to 36, indicating a deep degree of chronic depression. We arbitrarily—but reasonably—collapse these values into three
categories, low (0–10), medium (11–20), and high (21–30).

Note that the chi square value given in Table 9-7 is significant with the probability
being given as 0.0045—that is, well below the standard alpha of 0.05. This means that we
can be confident that an association exists between these two variables because we could
only get the observed pattern of cases *by chance* 45 times of every 10,000 samples of similar size and composition. The other reported statistics inform us of the strength and direction of the association, which we will cover throughout the remainder of the chapter.

Gamma

We will begin our discussion of ordinal-level statistics with **gamma** because it is
perhaps the most popular statistic applied to this type of analysis. Gamma ranges
between −1.0 and +1.0 and compares similar pairs of scores with dissimilar pairs
but ignores tied pairs (see Box 9-1). By ignoring tied pairs, gamma informs us that as
one variable increases in value, the other increases, decreases, or stays the same.
When the number of similar pairs is greater than the number of dissimilar pairs, the
association is positive. When the reverse is true, the association is negative. The
formula for computing gamma is formula 9-4:

9-4

$$\gamma = \frac{N_s - N_d}{N_s + N_d}$$

Where N_s = number of similar pairs
N_d = number of dissimilar pairs

From a visual inspection of Table 9-7 we note that a low level of social restriction is
associated with a low level of depression and that a high level of restriction is associated
with a high level of depression. We would know before looking at the statistics, then,
that the association is positive. If we were to predict a person's position in terms of low,
medium, and high on depression, it helps to know his or her level of social restriction.
For those low on social restriction we predict the same rank order on depression, that is,
low. Of the 38 individuals who are low on social restriction, 20 are low on depression

(cell A). We cannot pair this group of 20 people with people in any of the other cells sharing the same row (depression) or column (low social restrictiveness) because these cells are tied, and gamma does not consider tied pairs in its computation.

The first thing to do is to determine the similar and dissimilar pairs. To reiterate, similar pairs are all pairs that are not tied on one or the other of the conditions of the two variables. Thus, all those cells that are below and to the right of the upper left-hand cell constitute similar pairs because they are not tied in any way with those cells. We compute the number of similar pairs by multiplying the value of the upper left-hand cell with the sum of all cells below and to the right of it. This procedure is repeated for every cell in the table that has cells both below it and to the right. This process is much easier to grasp visually, as in Figure 9-2:

STEP 1: The following table indicates the first set of pairs to be calculated, starting with the *target* cell (low social restriction/low depression) and the cells below and to its right that are to be summed.

FIGURE 9-2
Visualizing pairs

A 20	B	C
D	E 23	F 14
G	H 24	I 14

N_s for cell A = (A)(E + F + H + I) = (20)(23 + 14 + 24 + 14) = (20)(75) = 1500

STEP 2: The next step uses cell D as the target cell:

A	B	C
D 14	E	F
G	H 24	I 14

(D)(H + I) = (14)(24 + 14) = (14)(38) = 532

STEP 3: The next step uses cell B as the target cell:

A	B 14	C
D	E	F 14
G	H	I 14

(B)(F + I) = (14)(14 + 14) = (14)(28) = 392

STEP 4: Finally, use cell E as the target cell (the only cell left with a cell that is both below and to the right of it):

A	B	C
D	E 23	F
G	H	I 14

(E)(I) = (23)(14) = 322. We now sum these quantities: N_s = 1500 + 532 + 392 + 322 = 2746.

STEP 5: We now have to find the dissimilar pairs by *working in reverse*. This time we start with the upper right-hand cell (cell C) and sum the values found in the cells below and to the left of it.

$$\text{cell C} = (8)(23 + 14 + 24 + 4) = (8)(65) = 520$$

$$\text{cell B} = (14)(14 + 4) = (14)(18) = 252$$

$$\text{cell F} = (14)(24 + 4) = (14)(28) = 392$$

$$\text{cell E} = (23)(4) = 92$$

$$\text{Total } N_d = 1256$$

STEP 6: Finally, we now put the values of N_s and N_d into the formula for gamma:

$$y = \frac{N_s - N_d}{N_s + N_d} = \frac{2{,}746 - 1{,}256}{2{,}746 + 1{,}256} = \frac{1{,}490}{4{,}002} = 0.372$$

STEP 7: Now, we can interpret our measure of association: there is a weak to moderate positive relationship between the degree of social restriction and feelings of social isolation. Since we are dealing now with ordinal variables with an inherent ordered structure, direction of association has a definite meaningful interpretation. We are saying that as social restriction gets more severe on an ordered scale, there is a tendency for prisoners to feel a greater degree of depression.

Lambda

As we see from the computer printout, the value of lambda varies with which variable is taken as dependent. As we have mentioned, lambda is an asymmetric statistic. Because the degree of social restriction is obviously not dependent on depression (at least not in this example), we calculated lambda with depression as the dependent variable. The third value of lambda in the computer printout, *symmetric* lambda, can be thought of as an average of the two asymmetric lambdas and is not much use to us.

We will not repeat the computation of lambda with these data. Instead we will consider a particularly vexing liability. *The problem is that lambda can yield a value*

TABLE 9-8. *Hypothetical Distribution and the Inherent Flaw in Lambda*

			Totals
100	90	60	250
40	50	60	150
Totals 140	140	120	400

of zero when there is, in fact, an association between the variables. This result occurs when the $E_1 = E_2$. And this occurs whenever all modal column scores occur in the same row. Consider the 3×2 distribution in Table 9-8.

Using our formulas from above,

$$E_1 = 400 - 250 = 150$$

$$E_2 = 40 + 50 + 60 = 150$$

$$\lambda = \frac{150 - 150}{150} = 0$$

But if we compute gamma for these data we find there is indeed a relationship (albeit not a very impressive one).

$$\gamma = \frac{16,400 - 9,000}{16,400 + 9,000} = \frac{7,400}{25,400} = 0.291$$

Somer's d

Somer's d is a measure of association that, although quite similar to gamma, is more restrictive in that it takes into account *pairs that are tied on the dependent variable.* Taking the tied pairs into account has the effect of weakening the numeric value of the association, as will be seen from the formula. By taking into account pairs tied on the dependent variable, we gain more information than gamma reveals. Somer's *d* is an asymmetric statistic, like lambda. The formula for Somer's *d* is formula 9-5:

9-5

$$d = \frac{N_s - N_d}{N_s + N_d + T_y}$$

Since the dependent variable is arrayed across the rows, pairs that are tied on y are located across the rows. Taking cell A as our first target cell, we find that pairs to the right of it with values of 14 and 8 are tied with it. We calculated T_y by multiplying the value of the target cell by all tied cases to the right of it (similar to what we did in Figure 9-2 above).

$$\text{cell A} = (20)(14 + 8) = 440$$

$$\text{cell B} = (14)(8) = 112$$

$$\text{cell D} = (14)(23 + 14) = 518$$

$$\text{cell E} = (23)(14) = 322$$

$$\text{cell G} = (4)(24 + 14) = 152$$

$$\text{cell H} = (24)(14) = 336$$

$$\text{Total } T_y = 1{,}880$$

We already have N_s and N_d values from gamma so all that we have to do is put T_y into the formula:

$$d = \frac{2{,}746 - 1{,}256}{2{,}746 + 1{,}256 + 1{,}880} = \frac{1{,}490}{5{,}882} = 0.2533$$

Thus, with d, as well, the relationship between depression and social restriction, although statistically significant (remember chi square), is not that impressive.

Tau b

Tau b is even more restrictive than Somer's d in that it includes pairs tied on the in-dependent variable (x) but not on the dependent variable (y) and pairs tied on y but not on x, that is, ties on one variable or the other but not on both. What this means is that tau b can only reach −1.0 or +1.0 when *all the frequencies fall on the diagonal*. Tau b is appropriately used when the number of rows and columns in a table are equal, as in the present case. Like gamma and Somer's d, tau b uses the difference between N_s and N_d as the numerator. The formula for tau b is formula 9-6:

9-6

$$b = \frac{N_s - N_d}{\sqrt{(N_s + N_d + T_y)(N_s + N_d + T_x)}}$$

We have already calculated all values except T_x. T_x is calculated just like T_y except that now we work *down* the columns of the independent variable instead of across the row of the dependent variable. Again taking cell A as the target cell, we multiply cell A by the pairs in each cell immediately below it.

$$\text{cell A} = (20)(14 + 4) = 360$$

$$\text{cell B} = (14)(23 + 24) = 658$$

$$\text{cell C} = (8)(14 + 14) = 224$$

$$\text{cell D} = (14)(4) = 56$$

$$\text{cell E} = (23)(24) = 552$$

$$\text{cell F} = (14)(14) = 196$$

$$\text{Total } T_x = 2{,}046$$

Putting the values in formula 9-6:

$$b = \frac{2{,}746 - 1{,}256}{\sqrt{(2{,}746 + 1{,}256 + 1{,}880)(2{,}746 + 1{,}256 + 2{,}046)}}$$

$$b = \frac{1{,}490}{\sqrt{5{,}882 \times 6{,}048}} = \frac{1{,}490}{\sqrt{35{,}574{,}336}} = \frac{1{,}490}{5{,}964.422} = 0.2498$$

This value corresponds identically (essentially) to all the previous measurements of association we have run on the relationship between social restrictions and depression in prison.

Because the printout supplies a probability that tau b is 0.0006, we take this opportunity to reinforce your knowledge of probability and the normal curve. We can test tau b for significance using the z distribution according to formula 9-7:

9-7

$$z = \frac{b}{\sqrt{\dfrac{4(r+1)(c+1)}{9nrc}}}$$

where r = number of rows

c = number of columns

Putting in the numbers we get the following:

$$z = \frac{0.2498}{\sqrt{\dfrac{4(3+1)(3+1)}{9(135)(3)(3)}}} = 3.26$$

A z of 3.26 is associated with an area of 0.4994. Adding this figure to the 0.5000 from the other side of the curve, we get 0.9994, and $1.000 - 0.9994$ leaves only 0.0006, or 0.06 percent of the area under the normal curve beyond a z of 3.26. Since this number far exceeds $z = 1.96$, you can safely reject the null that this relationship is only by chance.

THE ODDS RATIO AND YULE'S Q

A statistic known as the **odds ratio** is a useful measure that can be computed from tabular data. Additionally, it is an effect size that you'll run across repeatedly in more advanced statistics (c.f., Appendix A). The odds ratio is associated with an advanced method of contingency table analysis known as logistic regression and thus is rarely addressed in elementary statistics texts. However, it is a simple statistic to compute, and it provides valuable additional information concerning the relationship between two variables if we were attempting to explain our findings to someone without any statistical training. It is much easier to talk about odds for or against something occurring than to talk about chi square values, levels of significance, and measures of association. Further, master the odds ratio now and you'll have less to tackle when we discuss the behemoth that is the **generalized linear model**.

As all gamblers know, the *odds* is simply the ratio of the probability of an event occurring *versus* the probability of it not occurring. Symbolically, it is expressed as

9-8

$$\text{odds} = \frac{P}{Q}$$

Where P = the probability of an event occurring
Q = the probability of an event not occurring, which, as we know from chapter 3, is always equal to $1 - P$. So we can also express formula 9-8 as

$$\text{odds} = \frac{P}{1 - P}$$

For instance, the odds of throwing a 4 or a 5 with one throw of a fair die is a ratio formed by the probability of the stated event occurring (2/6 or 0.333) and the probability of the event not occurring (4/6 or 0.666). The ratio formed by these two probabilities is the odds (0.333/0.666 = 0.5), or 2:1 against. Note that anytime we obtain an odds ratio of less than 1.0 we can reverse the process (0.666/0.333 = 2.0) and say that the odds are *against* the event occurring.

The odds ratio is the ratio of two odds based on the independent variable from a contingency table. To illustrate the computation of the odds ratio and its meaning, reconsider Table 9-3 above. What are the odds that an inmate will be released, regardless of a psychologist's recommendation? We determine this figure by computing the marginal probability: 95/195 = 0.487. If $P = 0.487$, then $Q = 1 - 0.487 = 0.513$. The ratio of these two values is 0.487/0.513 = 0.949. Let us just say that the odds of being released versus not released are close to even. As you've already seen, *as the odds approach a value of 1, any given outcome becomes just as likely as the other outcome.* Now, returning to the odds *ratio*: because the odds ratio deals with the independent variable, we are talking about *conditional probability* converted into *conditional odds* (that is, the odds are conditioned by the presence of the independent variable). The **conditional odds** for this example are the odds of being released given that a psychologist recommended for or against it. The odds of being released given a positive recommendation are 85/25 = 3.4:1 in favor. Given a negative recommendation, the odds are 10/75 = 0.133:1, or (reversing things to make more intuitive sense of the numbers) 7.5:1 against. The odds ratio therefore provides a summary statistic that is the ratio of the two conditional odds:

9-9

$$OR = \frac{A/C}{B/D}$$

Where A/C represents the first odds we are interested in and B/D represents the second odds we are interested in. Thus, OR = 3.4/.133 = 25.5:

$$OR = \frac{85/25}{10/75} = \frac{3.4}{0.133} = 25.5$$

By default, the odds ratio is set to compare the final quotient to 1. That is, our answer above can be read as 25.5:1. This value indicates that the odds of an inmate who receives a favorable recommendation for release from a psychologist *being* released is 25.5 times greater than the odds of an inmate who received a "no release" recommendation for being released. (This is not the same as saying that an inmate who receives a favorable recommendation is 25.5 times more likely to be released than an inmate who receives an unfavorable recommendation—see Box 9-2.) Of those 95 who were actually released, 85 received a positive recommendation and 10 received a negative recommendation, so those who received a positive recommendation were 8.5 times more likely to be released than those who did not. The odds ratio is merely a measure of the *relative* risk derived from examining *both* conditions of the independent variable.

Another useful property of the odds ratio is that it can be easily converted into the traditional measure of association for 2 × 2 tables, Yule's Q. Yule's Q is simply a special case of gamma applicable to 2 × 2 tables. It may also be considered a standardized odds ratio that is constrained to range between −1.0 and +1.0, which the odds

---

Box 9-2
The Odds and Probability

It is important not to confuse odds with probability. To illustrate, the probability of a head in a single toss of a fair coin is 0.5, but the odds are 0.5/0.5 = 1—in other words, with a coin, the odds are not stacked against either a heads or a tails. Similarly, the probability of drawing a diamond out of a deck of cards is 13/52 = 0.25, but the odds are 0.25/0.75 = 0.333, or three-to-one against.

ratio is not—rather the odds ratio is bound between 0 and infinity (which is to say that it is basically unbound). As with gamma, the computation of Q involves only cell frequencies, ignoring marginal frequencies. The formula is identical in that the value of Q is derived from dividing the preponderance of similar or dissimilar cases by the total number of similar and dissimilar cases.

9-10

$$Q = \frac{AD - BC}{AD + BC}$$

The letters here refer to the cells such as outlined above in Table 9-7. From the data in Table 9-3, then, Yule's Q is

$$Q = \frac{AD - BC}{AD + BC} = \frac{(85)(75) - (10)(25)}{(85)(75) - (10)(25)} = 0.925$$

We may interpret the computed value of Q as indicating a strong relationship between our two variables, because it is bound between ±1, and the closer to 1 the value is, the stronger the relationship. Now let us see how Q is related to the odds ratio. To obtain Yule's Q directly from the odds ratio, we use formula 9-11:

9-11

$$Q = \frac{OR - 1}{OR + 1} = \frac{24.5}{26.5} = 0.925$$

This value may be interpreted as a 92.5 percent *proportional reduction in error* given knowledge of the independent variable.

You may be wondering why there is such a big difference between the value of lambda and the value of Q for these data. The difference is that Q does not consider tied cases either correct predictions or errors and is simply a ratio of similar ordered pairs minus dissimilar ordered pairs to the total number of untied pairs, because it is based on gamma.

The computation of odds ratios is not necessarily limited to 2 × 2 tables. We can make multiple comparisons from large tables as long as we identify *four cells with two columns and two rows*. We can then use the odds ratio to make comparisons piecemeal according to our research interests. For instance, considering Table 9-7, who has the greatest odds of suffering from depression: inmates with low or high social

TABLE 9-9. *Odds Ratio for Larger Tables Illustration*

DEPRESSION	SOCIAL RESTRICTIONS		
	Low	**High**	**Total**
Low	20	8	28
High	4	14	18
Total	24	22	

restrictions? For this example, let's assume we're only interested in inmates with very low and very high depression. Thus we can rearrange Table 9-7 to look like Table 9-9.

Let's first compute our odds ratio.

$$OR = \frac{A/C}{B/D}$$

$$OR = \frac{20/4}{8/14} = \frac{5}{0.571} = 8.757$$

So we know that the inmates with less social restrictions are 8.757 times less likely to be depressed than those with more social restrictions. Now, for our Yule's Q:

$$Q = \frac{OR - 1}{OR + 1}$$

$$Q = \frac{8.757 - 1}{8.757 + 1} = \frac{7.757}{9.757} = 0.795$$

Thus the relationship between depression and social isolation is quite strong, with an effect size of $Q = 0.795$. This results in a 79.5 percent reduction in error in predicting one's depression when we know their social isolation situation.

SPEARMAN'S RANK ORDER CORRELATION

Sometimes social science data are in the form of rankings. **Spearman's rank order correlation (rho)** is ideal for measuring association between two variables with values that have been ordered into ranks on a case-by-case basis rather than into nominal categories, as are the other measures discussed here. We are essentially asking whether a case's rank on one variable can predict its rank on another

TABLE 9-10. *Rank Order of Students on ACT English and Math Scores*

	MATH SCORE		ENGLISH SCORE			
	X	Rank	x	Rank	D	D²
Jane	20	1	17	3	−2	4
Frank	19	2	20	1	1	1
Jose	17	3	13	4	−1	1
Ray	14	4	18	2	2	4
Sheila	12	5	8	7.5	−2.5	6.25
Tony	11	6	8	7.5	−1.5	2.25
Kurt	10	8	10	5	3	9
Ahmed	10	8	9	6	2	4
Joyce	10	8	6	10	−2	4
Martin	7	10	7	9	1	1
Sums					0	36.5

variable. To borrow an example from education, suppose that we have 10 high school students who have taken the ACT college entrance exam in math and English and have obtained the scores in Table 9-10. Our first task is to rank order these scores from highest to lowest. Jane's score of 20 on the math test is the highest, so she is ranked number 1 on this variable. Her score of 17 on the English is the third highest, so she is ranked number 3 on this variable. Each student is so ranked. Kurt, Ahmed, and Joyce all scored 10 on the math exam. In the case of tied ranks such as these, we assign each case the average of the three ranks they would have occupied had their scores not been tied. These three subjects would have occupied ranks 7, 8, and 9. The average of these three ranks is 8, so they are all assigned this rank. Similarly, Sheila and Tony both scored 8 on the English test and are assigned the average of the two ranks they would have occupied had they not tied: $(7 + 8)/2 = 7.5$.

After we have determined the appropriate rankings, we subtract the rank on the English exam from the rank on the math exam for each case and enter that value under *D* for *rank difference*. Note that the sum of *D* is always zero. This is analogous to subtracting the mean from each raw score, as we did in chapter 3, for the standard deviation. The positive and negative differences will cancel each other out. We then square the differences to arrive at the *D squared* values, which are then summed. This value is entered into formula 9-12.

9-12

$$r_s = 1 - \frac{6(\Sigma D^2)}{N(N^2 - 1)}$$

Where N = number of paired observations
ΣD^2 = sum of the squared differences
6 = a constant

So to solve Spearman's rho for the information in Table 9-9:

$$r_s = 1 - \frac{6(36.5)}{10(100 - 1)} = 1 - \frac{219}{990} = 1 - 0.2212 = 0.779$$

Spearman's rho ranges from −1.0 to +1.0 and is an index of the strength of association between two rank-ordered variables. A perfect positive association would exist in the case of perfect agreement among the ranks, and a perfect negative association would exist for perfect disagreement among the ranks. Rho has a PRE interpretation when squared. If we square 0.779 we get 0.607, which means that our error is reduced by 60.7 percent when predicting rank with knowledge of one variable from rank on the other compared to predicting rank without knowledge of the other variable.

Assuming that these 10 cases are a random sample from the population, we can determine whether the sample finding can be generalized to the population. Since we have only 10 cases, the z distribution would not be appropriate for our test of significance. Fortunately, when the number of cases is 10 or more, the distribution of rho approximates the t distribution. We now test for significance with the t distribution using formula 9-13:

9-13

$$t = r_s \sqrt{\frac{n - 2}{1 - r_s^2}}$$

Plugging in our numbers, we get:

$$t = 0.779\sqrt{\frac{10-2}{1-0.607}} = 0.799\sqrt{\frac{8}{0.393}} = 0.799 \times 4.512 = 3.51$$

Turning to the t distribution table (see p. 344), we look at the 8 df column ($n - 2$), and we see that a t value of 2.896 is required to reject the null hypothesis with a one-tailed test and alpha set at 0.01. Our computed t exceeds this critical value and we can thus reject the null and conclude that it is unlikely that these data came from a population in which Spearman's rho is zero. Stated otherwise, our PRE of 60.7 percent is most likely an accurate representation of how much better we can predict one ACT score from another.

WHICH TEST OF ASSOCIATION SHOULD WE USE?

We suffer from such an embarrassment of riches when it comes to measures of association for nominal and ordinal data that it is understandable to ask, "Which one do we use?" There are no hard and fast rules to guide us in answering that question except to say that *you should choose the measure according to substantive theoretical context and to the type of data.* In the case of a 2 × 2 table we strongly favor phi because when squared (ϕ^2) it has both PRE and variance-explained interpretations. We also highly recommend including the *odds ratio* with such tables because of the intuitive interpretation it provides.

For tables larger than 2 × 2 we favor tau b with square tables (that is, those with an equal number of rows and columns). Because gamma ignores ties in its computation, we do not recommend it if there are a large number of ties in the data. Somer's d is an excellent choice if the researcher has hypothesized a strictly one-way asymmetric relationship between two variables in which one is clearly dependent and the other clearly independent. Nevertheless, tau measures may be preferable because they are more conservative in that they consider ties on both the independent and the dependent variables. We do not favor any measure (such as the contingency coefficient discussed in chapter 8) that does not have a PRE interpretation.

Finally, with rank-ordered data Spearman's rho is an excellent measure. However, if the data are ranked on the basis of accessible raw scores it is better to use the Pearson correlation coefficient, which we discuss in a future chapter. What we do when we transform interval- or ratio-level data (such as math and English scores in our example above) into ranks is to commit a statistical sin. Techniques applied to rank-ordered data are less powerful than techniques we can apply to interval or ratio data, because we hide so much of the good data (see chapter 3 for a review on moving between levels of measurement), so unless there is a good theoretical reason for applying less powerful techniques to the data, we should not.

Journal Table 9-1 provides a good example of measures of association for non-parametric statistics. The table is from the article "Self-attitudes and deviant response" by Kaplan (1976). For this study, the researcher tested the hypothesis that antecedent negative self-attitudes significantly increase the probability of subsequent use of deviant responses using participants who had already adopted deviant response patterns. In this table, we can see a summary of findings. The analysis reveals that of the 22 deviant acts that are listed, there is no relationship between antecedent self-derogation and subsequent performance of deviant behavior that should be rejected (see the table for instances where $p < 0.001$, $p < 0.01$, and $p < 0.05$). The degree of association for each item and category reveals that although all gammas are significant, the magnitudes are low to moderate. For example, the author found that there is a moderate degree of association for someone thinking about or threatening to take their own life (gamma = 0.34) and a low degree of association for someone who took something that was less than $2.00 (gamma = 0.09).

SUMMARY

Association refers to the connectedness or relatedness of two or more variables. We use various statistics to determine whether an association exists, its strength, and its direction. We have examined various techniques for making these determinations in cases where the variables are measured at the nominal and interval levels. Most of these techniques are based on simple ratios of similar and dissimilar pairs (agreement to disagreement) of cases. Lambda is rarely used, but it is useful for illustrating the logic of proportional reduction in error. PRE means, in essence, that knowing how one variable is distributed improves our ability to predict values on another variable. Any PRE measure is a ratio of errors made in predicting values of one variable made without knowledge of a second variable to errors made with knowledge of the second variable.

Gamma, Somer's *d*, and the tau measures differ in terms of how they deal with tied cases. Gamma ignores them completely and thus yields the most liberal index of association, and tau *b* yields the most conservative index. Spearman's rho is an index of the strength of association between two variables that have been rank ordered on

JOURNAL TABLE 9-1. *Percentage of Students Reporting Performance of Deviant Behaviors during the One-year Interval between the First and Second Test Administration by Self-derogation Level at First Administration among Students Indicating Nonperformance of the Behavior during a Specified Period Prior to the First Test Administration*

Deviant Behavior	SELF-DEROGATION LEVEL AT FIRST ADMINISTRATION		
	Low	Medium	High
3 Took things worth between $2 and $50 (0.22) †††	7.8	10.7	14.2***
	1672	1452	1265
7 Took things worth less than $2 (0.09) ††	19.5	21.9	24.1*
	1547	1248	1022
10 Thought about or threatened to take your own life (0.34) †††	9.4	13.9	22.9***
	1624	1306	1025
14 Became angry and broke things (0.17) †††	21	27.3	30.8***
	1462	1185	917
17 Carried a razor, switch blade, or gun as a weapon (0.15) †††	7.3	11.5	11.1***
	1626	1397	1217
24 Sold narcotic drugs (dope, heroin) (0.18) ††	3.1	4.4	5.3*
	1661	1461	1279
26 Received a failing grade in one or more school subjects (0.16)†††	15.9	22.8	23
	1408	1047	831
28 Used wine, beer, or liquor more than two times (0.12) †††	18.2	23.1	23.8***
	1574	1318	1143
29 Cheated on exams (0.16) †††	31.7	37.7	42.6***
	1528	1283	1043
31 Attempted suicide (0.30) †††	5	7.5	11.5***
	1688	1390	1163
33 Started a fist fight (0.11) ††	11.5	12.8	15.5***
	1536	1296	1104

(Continued)

JOURNAL TABLE 9-1. *(Continued)*

Deviant Behavior	SELF-DEROGATION LEVEL AT FIRST ADMINISTRATION		
	Low	Medium	High
38 Took narcotic drugs (0.19) †††	8.1	11.1	13.5
	1638	1455	1250
44 Skipped school without an excuse (0.15) †††	13.9	19.8	20.0***
	1637	1427	1212
50 Took part in gang fights (0.14) ††	6.1	8.2	9.1**
	1651	1410	1228
57 Used force to get money or valuables (0.25) †††	3	5.7	6.4***
	1651	1427	1243
61 Broke into and entered a home, store, or building (–0.16) ††	3.2	5.6	5.2**
	1656	1464	1295
64 Damaged or destroyed public or private property on purpose (–0.24) †††	5.3	9.1	10.4***
	1652	1414	1213
69 Stole things from someone else's desk or locker (–0.18) †††	10	12.3	16.4***
	1608	1374	1155
72 Used a car without the owner's permission (–0.21) †††	4.3	5.9	7.9***
	1666	1457	1279
75 Beat up someone who did nothing to you (–0.19) †††	5	7.3	8.5***
	1633	1393	1198
78 Took things worth $50 or more (–0.14) †	2.6	4.6	3.9*
	1677	1471	1297
82 Smoked marijuana (–0.12) †††	11.8	13.8	16.3
	1617	1430	1222

† Indicates Goodman and Kruskal's gamma, found in parentheses: †$p < 0.05$; ††$p < 0.01$; †††$p < 0.001$.

* Indicates significance level for chi square analysis ($df = 2$); *$p < 0.05$; **$p < 0.01$; ***$p < 0.001$.

a case-by-case basis on some attribute. When squared, it is a PRE measure. All the measures are valid, but before choosing one you should be concerned with the theoretical context of your research and with the form and nature of the association. Choosing a measure simply to maximize the strength of the association is dishonest and choosing one for no other reason than to be conservative is naive.

REFERENCE

Kaplan, H. B. (1976). Self-attitudes and deviant response. *Social Forces* 54(4), 788–801.

PRACTICE APPLICATION: NONPARAMETRIC MEASURES OF ASSOCIATION

What difference does the victim's sex make in the sentencing of sex offenders? We have 368 offenders who offended against females and 63 who offended against males. A low sentence is defined as one in which the offender was placed on probation from zero to 90 days. A medium sentence is defined as probation beyond 90 days with any jail sentence, and a high sentence is defined as any prison sentence. We find the following statistically significant distribution:

	Victim's sex		
Sentence	Female	Male	
Low	128	8	136
Medium	57	13	70
High	183	42	225
	368	63	431

$$\chi^2 = 12.15, p < 0.01$$

Calculate lambda.

Since all the modal cell category scores are in the same category of the independent variable, lambda will be zero.

$$E_1 = 206 \qquad E_2 = 185 + 21 = 206 \qquad 206 - 206/206 = 0$$

Compute gamma.

$$N_s = 128(13 + 42) = 7{,}040 \qquad\qquad N_d = 8(57 + 183) = 1{,}920$$
$$57(42) = 2{,}394 \qquad\qquad 13(183) = 2{,}379$$
$$\text{Total} = 9{,}434 \qquad\qquad \text{Total} = 4{,}299$$

$$\gamma + \frac{N_s - N_d}{N_s + N_d} = \frac{9{,}434 - 4{,}299}{9{,}434 + 4{,}299} = \frac{5{,}153}{13{,}733} = 0.374$$

Compute Somer's d. We have N_s and N_d; compute T_y.

$$(128)(8) \ = 1{,}024$$
$$(57)(13) \ = 741$$
$$(183)(42) = \underline{7{,}686}$$
$$\text{Total } T_y \ = 9{,}451$$

$$\gamma = \frac{N_s - N_d}{N_s + N_d + T_y} = \frac{9{,}434 - 4{,}299}{9{,}434 + 4{,}299 + 9{,}451} = \frac{5{,}135}{23{,}184} = 0.221$$

Compute tau b. We have N_s, N_d, and T_y; compute T_x.

$$128(57 + 183) = 30{,}720$$
$$57(183) = 10{,}431$$
$$8(13 + 42) = \ \ 440$$
$$13(42) = \ \underline{\ \ 546}$$
$$\text{Total } T_x = 42{,}137$$

$$b = \frac{N_s - N_d}{\sqrt{(N_s + N_d + T_y)(N_s + N_d + T_x)}}$$
$$= \frac{9{,}434 - 4{,}299}{\sqrt{(9{,}434 + 4{,}299 + 9{,}451)(9{,}434 + 4{,}299 + 42{,}137)}}$$
$$= \frac{5{,}135}{\sqrt{(23{,}184)(55{,}870)}} = \frac{5{,}135}{\sqrt{1{,}295{,}290{,}080}} = \frac{5{,}135}{3{,}590.1} = 0.143$$

Test *tau b* for significance, with alpha = 0.05, two-tailed test. H_0: tau b = 0

$$z = \frac{b}{\sqrt{\dfrac{4(r+1)(c+1)}{9nrc}}}$$

$$= \frac{0.143}{\sqrt{\dfrac{4(3+1)(2+1)}{9(431)(3)(2)}}} = \frac{0.143}{\sqrt{\dfrac{4(12)}{9(2,586)}}} = \frac{0.143}{\sqrt{0.0020624}} = \frac{0.143}{0.0454} = 3.15$$

Reject the null: computed z (3.15) exceeds critical z (1.96)

All computed measures indicate a weak but statistically significant association between the victim's sex and sentence type.

The Odds Ratio: Let us recode offenders who were not sentenced to prison (the low and medium categories) into one category and compute the odds ratio for receiving probation for offenders who offend against males versus against females.

Sentence	Victim's sex		
	Female	Male	
Low	185	21	206
High	183	42	225
	368	63	431

The odds of receiving probation for all 431 offenders is 0.915, or 1.09:1 against. For those who offended against females (185/183 = 1.01), the odds are essentially even, but for those who offended against males (21/42 = 0.5) they are 2:1 against. The ratio of these two odds is 1.01/0.5 = 2.02. Computing straight from raw numbers:

$$OR = \frac{(B)(C)}{(A)(D)} = \frac{(185)(42)}{(183)(21)} = \frac{7,700}{3,843} = 2.02$$

Compute Yule's Q:

$$Q = \frac{OR-1}{OR+1} = \frac{1.02}{3.02} = 0.338$$

The odds of receiving probation if a sex offender offends against a female are twice the odds of receiving probation than offenders who offend against males.

Sprearman's rho: A researcher asks a number of men and women to rank the seriousness of 11 crimes. The researcher notes that although males tend to rank property crimes higher, females tend to rank personal crimes as more serious. Compute Spearman's rho to determine how these rankings agree or disagree.

Crime	Males Rank	Females Rank	D	D²
Robbery	1	6	−5	25
Burglary	2	7	−5	25
Child molesting	3	2	1	1
Auto theft	4	11	−7	49
Rapes	5	1	4	16
Drug trafficking	6	10	−4	16
Assault	7	8	−1	1
Indecent exposure	8	9	−1	1
Trafficking in pornography	9	5	4	16
Wife beating	10	3	7	49
Dog fighting	11	4	7	49
		Sums	0	248

$$r_s = 1 - \frac{6(\Sigma D^2)}{N(N^2 - 1)} = 1 - \frac{6(248)}{11(120)} = 1 - \frac{1,488}{1,320} = 1 - 1.127 = -0.127$$

Test r_s for significance, with alpha = 0.05, two-tailed test.

$$t = r_s \sqrt{\frac{N-2}{1-r_s^2}} = -0.127\sqrt{\frac{9}{1-0.0161}} = -0.127\sqrt{\frac{9}{0.9839}}$$

$$= -0.127\sqrt{9.14739} = (-0.127)(3.024) = -0.384$$

Do not reject null: computed t (−0.384) is less than critical t (2.08). There is insufficient evidence that males and females differ in their rank ordering of crime seriousness.

CHAPTER 10

Elaboration of Tabular Data and the Nature of Causation

LEARNING OBJECTIVES:

After reading this chapter, the student will understand the following concepts:

- The nature of causality and how it is empirically established
- The difference between necessary and sufficient causes
- How to use tabular analysis to eliminate spuriousness between two variables
- The distinction between *explanation* and *interpretation* in tabular analysis and how to test for both
- How to calculate and understand partial gamma, as well as its limitations
- General limitations with tabular elaboration

INTRODUCTION

At their core, statistical models are tools for uncovering new knowledge and reducing uncertainty—just think of the very phrase, *proportional reduction in error*. Nowhere is this tool more important than when looking for causal relationships between two variables (for a quick primer on the difference between a *variable* and a *constant*, see Box 10-1). Now, Hubert Blalock states that causality is really a theoretical construct that cannot be demonstrated empirically. Yet he goes on to say, "But this does not mean that it is not helpful to think causally and

Box 10-1
Variables versus Constants

Now is a good time to review the concepts of *variables* and *constants*. A variable is anything that can change, whereas a constant is something that does not change. For example, if we are interested in the crime rates of boys and girls in Utah, *crime rate* and *gender* are our variables, whereas *location*—Utah—is a constant. For any given study, the constants cannot be considered explanatory because we are unable to establish *any* of the elements associated with either association or causality. For example, because *location* does not change, we cannot determine whether it affects the delinquent behavior of boys and girls. To be clear, this is a methodological artifact. Location most likely *does* matter when it comes to crime rate—perhaps not at the state level, but certainly at the municipal level, where delinquency is higher in urban as opposed to rural areas. But in a Utah study that measures the crime rate of boys and girls, location is taken out of the picture. We would need another study to establish the predictive value of location. For example, we could extend this study to include Utah, Wyoming, Arizona, and Idaho—now location is a variable and can enter into the predictive picture.

to develop causal models that have implications that are indirectly testable" (1961, p. 6). What this means is that we can never truly know whether *A* causes *B* in the social world—it will always remain a *theoretical* question. However, using probability can help us think in terms of causality in a way that is correct and clear. Therefore, we say such things as, "*A* is assumed to be a causal factor of *B* if the presence of *A* increases the probability that *B* will occur" given that certain criteria can be established. That is a far cry from saying that *A* causes *B*. Indeed, statements of this kind are not saying that changes in *A will* cause changes in *B* in a completely prescribed way. We operate in a probabilistic, not deterministic, world—as the very title of this book suggests. We will now examine this important concept of causality within the framework of the elaboration of tabular data. This discussion is all in preparation for the next chapter, when we consider one of the most popular measures of association, *Pearson's r*. As with the previous chapter, the material covered here can become complex quite quickly, and at times our explanations may seem unduly lengthy. Don't let this overwhelm you—stay undeterred and remember the old Russian maxim: repetition is the mother of all learning.

CRITERIA FOR CAUSALITY

To establish that something "causes" something else, there are a few things we must establish: association, temporal order, and nonspuriousness. We will only review these topics here because they are best suited for a methods textbook.

Association

The first criterion for causality is that an association must exist between the presumed cause and its effect. It is obvious that if two variables do not covary, neither can be considered a candidate to exert causal influence on the other. For example, sexual intercourse increases the probability that conception will occur. That is, if sexual intercourse is associated with conception, conception must at least occasionally occur when sexual intercourse occurs. Conversely, if sexual intercourse can occur infinitely and conception has never been known to follow, it cannot be said to be a cause of conception. The sexual intercourse/conception association is a good example for examining the concept of causality because almost everyone thinks that the relationship between them is strong. Actually there is a weak association because there are numerous intercourse events that are not followed by conception and that do not include contraceptive prophylactics of any sort.

As we have seen, variables are related to one another in varying degrees, which underscores the probabilistic nature of causality and the importance of measures of association. A perfect positive relationship exists when we observe a one-to-one correspondence between the two variables being explored. A perfect relationship between sexual intercourse and conception would be one in which every act of intercourse, without exception, resulted in conception. A perfect negative association would be one in which every increase in event A produced a corresponding decrease in event B. The overwhelming majority of the time, however, events occur that only *occasionally* result in the occurrence of other events. But as long as *some* sort of consistency is observed between events A and B, we have a candidate for causal (albeit probabilistic) inference.

Temporal Order

For variable A to be considered a causal candidate for the occurrence of B, it must occur before B in time. Causal order does not present much of a problem in the physical sciences. We can say without fear of contradiction that the sun shining on the window causes the glass to be warm, but it would be absurd to say that the warmth of the glass causes the sun to shine on it. Temporal order in the social and behavioral sciences is often obvious, but because of the feedback nature of many of the things we study it is not always easy. Consider the relationship between a nurturing parenting style and the delinquent behavior of a child. It has been well demonstrated that these two variables vary inversely together. But which is causally prior? Each variable can cause a decrease in the other in a felicitous spiral of type of parenting and juvenile behavior without ever actually determining which was ultimately responsible for setting the spiral in motion. Indeed, much research bears this out: just as parenting influences the behavior of children, so too does the behavior of a child influence the behavior of her parents. Note our word choice in that last sentence: we have chosen *influence* over *cause*. Why might we have done so?

Spuriousness

The third criterion is that the relationship between *A* and *B* must not statistically disappear when the influence of other variables is considered. For instance, there is a moderately strong positive correlation (about 0.45) between a school's average ACT or SAT scores and its proximity to Canada. In other words, the closer a U.S. school is located to the Canadian border, the better its students do on scholastic tests. Do you think the effect is real; that is, do you think being close to the U.S./ Canadian border exerts some *causal* power? Could it perhaps be that the closer we move to Canada the farther we are away from the mind-numbing urban centers of our nation and that accounts for the correlation? Latitude, although associated with scholastic performance, has *no causal influence on it at all*; the two variables are coincidentally linked but not causally connected.

Do note that although a variable can be dismissed as a causal explanation, we need not dismiss it as a *predictor*—the two terms are not necessarily synonymous. As long as the association between them is consistently and reliably found, we can use latitude to predict level of student ACT and SAT scores or even vice versa. Because an association is spurious it does not mean that it is false; a measure of association *is* what it is. Spuriousness means that the *interpretation* of the association, not the association itself, is false.

NECESSARY AND SUFFICIENT CAUSES

If we look back to our example of sexual intercourse and conception, it is clear that (barring artificial means) coitus is necessary to conceive. It is not, however, sufficient. A **necessary cause** or condition is one that *must* be present for an effect to follow. That is, if *A* is not present, there is no known incidence in which *B* has occurred. Immaculate conception and the newly developed technique of *in vitro* fertilization notwithstanding, intercourse is a necessary cause of conception. Certainly, being a female is necessary to being pregnant. Note that being a woman and experiencing intercourse *does not mean* that a woman will become pregnant; having intercourse is merely a necessary precondition for the possibility.

A **sufficient cause** is a cause or condition that by itself is able to produce an event. If other causal agents are needed to augment the nominated cause, it is not a sufficient cause. This does not mean that a sufficient cause is also a necessary cause. Being a convict or ex-convict is sufficient to cause stigma, discrimination, and a spoiled identity, but there are many other achieved and ascribed statuses, such as being a victim of a deforming disease, being a carrier of HIV, or being perceived as "crazy," that are themselves sufficient ways of acquiring a spoiled identity. Likewise, a cause can be necessary without being sufficient, as we've seen with both sexual intercourse and gender when it comes to conception. There are other variables in combination, such as the chemical environment of the womb, the absence of a contraceptive device, the fecundity of the female and the potency of the male, and so on, that are required to produce conception.

A cause is a **necessary and sufficient cause** if, and only if, it must be present for the effect to occur and has no help from other variables. Can you think of any nominated cause in criminology or criminal justice that meets this rigorous requirement for establishing a causal relationship between two variables? The (rather dubious) arguments of some low self-control researchers notwithstanding, neither can we; yet this is the implied demand of laypersons who point out exceptions to causal statements made by social scientists when they assert a causal connection between two variables. "Poverty, prejudice, unemployment, and a brutal childhood are not causes of crime because there are millions who suffer these privations without resorting to crime," they say. What they are really saying is that if we cannot produce necessary and sufficient causes of the phenomena we study, the whole enterprise of social science is useless and cannot tell us anything of value. We cannot satisfy the necessary and sufficient criterion of causality and we never will. A necessary and sufficient cause would be one in which all *A*'s are *X*'s, and no *B*'s are *X*'s. In statistical terms, all cases would be either in the primary or in the secondary diagonal of a cross tabulation table, chi square would be equal to *n*, and phi square would be 1.0, indicating that no other variable is required to account for variance. This is not possible, nor is it necessary, because of the probabilistic nature of social science statistics.

Let us consider a much more plausible example of what a tabular analysis would look like with a sample of boys, where experiencing poverty may or may not have

TABLE 10-1. *Examining Tabular Causality*

| | EXPERIENCED POVERTY | | |
Delinquency	Yes	No	Totals
Yes	235	65	300
No	35	265	300
Totals	270	330	600

$\chi^2 = 269.36, p < 0.05, \phi^2 = 0.449$

resulted in delinquent behavior at some point in their adolescence. The numbers presented in Table 10-1 are, of course, hypothetical for the sake of illustration.

What does this table tell us? First, there is a clear positive association between poverty and delinquency: of 270 delinquents, a full 235 experienced poverty, and of 330 nondelinquents, a full 265 did not experience poverty. Note that this relationship is not perfect: 35 boys in poverty did not engage in delinquency, and 65 boys who did not experience poverty did engage in delinquency. Although the chi square (269.36) is ridiculously large (and statistically significant), more impressive is the PRE, in this case phi square (0.449). This phi square means that knowing one's experience with poverty will decrease errors made in predicting that boy's delinquent behavior by 44.9 percent. Not perfect, but as far as social sciences go, pretty darn good.

Of course, none of this means that there is any causal relationship whatsoever here. Certainly, the variables covary, but what of temporal order? There is nothing about which came first: did the boys grow up in poverty and then start committing crime, or did they commit crime and then eventually start to live in poverty? Further, what of spuriousness? This is a simple 2 × 2 table; the possibilities for a third variable intervening are almost infinite at this point. All this being said, we should not be so quick to dismiss the *association*. For instance, unemployment is often dismissed as a cause of crime because the vast majority of those who become unemployed do not commit crimes; that is, it is not *characteristic* of the unemployed to commit crimes. Many other factors differentiate the unemployed who do and who do not commit crimes. As we have just seen, intercourse is not characteristically followed by pregnancy, but who among us who dismiss sexual intercourse as *the* cause of pregnancy would also dismiss it as *a* cause? The importance of one variable in explaining another lies not in whether it is characteristic but rather in *how much* of the variance it can uniquely account for in the dependent variable or how much it reduces prediction error. Although poverty does not *uniquely* explain some 45 percent of the variance in delinquency (after all, we have not controlled for other variables—more on this below), 45 percent is still a large PRE.

The whole point of the preceding discussion is to demonstrate that although there are few, if any, variables in social science that must necessarily be present to produce a specific effect, we are not necessarily precluded from engaging in causal analysis. What we can do is intelligently and accurately identify clusters of variables that in combination increase the probability of an event's occurrence. This is done in something known as multivariate analysis; to introduce you to this idea, we consider multivariate contingency analysis, which makes use of two or more contingency tables.

MULTIVARIATE CONTINGENCY ANALYSIS

If no single independent variable can account for all the variance observed in the dependent variable, other variables as yet unexamined must also be affecting the distribution of the dependent variable. Perhaps it is even the case that the association observed in the bivariate table is spurious, meaning that some third variable affects both the dependent and the independent variables in such a way that if its effects were to be removed, any observed relationship between the initial two variables would disappear. The classic example of **spuriousness** is the strong association between the number of firefighters at a fire and the magnitude of the dollar loss resulting from the fire (the more firefighters at the fire, the greater the dollar loss). Does this strong association mean that there is a cause-and-effect relationship operating? Of course not; a third variable, namely, the size of the fire, determines both the number of firefighters attending the fire and the magnitude of the dollar loss.

Taking the size of the fire into account is an example of what is known as *controlling for*, or *holding constant*, the effects of a third variable (sometimes you come across the more ostentatious *net of controls*). We can accomplish this by physically dividing a sample into subsamples based on categories of the third variable that we call a **control variable**. We then examine the relationship between the original two variables within the categories of the control variable. By *controlling for* or *holding constant*, we mean that categories of the third variable are fixed so that they are no longer free to vary. The *size of fire* variable, for instance, is free to vary between large and small or perhaps small, medium, and large. But once we determine the categories of the third variable and then reexamine the original relationship within those categories, we have essentially controlled its variability by changing it into a constant. When reexamining the basic bivariate relationship within any given category of the control variable, now no longer free to vary, we have in effect eliminated the influence of the third variable in each partial table by transforming it into two or more constants. The influence of the third variable can be ascertained only when we compare the outcomes of the bivariate relationship across tables formed from its categories. Confused? No need to be: read on.

Where do control variables come from, and how do I know which one(s) to use? *There is no substitute for a deep theoretical knowledge of your subject matter and good common sense when selecting control variables.* In the firefighters/dollar loss example it would not make sense to control for, say, socioeconomic class of the firefighters. If you are hypothesizing something novel or controversial, you must *always* control for variables already known to affect the dependent variable. For instance, if you propose that type A personalities have higher blood pressure levels than type B personalities, your results would not be taken seriously unless you showed that you controlled for variables already known to be related to blood pressure levels, such as age, gender, weight, and so forth.

Introducing a Third Variable

Let's take a look to see how controlling a third variable using tabular data works. To illustrate this process, we consider an example from our offender data. Let us suppose we want to examine the effects of the relationship of the offender to the victim on the type of sentence (probation or prison) received by sex offenders. We might be convinced that the courts deal more harshly with offenders who are acquainted with their victims because we see sexual offending against persons known to the offenders as a violation of trust. We divide these offender/victim relationships into two gross categories, *strangers* and *acquaintances*, and compute chi square and gamma. The results are given in part A of Table 10-2. We observe that this relationship is highly significant (chi square = 25.1), although it is contrary to our expectation: strangers, not acquaintances, are more likely to be imprisoned. We swallow our disappointment and then ask ourselves what else besides victim/offender relationship could influence sentence type. The most obvious answer is the seriousness of the crime. To convince ourselves of this, we cross tabulate sentence type with crime seriousness, which we also divide into two gross categories (high and low) from an original measure of crime seriousness that ranged from 1 to 10 (see the sentencing guidelines in chapter 1 for operational definitions). We obtain the results in part B of the table. These results show a much stronger association between crime seriousness and sentence type than between offender/victim relationship and sentence type.

TABLE 10-2. *Using Tabular Data to Establish Nonspuriousness*

ZERO-ORDER TABLES

	A				B		
Sentence Type	**Offender/Victim Relationship**				**Crime Seriousness**		
	Stranger	**Acquaintance**	**Total**		**Low**	**High**	**Total**
Probation	32	174	206		200	6	206
Prison	83	142	225		102	123	225
Total	115	316	431		302	129	431
	$\chi^2 = 25.1, p < 0.05$				$\chi^2 = 137.3, p < 0.05$		

CONDITIONAL (FIRST-ORDER) TABLES

	C						
	Low Crime Seriousness				**High Crime Seriousness**		
Sentence Type	**Offender/Victim Relationship**				**Offender/Victim Relationship**		
	Stranger	**Acquaintance**	**Total**		**Low**	**High**	**Total**
Probation	30	170	200		2	4	6
Prison	18	84	102		65	58	123
Totals	48	254	302		67	62	129
	$\chi^2 = 0.35$, ns				$\chi^2 = 0.87$, ns		

ASSOCIATION BETWEEN OFFENDER/VICTIM RELATIONSHIP AND CRIME SERIOUSNESS

	D		
	Offender/Victim Relationship		
Crime Seriousness	**Stranger**	**Acquaintance**	**Total**
Low	48	254	302
High	67	62	129
Totals	115	316	431
	$\chi^2 = 60.0, p < 0.05$		

We can now examine the association between sentence type and offender/victim relationship within the two categories of crime seriousness, a factor that is now no longer free to vary because we have made it two separate constants. Part C presents two tables assessing this association within low and high categories of crime seriousness. We see that when crime seriousness is taken into account, the association between sentence type and offender/victim relationship is nonsignificant (both conditional chi square values are far from the critical value of 3.841). Thus, the initially observed relationship was not a causal one. It appears that strangers are sentenced more harshly because they commit more serious crimes (they tend to use force and to harm their victims more so than offenders who are known to their victims). The table in Part D assessing the association between offender/victim relationship and crime seriousness confirms this proposition. We see that 67 of the 115 stranger assaults (58.3%) are in the high crime seriousness category as opposed to only 62 (19.6%) of the 316 acquaintance assaults.

The crime seriousness variable emerges as the variable that helps us to interpret the initially bivariate relationship of acquaintanceship and sentence severity. Strangers are not punished more severely *because* of their relationship with their victims but because they commit more serious crimes. Note that the *n*'s in the two conditions of crime seriousness sum to the *n* for the zero-order table (302 + 129 = 431) and that each of the respective cells sum to their zero-order value. A **zero-order relationship** is one without any controls. *Introducing a control variable does not change the distribution of the cases.* For instance, 142 offenders who were acquainted with their victims were shown to have been sentenced to prison in the zero-order table. When we placed these individuals into the low and high categories of crime seriousness in the conditional tables we still observe that 142 offenders who were acquainted with their victims were sentenced to prison, 84 in the low crime seriousness condition and 58 in the high crime seriousness condition. Tables produced in this manner are called *conditional* or *partial* tables, and the observed relationships are called *partial relationships* (this will segue later in the book to **partial correlation** *coefficients*).

EXPLANATION AND INTERPRETATION

When a bivariate relationship disappears (becomes nonsignificant) after a third variable is controlled for, we see the only reason for the initially observed relationship is that it was caused by one or more other variables. Such outcomes can be subdivided into outcomes known as *explanation* and *interpretation*. An outcome is called an **explanation** when the original relationship is explained away by an

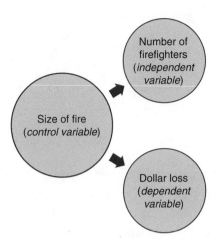

FIGURE 10-1
Moderating
relationships

antecedent variable, that is, a variable that precedes both the dependent and the independent variables in time. In the classic example of the number of firefighters and dollar loss, the relationship is explained away by a variable that clearly occurred before both the dollar loss and the number of firefighters dispatched, the size of the fire. Figure 10-1 illustrates the relationship between an antecedent control variable and the dependent and independent variables in the context of this example. Explanation is often referred to as a **moderating relationship**.

Interpretation occurs when the initial bivariate relationship is rendered nonsignificant by an intervening variable. In the sentence type and offender/victim relationship it is obvious that crime seriousness is not an antecedent variable. The relationship between victim and offender existed before the crime occurred. Crime seriousness is therefore a variable *intervening* between relationship and sentence type. Note that the association between crime seriousness and victim/offender relationship goes a long way in helping us to interpret the association between victim/offender relationship and sentence type; that is, those who offend against strangers commit more serious crimes, and more serious crimes result in more punitive sentences. Because the introduction of an intervening variable specifies a process by which the independent variable affects the dependent variable, an interpretation outcome is not a spurious one in the sense that an explanation outcome is. The independent variable "causes" the intervening control variable, which "causes" the dependent variable. In the present example, offender/victim relationship would be seen as "causing" crime seriousness, which then "causes" sentence type. The following figure illustrates the relationship between an intervening variable and the independent and dependent variables in the context of this example. Interpretation is often referred to as a **mediating relationship** (Figure 10-2).

FIGURE 10-2
Mediating
relationships

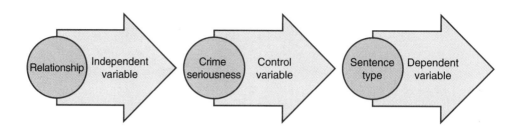

The differences between explanation and interpretation are often theoretical assumptions relating to the time ordering of the test variable. If a test variable exerts
influence before both the independent and the dependent variables, it is antecedent;
if it exerts influence after the independent variable but before the dependent variable, it is intervening. To give a further simple example, suppose we find a significant relationship between broken homes and delinquency rates among a sample of
schoolchildren. We then introduce a variable we shall call "quality of relationship
with parent(s)" as a control variable and find that the initial relationship disappears.
We might then say that among children who enjoy a good relationship, delinquency
rates are not affected by whether they come from a broken home. Similarly, we
might find among children with a poor relationship that delinquency rates do not
differ across categories of broken/intact homes. We thus conclude that it is the association between broken homes and quality of relationship that produced the bivariate association; that is, poor-quality relationships increase the probability of
delinquency *and* the probability that the home will be broken.

We emphasize that the difference between explanation and interpretation is
theoretical, not statistical. Researchers decide what type of outcome they observe
according to their understanding of what is going on theoretically within the data.
The statistics will only inform us of what happens to the initial relationship when
we control for other variables, not why it happened. For instance, the data on delinquency, broken homes, and quality of relationship could reflect processes going
in any and all directions. Delinquency could actually be the cause of poor relationships between child and parents rather than the other way around. Further, a
child's delinquency could lead to a broken home because of mutual parental re-
criminations regarding the child's behavior. Only a strong sense of theoretical ordering and the ability to dig deeply into the data will lead researchers to a
reasonable conclusion. As we have emphasized throughout this text, statistics are
only tools—only numbers. You need theory and experience to make sense of them.
(For more on digging more deeply into the numbers, see Box 10-2 on replication
and specification.)

Box 10-2
Replication and Specification

Suppose we observe a strong association between gender and frequency of crime among a sample of men and women, with men committing crime more often. We then divide the sample into subsamples based on race (white/black) and reexamine the relationship and find that it remained strong in both the black and the white categories of the control variable, thus replicating our original finding. The race variable did not affect the relationship between gender and frequency of crime in any way. Men commit more crime than women regardless of race. This is referred to as replication. **Replication** occurs when partial relationships are essentially of similar magnitude as the bivariate relationship, meaning that the third variable has no effect on the relationship between the zero-order variables.

Specification occurs when a third variable enables the researcher to specify under what conditions the bivariate relationship is true and when it is not true. In such a case, one partial relationship may result in the replication of the bivariate correlation or even in a dramatic increase, whereas the other partial relationship is near zero or may even have changed direction (from positive to negative or vice versa). This is essentially the same concept as *interaction*, which we covered in the previous chapter. It is important to note that the specification of an intervening variable does not negate any assumed causal relationship between *A* and *B*. Rather, the intervening variable *C* specifies a process by which *A* influences *B*. See Box 10-3 for more on this phenomenon.

ILLUSTRATING ELABORATION OUTCOMES

Let's take another example by further using our data on the sentencing of sex offenders. We first examine the bivariate relationship between offender type (sex and non-sex) and sentence (probation and prison), which is shown in Table 10-3. Only the gamma measure of association is given in the table. Column percentiles are also provided.

Controlling for One Variable

We see from Table 10-3 that sex offenders are significantly more likely to be sentenced to prison than are non-sex offenders. The probability of any convicted criminal being sent to prison is $281/637 = 0.441$; for a sex offender it is $225/431 = 0.522$,

TABLE 10-3. *Sentences by Group*

	ZERO-ORDER		
	Categorized Sentence by Group		
Sentence	**Group**		
	Non-sex	**Sex**	**Total**
Probation	150	206	356
	72.8	47.8	55.9
Prison	56	225	281
	27.2	52.2	44.1
Total	206	431	637
$\chi^2 = 35.39, p < 0.05, \gamma = 0.49$			

and for a non–sex offender it is $56/206 = 0.272$. Computing the odds ratio, we find that the odds of a sex offender being sentenced to prison are 2.9 times the odds that a non–sex offender will be sent to prison.

This does not necessarily mean that sex offenders are the victims of discriminatory sentencing because there are other variables besides the type of offense that influence sentencing. Crime seriousness is certainly one of them. We divide our crime seriousness scores into two categories. Offenders who scored 3 (the mean of the crime seriousness variable) or below are placed into a low seriousness category, and those who scored 4 or above are placed into a high seriousness category. We then recompute our statistics within these separate categories as in Table 10-4.

We are now examining the bivariate relationship between offender type and sentence under conditions of one control variable, an operation referred to as examining

TABLE 10-4. *Relationship Between Offender Type and Sentence Controlling for Crime Seriousness*

LOW CRIME SERIOUSNESS				**HIGH CRIME SERIOUSNESS**			
Sentence	**Group**			**Sentence**	**Group**		
	Non-sex	**Sex**	**Total**		**Non-sex**	**Sex**	**Total**
Probation	118	200	318	Probation	32	6	38
Prison	13	102	115	Prison	43	123	166
Total	131	302	433	Total	75	129	204
$\chi^2 = 26.6, p < 0.05, \gamma = 0.645$				$\chi^2 = 45.2, p < 0.05, \gamma = 0.877$			

the **first-order partial relationship.** A first-order relationship is one where controls are introduced. The partial relationship shows that within the low seriousness category we have replicated the original zero-order bivariate relationship. Gamma has increased for this conditional table from the zero-order value of 0.49 to 0.645. Note that although gamma has increased, the chi square value has decreased from 35.4 to 26.6 because the sample size has decreased (remember, like many statistics, chi square is largely a product of sample size).

The association between offense type and sentence type becomes much stronger within the high seriousness category and slightly higher within the low seriousness category when compared with the zero-order association between sentence type and offense type. This result indicates that crime seriousness has been acting as a **suppressor variable**, hiding the true relationship between offense type and sentence type. On average, sex offenders receive harsher sentences, but they also tend to commit less serious crimes as seriousness is defined in this jurisdiction (see sentencing guidelines in chapter 1). The sentence type/offense type relationship is suppressed *unless* crime seriousness is controlled for. The outcome of this elaboration both is a replication (the original relationship and its direction remain) and specifies that the relationship is particularly true within one of the categories of the control variable.

Criminal record is another variable that is considered in sentencing decisions. Criminal record is measured in this jurisdiction by an ordinal measure ranging from 0 to 27. If we did not want a 2 × 10 table, we surely do not want a 2 × 27 table. So again we collapse our ordinal variable into two dichotomous variables: first offenders and repeat offenders. We then repeat the same procedure with prior record that we went through with crime seriousness. This is presented in Table 10-5.

Table 10-5 illustrates a specification outcome; the relationship between type of offender and type of sentence is true only among repeat offenders. The low prior

TABLE 10-5. *Relationship Between Offender Type and Sentence Controlling for Prior Record*

LOW PRIOR RECORD				HIGH PRIOR RECORD			
Sentence	Offender Type			Sentence	Offender Type		
	Non-sex	Sex	Totals		Non-sex	Sex	Totals
Probation	69	112	181	Probation	81	94	175
Prison	12	32	44	Prison	44	193	237
Totals	81	144	225	Totals	125	287	412

$\chi^2 = 1.8$, ns $\chi^2 = 36.6, p < 0.05, \gamma = 0.530$

record partial relationship is nonsignificant, and the high prior record partial relationship has increased in magnitude over the computed bivariate gamma. No gamma is calculated for the low prior record group because we have accepted the null that no relationship exists. In other words, we observe an interactive effect because the effect of offender group on sentence type differs markedly over the two categories of the control variable.

Further Elaboration: Two Control Variables

Knowing the seriousness of the crime committed and the offender's criminal record will improve your ability to predict the sentence he will receive over what you would have predicted knowing only his offense type. Of course, each offender is sentenced

---

Box 10-3

Simpson's Paradox

Understanding third variables is important for another reason: subgroups often act differently than the group itself. This reality can play out in your statistics. As mentioned in Box 10-2, the specification of an intervening variable does not negate any assumed causal relationship between *A* and *B*. Rather, the intervening variable *C* specifies a process by which *A* influences *B*. This could mean that your group association may be positive, but your subgroup associations may be *negative*. To illustrate this, we'll use a real-life example: batting averages in baseball. In his book *A Mathematician at the Ballpark: Odds and Probabilities for Baseball Fans*, Ken Ross (2004) compares the batting averages of Derek Jeter and David Justice from the years 1995, 1996, and 1997:

	1995		1996		1997		Combined	
Derek Jeter	12/48	0.250	183/582	0.314	190/654	0.291	385/1284	0.300
David Justice	104/411	0.253	45/140	0.321	163/495	0.329	312/1046	0.298

Looking at their batting averages from year to year, Justice has the higher batting average. But when we consider their combined effect, Jeter comes out on top. What's causing this? The answer lies in the denominator: note how much more often Jeter went to bat when compared to Justice.

Such occurrences are common in social science: be aware of them and what they mean for how you interpret not just causal relationships, but all associations.

according to his felony sentencing worksheet score on both of these variables at the same time. It is artificial, therefore, to attempt to predict sentence by either of these variables in isolation. To examine the *joint* effects of these variables on the offender type/sentence type relationship requires the computation of four partial relationships:

- Low crime seriousness × low prior record
- High crime seriousness × low prior record
- Low crime seriousness × high prior record
- High crime seriousness × high prior record

These four partial tables are presented in Table 10-6.

When the basic bivariate relationship is examined under the various conditions of two control variables, it is called **second-order partial relationship.** Having

TABLE 10-6. *Relationship Between Offender Type and Sentence Controlling for Prior Record and Crime Seriousness*

LOW CRIME SERIOUSNESS × LOW PRIOR RECORD				HIGH CRIME SERIOUSNESS × LOW PRIOR RECORD			
Offender Type				Offender Type			
Sentence	Non-sex	Sex	Totals	Sentence	Non-sex	Sex	Totals
Probation	56	108	164	Probation	13	4	17
Prison	1	16	17	Prison	11	16	27
Totals	57	124	181	Totals	24	20	44

$\chi^2 = 5.7, p < 0.05, \gamma = 0.785$ $\chi^2 = 5.4, p < 0.05, \gamma = 0.651$

LOW CRIME SERIOUSNESS × HIGH PRIOR RECORD				HIGH CRIME SERIOUSNESS × HIGH PRIOR RECORD			
Offender Type				Offender Type			
Sentence	Non-sex	Sex	Totals	Sentence	Non-sex	Sex	Totals
Probation	62	92	154	Probation	19	2	21
Prison	12	86	98	Prison	32	107	139
Totals	74	178	252	Totals	51	109	160

$\chi^2 = 22.7, p < 0.05, \gamma = 0.657$ $\chi^2 = 38.2, p < 0.05, \gamma = 0.939$

controlled for the two legally relevant variables that are *supposed* to influence sentencing, we can now assess the effects of *group* (sex offender and non–sex offender). Consulting Table 10-6, our findings from above hold true: all things equal, sex offenders are significantly more likely than non–sex offenders to be imprisoned regardless of which of the four partial relationships we examine. The relationship is particularly strong in the high crime seriousness/high prior record category (where $\gamma = 0.939$) but weaker in the high crime seriousness/low prior record category ($\gamma = 0.651$).

Partial Gamma

To summarize the relationship between offender group and type of sentence received, we have had to make four separate statements with reference to four sets of computed statistics. It would be nice if we could boil these statements down to one succinct statement about the relationship between offender group and type of sentence controlling for crime seriousness and prior record. One technique that allows us to do so is known as **partial gamma**, which is obtained by the simple method of combining the separate computations from each conditional table into a single measure of association. Recall that the formula for gamma is

$$\gamma = \frac{N_s - N_d}{N_s + N_d}$$

The formula for partial gamma is therefore an extension of this, as seen in formula 10-1:

10-1

$$\gamma_p = \frac{\Sigma N_s - \Sigma N_d}{\Sigma N_s + \Sigma N_d}$$

Where ΣN_s = the similar pairs summed across all conditional tables
ΣN_d = the dissimilar pairs summed across all conditional tables

The zero-order gamma for our offender type/sentence type data was 0.490. The respective gammas for the low crime seriousness and the high crime seriousness conditional relationships were 0.645 and 0.877. We now wish to transform these separate gammas into a single summary statistic. The computations for the two separate gammas can be found in Table 10-6, but we can recreate them ourselves to demonstrate the logic behind partial gamma:

$$\text{low crime seriouness } \gamma = \frac{12{,}036 - 2{,}600}{12{,}036 + 2{,}600} = \frac{9{,}436}{14{,}636} = 0.645$$

$$\text{high crime seriousness } \gamma = \frac{3{,}936 - 258}{3{,}936 + 258} = \frac{3{,}678}{4{,}194} = 0.877$$

To obtain partial gamma we sum as directed:

$$\Sigma N_s = 12{,}036 + 3{,}936 = 15{,}972$$
$$\Sigma N_d = 2{,}600 + 258 = 2{,}858$$
$$\gamma_p = \frac{15{,}972 - 2{,}858}{15{,}972 + 2{,}858} = \frac{13{,}114}{18{,}830} = 0.70$$

The first-order gamma of 0.70 indicates that knowledge of the distribution of crime seriousness, as well as knowledge of type of offense, proportionately improves our ability to predict the type of sentence by 70 percent over what our predictions would be without knowledge of these two variables in tandem. (It is important to note, however, that crime seriousness has been controlled for in an arbitrary fashion. If we had used more categories of this variable, such as low, medium, and high, somewhat different results may have been obtained.) Now, we will apply the same logic and solve for partial gamma step by step.

STEP 1: Now that you are aware of the logic involved, we will proceed directly to the computation of the second-order partial gamma. The computations of gamma for the four separate tables are as follows:

$$\text{low crime seriousness} \times \text{low prior record} = \frac{896 - 108}{896 + 108} = \frac{788}{1{,}004} = 0.785$$

$$\text{low crime seriousness} \times \text{high prior record} = \frac{5{,}332 - 1{,}104}{5{,}332 + 1{,}104} = \frac{4{,}228}{6{,}436} = 0.657$$

$$\text{high crime seriousness} \times \text{low prior record} = \frac{208 - 44}{208 + 44} = \frac{164}{252} = 0.651$$

$$\text{high crime seriousness} \times \text{high prior record} = \frac{2{,}033 - 64}{2{,}033 + 64} = \frac{1{,}969}{2{,}097} = 0.939$$

STEP 2: Now, we sum the N_s and N_d together:

$$\Sigma N_s = 896 + 208 + 5{,}332 + 2{,}033 = 8{,}469$$
$$\Sigma N_d = 108 + 44 + 1{,}104 + 164 = 1{,}320$$

STEP 3: We finish things off by solving for γ_p:

$$\gamma_p = \frac{8{,}469 - 1{,}320}{8{,}469 + 1{,}320} = \frac{7{,}149}{9{,}789} = 0.73$$

STEP 4: We are now in a position to interpret partial gamma. We have arrived at a single statistic summarizing the relationship between sentence type and offender type, controlling for crime seriousness and prior record as we have measured and categorized these variables. Since gamma is a PRE measure, we may conclude that we have proportionately reduced error in predicting type of sentence by 73 percent given our knowledge of offense type, crime seriousness, and prior record. Note that with knowledge of offense type only, we were able to proportionately reduce prediction errors by 49 percent (zero-order gamma). With the additional information provided by crime seriousness we were able to reduce errors by 70 percent (first-order gamma). With knowledge of prior record we were able to proportionately reduce errors by another 3 percent. Knowledge of offense type, crime seriousness, and prior record proportionately reduces the errors we would make in predicting an offender's sentence type without this information by 73 percent. Such global measurements of association will crop up again in future chapters. Further, for an important note on when *not* to compute partial gamma, see Box 10-4.

PROBLEMS WITH TABULAR ELABORATION

As we moved from an examination of the zero-order to the second-order relationship we noted that the number of cases in each cell diminished severely. For instance, 4 of our 16 cells in the second-order examination of offender type and sentence type contained fewer than five cases, although we have a relatively large sample. If we wished to add a further dichotomous control variable (third-order), each of our four partial relationships would have to be examined under the two

Box 10-4
When Not to Compute Partial Gamma

In Table 10-6 all partial tables convey essentially the same information: sex offenders are significantly more likely to be sentenced to prison than non-sex offenders. Given this consistency, partial gamma is a useful summary statistic. However, we would not want to compute partial gamma if we found a specification outcome (see Box 10-2). The very reason for elaboration is to uncover interesting specifications. Having gone through the process of elaboration and discovering that your control variable has an interactive effect on the bivariate relationship, we would not want to cover it up again by reporting partial gamma.

To illustrate, suppose we have a teacher concerned with inappropriate activity (fidgeting, talking, fighting, moodiness, not completing assignments, smoking, and various kinds of horseplay) in school. On the basis of various measures and other information, the teacher divides a sample of 200 boys into categories based on their activity level, coded high and low, and on whether they are considered *problem children* and finds that the computed chi square is nonsignificant at 2.66 and that the zero-order gamma is 0.263. Since there was a nonsignificant chi square, the teacher may accept the null that there is no difference in activity level between children defined as problem and nonproblem children and leave it at that.

But suppose the teacher realizes that all children had recently completed a scale measuring extroversion/introversion and decides to elaborate her initial finding using those data. You might think that because she accepted the null there is no point in doing this, but there is. Can you think why she is justified in doing this based on something we addressed earlier in this chapter? A control variable may be suppressing the nature of the relationship, and once that variable is introduced, the "true" nature of the independent variable on the dependent variable is uncovered. Thus the teacher divides the sample into extroverts and introverts and finds that the hypothesized relationship is strongly supported ($\chi^2 = 20.5$, $p < 0.05$, $\gamma = 0.881$) among extroverts. Among the extroverts problem children are significantly more likely than nonproblem children to have high activity levels. There is also a significant relationship among the introverts ($\chi^2 = 3.97$), but it is in the opposite direction ($\gamma = -0.429$). That is, whereas extroverted problem children are strongly prone to high levels of activity, introverted problem children are less prone to high activity levels than nonproblem children. It is obvious that the independent variable (*problem child*) has different and interesting effects on the dependent variable under the two conditions of the control variable. The relationship attains statistical significance under both conditions, the strength of the association increases, and the relationship among the introverts is reversed. The teacher would never have uncovered these interesting findings if the analysis had ceased because of the initial nonsignificant bivariate result.

Zero-Order Relationships

	Problem Child		
Activity	Yes	No	Totals
High	80	70	150
Low	20	30	50
Totals	100	100	200

Conditional Relationships

Extroverts Problem Child				Introverts Problem Child			
Activity	Yes	No	Total	Activity	Yes	No	Total
High	50	20	70	High	30	50	80
Low	5	20	25	Low	15	10	25
Totals	55	40	95	Totals	45	60	105

Computing partial gamma from these data we obtain 0.209, which provides us with a totally misleading impression of the nature of the relationship between the independent and the dependent variables. Any reader might conclude on the basis of that measure that the initial relationship is replicated (it is still nonsignificant), although attenuated, when controlling for the extrovert/introvert variable. Computing partial gamma after uncovering such interesting specifications is rather like digging up the pirate gold and then burying it again. The extrovert/introvert dimension is a suppressor variable masking the true nature of the relationship between activity level and the designation *problem child*.

conditions of the added control variable. Instead of 16 cells, we would now have 32. The effect of this change on cell frequency is obvious. Results would become increasingly less meaningful as our cells became increasingly deprived of case frequencies. And recall that the behavior of chi square becomes unwieldy when expected cell frequencies drop below five. Even if we doubled our sample size, a costly and time-consuming strategy, the task of summarizing so many tables into a succinct statement about how the variables are related would be messy. The problems of elaboration render it a relatively inefficient method of multivariate analysis for all but the most simple substantive problems and small sample sizes.

A further problem arises when we collapse interval-level data into a limited number of categories. Although collapsing was necessary to arrive at manageable tables, doing so cost us a loss of information. With crime seriousness, for instance, offenders who had 4 crime seriousness points were categorized with those who had 10 crime seriousness points. Our statistics were then computed as if these people had committed crimes of equal gravity, which they had not. In other words, it is reasonable to suppose that an offender with 10 crime seriousness points will receive a harsher sentence than will an offender with 4 crime seriousness points. However, we cannot determine this result from the analysis we have conducted because we have artificially placed them (along with offenders with 5, 6, 7, 8, and 9 points) into a single category.

It is for this reason that collapsing data measured at the interval and ratio levels into limited nominal or ordinal categories to accommodate weaker methods of statistical analysis when the data are suitable for more efficient and powerful techniques is problematic because we lose valuable variation in the data. Other methods to be examined in chapter 12 and Appendix A are more efficient methods of multivariate analysis because they do not require the physical placement of cases into subtables and because they utilize all cases simultaneously. However, we believe that it is easier to get a better intuitive grasp of multivariate analysis if it is first presented in tabular form because we are able to see how the cases are physically moved around into the various categories of the control variable(s). The principles and concepts you learned in this chapter about interaction, specification, interpretation, and control will serve you well in future chapters.

SUMMARY

The concept of causality is a difficult one. There are three basic criteria for establishing causality: (1) a statistically significant association, (2) temporal order, and (3) nonspuriousness. We differentiated between necessary and sufficient causes and causes that are both necessary and sufficient. It is impossible to satisfy the necessary and sufficient criteria for causality because no one thing is the sole cause of anything; rather, variables often act in conjunction to bring about an effect. To explore the effects of an independent variable on a dependent variable when performing tabular analysis, we must examine the association within categories of a theoretically meaningful control variable in a process called *elaboration*.

When we examine the effects of additional variables on the bivariate relationship we observe various kinds of elaboration outcomes: replication, explanation, interpretation, or specification. Replication means that the addition of another variable did not appreciably alter the zero-order outcome. Explanation means that the control variable completely eliminates (explains away) the initially observed relationship. Interpretation means that the introduction of the control variable weakens or eliminates the strength of the bivariate association. An explanation outcome means that the relationship observed between two variables is entirely coincidental and that the control variable, which precedes both the dependent and the independent variables in time, "causes" both. Interpretation means that the control variable intervenes between the independent and dependent variables and helps us to interpret the relationship between them.

Partial gamma, which we examined with our sex offender data, is an index of the strength of association between two variables, controlling for the effects of one or more additional variables. Partial gamma offers us a single statistic that sums up the findings of multiple tables. However, if interesting specifications are uncovered by the elaboration method, they should be noted and not covered up again by partial gamma. Further, other problems of bivariate elaboration include rapid depletion of cell sizes as more control variables are added and the somewhat arbitrary categories that sometimes have to be created.

REFERENCES

Blalock, H. M., Jr. (1961). *Causal inference in nonexperimental research.* Chapel Hill, NC: University of North Carolina Press.

Ross, K. (2004). *A mathematician at the ballpark: Odds and probabilities for baseball fans.* New York: Penguin.

PRACTICE APPLICATION: BIVARIATE ELABORATION

Let us turn back to our 3×2 chi square in Table 8-5. In it we found that birth order was significantly related to having committed a violent crime among a sample of 585 juvenile delinquents. We now wish to go a little further and see whether this result is true for both boys and girls. We have to make two 3×2 tables now, one for the boys and one for the girls. We go back into the data to find the distributions on birth order/violent crime for each gender and compute chi square for each separate table.

	Boys					**Girls**			
	Birth Order					**Birth Order**			
Violent offense									
	First	Middle	Last	Total		First	Middle	Last	Total
No	69	65	50	184		32	17	6	55
Yes	79	174	74	327		6	10	3	19
Total	148	239	124	511		38	27	9	74

Compute chi square.

$$\chi^2 = \Sigma\frac{(O - E)^2}{E} \quad \text{where } E = \frac{r \times c}{n}$$

Expected Frequencies

Boys	*Girls*
A. $148 \times 184/511 = 53.29$	A. $38 \times 55/74 = 28.24$
B. $239 \times 184/511 = 86.06$	B. $27 \times 55/74 = 20.07$
C. $124 \times 184/511 = 44.65$	C. $9 \times 55/74 = 6.69$
D. $148 \times 327/511 = 94.71$	D. $38 \times 19/74 = 9.76$
E. $239 \times 327/511 = 152.94$	E. $27 \times 19/74 = 6.93$
F. $124 \times 327/511 = 79.35$	F. $9 \times 19/74 = 2.31$

Chi Square Boys

Cell	Obs.	Exp.	$(O - E)$	$(O - E)^2$	$(O - E)^2/E$
A	69	53.29	15.71	246.80	4.63
B	65	86.06	−21.06	443.52	5.15
C	50	44.65	5.35	28.62	0.64
D	79	94.71	−15.71	246.80	2.61
E	174	152.94	21.06	443.52	2.90
F	74	79.35	5.35	28.62	0.36
	511	511	00.00		16.29

$\chi^2 = 16.29$

Is it significant? With 2 degrees of freedom [$(R - 1)(C - 1) = 2$], it exceeds the critical value for significance at 0.05 (5.99). It also exceeds the critical value for the 0.01 level (9.210). Therefore, it is highly unlikely that our sample comes from a population where the probability of committing a violent crime is the same for each birth-order group.

Chi Square Girls

Cell	Obs.	Exp.	$(O - E)$	$(O - E)^2$	$(O - E)^2/E$
A	32	28.24	3.76	14.14	0.50
B	17	20.07	−3.07	9.42	0.47
C	6	6.69	−0.69	0.48	0.07
D	6	9.76	−3.76	14.14	1.45
E	10	6.93	3.07	9.42	1.36
F	3	2.31	0.69	0.48	0.21
	74	74	0.00		4.06

$\chi^2 = 4.06$

With 2 *df* we need a chi square value of 5.991 to reject the null hypothesis. Our computed value of 4.06 falls below this figure. Therefore, we do not reject the null. The sample could have come from a population in which the probability of committing a violent crime is the same for all three female birth-order groups. We have a specification result: the association between birth order and violent crime is true only for delinquent boys.

Compute the contingency coefficient for both subsamples:

Boys

$$\text{Boys } C = \sqrt{\frac{x^2}{x^2 + N}}$$

$$= \sqrt{\frac{16.29}{16.29 + 511}} = \sqrt{\frac{16.29}{527.29}} = \sqrt{0.0309} = 0.1725$$

Girls

$$\text{Girls } C = \sqrt{\frac{4.06}{4.06 + 74}} = \sqrt{\frac{4.06}{78.06}} = \sqrt{0.0520} = 0.228$$

The contingency coefficient is actually stronger for girls than it is for boys. If we had an equal number of boys and girls, and assuming constant cell percentages, we would conclude that the relationship between birth order and the commission of a violent offense is stronger for girls than for boys. This does not mean that girls are more violent than boys. The percentage of girls convicted of a violent offense is 25.7, but for boys it is 64. It simply means that being convicted of a violent crime is more dependent on birth order for girls than it is for boys. Remember also that this could possibly be a simple chance finding since we have a chi square that did not attain statistical significance.

CHAPTER 11

Bivariate Correlation and Regression

LEARNING OBJECTIVES:

After reading this chapter, the student will understand the following concepts:

- Pearson's *r* correlation coefficient, including its computation formula, underlying logic, and interpretation
- How to calculate and interpret bivariate regression, including the intercept, slope, and *b* coefficient
- The meaning of *error* and *residuals* in bivariate regression
- How to use a scattergram to plot regression lines
- The utility and versatility of bivariate regression in relation to previously explored statistical techniques

INTRODUCTION

This chapter presents two powerful techniques for analyzing the linear relationship between two variables measured at the interval or ratio levels. Although these techniques differ somewhat in logic from those we have examined so far, they are designed to answer many of the same questions. Correlation and regression are the "meat and potatoes" of contemporary social science—particularly criminology and criminal justice—so it is imperative to introduce students to these methods as soon as possible. Because they are fundamental, we devote proportionately more space to these than to other techniques.

Regression techniques are used to "predict" the value of one variable from knowledge of another. **Correlation** tells us how accurate these predictions are and describes the nature (strength and direction) of the relationship. The indispensable nature of regression to scientific research has been aptly put by Pedhazur (1982, p. 42): "The regression model is most directly and intimately related to the primary goals of scientific inquiry: explanation and prediction of phenomena." Correlation and regression techniques are more powerful than the statistics discussed in chapter 9. Statistics such as gamma allow us only to predict a case's category on one variable given knowledge of its category on another. Correlation and regression are more precise in that they enable us to *predict the specific value* or score of a case on one variable from a value or score on another. Since the purpose of regression is essentially prediction, many researchers use the term **predictor variables** for independent variables and **criterion variable** for the dependent variable. Nevertheless, we urge you to remember that causality is a methodological issue more than it is a statistical one. No matter how sophisticated your statistics are, if your method is flawed, so, too, will your statistical models be flawed.

LINEAR RELATIONSHIPS

As we saw in chapter 9, there is a positive relationship between two variables when high scores on variable Y are associated with high scores on variable X and low scores on Y are associated with low scores on X. Conversely, there is a negative relationship when high scores on Y are associated with low scores on X. With continuous data, these relationships can be approximated by a straight line—and any straight line is given by the classic algebraic equation $y = a + bx$. Consider the example of workers earning $10 per hour. A worker who works zero hours gets paid zero money, one who works two hours gets $20, and so on. The dependent variable (Y) is dollars earned and the independent variable (X) is hours worked. We can graph this relationship as in Figure 11-1.

The relationship is linear and perfect. As X increases so does Y in a perfectly linear fashion. For example, a 1.5 increase in X is associated with an increase of 15 in Y. In regression analysis, such straight lines are called **regression lines**. Depending on the distribution of the data, these lines have different **regression slopes**. The **slope** of a line is defined as the vertical distance divided by the horizontal distance between any two points on the line. This relationship is shown in formula 11-1.

11-1

$$b = \frac{\text{vertical distance}}{\text{horizontal distance}} = \frac{y_1 - y_2}{x_1 - x_2}$$

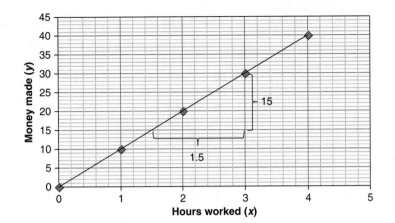

FIGURE 11-1
A perfect linear relationship

x	y
0	0
1	10
2	20
3	30
4	40

	x	y
Totals	10	100
Means	2	20

We can use the information from Figure 11-1 to find the slope of the relationship between hours worked and money made using formula 11-1. If we look at $y = 40$, we see that $x = 4$, and if we look at $y = 30$, $x = 3$. This provides us with the following numbers:

$$y_1 = 40$$

$$x_1 = 4$$

$$y_2 = 30$$

$$x_2 = 3$$

We substitute these values into the formula to obtain the slope:

$$b = \frac{40 - 30}{4 - 3} = \frac{10}{1} = 10$$

The slope of the line is 10; it will be 10 for this data set regardless of which two reference points we may choose. For example, let's choose the following numbers:

$$y_1 = 25$$

$$x_1 = 2.5$$

$$y_2 = 15$$

$$x_2 = 1.5$$

Then

$$b = \frac{25 - 15}{2.5 - 1.5} = \frac{10}{1} = 10$$

For the present example, the slope (which we will later know as the regression coefficient or *b*) informs us that *for each unit increase in the independent variable there is a 10-unit increase in the dependent variable.* This means we can make predictions of *y* using knowledge of *x*.

We said that the equation for a straight line is $y = a + bx$. We have *b*, so all we must do now is calculate *a*, which is the **y-intercept** (also known as the *constant*), or the point at which the slope intersects the Y-axis. We can determine visually from Figure 11-1 that $a = 0$ because both *Y* and *X* scores have values of zero in the distribution and because a score of zero on *X* corresponds exactly with a zero score on *Y*. (In other words, the *y*-intercept is always the value of *y* when $x = 0$.) Nevertheless, we will demonstrate that $a = 0$ by formula 11-2:

11-2

$$a = \bar{y} - b\bar{x}$$

We know that the mean of *y* is 20 and the mean of *x* is 2 and that $b = 10$. Thus

$$a = 20 - 10(2) = 20 - 20 = 0$$

Once we have the slope (*b*) and the intercept (*a*) for *any set of data* we can use the formula for a straight line to predict a *y* value for any given value of *x*. The *a* and *b* values are constants, so all we have to do to determine a predicted *y* value, symbolized as y' (read *y prime* or sometimes *y predicted*; some texts also prefer $\hat{y}$, *y hat*, or even y^*), is to specify a value of x. To predict the *y* value (number of dollars) for a worker who works eight hours (that is, where $x = 8$) we would calculate:

$$y' = a + bx = 0 + (10 \times 8) = 80$$

That is, working for eight hours would result in $80.

This looks like a horribly complicated way to arrive at a value that you could easily calculate in your head (8 hours at $10 per hour = 8 × 10 = $80), but this is a "perfect" example designed to convey the logic of linear prediction. Social science data are never as cooperative as this. The intersection of *y* and *x* scores never rises uniformly, as in this example. The plotted points representing the complexity of the real world will never fall on a straight line but will be scattered around it, so any predictions we make will be subject to error. The following example is more representative of this complexity.

Linearity in Social Science Data

We begin by constructing a scatterplot (see Box 11-1) for some simple data on the number of prior felony convictions and years of imprisonment for the latest offense. Suppose we have a sample of 10 convicted felons with different criminal

---

Box 11-1
The Scatterplot

When we examined the associations between variables measured at the nominal and ordinal levels, we noted that a useful preliminary technique was to examine the pattern of frequencies and percentages in the table cells. A similarly helpful technique when examining the association between two interval/ratio variables is to examine their joint distribution in a scatterplot. A **scatterplot** is a plot in which the position of each observation is designated at the point corresponding to its joint value on the dependent and independent variables—this is exactly what Figure 11-1 is. The independent variable is arrayed on the horizontal axis and the dependent variable on the vertical axis. If these plots bunch together like a thin tube along a steeply angled line, the association is strong. If they bulge out at all sides like a balloon, the association is weak or nonexistent. If the plots appear to be rising from the lower left-hand corner to the upper right-hand corner, the association is positive. If they appear to be going from the top left-hand corner to the lower right-hand corner, the association is negative. Presented below are three scatterplots illustrating possible patterns of associations between two interval/ratio-level variables.

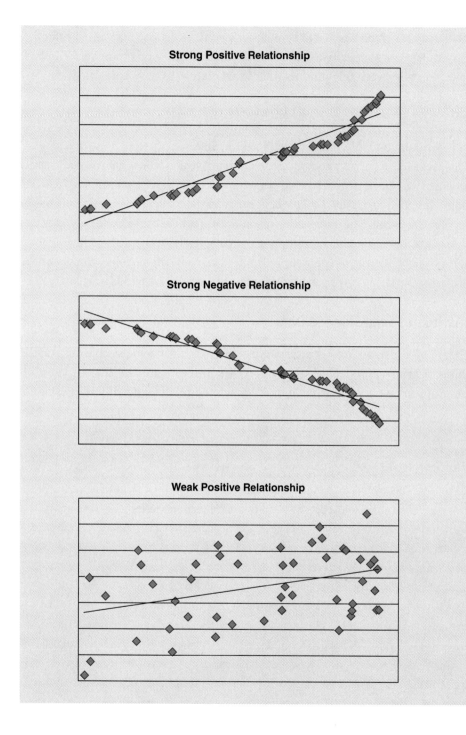

histories who received different sentences. We want to determine the impact that criminal record has on sentence severity. Our first task is to make a list of our 10 cases, noting the number of prior felony convictions for each individual along with the sentence he received in years for the latest offense. These data are shown in Table 11-1.

The data are plotted on the scatterplot shown in Figure 11-2 according to their joint position on both variables. This pattern of dots summarizes the nature of the relationship between the two variables. We can see that the relationship is positive and that it is linear; that is, as the number of prior convictions goes up, the number of years to which an individual is sentenced to prison also goes up in a constant manner. The pattern can be further clarified by drawing a straight line through the cluster of dots so that the line comes as close as possible to touching every dot. This is called **fitting the line**. To draw a line we need two reference points, the first of which is a, the y-intercept. The value of a has been calculated to be 0.86 (we will see the calculations later). The second reference point is the intersection of the means of the two variables. *Regardless of the value of the slope, the means of the two variables are always on the regression line.* The mean of y is 3.8 and the mean of x is 2.8. We find the

TABLE 11-1. *Raw Data on Prior Convictions and Sentences*

Case	Number of Prior Convictions (x)	Sentences in Years (y)
a	1	1
b	1	3
c	2	3
d	2	4
e	2	2
f	3	3
g	3	4
h	4	6
i	5	7
j	5	5
Totals	28	38
Means	2.8	3.8

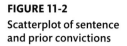

FIGURE 11-2

Scatterplot of sentence and prior convictions

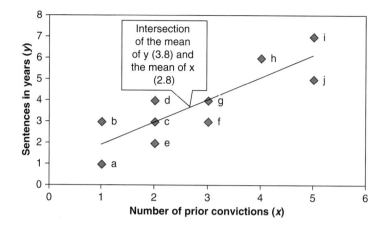

intersection of these two points and then connect it with the *y*-intercept. When we connect the two reference points with a straight line we have what is called the *least squares regression line.*

Note that not all dots are on the regression line. We call the difference between where a dot *is* and where we *expect it to be* the *residuals* (you can probably see how this is going to work, later on, in terms of discovering statistical significance and assessing model fit). These are calculated by taking the actual *y* score minus the predicted *y'* score (given symbolically as $y - y'$). In regression terminology we call these *errors from the regression line.* Think of the regression line like a mean and the residuals like deviation scores. As with the deviation scores from a mean, if we sum the errors, we will arrive at zero. We want the regression line placed where, if each residual is squared and summed (since if we do not square them they will equal zero), we will get the smallest value and hence the smallest prediction errors (that is, the greatest PRE). In other words, the *squared distance* between the regression line and an observed score is the error we make in predicting the value of that observation when we use the regression line. (Hence the term *least squares* and the term ordinary least squares regression for the statistical technique we present here.) Our regression line is a graphic representation of our prediction of *y* given *a, b,* and *x.*

Computing *b* and *a*

We will begin by computing *b* because we need it to compute *a* (recall formulas 11-1 and 11-2 above). In addition to conceptualizing *b* as a ratio of vertical to horizontal distance we also conceptualize it as a ratio of the sum of squares of the cross-products of *y* and *x* to the sum of squares of *x.* That is a mouthful. The sum of squares of the cross-product of *x* and *y* refers to their covariation, whereas the sum of squares of *x* refers to the sum of all residual terms when squared (as discussed above). In formula terms, it looks like formula 11-3:

11-3

$$b = \frac{SS_{yx}}{SS_x}$$

As has already been the case with the standard deviation, the computational formula for b is easier to work with:

11-4

$$b = \frac{N\Sigma XY - (\Sigma X)(\Sigma Y)}{N\Sigma X^2 - (\Sigma X)^2}$$

All of the information we need to compute this equation is in Table 11-1. Table 11-2 will help us compute b as well. We will need five numbers and, therefore, five columns: the sum of all x's, the sum of all y's, the sum of the product of x and y (that is, we multiply them together), the sum of x^2, and the sum of y^2. These calculations are completed in Table 11-2.

TABLE 11-2. Computations for b and r

Case	x	y	x²	y²	xy
a	1	1	1	1	1
b	1	3	1	9	3
c	2	3	4	9	6
d	2	4	4	16	8
e	2	2	4	4	4
f	3	3	9	9	9
g	3	4	9	16	12
h	4	6	16	36	24
i	5	7	25	49	35
j	5	5	25	25	25
Totals (Σ)	28	38	98	174	127

Putting the numbers into formula 11-4, we get

$$b = \frac{10(217) - (28)(38)}{10(98) - 784} = 1.05$$

We know that b gives an average estimate of how much change in the dependent variable accompanies a one-unit change in the independent variable. Therefore, our computed slope of 1.05 tells us that for each unit change in x there is an average change of 1.05 units of y. In this example, it means that for every additional felony conviction, an offender can expect, on the average, an additional 1.05 years of imprisonment. Take note of the repetition of the term *average*. We do not expect that an additional conviction for any particular offender will result in exactly 1.05 years of imprisonment; we only mean that averaged over all offenders the expected additional time per additional felony charge will be 1.05 years. It is often forgotten in regression models, but the slope coefficients are nothing more or less than *averages of the dependent variable holding the independent variable constant, net of controls.*

The Intercept

To find the intercept (a), we need two additional computations, the mean of x and the mean of y. From Table 11-1, we see that the mean of x is 2.8, and the mean of y is 3.8. Along with our computed b, these figures are put into formula 11-2:

$$a = 3.8 - 1.05(2.8) = 0.86$$

The regression line intercepts the y coordinate at a value of 0.86 and represents the average predicted value of y when x equals zero. It is a fixed or *constant* effect, which must be taken into account when predicting the value of y given x. Think of it as y's starting point. In our example, an offender without any prior convictions can expect, on average, to receive a little less than a year imprisonment. Unfortunately, we have no offender in our sample with no prior convictions. Thus we are already making predictions beyond the range of the data, which is risky. Of course, in any real-life sample many times larger than our hypothetical sample, there will be many offenders with no prior felony convictions.

Now that we have all of the values for the regression line, we can use it to predict scores on the dependent variable (y) for a given value on the independent variable (x). Since both a and b values are constants, the only unknown value is x. We give x the value of a case of interest to us. Suppose we wanted to predict the number of years to which an individual with six prior convictions would be sentenced (designated by y' to indicate that it is a predicted value of y rather than an actual value of y).

$$y' = a + bx = 0.86 + 1.05(6) = 7.16$$

Our hypothetical offender would expect to get 7.16 years imprisonment. Note that for an offender with no prior convictions the b value would drop out of the equation, leaving 0.86: 0.86 + (1.05)(0) = 0.86 + 0 = 0.86. This illustrates that the y intercept (a) is the value of the dependent variable (y) when the value of the independent variable (x) is zero.

THE PEARSON CORRELATION COEFFICIENT (r)

Now that we have learned how to fit a regression line to paired data, our next step is to determine how well the line actually fits. Since b is a measure of the effect of x on y, we already have some idea about the nature of the relationship. We know, for instance, that the relationship between prior convictions and sentence is positive, and we can assume with confidence that this relationship is quite strong because we have minimal scatter around the regression line shown in Figure 11-2. We need to compute a further statistic because although the value of b is a function of the strength of the relationship, it is not standardized. Rather, it depends on our scale. The computed value of b depends on how we have measured the dependent variable. For instance, if we had measured sentence severity in months instead of years, the value of b would be quite different—indeed, it would be roughly 12 times larger because there are 12 months in a year. This is useful for interpretation, but not for discussing strength of association, necessarily. For this, we use **Pearson's r**, also known as the **correlation coefficient**.

The correlation coefficient would be the same regardless of how we measured sentence severity. In other words, r is independent of how we have measured y; b is not. If we had measured sentence severity in months, the value of b would have been 12.6 (1.05 × 12 = 12.6 months) instead of 1.05. Scale does not affect r because it is calculated using the scatter around the line, which never changes regardless of how our dependent variable is measured. If we did measure y in terms of months, the regression line would be steeper (because of more change), thus increasing the size of b. But this increase would only be proportional. For example, 1.05 = 12.6 months, and 12.6 months = 54.6 weeks, which in turn equal 382.2 days. In the first case, we multiply our b by 12, then by about 4.3, then 54.6 by 7. In other words, we are only changing the scale, not the pattern. The proportional difference between y and x remains the same, even if the raw magnitude does not. As such, the squared differences between the plotted paired cases and the regression line will remain constant. This equivalence is recognized by r since the scatter around the regression line would be exactly the same—even if the values differ, the *pattern* does not. The function of r is to indicate the strength of the relationship so that we can predict, and our prediction would be exactly the same whether we called it 1.05 years, 12.6 months, 54.6 weeks, or 382.2 days.

Another reason for computing Pearson's r in addition to b is that we cannot directly compare slopes for a number of different variables if they are all measured in different units, as we will see in the next chapter. We can compare correlation coefficients, however, regardless of how the variables they describe are measured because r is standardized between ±1. This important property of correlation coefficients renders them comparable.

Formula 11-5 is the computational formula for the Pearson correlation coefficient.

11-5

$$r = \frac{N\Sigma XY - (\Sigma X)(\Sigma Y)}{\sqrt{[N\Sigma X^2 - (\Sigma X)^2][N\Sigma Y^2 - (\Sigma Y)^2]}}$$

Note that the numerator of r is the same as the numerator of b. We call this formula the **covariance** of y and x. The covariance is the joint variation of two sets of scores from their respective means. (Remember that when we are interested in joint probabilities, we invoke multiplication. For information on how to calculate covariance, see Box 11-2.) The more the two variables covary, the stronger r will be. Similar to other equations we have done, we standardize the covariance (to find r) by dividing the covariance by the paired standard deviations of the two variables. Thus, r can be operationally defined as the ratio of the product of the standard deviations of y and x to the covariance of y and x:

$$r = \frac{\text{covariance of } x \text{ and } y}{(\text{standard deviation of } y)(\text{standard deviation of } x)}$$

We can also write this equation with the following, relatively conventional notation:

$$r = \frac{COV(XY)}{s_x s_y}$$

Let's use the numbers from Table 11-2 to find the correlation coefficient for the data. Let's return to our typical pattern of hypothesis testing, but with an interlude before we discuss finding significance for b and r.

Box 11-2
Calculating Covariance

The formula for covariance (11-6) looks like this:

11-6

$$COV(XY) = \frac{\Sigma XY - \frac{(\Sigma X)(\Sigma Y)}{n}}{n - 1}$$

For our purposes here, we will stick to the computation formula for *r* found in 11-5. Stated in equation form, then:

$$COV(XY) = N\Sigma XY - (\Sigma X)(\Sigma Y) = \frac{\Sigma XY - \frac{(\Sigma X)(\Sigma Y)}{n}}{n - 1}$$

STEP 1: First, we state our hypothesis and set our alpha level. *Do not neglect to state the null hypothesis*, which in this case is $r(y, x) = 0$. We hypothesize that more prior convictions will increase the number of years a convict is sentenced to prison. This is a directional test, but we decide to use a two-tailed test to be conservative and careful. Thus our alpha level is set at the conventional 0.05.

STEP 2: Now, we revisit Table 11-2 to acquire all the pieces we need for formula 11-5:

$$\Sigma X = 28$$
$$\Sigma Y = 38$$
$$\Sigma X^2 = 98$$
$$\Sigma Y^2 = 174$$
$$\Sigma XY = 127$$

We now plug these numbers into our computation formula for *r*. Recall that $n = 10$:

$$r = \frac{(10)(127) - (28)(38)}{\sqrt{[(10)(98) - 28^2][(10)(174) - 38^2]}}$$

We now solve for *r* using this equation:

$$r = \frac{206}{240.865}$$

$$r = 0.855$$

STEP 3: We now interpret *r*. The correlation coefficient of 0.855 indicates that there is a strong positive relationship between the number of prior felony convictions and the number of years sentenced to prison (recall our rules of thumb from previous chapters concerning determining strength from a measurement of association). That is, as the number of prior convictions increases, the severity of the sentence imposed increases. We remind you again that a correlation never proves causality. It is a mathematical relationship that may or may not be indicative of some underlying causal relationship. What a correlation coefficient does is support (or fail to support if it is not significant—more on this below) an explanation that the researcher can justify on *theoretical* grounds.

r^2 as a Proportional Reduction in Error

We can go beyond interpreting a correlation as strong, moderate, or weak by calculating r^2, which is simply the square of the correlation coefficient. Thus, r^2 for our data is 0.731 (0.855 × 0.855 = 0.731), which is interpreted as 73 percent of the variance in sentence severity is accounted for by number of prior convictions. This value can also be interpreted as a proportional reduction in error. That is, we can say that when knowledge of the independent variable (prior felony convictions) is taken into account, we improve our ability to predict values on the dependent variable (sentence in years) by a factor of 73.1 percent. This is considerably better than what we could do without knowledge of any independent variables.

To demonstrate the logic of r^2 as a PRE, we must consider just how poorly we would predict the dependent variable without knowing the independent variable. Without knowledge of the independent variable, our best prediction of the number of years a given offender would receive would be the mean of the sentence distribution—the value that explains the most common outcome. As we saw earlier, the scores vary less

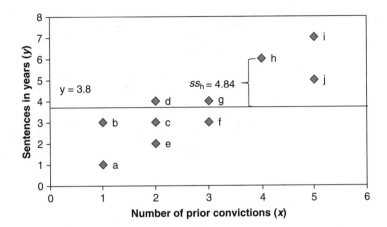

FIGURE 11-3
Scatterplot showing
total variation around
the mean of y

around the mean than around any other point. In other words, we would predict a sentence of 3.8 years for all offenders, and our line of prediction would run parallel with the line when $x = 0$, called the abscissa. This line would start from the mean of y. This is shown in Figure 11-3.

To find out how much prediction error we would have, we must compute the total variation in the same way we compute ANOVA—in other words, we compute the total sum of squares, or $\Sigma(y - \bar{y})^2$. This is found in Table 11-3.

This value, 29.6, is the total amount of (squared) errors we would have if we knew absolutely nothing about the relationship between prior convictions and years sentenced. We call this, as in ANOVA, the total sum of squares. This is the first piece of the puzzle. The second piece is figuring out how well we actually did with knowledge of the independent variable. To do this, we need to compute the error based on the regression equation, that is, the error we will make in predicting sentence severity given that we now have knowledge of the distribution of the independent variable. These errors are labeled $(y - y')$ and are known as **residuals**.

The sum of these squared residuals, $(y - y')^2$, is known as the **unexplained variance**. In other words, this is the variation in the dependent variable that we're unable to explain even with knowledge of the independent variable. To obtain this value we first compute the predicted value for *each case* using the formula we learned above for regression, the classic algebraic expression $y' = a + bx$. This will give us y'. Then, we subtract that value from the actual value. To get the sum of residuals, we'll first

TABLE 11-3. r^2 *as a PRE, Part 1*

Case	x	y	$y - \bar{y}$	$(y - \bar{y})^2$
a	1	1	2.8	7.84
b	1	3	0.8	0.64
c	2	3	0.8	0.64
d	2	4	−0.2	0.04
e	2	2	1.8	3.24
f	3	3	0.8	0.64
g	3	4	−0.2	0.04
h	4	6	−2.2	4.84
i	5	7	−3.2	10.24
j	5	5	−1.2	1.44
Totals (Σ)	28	38	0	29.6

have to square these differences, just as we would for the standard deviation and sums of squares—if we don't square them, they will sum to 0. These steps are demonstrated in Table 11-4. The final total error term is 7.95. We call this the **error sum of squares**. This is substantially smaller than the 29.6 we would have to deal with given no predictors. Consider also the case *h* in both Figures 11-3 and 11-4: note that without knowledge of prior convictions, our prediction for how many years *h* would be sentenced is terribly underestimated—by almost 5 years. However, when we include prior convictions, we underpredict by less than 1 year (see Figures 11-3 and 11-4).

We now have the total sum of squares (29.60) and the error sum of squares (7.95). We can now use these values to arrive at the total amount of variance we *do* explain (again, as with ANOVA):

$$SS_{total} = SS_{explained} + SS_{error}$$

$$29.60 = SS_{explained} + 7.95$$

$$21.65 = SS_{explained}$$

TABLE 11-4. r^2 as a PRE, Part 2

Case	x	y	y'	y − y'	(y − y')²
a	1	1	1.91	−0.91	0.83
b	1	3	1.91	1.09	1.19
c	2	3	2.96	0.04	0.00
d	2	4	2.96	1.04	1.08
e	2	2	2.96	−0.96	0.92
f	3	3	4.01	−1.01	1.02
g	3	4	4.01	−0.01	0.00
h	4	6	5.06	0.94	0.88
i	5	7	6.11	0.89	0.79
j	5	5	6.11	−1.11	1.23
Totals (Σ)	28	38			7.95

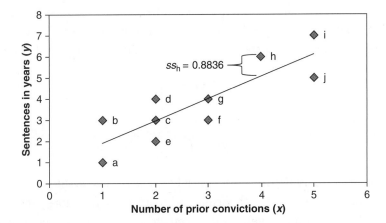

FIGURE 11-4
Scatterplot showing total variation around y'

Since r^2 represents the proportional reduction in error by moving from estimating the mean of y for all y values to predicting each y value from the regression equation, we can determine how much we have reduced our prediction error when knowledge of the independent variable is taken into consideration. We take the two components we have just computed and put them into the standard PRE formula given in chapter 9 as

$$PRE = \frac{E_1 - E_2}{E_1}$$

Recall that E_1 is the total variance (or sum of squares) and E_2 is the error variance (or error sum of squares). Thus,

$$\text{PRE} = \frac{29.6 - 7.95}{29.6} = \frac{21.65}{29.6} = 0.731$$

Thus, the coefficient of determination (r^2) is a PRE measure because our computed PRE is exactly the same value as r^2; in fact it is r^2 determined by another method. The proportion of variance in the dependent variable left unexplained by the independent variable is simply $1 - r^2$. In our present example it is $1 - 0.731 = 0.269$. Recall that in ANOVA we called the variance left unexplained by the independent variable the within-group sum of squares—for r (and for some textbooks, ANOVA), it is called the error sum of squares.

Significance Testing for Pearson's r

To complete our hypothesis test from above, we would need to add a final step: significance testing. As with other measures of association, we need to determine whether the observed sample relationship can be assumed to exist in the general population from which the sample was drawn. The usual method of testing r for statistical significance is the t statistic, which is computed with formula 11-7.

11-7

$$t = r\sqrt{\frac{n-2}{1-r^2}}$$

Recall that t tests are used to find differences between means. In this case, remember that we are actually working with means and that we are therefore comparing the means we observe with the means we can create using chance—that is, using the theoretical normal curve. The t test for our calculated r^2 from above is therefore

$$t = 0.855\sqrt{\frac{10-2}{1-0.855^2}}$$

$$t = 0.855\sqrt{29.74}$$

$$t = 0.855 \times 5.45 = 4.66$$

Turning to the t distribution (see p. 344), with 8 degrees of freedom ($df =$ $n -$ variables involved $= 2$), we find that our computed t of 4.66 exceeds the critical value at the 0.05 level. We thus reject the null hypothesis and conclude that the variables are also related in the population from which our sample was drawn.

We can rearrange formula 11-7 to determine the minimum r necessary to reject the null hypothesis that the population $\rho = 0$. The first thing we do is turn to page 344 and find the critical t value required to reject the null with 8 degrees of freedom and a given alpha level. Let us say that we are conducting a two-tailed test and that we set alpha at 0.05. You will find the critical t value under these conditions to be 2.306. We then put this value into formula 11-8 (which simply rearranges formula 11-7) to determine the critical r:

11-8

$$r = \frac{t_{\text{critical}}}{t^2_{\text{critical}} + df}$$

Doing the math,

$$r = \frac{2.306}{5.3176 + 8} = \frac{2.306}{3.649} = 0.632$$

The minimum value of r required to reject the null at the 0.05 level (two-tailed test) with a sample of 10 is 0.632. Box 11-3 discusses the role of the standard error in determining the statistical significance of r.

Box 11-3
Standard Error of r

If we drew 10 further samples of 10 convicted felons we would not expect to get a correlation between the number of convictions and the years of imprisonment of exactly 0.855. This value is simply an estimate of the population correlation coefficient (symbolized as ρ, the Greek letter *rho*), and other r's will vary as a result of sampling variation. As is the case with sample means, if we draw an infinite number of random samples from the same population and compute r for the two variables of interest, we would have a sampling distribution of r's. Just as 68 percent of sample means will lie within plus and minus

1 standard error of the true population mean, 68 percent of sample correlations will be within plus and minus 1 standard error of the true population correlation, and 95 percent will be between plus and minus 1.96 standard errors (i.e., z scores). We can thus place confidence intervals around our sample r using formula 11-9:

11-9

$$s_r = \frac{1-r^2}{\sqrt{n}}$$

We can use this for our r^2 from above:

$$s_r = \frac{1-0.855^2}{\sqrt{10}} = \frac{0.269}{3.162} = 0.085$$

The standard error of 0.085 means that 95 percent of the samples of the same size taken from the same population will yield a correlation of .855 plus or minus (1.96)(0.085) = 0.167, or between 0.688 and 1.022. Since we cannot obtain a correlation of greater than unity (read 1), we would say between 0.688 and 1.00.

THE INTERRELATIONSHIP OF b, r, AND, β

It is interesting to note that the regression slope can be expressed by formula 11-10:

11-10

$$b = r\left[\frac{s_y}{s_x}\right]$$

The slope is equal to the correlation between y and x multiplied by the standard deviation of y divided by the standard deviation of x. We substitute these previously calculated values into the formula and get

$$b = 0.855\left[\frac{1.8135}{1.4757}\right] = 0.855 \times 1.229 = 1.05$$

We can also use the standard deviations and the regression slope to calculate the **standardized beta** (β). The standardized beta, more fully explained in the next chapter, is used in multiple regression analysis. One difference between the unstandardized b and the standardized beta to know at this point is that the former is in the actual measured units of the dependent variable and the latter is given in standard deviation units—that is, it is standardized and therefore more readily comparable across regression models. In bivariate regression (but not in multiple regression) β is analogous to Pearson's r. Standardized beta is calculated with formula 11-11.

11-11

$$\beta = b\left[\frac{s_x}{s_y}\right]$$

Thus, from our example,

$$\beta = 1.05\left[\frac{1.4757}{1.8135}\right] = 1.05 \times 0.8137 = 0.855$$

This demonstrates that r and β are equivalent in the bivariate case (for more on this topic, see Box 11-4).

Box 11-4
Summarizing the Properties of r, b, and β

- r ranges between −1.0 (a perfect negative relationship) and +1.0 (a perfect positive relationship). A value of zero indicates no linear relationship between y and x.
- The value of r is independent of the scale of measurement.
- When squared, r indicates the proportion of variance in y accounted for by x.
- b indicates the change in y per unit change in x.
- The value of b depends on the scale of measurement.
- β indicates the change in standard deviation units of y per standard deviation unit change in x.
- r and β are identical in a bivariate regression/correlation model.
- r, b, and β must have the same sign. In addition, when $r = 0$, b and $\beta = 0$.

STANDARD ERROR OF THE ESTIMATE

Another statistic for assessing the accuracy of predictions is called the **standard error of the estimate**. This statistic informs you of the average prediction error in predicting Y from X. The definitional formula for the standard error of estimate is formula 11-12:

11-12

$$s_{y.x} = \sqrt{\frac{\Sigma(y - y')^2}{n - 2}}$$

The formula for $s_{y.x}$ is quite similar to the formula for the standard deviation except that we divide by $n - 2$ rather than $n - 1$. It is conceptually similar also in that it reflects variability, but variability around the regression line rather than about a mean. Because $s_{y.x}$ involves fitting the data to a straight line, which requires the estimation of the slope and the intercept and thus the calculations of y and x, we lose $2\ df\ (n - 2)$. Since we already have all of the values necessary to compute $s_{y.x}$, we will simply put them in as follows:

$$s_{y.x} = \sqrt{\frac{7.95}{8}} = \sqrt{0.99375} = 0.997$$

Under the assumption that the array of y scores associated with each value of x forms a normal distribution, the standard error of the estimate may be interpreted in terms of area under the normal curve. Thus, we can say that about 68 percent of our predictions will be within plus or minus 1 $s_{y.x}$ and that 95 percent will be within plus or minus 2. Be aware that we are talking about *average* error, not the error for any particular prediction of y from x. $s_{y.x}$ will underestimate the error in predicting y from x values as X departs markedly from the mean of S. There are formulas that adjust for this error, but as with many other adjustments for error we have looked at, the amount of error becomes negligible with large samples.

SUMMARIZING PREDICTION FORMULAS

Table 11-5 summarizes the operations we would perform in making predictions for any score with and without knowledge of the distribution of an independent

TABLE 11-5. *Summary of Prediction Computations*

Operation	Without Knowledge of x	With Knowledge of x
Best prediction of a score	$\bar{y} = \dfrac{\Sigma Y}{n}$ The mean	$y' = a + bx$ The regression line
Error of prediction score	$y - \bar{y}$ Deviation	$y - y'$ Residual
Average error in predicting a score	$s = \sqrt{\dfrac{\Sigma x^2 - \dfrac{(\Sigma x)^2}{n}}{n-1}}$ Standard deviation	$s_{y.x} = \sqrt{\dfrac{\Sigma(y - y')^2}{n-2}}$ Standard error of estimate

variable. Without knowledge of the independent variable, the best prediction would always be the mean. With knowledge of the distribution of the independent variable, the regression equation provides the best prediction since it minimizes the sum of squares around the regression line. The error in making predictions other than the mean over all predictions is the standard deviation. In a bivariate distribution the error averaged over all predictions is the standard error of the estimate. We have shown that for any two variables that are linearly related, knowledge of their joint distributions improves our ability to predict one variable from the other.

A COMPUTER EXAMPLE OF BIVARIATE CORRELATION AND REGRESSION

We now use our sex offender data to demonstrate bivariate correlation. When we performed a *t* test in chapter 6 with sentence severity as the dependent variable and group (non-sex/sex) as the independent variable we saw that the variances of the two offender groups were unequal. It is technically incorrect to perform regression with these data because regression analysis assumes equal variances. However, as is the case with the *t* test, when the larger sample has the greatest variance, as is the case here, regression is conservative with respect to committing type I errors. In other words, we have greater protection against committing a type I error even when we are breaking assumptions (more on assumptions for regression in the following chapter).

Table 11-6 presents the correlation between sentence severity and group. The first piece of information is the number of cases and the means and standard deviations of each variable. We are then given the cross-product deviation and the

TABLE 11-6. *Partial Computer Printout for Pearson Correlation*

VARIABLE	CASES	MEAN	STD DEV
SENSEV	637	492.002	727.3945
GROUP	637	0.6766	0.4681

VARIABLES	CASES	CROSS-PROD DEV	VARIANCE–COVAR
SENSEV GROUP	637	34584.5275	54.3782

CORRELATION COEFFICIENTS		
	SENSEV	GROUP
SENSEV	1	0.1597
	(637)	(637)
		$p = 0.000$

covariance. The cross-product deviation is divided by $n - 1$ to yield the covariance (34584.5275/636 = 54.3782). Dividing the covariance of x and y by the product of their standard deviations results in a correlation coefficient of 0.1597, which is the value given in the table. The number beneath the coefficient is the number of cases on which the calculation is based (637), followed by the exact one-tailed significance of r. The group variable is coded as 0 = non–sex offenders, 1 = sex offenders; thus the mean value for the group variable (0.6766) means that 67.66 percent of the 637 cases in the sample were sex offenders.

Table 11-7 is a computer printout for a bivariate regression regressing *Group* on *Sensev*. We note that a one-unit change in *Group* (coded 0 for non–sex offenders and 1 for sex offenders) results in a 248.128 unit change in the dependent variable (sentence severity). If you turn back to the *t* test in Table 6-2, you will see that the difference between sentence severity means for the two offender groups is exactly the value given for b in Table 11-7. Also note that the *t* value based on the assumption of equal variances is the same.

Note that the *y*-intercept (labeled "Constant" in Table 11-7) is 324.136. Recall that the *y*-intercept is the point at which the slope crosses the *y*-axis and is the value of *y* when $x = 0$. Because non–sex offenders were coded zero, this represents the mean sentence severity score for non–sex offenders. A one-unit change in x (moving from non–sex offenders to sex offenders) results in a 248.128 unit increase in *y*. If we add

TABLE 11-7. Partial Printout for Bivariate Regression for the Effects of Offender Group on Sentence Severity

VARIABLE	B	SE B	BETA	T	SIG T
GROUP	248.128	60.869	0.1597	4.076	0.001
(CONSTANT)	324.136	50.069		6.474	0

the value of the y-intercept to the value of the slope, we get the mean sentence severity score for sex offenders (324.136 + 248.128 = 572.264). In general terms, the formulas for calculating the means of a dichotomous independent variable (which we call dummy coding and is typically coded as 0 and 1) from regression results are

$$\bar{y}_0 = a + b_0$$

and

$$\bar{y}_1 = a + b_1$$

So for non–sex offenders $\bar{y}_0 = 324.136 + 0 = 324.136$, and for sex offenders $\bar{y}_1 = 324.136 + 248.128 = 572.264$.

We have determined therefore the respective group means from the regression analysis. Go back to Table 6-2 and check these means with those obtained from the *t* test procedure. This illustrates that for a dichotomous independent variable subjected to bivariate regression, the difference between the means of the two categories is the value of the slope (the unstandardized *b*). Remember, *b* coefficients are, at the end of the day, averages.

We can use the standard error to establish confidence intervals around the slope. The reported *b* is a specific value or point estimate around which may be placed an interval estimate. The logic of setting confidence intervals around the regression slope is identical to setting confidence intervals around the mean:

11-13

$$CI = b \pm tSE_b$$

Thus, with an alpha level of 0.05, where a critical *t* would be 1.96,

$$CI = 248.128 \pm 1.96 \times 60.87 = 119.3$$

We can therefore state with 95 percent confidence that the parameter lies somewhere between 248.128 ± 119.3, that is, between 128.828 and 367.428.

The next value is the standardized beta (β: BETA in the printout). As previously stated, in a bivariate regression β is equal to the bivariate correlation. Note that β is also equal to the square root of the η^2 we computed for these data in chapter 6. Squaring β yields the same variance-explained interpretation as the squares of eta and the Pearson correlation coefficient. The standardized beta is followed by the t value and the significance of t. In chapter 6 we defined t as the difference between means divided by the standard error of the difference. The unstandardized beta in this example is the difference between the means of our dichotomous variable. Therefore,

$$t = \frac{\text{difference between means}}{\text{standard error of difference}} = \frac{\beta}{\text{standard error of } \beta} = \frac{248.128}{60.869} = 4.076$$

Because we will need to refer back to bivariate regression values for crime seriousness and prior record when we discuss multiple correlation and regression in the next chapter, we will present these values now in the partial printouts in Table 11-8. Note that both crime seriousness and prior record are more powerfully related (as indicated by their respective β's) to sentence severity than is offender group. Further discussion is deferred until chapter 12.

TABLE 11-8. *Partial Printouts for Bivariate Regressions for the Effects of Crime Seriousness and Prior Records on Sentence Severity*

		CRIME SERIOUSNESS			
VARIABLE	B	SE B	BETA	T	SIG T
CRSER	265.6400	10.2730	0.7160	25.8590	0.0000
(CONSTANT)	−303.2329	36.7560		−8.2500	0.0000

		PRIOR RECORD			
	B	SE B	BETA	T	SIG T
PRREC	64.3921	5.2980	0.4344	12.1570	0.0000
(CONSTANT)	235.0600	33.4950		7.0180	0.0000

SUMMARY

Correlation and regression techniques are used to analyze linear relationships between interval or ratio variables. Regression is a method of predicting values on the dependent variables from knowledge of the independent variable using the linear equation. Correlation tells us how accurate these predictions are. A preliminary stage in regression analysis is the examination of plotted values on a scattergram. The regression line in a scattergram functions as a kind of floating mean in that predictions made on the basis of the line minimize prediction error (residuals). The regression is a function of a (the y-intercept) and b (the slope). The y-intercept is the value of y when $x = 0$, and the slope reveals how much the dependent variable increases or decreases in a constant manner per unit increase in the independent variable. The slope and the intercept are constants in the prediction equation and are used to make predictions about y from a given value of x.

The correlation coefficient, an index of the strength and direction of the association, ranges from -1.0 to $+1.0$. The correlation coefficient is defined as the ratio of the covariance of y and x to their respective standard deviations. When squared, the correlation is interpreted as the percentage of variance in the dependent variable accounted for by the independent variable, also interpreted as a PRE statistic. It is tested for statistical significance using the t distribution. The standard error of the estimate tells us the average prediction error in predicting y from x. It functions similarly to the standard deviation in a univariate distribution in that it gives the average deviation of scores from the regression line.

We demonstrated the diversity and usefulness of bivariate regression using our sex offender data. We saw how regression results can supply us with all the information (strength and direction of a relationship, significance of the relationship, category means with an independent variable coded 0 and 1) contained in other techniques, plus the information unique to it (that is, the change in y per unit change in x). The greatest utility of regression, however, lies in its ability to assess the impact of a large number of predictor variables simultaneously. This is the subject of the next chapter.

Journal Table 11-1 is an example of bivariate correlations and regression. This table is from the article "Rehabilitation and repression: Reassessing their ideological embeddedness" by Mascini and Houtman (2006). In this study, the researchers analyzed whether public support for rehabilitation is the converse of that for repression. The researchers hypothesized that support for rehabilitation and support for repression are not correlated negatively and significantly and that support for decriminalization and support for repression are correlated strongly and negatively. This table

JOURNAL TABLE 11-1. *Correlations between Support for Repression, Rehabilitation, and Decriminalization*

	Repression	Rehabilitation	Decriminalization
Repression	1		
Rehabilitation	−0.06	1	
Decriminalization	−0.52*	0.05	1

*$p < 0.001$.

shows correlations between support for repression, rehabilitation, and decriminalization. In their study, the researchers found evidence in support of their hypothesis that there is no significant relationship between rehabilitation and repression or between rehabilitation and decriminalization. There is, however, a statistically significant relationship between decriminalization and repression (−0.52) at the $p < 0.001$ level (Mascini and Houtman, 2006). How would you categorize the strength of the effect size?

REFERENCES

Mascini, P., & Houtman, D. (2006). Rehabilitation and repression: Reassessing their ideological embeddedness. *British Journal of Criminology* 46, 822–836.

Pedhazur, E. (1982). *Multiple regression in behavioral research: Explanation and prediction.* New York: Holt, Rinehart and Winston.

PRACTICE APPLICATION: BIVARIATE CORRELATION AND REGRESSION

A researcher wants to determine whether a desire to bully homosexual persons is related to social distance from homosexuals. Two scales are administered to 10 subjects. The "bullying propensity" is reverse coded such that a score of zero suggests high propensity and a score of 40 indicates low propensity. The social distance scale ranges from zero (total nonacceptance of homosexuals) to 10 (complete acceptance).

	Bullying Propensity		Social Distance		
Case	X	Y	X	Y²	XY
a	20	4	400	16	80
b	22	3	484	9	66
c	29	8	841	64	232
d	25	5	625	25	125
e	32	7	1024	49	224
f	25	7	625	49	175
g	25	5	625	25	125
h	30	9	900	81	270
i	30	8	900	64	240
j	32	8	1024	64	256
	$\Sigma X = 270$	$\Sigma Y = 64$	$\Sigma X^2 = 7,448$	$\Sigma Y^2 = 446$	$\Sigma XY = 1,793$
	$\overline{X} = 27$	$\overline{Y} = 6.4$			

Compute the slope (b), the Y intercept, and the correlation coefficient. The slope (b) is

$$b = \frac{N\Sigma XY - (\Sigma X)(\Sigma Y)}{N\Sigma X^2 - (\Sigma X)^2}$$

$$= \frac{10(1,793) - (270)(64)}{10(7,448) - (72,900)} = \frac{17,930 - 17,280}{74,480 - 72,900} = \frac{650}{1,580} = 0.411$$

The slope of 0.411 tells us that for each one-unit change in bullying propensity there is a 0.411 unit change in the acceptance of homosexuals.

The Y intercept (a) is $a = \overline{Y} - b\overline{X} = 6.4 - (0.411)(27) = 6.4 - 11.097 = -4.7$

If a person has a bullying propensity score of 35, what level of homosexual acceptance would you predict for him or her?

$$Y' = a + bX = -4.7 + 0.411(35) = -4.7 + 14.385 = 9.685$$

The correlation coefficient is

$$r = \frac{N\Sigma XY - (\Sigma X)(\Sigma Y)}{\sqrt{[N\Sigma X^2 - (\Sigma X)^2][N\Sigma Y^2 - (\Sigma Y)^2]}}$$

$$= \frac{(10)(1{,}793) - (270)(64)}{\sqrt{[(10)(7{,}448) - 72{,}900][(10)(446) - 4{,}096]}} = \frac{17{,}930 - 17{,}280}{\sqrt{(74{,}480 - 72{,}900)(4{,}460 - 4{,}096)}}$$

$$= \frac{650}{\sqrt{(1{,}580)(364)}} = \frac{650}{758.37} = 0.857$$

Compute the significance level using t.

$$t = r\sqrt{\frac{N-2}{1-r^2}}$$

$$= (0.857)\sqrt{\frac{10-2}{1-0.857^2}} = (0.857)\sqrt{\frac{8}{1-0.734}} = (0.857)\sqrt{30} = (0.857)(5.484) = 4.7$$

The variables are strongly positively correlated. Acceptance of homosexuals increases as the reverse coded bullying propensity score also increases. The coefficient of determination is 0.734, indicating that 73.46 percent of the variance in the acceptance of homosexuals is explained by bullying propensity. The computed t value (4.7) with 8 df exceeds the critical t (2.306) for a two-tailed test with alpha set at 0.05.

CHAPTER 12

Multivariate Correlation and Regression

LEARNING OBJECTIVES:

After reading this chapter, the student will understand the following concepts:

- How to control for confounding variables using multivariate correlation and regression
- The assumptions underlying multivariate statistics for the general linear model
- The interrelatedness and differences between r, b, and β
- The calculation and interpretation of regression models, including b, β, and R^2 (as well as adjusted R^2)
- How to include interaction terms in a multivariate regression model

INTRODUCTION

This chapter introduces multivariate statistical techniques for variables measured at the interval/ratio level. As we saw in chapter 10, several factors typically combine to influence variation in a dependent variable. The basic logic of multivariate correlation and regression is the same as it is for partial gamma, except we mathematically control for *additional* predictor variables rather than physically moving cases into categories of a control variable. This enables control for any number of other variables without encountering the problems discussed in chapter 10. The more *theoretically* meaningful variables that are introduced into our models, the better we should be able to understand our data and the fewer prediction errors we should make. As you can imagine, this is not always a straightforward process. The key is to start and end with solid theoretical reasons and to carefully follow all the steps necessary to complete the statistical model—keeping in mind everything you have learned up to this point.

You may recall from learning about ANOVA that we mentioned that higher-level statistics—like those you are about to learn—carry with them a suite of assumptions that must be met to have confidence in their findings. You may also remember that we mentioned that ANOVA, r, and regression analysis are intimately related to each other. Thus, the assumptions for ANOVA are the same for regression and correlation, with a few additional assumptions for the multivariate versions of these models.

- The samples are randomly selected from a population and are independent of each other.
- Similarly, within a sample, the subjects are independent of each other.
- Data are continuous (or nearly); predictors can also be binary).
- The distribution of all cases creates a normal curve that approximates the standardized normal curve.
- The independent variables are also independent of each other.

The last bullet point is the new assumption: the independent variables are also independent of each other. This does not mean that they are completely uncorrelated with each other—given that they are most likely correlated with the dependent variable, they *must* correlate together at some level. Rather, it means that when two (or more) independent variables are *so* correlated with each other that they are essentially the *same* variable, we have a problem. As an extremely hyperbolic example, imagine if we have two independent variables—police officer (0 = no, 1 = yes) and uniform color (0 = no uniform, 1 = blue)—which we use to predict likelihood of retiring within 20 years. If someone is a police officer, they are likely to have a blue uniform—*extremely likely*. So likely that the r between police officer and uniform color is likely to approach 1.0. In effect, then, police officer and uniform color are the same variable for statistical purposes. The effect on our statistical model can be described as *double dipping*, which will have the effect of artificially inflating how well our model does in predicting likelihood of retiring within 20 years.

In truth, this really is not *that* new of an assumption. A careful reading of the section on two-way ANOVA will reveal that any two factors in ANOVA also cannot be so highly correlated as to be the same variable. We will expand on these concepts throughout the chapter; for now, keep these assumptions in mind as you read further. Breaking assumptions is not the end of the world; it simply means that we can't fully trust our statistical models. And, as you'll learn, ordinary least squares regression can happily break almost *any* assumption and remain relatively accurate. For this reason, ordinary least squares regression is considered a **robust** statistical model.

PARTIAL CORRELATION

Let's start things off by extending an example from the previous chapter. Let us see what happens to the zero-order correlation of 0.855 between the number of prior felony convictions and the number of years imprisonment computed in chapter 11 when we control for a third variable, *seriousness of criminal charge*. This variable is coded 1 for the least serious charge, 2 for the next most serious, 3 for the next, and 4 for the most serious charge. The data from Table 11-1 are reproduced in Table 12-1, with the crime charge (*v*) variable added.

From this table, we can calculate three separate bivariate correlations: between the number of convictions (*x*) and the sentence (*y*), between number of convictions

TABLE 12-1. *Paired Data for Prior Convictions, Sentence in Years, and Seriousness of Criminal Charge*

Case	Number of Prior Convictions (x)	Sentence in Years (y)	Seriousness of Criminal Charge (v)
a	1	1	1
b	1	3	2
c	2	3	2
d	2	4	4
e	2	2	1
f	3	3	3
g	3	4	3
h	4	6	4
i	5	7	4
j	5	5	3
Totals	28	38	27

(x) and the seriousness of the charge (v), and between sentence (y) and the charge (v):

$$r_{yx} = 0.855$$

$$r_{xv} = 0.675$$

$$r_{yv} = 0.867$$

When we examine the effect of the number of prior convictions on sentence length controlling for the effects of crime charge, it is expressed symbolically as $r_{yx.v}$. The formula for partial correlation is formula 12-1:

12-1

$$r_{yx.v} = \frac{r_{yx} - (r_{yv})(r_{xv})}{\sqrt{1 - r_{yv}^2}\sqrt{1 - r_{xv}^2}}$$

The numerator in formula 12-1 tells us to subtract the combined effects of crime charge (v) on both sentence length and prior convictions (the product of r_{yv} and r_{xv}) from the effects of prior convictions on sentence length (r_{yx}). In effect we are considering *only* the covariance of sentence length and prior convictions remaining *after* crime charge has operated on them both. This value is then divided by what we might consider the average value of the coefficient of *non*determination, where $1 - r_{yv}^2$ equals the proportion of variance in sentence length not explained by crime charge and $1 - r_{xv}^2$ equals the proportion of variance in crime charge not explained by prior convictions. There is an important point found in this formula: to understand the unique effect of any given independent variable on a dependent variable, all we do (both conceptually and mathematically) is subtraction. The math looks more frightening than that, but at its heart, that is what we are doing.

Using these three correlations, we can now determine the effect of prior convictions on sentence length, controlling for the effects of seriousness of crime charge. Consider the bivariate correlations and try to determine logically what you think will happen. Will the partial correlation remain roughly the same, increase, or decrease? Use your answer to formulate a hypothesis, set at the 0.05 alpha level. Rather than take things step by step, we simply plug the numbers above into formula 12-1.

$$r_{yx.v} = \frac{0.855 - (0.867)(0.675)}{\sqrt{1 - 0.867^2}\sqrt{1 - 0.675^2}} = 0.734$$

As we hope you anticipated from noting the high correlation between prior convictions and seriousness of crime charge, the relationship between prior convictions and sentence length has diminished from 0.855 to 0.734. This is because part of the reason people with a greater number of convictions get more time is that they also tend to have more serious charges. Partial correlation eliminates the overlap and gives us a "pure" (so to speak) association between prior conviction and sentence length.

We can test the partial correlation for significance using the t distribution and computing t according to formula 12-2:

12-2

$$t = \frac{r_{yx.v}\sqrt{n - q - 2}}{\sqrt{1 - r_{yx.v}^2}}$$

The expression $n - q - 2$ is our degrees of freedom. In this equation, q is the number of variables held constant, in this case, 1, v. Thus we have 7 degrees of freedom.

$$t = \frac{0.734\sqrt{7}}{\sqrt{1 - 0.734^2}} = 2.865$$

Turning to the t distribution table we find that with 7 degrees of freedom at an alpha of 0.05, our t critical is 2.365. Our t calculated of 2.865 beats t critical, and therefore the partial correlation is significant. We can therefore say that, *net of crime seriousness*, prior convictions remains correlated with sentence in years at $r = 0.734$.

COMPUTER EXAMPLE

We will now explore partial correlation further with a more complex computer example using our sex offender data. Table 12-2 is a correlation matrix (a row-by-column display) of zero-order correlations between all the relevant variables. In the present case, the variables are sentence severity, offender group (non–sex

TABLE 12-2. *Matrix of Pearson Correlation Coefficients*

Variable	CASES	MEAN	STD DEV	
SENSEV (Y)	637.0000	492.0220	727.3945	
GROUP (X)	637.0000	0.6766	0.4681	
CRSER (V)	637.0000	2.9937	1.9611	
PRREC (W)	637.0000	3.9906	4.9073	
	SENSEV	**GROUP**	**CRSER**	**PRREC**
SENSEV	1.000	0.1597*	0.7162*	0.4334*
GROUP		1.000	−0.1666*	0.0582
CRSER			1.000	0.3150*
PRREC				1.000

*$p < 0.05$.

and sex), crime seriousness, and prior record. The top of the table lists the variable code names, number of cases, and means and standard deviations of all variables. Note that the mean given for the group variable (dummy coded) is simply the proportion of sex offenders in the data set (431/637 = 0.6766), with non–sex offenders coded 0 and sex offenders coded 1.

Reading along the top row of the correlation matrix, we learn that sentence severity is weakly but significantly related to offender group (0.1579), that the correlation between sentence severity and crime seriousness is strong at 0.7162, and that the correlation between sentence severity and prior record is moderate at 0.4344. Given this information, we might be led to conclude that crime seriousness is the most important variable determining sentence severity, followed by prior record, and last by offender group.

Tracing along the next row, we find that offender group is negatively and significantly related to crime seriousness (−0.1666) and positive but nonsignificantly related to prior record (0.058). That is, as these two legal variables are measured by the courts, sex offenders commit the less serious crimes but have the more serious prior records. However, since the correlation between offender group and prior record is not significant at less than an alpha level of 0.05, we cannot assume that this is true in the population of sex offenders in this jurisdiction.

The direction of a relationship involving a dichotomous variable depends on how we code the dichotomous variable. If we had coded offender group as sex = 0, non–sex = 1, the correlation between sentence severity and offender group would have been −0.1597, the correlation between offender group and crime seriousness would have been 0.1666, and the correlation between offender group and prior record would have been −0.058. Thus, although the coding is arbitrary with nominal variables, such as offender group, and does not affect the statistical computations, it must be shown in the table so that the reader may properly interpret the results. This is not the case with correlating two continuous variables, where the value of r is always symmetrical. The last correlation reported in the table is the one between crime seriousness and prior record (−0.315), indicating a moderate statistically significant tendency for those with the more serious criminal histories to commit the more serious crimes.

We will now compute the partial correlation between offender group and sentence severity, controlling for crime seriousness. Given that we know that sex offenders receive significantly harsher sentences than non–sex offenders ($r_{yx} = 0.1597$), but also that they commit significantly less serious crimes ($r_{yv} = -0.1666$), what effect do you think that controlling for crime seriousness will have on the basic offender group/sentence severity relationship? Will the association increase or decrease? Generate a hypothesis and set the alpha threshold at 0.05. Computing for partial r:

$$r_{yx.v} = \frac{0.1597 - (0.7162)(0.1666)}{\sqrt{1 - 0.7162^2}\sqrt{1 - \left(-0.1666\right)^2}} = 0.406$$

If you thought that controlling for the effects of crime seriousness would increase the strength of the relationship between sentence severity and offender group, you were right. It makes sense that this should be so since sex offenders who were already receiving harsher sentences also had lower crime seriousness scores, a variable that contributes powerfully to sentence severity. As we pointed out in chapter 10, crime seriousness is acting as a suppressor variable masking the true strength of the relationship between offender group and sentence severity. In other words, the punishment cost of being a sex offender rather than a non–sex offender is greater than the mean difference of 248.1 sentence severity points that separates the groups as determined by the t test in chapter 6. As an exercise, see whether you can compute t to determine whether the partial r is statistically significant.

SECOND-ORDER PARTIALS: CONTROLLING FOR TWO INDEPENDENT VARIABLES

As stated in chapter 10, controlling for crime seriousness or prior record alone leaves an incomplete picture of what is going on in the sentencing world. Since they operate jointly in the real world, we must assess their *joint* effects. That is, we need to determine the relationship between group and sentence severity controlling for both legal variables simultaneously—symbolically, $r_{yx.vw}$. Before you can compute this second-order partial, two final first-order correlations must be computed: the relationship between sentence severity and prior record, controlling for crime seriousness ($r_{yw.v}$), and the relationship between offender group and prior record, controlling for crime seriousness ($r_{xw.v}$). These values have been computed as $r_{yw.v}$ = 0.315 and $r_{xw.v}$ = 0.119. We will put them into formula 12-3 along with $r_{yx.v}$ (0.407) to demonstrate that the logic of computing **second-order partials** is the same as that for computing first-order partials.

12-3

$$r_{yx.vw} = \frac{r_{yx.v} - (r_{yw.v})(r_{xw.v})}{\sqrt{1 - r_{yx.v}^2}\sqrt{1 - r_{xw.v}^2}}$$

Plugging in all of our r values from above,

$$r_{yx.vw} = \frac{0.407 - (0.315)(0.119)}{\sqrt{1 - 0.135^2}\sqrt{1 - (-0.119)^2}} = 0.392$$

The relationship between offender group and sentence severity, controlling for crime seriousness and prior record, is 0.392. The simultaneous control of the two legally relevant variables (the "only" two variables that are supposed to determine sentencing decisions) with partial correlation analysis will allow us to make statements about the sentencing of sex offenders that other techniques just hint at. Since we have controlled for the only two variables that are legally supposed to influence sentencing decisions, we can state with confidence that sex offenders receive discriminatory sentencing relative to non–sex offenders in this jurisdiction. The process of finding statistical significance is replicated as above, with $n - q - 2$ degrees of freedom.

THE MULTIPLE CORRELATION COEFFICIENT

When using partial correlations we are only interested in the association of y and x net of controls. A partial correlation is an estimate of the correlation between two variables in a population with the effects of one or more other variables controlled for, or partialed out. It is the correlation between y and x uncontaminated by v, w, and so on. When we use **multiple correlation**, on the other hand, we are interested in the *combined* effects of a set of independent variables on y. This gives us an idea of how well our statistical model fits the data—and so it is sometimes referred to as a goodness-of-fit statistic.

In chapter 11 we noted that the squared zero-order correlation coefficient is the proportion of variance in the dependent variable accounted for by the independent variable. In terms of our offender data, crime seriousness explains 51.3 percent of the variance in sentence severity ($0.716^2 = 0.513$) and offender group explains 2.56 percent ($-0.16^2 = 0.0256$). You might think that all you have to do to determine the percentage of the variance that they jointly account for is to add these percentages ($51.3 + 2.56$) to arrive at 53.86 percent. But we have already seen that when we take crime seriousness into account, the correlation between sentence severity and offender group actually *increases*. Therefore, the percentage of variance in sentence severity jointly accounted for by these two independent variables should be *greater* than the sum of their zero-order contributions. Formula 12-4 is used to calculate the multiple correlation coefficient, symbolized by a capital R.

12-4

$$R_{y.xv} = \sqrt{\frac{r_{yx}^2 + r_{yv}^2 - 2r_{yx}r_{yv}r_{xv}}{1 - r_{xv}^2}}$$

We already have the numbers for these values, so let's plug them in the formula:

$$R_{y.vx} = \sqrt{\frac{0.160^2 + 0.716^2 - 2(0.160)(0.716)(-0.167)}{1 - (-0.167)^2}} = 0.77$$

The multiple correlation coefficient is 0.77, and its squared value (0.593) is the percentage of the variance in sentence severity jointly accounted for by the two variables—that is, the total amount of variance explained by the model. In common statistical parlance, we refer to the squared multiple correlation coefficient as R^2. Note that if the correlation between offender group and crime seriousness had been zero (if they were independent events), the multiple correlation coefficient obtained from this laborious process *would* have been exactly the value obtained from simply adding together the zero-order contributions (53.86 percent). But, as is almost *always* the case in the social world, this is not the case.

A diagrammatic illustration of a simple example may help you to visualize the nonadditivity, and hence redundancy, of some of the variance explained in y by two correlated independent variables. In situation A in Figure 12-1 both x and v are

FIGURE 12-1
Visualizing R^2

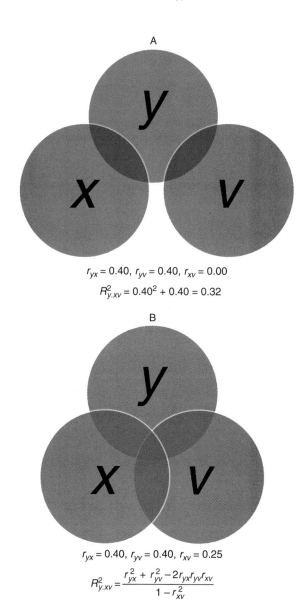

A

$r_{yx} = 0.40$, $r_{yv} = 0.40$, $r_{xv} = 0.00$

$R^2_{y.xv} = 0.40^2 + 0.40 = 0.32$

B

$r_{yx} = 0.40$, $r_{yv} = 0.40$, $r_{xv} = 0.25$

$$R^2_{y.xv} = \frac{r^2_{yx} + r^2_{yv} - 2r_{yx}r_{yv}r_{xv}}{1 - r^2_{xv}}$$

correlated with y but are uncorrelated with each other. We can simply sum the separate proportions of variance explained by x and v to get 16 percent + 16 percent = 32 percent. In situation B, x and v are correlated. We cannot sum their contributions to variance in y because they account for a certain proportion of common variance. This shared variance, represented by the overlapped darker blue area, is the redundant information that must be subtracted. The multiple correlation coefficient can also be extended to include any number of independent variables, but you can safely leave the busy work to the computer as long as you understand the logic behind the process. R^2 becomes especially important for multiple (or multivariate) regression, which we now consider.

MULTIPLE REGRESSION

As neat and tidy as partial correlation is for summarizing the relationship between two variables controlling for a number of other variables of theoretical importance, we still need other techniques to fully understand our data. Which of the three variables (group, crime seriousness, or prior record) is of most or least importance in explaining variance in sentence severity, taking into consideration their simultaneous presence? How much of the variance in sentence severity do the three variables taken together explain? These questions, and more, can be answered by multiple regression. **Multiple regression** (also known as multivariate regression) is a basic tool for evaluating the overall dependence of a variable on a set of independent variables. It is, quite simply, the workhorse of all social science statistics and will be the launching point for all advanced statistics beyond the general linear model.

The Unstandardized Partial Slope

We saw in chapter 11 that the best way to describe the linear relationship between two interval-level variables is the least-squares regression line: $y = a + bx$. *This regression line can be extended to include any number of other independent variables, even those that are measured at the nominal level.* The general formula for multiple, ordinary least squares regression, is given as formula 12-5:

12-5

$$y = b_0 + \Sigma b_p x_p + e$$

Where y = the dependent variable, or the criterion
b_0 = a from the bivariate regression equation, that is, the constant or y-intercept
b_p = the slope for a given independent variable (or **predictor**) p
x_p = the value of a predictor p
e = the error or residuals, as discussed in the previous chapter

Applying this to the question at hand, we have three predictors: group, crime seriousness, and prior record. Therefore,

$$y'_{\text{sentence severity}} = b_0 + b_{\text{group}}x_{\text{group}} + b_{\text{crime seriousness}}x_{\text{crime seriousness}} + b_{\text{prior record}}x_{\text{prior record}} + e$$

b is our *understandardized partial slope* and is analogous to the slope we calculated in the previous chapter. The difference is that now, for each predictor, we partial out the variance that it explains in criterion.

We saw in chapter 11 that a regression slope shows the amount of change in the dependent variable per unit change in the independent variable. We also saw in the bivariate regression of crime seriousness on sentence severity in Table 11-8 that each unit increase in crime seriousness resulted in an increase of 265.6 days in prison. In multiple regression the regression slope is an **unstandardized partial regression slope**, which indicates the amount of change in the dependent variable per unit change in the independent variable controlling for the effects of all other independent variables in the equation. The partial slope is obtained by formula 12-6.

12-6

$$b_p = \left[\frac{S_y}{S_x}\right]\left[\frac{r_{yx} - (r_{yv})(r_{vx})}{1 - r_{vx}^2}\right]$$

Where b_p = the partial slope of v (crime seriousness) on y (sentence severity)
s_y = the standard deviation of y (sentence severity)
s_x = the standard deviation of x (offender group)
r_{yv} = the zero-order correlation between sentence severity and crime seriousness
r_{yx} = the zero-order correlation between sentence severity and offender group
r_{vx} = the zero-order correlation between crime seriousness and offender group

The information needed to compute these partial slopes is reproduced in Table 12-3. Let's use these data to figure out the partial slope for crime seriousness (v):

$$b_v = \left[\frac{727.39}{1.96}\right]\left[\frac{0.716 - (0.16)(-0.167)}{1 - (-0.167)^2}\right] = 283.5$$

We can also use the same formula to figure out the partial slope for offender group (x).

$$b_x = \left[\frac{727.39}{0.468}\right]\left[\frac{0.16 - (0.716)(-0.167)}{1 - (-0.167)^2}\right] = 447.6$$

TABLE 12-3. *Data for the Calculation of the Partial Slope*

	Sentence Severity (y)	Crime Seriousness (v)	Offender Group (x)		Correlations (r)
Mean	492.00	2.99	0.667	r_{yv}	0.716
Std dev	727.39	1.96	0.468	r_{yx}	0.160
				r_{vx}	−0.167

The first partial slope tells us that there is a change of 283.5 units in the dependent variable (283.5 sentence severity points) per unit increase in crime seriousness points when the influence of group is held constant. When group is controlled for there is an increase of just under 20 points over the 265.6 value noted in the unstandardized slope in Table 11-8. In the second case there is a 447.6 unit increase in sentence severity per unit change in group (moving from 0 = non–sex to 1 = sex) when the influence of crime seriousness is held constant. This value is an increase of 199.4 over the bivariate slope for sentence severity and group ($b = 248.1$) noted in chapter 11.

The Standardized Slope (β)

We cannot determine from the unstandardized partial slopes which of the independent variables in the model has the *most* powerful impact on sentence severity. In the bivariate regressions in Tables 11-7 and 11-8, we saw that the slope for crime seriousness is 265.6; for offender group, 248.1; and for prior record, 64.4. We cannot assume from these figures that since the slopes for crime seriousness and offender group are almost equal, they are approximately of equal importance in determining sentence severity, nor can we assume that either one of them is about four times more important than the prior record. This is because they are all measured differently. In chapter 11 we explained that the value of b depends on how we measured the dependent variable. It also depends on the range of the independent variable. Recall also that the slope indicates the change in y *per-unit* increase in the independent variables(s), so if there are more units in one variable than in another we cannot directly compare their per-unit impact on y. For example, the offender group variable only has to split the sentence severity variance it explains two ways; that is, into sex or non–sex categories. Crime seriousness points range from 1 to 10, and prior record points range from zero to 27, which means that they have to split the variance they account for 10 and 28 ways, respectively.

To assess the relative importance of the independent variables in explaining variance in y we have to convert them to a common scale, that is, standardize them. To do so we use the standard deviation to calculate the **standardized slope** (β); this informs us of the change (increase or decrease) in the dependent variable in standard deviation units per standard deviation change in the independent variable. It also allows us to determine which predictor has the strongest impact on the criterion. The formula for standardizing a regression slope is given in formula 12-7:

12-7

$$\beta_p = b_p \left[\frac{s_v}{s_y} \right]$$

For crime seriousness:

$$\beta_v = 265.6 \left[\frac{1.96}{727.39} \right] = 0.714$$

For offender group:

$$\beta_x = 248.1 \left[\frac{0.468}{727.39} \right] = 0.1595$$

A similar computation for prior record is 0.43. The computed values for the standardized betas are, within the limits of rounding error, analogous to the zero-order correlations between these pairs of variables given in Table 12-2. But we still cannot tell which of the three independent variables has the most important impact on sentence severity from these standardized betas any more than we could from the zero-order correlations. To do so we must compute the **standardized partial regression slopes** for these variables.

The standardized partial regression slope, referred to as the *standardized beta* from now on, indicates the average standard deviation change in the dependent variable associated with a standard deviation change in the independent variable, holding constant all other variables in the equation. The formula for computing the standardized beta is given in formula 12-8.

12-8

$$\beta_{yv.x} = b_{yv.x} \left[\frac{s_x}{s_y} \right]$$

where $\beta_{yv.x}$ = the standardized partial beta
$b_{yv.x}$ = the unstandardized partial b

As you can see, the standardized beta formula is essentially the same as the partial beta above. So the standardized beta for crime seriousness is

$$\beta_{yv.x} = 283.5\left[\frac{1.96}{727.39}\right] = 0.763$$

This value of 0.763, with tolerance for rounding, is identical to the value we computed for the multiple correlation coefficient from formula 12-4. A similarly computed partial *standardized beta* for offender group, controlling for crime seriousness, is 0.289. We are sure at this point that crime seriousness is more important to sentencing decisions than offense type (group). However, we still do not know whether *group* or *prior record* is the second most powerful predictor. The answer to this question requires us to extend the equation to include *prior record*. In the interest of brevity we will not compute this step, but the logic is analogous to that involved in computing second-order partial correlation coefficients. We will now discuss the computer readout for the regression model assessing the combined effects of offender group, crime seriousness, and prior record on sentence severity.

A COMPUTER EXAMPLE OF MULTIPLE REGRESSION

We are now in a position to assess the simultaneous effects of all three predictor variables on sentence severity. It will be useful to look at three successive printouts so that you can see the changes in the various statistics as we add new variables and to reinforce what you have learned about regression in the last two chapters. The first panel in Table 12-4 is a simple bivariate regression of crime seriousness on sentence severity. The second panel shows the regression results with offender group added to the equation, and the third panel shows the full three-variable model (crime seriousness, group, and prior record regressed on sentence severity).

INTERPRETING THE PRINTOUT

In the two-variable regression model in panel 2, the first statistic encountered is multiple *R*, the correlation between a dependent variable and two or more independent variables. In the present case it is the multiple correlation between sentence severity

TABLE 12-4. *Regression Models Progressively Entering Control Variables*

Panel 1. Bivariate regression of crime seriousness on sentence severity

MULTIPLE R	0.71618			ANALYSIS OF VARIANCE	
R SQUARE	0.51291		DF	SUM OF SQUARES	MEAN SQUARES
ADJUSTED R SQUARE	0.51215	REGRESSION	1	172599964.1	172599964.1
STANDARD ERROR	508.06003	RESIDUAL	635	163909373.3	258124.99
F = 668.66815	SIGNIF F = 0.000				

VARIABLE	B	SE B	BETA	T	SIG T
CRSER	265.64	10.273	0.716	25.859	0
(CONSTANT)	−303.231	36.756		−8.250	0

Panel 2. The addition of offender group to the model

MULTIPLE R	0.77006			ANALYSIS OF VARIANCE	
R SQUARE	0.59299		DF	SUM OF SQUARES	MEAN SQUARES
ADJUSTED R SQUARE	0.59171	REGRESSION	2	199547814.1	99773907.03
STANDARD ERROR	64.78774	RESIDUAL	634	136961523.6	258124.99
F = 461.85714	SIGNIF F = 0.000				

VARIABLE	B	SE B	BETA	T	SIG T
CRSER	283.378	9.531	0.764	29.732	0
GROUP	445.937	39.927	0.287	11.169	0
(CONSTANT)	−658.059	46.23		−14.225	0

Panel 3. The addition of prior record to the model

MULTIPLE R	0.79265			ANALYSIS OF VARIANCE	
R SQUARE	0.62829		DF	SUM OF SQUARES	MEAN SQUARES
ADJUSTED R SQUARE	0.62653	REGRESSION	3	211424782.8	70474927.59
STANDARD ERROR	444.52889	RESIDUAL	633	125084554.9	197605.93
F = 365.64379	SIGNIF F = 0.000				

VARIABLE	B	SE B	BETA	T	SIG T
CRSER	258.685	9.656	0.697	26.79	0
GROUP	410.668	38.456	0.264	10.679	0
PRREC	29.548	3.811	0.199	7.753	0
(CONSTANT)	−678.185	44.319		−15.302	0

and crime seriousness and offender group given their simultaneous presence in the model. Note that this value is identical to the value we computed for $R_{y.xv}$.

The next statistic is R squared, which is the square of multiple R (0.77) = 0.593 (rounded). It is important to note the change in the R^2 value from that given in panel 1 to the value given in panel 2. It has increased from 0.51291 to 0.59299, an increment of 0.0801. This increase indicates that after crime seriousness has been allowed to explain all the variance that it can, offender group explains an additional 8 percent. In panel 3 you can see a further increase in R^2 of 0.0353, for a total R^2 for the model of 0.62829. (For a comment on what's known as the "adjusted R^2", see Box 12-1.)

The next value is the standard error, or standard error of the estimate. Recall from chapter 11 that this is an estimate of the average prediction error, and it is defined as the standard error of actual y values from the predicted y' values based on the regression equation. Also recall that the standard error of the estimate is also the standard deviation of the residuals. The residual or unexplained sum of squares is printed out as 125084554.9 in panel 3. If we divide this by the df for $SS_{residual}$, defined as $n - k - 1 = 633$, we get the variance of the residuals. The square root of the residuals is the standard deviation of the residuals, or the standard error of the estimate. For reference, this is given as formula 12-9:

12-9

$$S_{y.xvw} = \sqrt{\frac{SS_{residual}}{df}}$$

To the right of these statistics is the analysis of variance. The sum of squares explained by the regression is analogous to the term *explained sum of squares* in ANOVA, and the residual sum of squares means exactly the same as it does in ANOVA (i.e., the unexplained variance in the model). Dividing the regression mean square by the residual mean square we obtain the F ratio observed in panel 3.

Box 12-1
The Adjusted R^2

The adjusted R^2 is a conservative estimate of explained variance that adjusts for sample size and/or number of predictor variables. It is always preferable to report the adjusted R^2 whenever our number of predictor variables becomes quite large. The computation of the adjusted R^2 found in panel 3 is illustrated by formula 12-10.

12-10

$$\text{adjusted } R^2 = 1 - (1 - R^2)\frac{n-1}{n-k-1}$$

In this formula, k is the number of predictors in the model. Thus, for Table 12-4, panel 3,

$$\text{adjusted } R^2 = 1 - \left(1 - 0.79265^2\right)\frac{637-1}{637-3-1} = 0.6253$$

Although the R^2 value will always increase with the addition of variables to the regression equation, the *adjusted* R^2 may begin to *decrease* in value. When there is a *serious* decrease, we are being warned that we have added variables that are not useful in helping us to understand our data. Note that the adjusted R^2 value in panel 3 is only *slightly* lower than the unadjusted R^2 value. This is a relatively good (albeit crude) indication of model fit.

$$F = \frac{70474927}{197605.93} = 356.64379$$

Comparing this value to the F table (see pp. 345–346), we can safely conclude that the regression model clearly explains a highly significant proportion of the variance in sentence severity.

The Predictor Variables: b, β, and t

Below the summary model statistics is information regarding the contributions of each specific variable in the model. Reading from left to right, the first statistic is the partial unstandardized b for sentence severity and crime seriousness, controlling for other variables in the model, which is only offender group in panel 2. Note that the unstandardized b has increased from 256.6 in panel 1 to 283.4 in panel 2. Within the limits of rounding error, this is the value we computed above. In panel 3, the partial slope for crime seriousness declines to 258.68 because prior record is significantly and positively correlated with crime seriousness. Those who commit the more serious crimes tend to have the more serious prior records. The unstandardized partial slope of 258.68 in panel 3 is interpreted as meaning that for each unit increase in crime seriousness there is an average increase of 258.68 sentence severity points when the effects of offender group and prior record are held constant.

The next statistic is the standardized partial slope (beta) for crime seriousness, reported as 0.697 in panel 3. This value tells you how much a 1 standard deviation change in x will affect y, also in standard deviation units, controlling for the effects of the other variables in the model. This is an important statistic because, unlike the unstandardized partial slope, it is a measure of the relative importance of the independent variables in the model. The statistical significance of each variable is assessed by the t test. We see that all variables contribute significantly to the model.

We now move down to the second row, containing the statistics relevant to offender group. The unstandardized partial slope of 410.7 given in panel 3 indicates that the effect on sentence severity of being a sex offender as opposed to a non–sex offender is 410.7 sentence severity points. This is a dramatic increase from the 248.1 points difference observed when we did not take the two legally relevant variables into account. With the addition of prior record in panel 3, both the standardized b's and the unstandardized betas for crime seriousness and offender group have diminished. Again, this is intuitively reasonable if we recall from the matrix of zero-order correlations that prior record is positively related to both crime seriousness and offender group. We finally know what being a sex offender versus not being a sex offender means in terms of sentence severity. It tells us more than a simple multiple correlation could because we can easily translate the unstandardized partial slope into substantive terms (i.e., days incarcerated).

Multiple regression allowed us to determine the ranking of the independent variables in terms of how they affect sentencing. It is now obvious from the standardized betas that offender group ($\beta = 0.264$) has a more powerful effect than does prior record ($\beta = 0.199$). We would have been misled into thinking that prior record was the more important of the two had we not performed a regression analysis. The relative importance of these three predictor variables can be determined by taking the ratio of the squares of their standardized betas. The squares (rounded to two places) of our three predictors are crime seriousness $= 0.49$, offender group $= 0.07$, and prior record $= 0.04$. Crime seriousness accounts for 7 times more variance ($0.49/0.07 = 7$) than offender group and just over 12 times more than prior record. Finally, offender

Box 12-2
The y-Intercept

The final statistic is the y-intercept (CONSTANT), which represents the value of y when all of the independent variables have a value of zero. As we saw previously, the constant is used to predict the value of an individual score from given values of the independent variables in the equation. We can manipulate the value of the constant to make interpretation of the y-intercept easier. We did not do it here, but one of the most useful things you can do in a regression model (if it makes sense to do so), is to *mean center* your variables. To mean center a variable, you subtract the mean from each case's value. For example, imagine that you have five numbers: 1, 4, 6, 8, and 10. The mean is 5.8. The mean centered values are therefore

1	5.8	−4.8
4	5.8	−1.8
6	5.8	0.2
8	5.8	2.2
10	5.8	4.2

The average of the mean centered values is now 0. Recall that all b's and the a (that is, the y-intercept) are all *averages*: the y-intercept is the average value of y when all of the predictors equal 0. If the averages for each variable have been set to 0, then the y-intercept can be interpreted as the *average value of the dependent variable when all predictors equal their average*. For example, if you are interested in the effects of police officer age on police officer job satisfaction and you mean center all of the variables, the y-intercept can be interpreted as the average job satisfaction of the average-aged police officer.

group accounts for 1.75 times more of the variance (0.07/0.04 = 1.75) than prior record. (For information on understanding the "CONSTANT," see Box 12-2.)

A VISUAL REPRESENTATION OF MULTIPLE REGRESSION

To help you grasp the idea of multivariate regression, note what happens in Figure 12-2. The circle labeled y is the total variance in sentence severity. The first variable to enter

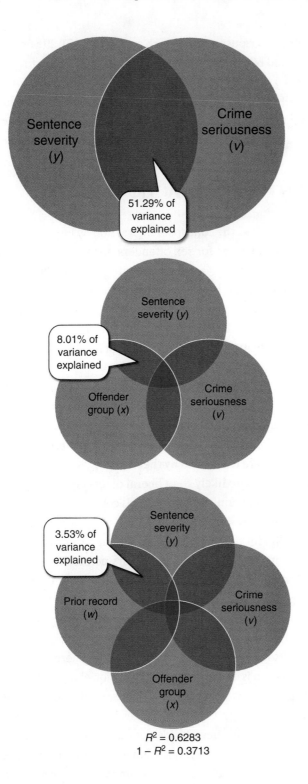

FIGURE 12-2
Visual representation of partitioning variance in multiple regression

the equation is crime seriousness (v), which accounts for 51.29 percent of the variance (visually represented by the shaded area). The next most powerful predictor, offender group (x), accounts for 8.01 percent of the *remaining* variance. Finally, prior record (w) takes out 3.53 percent of the variance in y after x and v have taken their share. Thus, the three predictor variables have taken a combined total of 62.83 percent of the variance in sentence severity, leaving 37.17 percent of the variance unexplained.

REGRESSION AND INTERACTION

In chapter 7 we illustrated the concept of interaction by looking at probation officers' sentencing recommendations for sex offenders, using victim/offender relationship and probation officer ideology as independent variables. The ANOVA model indicated significant interaction between the two independent variables, thus suggesting further exploration of the data for a more meaningful interpretation of the effects of the two independent variables on recommendations. Unlike ANOVA, regression does not explicitly reveal the existence of interaction, but it can be detected indirectly with a little extra effort.

If preliminary statistical analyses and/or our theoretical knowledge of the subject under investigation leads us to suspect significant interaction, we should create a new variable that is a composite of the two interacting variables. For instance, we already know from the two-way ANOVA results in chapter 7 that probation officers' sentencing recommendations are influenced by their ideology. Criminological theory tells us that conservatives are more likely than liberal officers to hold a just deserts position in terms of the purpose of punishment. If this is correct, we would expect to find that crime seriousness is more important in determining conservative officers' recommendations than liberal officers' recommendations. In other words, the effects of crime seriousness on recommendations will vary across officer category. To test this assumption we create an interaction term by multiplying (or having the computer multiply) ideology (IDEOL) by crime seriousness (CRSER). Why? Think back to our probability discussion: whenever we are interested in the probability of *two* events *co-occurring*, the multiplicative property directs us to multiply their individual probabilities. The same logic undergirds what we are doing here with regression.

This interaction term is entered into the regression equation with its two composite variables. That is, we now have three variables: crime seriousness, ideology, and crime seriousness × ideology. Crime seriousness and ideology are called the main effects, whereas crime seriousness × ideology is called the interactive effect. The regression model used to illustrate interaction in model C in Table 12-5 consists of one continuous dependent variable, *probation officer recommendation* (POREC), one

TABLE 12-5. *Illustrating Interaction Terms*

A. Liberal officers only

VARIABLE	B	SE	BETA	T	SIG
CRSER	178.7500	14.6600	0.5720	12.2000	0.0000
ADJUSTED R2	0.3250				

B. Conservative officers only

VARIABLE	B	SE	BETA	T	SIG
CRSER	290.8900	15.9200	0.7720	18.2700	0.0000
ADJUSTED R2	0.5940				

C. Ideology by crime seriousness interaction

VARIABLE	B	SE	BETA	T	SIG
CRSER	178.7400	16.4300	0.5020	10.8700	0.0000
IDEOL	−159.0400	77.6400	−0.1110	−2.0500	0.0410
CRSER × IDEOL	112.1400	21.6400	0.3520	5.1800	0.0000
(CONSTANT)	−159.5100	52.8900		−3.0200	0.0027
ADJUSTED R2	0.5280				

continuous independent variable, *crime seriousness* (CRSER), one dummy independent variable, *ideology* (IDEOL), and one *interaction term* (CRSER × IDEOL). If the regression results indicate no significant interaction, the prediction equation is simply additive with the form we have already learned above:

$$y' = b_0 + b_1 x_1 + b_2 x_2 + e$$

In this equation b_1 and x_1 refer to the slope and variable value (respectively) for crime seriousness, and b_2 and x_2 refer to the slope and variable value (respectively) for probation officer ideology. If interaction is significant, the additive model is no longer adequate to describe the data, and the equation must take the form

$$y' = b_0 + b_1 x_1 + b_2 x_2 + b_3 x_1 x_2 + e$$

In this model, $x_1 x_2$ refers to the interaction term, which has its own unique slope (b_3).

Table 12-5 presents three separate regression models. Models A and B are bivariate regression models of the effect of crime seriousness on recommendations for sex and non–sex offenders for liberal and conservative officers, respectively. The adjusted R^2 values (0.325 for liberals and 0.594 for conservatives) support our contention that crime seriousness is a more important determinant of the recommendations conservative officers make than it is for liberal officers. The impact of one additional crime seriousness unit results in an increase of 290.89 recommendation units ($b = 290.89$) for conservative officers but only 178.75 units for liberal officers ($b = 178.75$). Subtracting the slope for the liberal officers from that of the conservative officers we see a difference of 112.14 recommendation points.

Let us now look at model C, which is a multiple regression including both independent variables and the interaction term CRSER $\times$ IDEOL. Both independent variables are significant. The important point is the value of the unstandardized beta for the interaction term. We see that it is 112.14, the value we got from subtracting the slope in model A from the slope in model B. The test of statistical significance for the regression coefficient associated with the interaction term is a test of the statistical significance of the *difference of the two slopes defined by IDEOL*. The *t* value (5.18) for the interaction term is highly significant; thus the interaction effect is highly significant, and the additive prediction equation is inadequate. Note that IDEOL has a significant effect on recommendation severity even after the effects of the interaction term have been accounted for. (Note that sometimes, interaction effects are difficult to interpret. It is often useful to consult a scattergram or contingency table to better understand what is going on with the interaction terms.)

SUMMARY

Partial correlation allows us to assess the strength of the relationship between two variables controlling for the effects of one or more other variables. It is an effective technique if the researcher is concerned only with the relationship between x and y, with the effects of all other theoretically relevant variables removed. Multiple correlation is the correlation between a dependent variable and two or more variables. Squaring the multiple correlation gives the percentage of the variance in the dependent variable explained by all of the independent variables in the equation. Multiple regression is used to make predictions of the dependent variable from two or more independent or predictor variables. The unstandardized partial slope (beta) is an index of the amount of change in the dependent variable per unit change in an independent variable, controlling for the effects of the other independent variables in the model. The unstandardized partial slope values are given in their original measurement units. The standardized partial slopes convey the same information in terms of standard deviation units rather than the original metric. By standardizing the partial slopes we render them comparable in terms of the relative strength of each variable's impact on the dependent variable. The R^2 value represents the percentage of the variance explained in the dependent variable by all independent variables operating together.

Multiple correlation and regression are remarkably powerful and robust techniques for assessing the combined effects of a series of independent or predictor variables on a dependent variable, supplying researchers with a wealth of information. The multiple regression model is typically referred to simply as the general linear model. This terminology is drawn from the fact that the goal of regression is to fit the data as closely as possible to a line that extends from the y-intercept and through the mean of y and the predictor variables. For those interested, we draw on the logic underlying the general model to introduce you to the generalized linear model in Appendix A.

At first glance, this table *may not* be such a good example. But Journal Table 12-1 is not only a good example of ordinary least squares regression, but also a good example of when researchers will report variables as they were coded and display their coded names to readers, rather than the informal variable names. This table is from the article "The specific deterrent effect of higher fines on drink-driving offenders" by Weatherburn and Moffatt (2011). For this study, the researchers reported the results of an ordinary least squares analysis of the specific deterrent effect of high fines

JOURNAL TABLE 12-1. *Ordinary Least Squares Regression*

Variables	*b*	Std. Error	*t*	Sig.
(Constant)	4.697	0.026	182.44	0.000
SEVERITY_GP	0.069	0.001	56.246	0.000
AGEGROUP	0.009	0.003	2.85	0.004
GENDER	0.098	0.01	9.955	0.000
ARIA_GP	−0.062	0.005	−13.454	0.000
PCA_GP	0.388	0.005	78.44	0.000
PLEA_GP	0.13	0.014	9.169	0.000
LEGALREP	0.021	0.007	2.882	0.004
PRIORPCA_GP	0.189	0.01	19.62	0.000
$R = 0.68$				

on drunk-driving offenders in Australia, in which judicial severity served as the instrumental variable. The amount of the fine (LOGFINE—the "LOG" part indicates they took the natural log to help with the linearity assumption of the linear model) imposed for the offense was used as the dependent variable in the first stage of the analysis. The remaining control variables included in the study were age group (AGEGROUP), gender (GENDER), geographic location (ARIA_GP), plea (PLEA_GP), legal representation (LEGALREP), and prior convictions (PRIORPCA_GP). During the first state of the analysis, LOGFINE was regressed against the instrument (SEVERITY_GP) to assess how much of the variation in fines the instrument explained. Based on this information, it can be determined that all variables are significant. If we square their R value, we learn that 46.2 percent of these variables explain variation in the fine amount. Further, because this table reports beta coefficients, readers can see that PCA cases (PCA_GP) ($\beta = 0.388$) and prior convictions (PRIORPCA_GP) ($\beta = 0.189$) have a more powerful effect than does age group ($\beta = 0.009$).

REFERENCE

Weatherburn, D., & Moffatt, S. (2011). The specific deterrent effect of higher fines on drunk-driving offenders. *British Journal of Criminology* 51, 789–803.

PRACTICE APPLICATION: PARTIAL CORRELATION

We will now determine whether the correlation between bullying propensity and acceptance of homosexuals holds up with controlling for educational level (V). Refer back to the practice application from chapter 11 for details about this hypothetical study. All the necessary information to make our computations is in the following matrix. Remember that bullying propensity is *reverse coded*:

	Y	X	V	$\bar{X}$	s
(Y) Social distance	1.000	0.857	0.769	6.3	2.01
(X) Bullying propensity		1.000	0.850	27.0	4.19
(V) Level of education			1.000	13.1	2.56

What is the strength of the relationship between X and Y controlling for V?

$$r_{yx \cdot v} = \frac{0.857 - (0.769)(0.85)}{\sqrt{1-(0.769)^2}\sqrt{1-(0.85)^2}} = \frac{0.203}{(0.639)(0.529)} = 0.60$$

Is the partial relationship statistically significant? (Note: $df = 3$ because we are testing a first-order relationship).

$$t = r_{yx \cdot v}\sqrt{\frac{N-3}{1-r^2}} = 0.60\sqrt{\frac{7}{36}} = 0.60\sqrt{19.44} = 2.64$$

t critical with 7 df at the 0.05 level (two-tailed) is 2.365. Our calculated t exceeds this; reject the null that $\rho_{yx \cdot v} = 0.0$ in the population. Thus, controlling for education level weakens the bivariate relationship because of the strong correlation between bullying propensity and education level, but it remains fairly strong and is statistically significant.

Compute the multiple correlation coefficient.

$$R_{y \cdot xv} = \sqrt{\frac{r_{yx}^2 + r_{yv}^2 - 2r_{yx}r_{yv}r_{xv}}{1 - r_{xv}^2}}$$

$$= \sqrt{\frac{0.857^2 + 0.769^2 - 2(0.857)(0.769)(0.85)}{1-(0.85)^2}} = \sqrt{\frac{0.734 + 0.591 - 2(0.56)}{1 - (0.722)}}$$

$$= \sqrt{\frac{1.325 - 1.12}{0.2775}} = \sqrt{\frac{0.205}{0.2775}} = \sqrt{0.739} = 0.86$$

Squaring multiple R we find that bullying propensity and education jointly account for 74 percent of the variance in social distance from homosexuals. Bullying propensity by itself accounted for 0.734 percent of the variance (0.857^2). We added practically nothing to our understanding of the bullying propensity/social distance relationship by adding education to the model because education is highly correlated with self-esteem.

Calculate the unstandardized partial slope for bullying propensity:

$$b_1 = \left[\frac{S_y}{S_x}\right]\left[\frac{r_{yx} - (r_{yx})(r_{vx})}{1 - r_{vx}^2}\right]$$

$$= \left[\frac{2.01}{4.19} \right] \left[\frac{0.857 - (0.769)(0.85)}{1 - (0.85)^2} \right]$$

$$= (0.48) \left[\frac{0.857 - 0.654}{1 - 0.7225} \right] = (0.48) \left[\frac{0.203}{0.2775} \right] = (0.48)(0.7315) = 0.351$$

Calculate the unstandardized partial slope for education

$$b_2 = \left[\frac{2.01}{2.56} \right] \left[\frac{0.769 - (0.857)(0.85)}{1 - (0.85)^2} \right]$$

$$= (0.785) \left[\frac{0.769 - 0.728}{1 - 0.7225} \right] = (0.785) \left[\frac{0.041}{0.2775} \right] = (0.785)(0.148) = 0.116$$

Compute the standardized partial slope for bullying propensity:

$$\beta_1 = b_1 \left[\frac{S_x}{S_y} \right] = 0.351 \left[\frac{4.19}{2.01} \right] = 0.732$$

For education level:

$$\beta_2 = b_2 \left[\frac{S_x}{S_y} \right] = 0.116 \left[\frac{2.56}{2.01} \right] = 0.148$$

Calculate the y-intercept:

$$a = \bar{Y} - b\bar{X}_1 + b\bar{X}_2 = 6.4 - (0.351)(27) + (0.116)(13.1) = 6.4 - (9.48 + 1.52)$$
$$= 6.4 - 11 = -4.6$$

What social distance score would you predict for a person with a bullying propensity score of 34 and 16 years of education?

$$Y'a + b_1 X + b_2 X = -4.6 + (351)(34) + (0.116)(16)$$
$$= -4.6 + 11.93 + 1.86 = 9.19$$

Appendix A

Introduction to Regression with Categorical and Limited Dependent Variables

This appendix introduces you to new and fairly advanced statistics. We will not take time detailing how to calculate these statistics. Instead, we will focus on explaining when you might see these models pop up and how to interpret them. The most advanced models we have so far explored in this book—ANOVA, t test, Pearson's r, and ordinary least squares regression—are part of a family of statistical techniques called the general linear model, often abbreviated simply as LM for linear model. As the name suggests, LM statistics assume linearity—a relationship between criterion and predictor that can accurately be expressed as $y = a + bx$. For the LM to work, certain assumptions must be met. We have gone over several of these assumptions, already; one that we have somewhat glossed over is the need for our dependent variable to be continuous—to, at least hypothetically, have a distribution that is normal. Recall that a normal distribution is one that looks like a bell when plotted as a histogram. For truly continuous variables—such as the distribution of grades in any average college course—this distribution holds.

For many of our variables in criminology and criminal justice, this is not the case. Rather, our dependent variables, although perhaps technically continuous and asymptotic in their distributions, hardly approach a normal distribution. Instead, their distributions look more like that displayed in Figure A-1.

Such a distribution is skewed to the right and is commonly observed in criminology and criminal justice data. Criminological data are often skewed heavily to the right because we typically measure infrequent events. As much as the media and politicians would have us believe that serious and violent crime is happening all of the time and everywhere, this is simply not the case; statistically speaking, it is quite rare. Not only is it rare, but also it is hardly random. As a rule of thumb, only *random* data approach normality and, hence, a normally distributed histogram. Being

FIGURE A-1
A limited variable
distribution

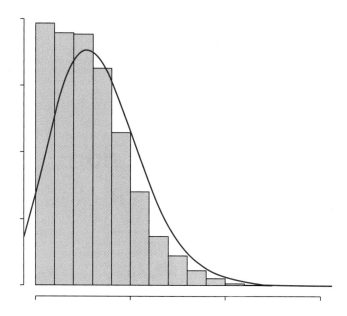

infrequent and nonrandom, crime (and other variables associated with crime and justice) is typically not normally distributed. Rather, it follows different sorts of distributions. This begs an important question: if our statistics are based on probability, which is itself based on the concept of randomness and normally distributed data, how can we use statistics to predict criminal justice events that are not randomly distributed? This is an excellent question, with a complex answer. Fortunately, our LM statistics are typically robust enough to deal satisfactorily with even nonrandomly distributed data. On occasion, however—for instance, when the distribution is extremely skewed to the right—the LM does not perform trustworthily with non-normally distributed data. For such occasions we must turn to what is known as the generalized linear model, or GLM.

The GLM was explicitly designed to deal with nonnormally distributed data. Although any sort of variable can, technically and theoretically, be nonnormally distributed, in criminology and criminal justice the most common type of nonnormally distributed variables fall into these categories: binary, nominal, ordinal, and count outcomes. Below, we go into each of these in detail. We collectively refer to these variables as *limited and categorical dependent variables*. We do so in part because they are, either by the nature of the phenomena or the nature of the measurement, bound by specific anchor points. For example, a binary outcome—such as "arrested" or "not arrested"—*only has two options*. It is therefore limited. One cannot take these descriptions too far. IQ is also, practically speaking, limited. But the distribution of IQ is normal; there is simply no possible way for a binary variable to be "normally" distributed. Indeed, if a binary variable were randomly distributed, the

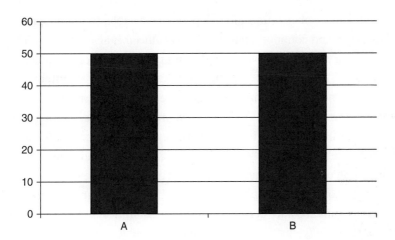

FIGURE A-2
A binary, random
distribution

distribution would look something like Figure A-2, with each category having a probability of 0.50.

Limited dependent variables, although perhaps appearing continuous on their surface, will always manifest themselves in terms of how they are distributed. This should become clearer as we discuss the models appropriate to each limited dependent variable below.

THE GENERALIZED LINEAR MODEL

At its most basic level, the GLM is trying to do one (conceptually) simple thing: convert a nonlinear dependent variable to a linear distribution and then apply the LM. Mathematically, the process can be quite complex and employs high-level calculus formulae. (In fact, the "conversion" process is so complex that it must often be repeated several times before the model "fits" the data—more on this below). The means of making this change is something called the *link*. The link is the part of the equation that takes the limited or categorical dependent variable and allows it to be treated (mathematically) as if it were normally distributed. As you can see from formula A-1, the basic structure of the GLM is identical (essentially) to ordinary least squares (OLS) regression (that is, to LM):

A-1

$$\eta = \beta_0 + \Sigma\beta_p X_p + \epsilon$$

The main difference is the y for the LM and the Greek letter eta found here in the GLM. Eta represents the link function, and what eta equals requires some complex math best left to the computer at this point in your statistical education.

We will introduce you to four limited dependent variables in this appendix: binary, nominal, ordinal, and count outcomes. A *binary outcome*, also called a dichotomous outcome, is one in which (as above) we only have two options, for example, "arrested" and "not arrested" or "convicted" and "not convicted." A **nominal** outcome is similar to a binary outcome (in fact, binary is simply one form of nominal), but can differ in that there can be more than two choices, for example, "Catholic," "Protestant," "Jew," "Muslim." An **ordinal** outcome is one that is categorical, but can be rank ordered, for example, "first degree murder," "second degree murder," and "manslaughter." Finally, a *count* outcome is one where the dependent variable does just that: counts the number of times something happens. In a sense, then, count variables *are* continuous in that they have an absolute zero and infinite possibilities. But count variables are distinct from *normally* distributed continuous variables in that they are heavily weighted toward the low end of the continuum, that is, near 0 and 1. In addition, because they count the number of times something happens, there are typically no negative values with count outcomes. A classic example in criminology research is "number of times someone was arrested." Even convicted offenders with long rap sheets have not been arrested enough to create a normal distribution. And in the general population, almost *nobody* has been arrested. This creates a special distribution called a Poisson distribution, which we discuss in some detail below.

Each type of limited or categorical dependent variable has its own link (that is, eta is calculated uniquely for each type of limited dependent variable), but they all work essentially the same. For example, the binary link (called the logit) takes the probability of a binary variable (expressed as the distribution in Figure A-3), which

FIGURE A-3
A binomial
probability
distribution

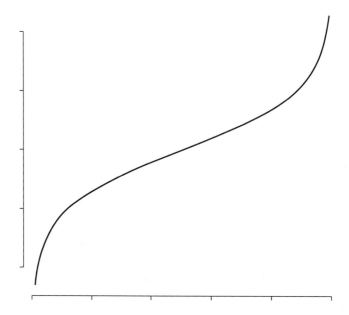

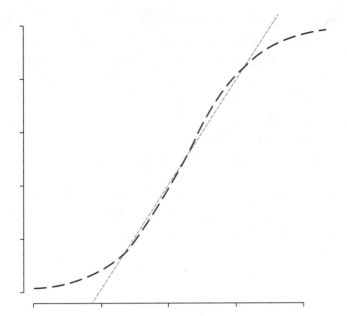

FIGURE A-4
A binomial probability distribution (long dashes) plotted against a linear logit link (short dashes)

is not at all linear, and converts it to a linear logit distribution that, as you can see in Figure A-4, is linear.

Binary, nominal, ordinal, and count outcomes each have their own link properties that transform them from something utterly nonlinear (such as Figure A-3 for a binary outcome) to something completely linear (such as that found in Figure A-4). We should note, however, that the demands placed on the data are more stringent for the GLM than for the LM. That is to say that the GLM is not as robust as the LM. The assumptions required by the LM can typically be bent and still have the models behave relatively well. This is usually not the case with the GLM. It is therefore important to keep in mind that if the data do not behave well, you might actually be better off using an LM than a GLM. Knowing when to make decisions like this will become clearer the more you read examples of good statistics and the more you practice calculating and interpreting statistics. For now, let's go over the four most popular GLM statistics you'll encounter in criminology and criminal justice research.

BINARY OUTCOMES: THE LOGIT

Whenever we have a binary outcome, the appropriate model to employ is a *logistic regression*, which uses a *logit* for its link. (This actually applies as well to the multinomial and ordered logit models, discussed below.) We can't really "distribute" binary outcomes because we have only two options. But we can consider the probability of each event happening (with the event of any of the two events being equal to one minus the probability of the other event, as in chapter 4). The logit takes this probability and interpolates a linear distribution. We then run a regression model following the same logic outlined in chapter 12. In a logistic model, we are no longer trying to account for the *variation* in y given x, net of controls. Instead, we are trying to figure out the *likelihood* of y given x, net of controls. In a (rather inaccurate) sense, we are essentially trying to predict the probability of the dependent variable.

Table A-1 is a typical logistic regression output that you might see from a computer program. For this model, we are interested in seeing whether owning a handgun predicts future risky behavior. Our variables are "owning a handgun," "age," "whether someone has a college degree," "household income," and their "political ideology," "race," and "gender." We measure risky behavior by asking whether they have cheated on their spouse in the past year. Note that we measure this variable a year *after* all other variables. We also control for any cheating behavior they may have engaged in during this prior year. Why do you think we made these choices?

This table should look similar to the computer printouts we went over in chapter 12: we have b coefficients and standard errors. But there are differences, too. We now have z scores rather than t scores, and we also have several lines of something called "iterations." Finally, we no longer have an R^2, but a pseudo-R^2. Let's break this table down to its component parts.

The "iterations" are almost never reported. The computer goes through a series of trial and errors until it calculates a best-fitting model with the data at hand—specifically, when the probability of the observed outcome given the predictors is greatest. This process is based on a statistical method called maximum likelihood. This topic is beyond the ken of this book, but it's something to tuck away for future statistics. (In fact, the typical way of calculating even LM regressions is to use maximum likelihood, rather than OLS.) *Likelihood* is an important concept in all GLMs, because it reflects what the GLM is trying to do: whereas LMs result in algebraically linear coefficients for each predictor, GLMs result in predicted probabilities—that is, predicted likelihoods. How well a GLM predicts a criterion's probability can be estimated using what we call the *log likelihood*. Note that the log likelihood is the same as the final iteration value, -188.97167. We can estimate a pseudo-R^2 using the log likelihood: if we take the log likelihood of the model and divide into the log likelihood of an intercept-only model, we can estimate a quotient that can roughly be interpreted in the same manner as an R^2 for a linear model. In this case, the pseudo-$R^2 = 0.3172$ (see Box A-1).

TABLE A-1. *An Example of Logistic Regression*

| Iteration 0: log likelihood = −276.75768 |
| Iteration 1: log likelihood = −196.07818 |
| Iteration 2: log likelihood = −189.21496 |
| Iteration 3: log likelihood = −188.97186 |
| Iteration 4: log likelihood = −188.97167 |
| Iteration 5: log likelihood = −188.97167 |

| Number of obs = 523 |
| LR chi2(10) = 175.57 |
| Prob > chi2 = 0 |
| Log likelihood = −188.972 |
| Pseudo-R2 = 0.3172 |

cheat_2b	B	SE B	Z	SIG Z
rhandgun	0.2839948	0.3459879	0.82	0.412
age_1	−0.0090608	0.0092731	−0.98	0.329
deg_1	0.2200182	0.3185203	0.69	0.49
income06_1	0.008554	0.0283732	0.3	0.763
lib	0.3524667	0.3296315	1.07	0.285
mod	−0.1496347	0.3257214	−0.46	0.646
white	0.6239997	0.463875	1.35	0.179
other	0.3115109	0.6851992	0.45	0.649
sex_1	0.3689	0.282913	1.3	0.192
cheat_1b	3.190388	0.281681	11.33	0
constant	−3.614342	2.317696	−1.56	0.119

You'll also want to consider the chi square value, given here as 175.57. GLMs are so complicated that we cannot use a randomized distribution as we would for LMs; rather, we estimate their distributions using either the *F* of chi square distributions, both of which you have already been introduced to. For logistic regression (and for all other models that we cover in this chapter), we use the chi square distribution.

Box A-1
About the Pseudo-R^2

One equation for a pseudo-R^2 looks like this (there are several equations under the umbrella term pseudo-R^2, but each serves the same purpose):

$$R^2 = 1 - \left[\frac{L(M_\alpha)}{L(M_\beta)}\right]^{2/N}$$

The numerator is a model with only an intercept (that is, a constant), and the denominator is the full model. N, of course, is the sample size.

Note that this is only *one* of several pseudo-R^2's. And this is one of the problems with pseudo-R^2's: there are several, and they all approach the issue differently. The issue that they are approaching is how to meaningfully measure the amount of variance explained in any given GLM model. Because pseudo-R^2's are based on probability and not variance explained, however, they can never explain the variation in the same manner that an LM's R^2 does. Trust us when we say this is a topic best left for an advanced statistics book.

As you can see from line under "LR chi2," this model is statistically significant ("Prob>chi2=0"). This is similar to the F test for OLS regression.

We can now move on to the actual coefficients. You'll note that there are four columns: "B," "SE B," "Z," and "SIG Z." These correspond to the LMs "B," "SE," "T," and "SIG T." "B" represents our linear probability; when we divide it by its standard deviation, we get a z score. As with all z scores, we want this to be larger than 1.96. If it is, we can declare it to be statistically significant at $p < 0.05$ (the exact probabilities are given in the "SIG Z" column). As they are presented, b coefficients in GLMs are uninterpretable. What does it mean that a one-unit change in owning a handgun results in a 0.28-unit change in the logit of cheating on one's spouse? (At least, with a 59 percent chance of being *incorrect* in this prediction.) The answer is *something*.

We can render this number more easily interpretable if we exponentiate it. Recall what GLMs are doing: taking the criterion and converting it to something linear. It will help us interpret our b coefficients if we can convert them, as well. We do this by exponentiating them by e—that is, raising e to the power of our coefficient. Like pi (π), e is a mathematical constant roughly equal to 2.718. When we take our linear probability coefficients from *any* GLM and raise e by them, we transform our coefficients into an odds ratio, which we have already discussed. The only coefficient that is statistically significant in Table A-1 is cheating at time 1: cheating at time 1 predicts cheating (on one's spouse, that is) at time 2, where $b = 0.287$. If we exponentiate this, we get an odds ratio (often abbreviated simply as OR) of $e^{0.287} = 1.332$. This means that the odds of cheating at time 2 are increased by 1.332 times if the respondent had cheated at time 1.

Take another look at the model in Table A-1. What do you think: is it a strong model or a weak one? Does it tell us anything interesting? What is the "best" predictor among *all* predictors?

NOMINAL OUTCOMES: THE MULTINOMIAL MODEL

Having been introduced to logistic regression, you are now ready to tackle multinomial logistic regression. For a dependent variable to be considered multinomial, it must be categorical, with more than two options, and must not be rank ordered. For example, imagine a multinomial criterion with three options: *incarceration status*, with the options *incarcerated, probation*, or *parole*. Multinomial logistic regression is basically several logistic regression models run simultaneously. You run a logistic regression model for each potential *pair* of categories in the dependent variable. So with our current example, to calculate a multinomial model, you run a logistic regression model for incarcerated versus probation, incarcerated versus parole, and probation versus parole. The key difference between actually running three logistic regression models for binary outcomes and running a single multinomial model is that the latter does this *simultaneously* across all three pairs.

For such a multinomial equation, you will therefore be presented with a table with two models. For any multinomial model, you must choose a reference category (like dummy variables). Thus there are two instead of three models. The probability of the nonreference category is then pitted against the probability of the reference category. An example will clarify this process. Table A-2 presents a typical computer output for a multinomial model. The question is the following: can we use race to predict whether one thinks the nation is doing too much, too little, or just enough about crime?

Note that all of the statistics we saw for the logistic regression model are here: iterations, *pseudo-R^2's, b*, standard errors, and *z* scores. Further, all of these are basically interpreted in the same fashion—and we can still convert *b* scores to odds ratios by raising *e* to the power of *b*. (This will apply to *all* of the models covered in this appendix.) What can become tricky—at least at first glance—is what do these odds ratios mean? First, remember that each model is comparing a pair of categories. According to Table A-2, the reference category is "*too_little*." Our first model

TABLE A-2. *An Example of a Multinomial Logistic Regression Model*

Iteration 0: log likelihood = −805.94953	
Iteration 1: log likelihood = −793.54656	
Iteration 2: log likelihood = −793.08602	
Iteration 3: log likelihood = −793.08453	
Iteration 4: log likelihood = −793.08453	

Multinomial logistic regression	Number of obs = 976
	LR chi2(4) = 25.73
	Prob > chi2 = 0.000
Log likelihood = −793.08453	Pseudo-R2 = 0.016

natcrime_1	B	SE B	Z	SIG Z
too_little	(base outcome)			
about_right				
white	−1.0571	0.24662	−4.29	0
other	−0.9825	0.31136	−3.16	0.002
_cons	2.46079	0.82797	2.97	0.003
too_much				
white	−0.0792	0.38568	−0.21	0.837
other	−0.7777	0.46708	−1.67	0.096
_cons	−0.7986	1.26006	−0.63	0.526

pits this against "*about_right*." Note that being white and being of another racial group are both statistically different (at $p < 0.05$) than being black and that these coefficients are negative. This means that being white or of another racial category decreases the likelihood that you think the government is doing just about the right amount of work toward decreasing the crime rate compared to being black.

Let's convert these to odds ratios to make this easier to see: for white, OR = $e^{-1.0571}$ = 0.347. For Latinos, the finding is almost the same: the OR = $e^{-0.9825}$ = 0.374. Stated clearly, but less precisely, whites and other races are more likely to believe the government isn't doing enough to decrease the national crime rate. The next model compares "*too_little*" with "*too_much*." For this model, none of the variables is

---

Box A-2
What about the Reference Category?

Although we only have two models, we still have three pairs. Why did our computer not give us the output for *about_right* versus *too_much*? For two reasons. First, it's redundant. As with dummy variables, so too with the multinomial model: we can use arithmetic to figure out the OR for this pair given our predictors. We will spare you the math and instead suggest that if you're really curious to know that particular model, instruct your statistical package either to include it in the output or to run the statistic again specifying a different referent category. Most statistical software will choose your referent category unless you instruct it differently. More than this, we'd advise you to be careful and thoughtful about choosing your referent category. It could be that your research question is only interested in what predicts whether people believe the government is not doing enough with a "rising" crime rate. If that is the case, then choose that as your reference category, and you need look no further.

---

statistically different. It is therefore in the middle ground where we find much disagreement according to racial grouping (see Box A-2).

Assess model fit on your own—does this model fit the data well or not? If you answered "not that well," why might this be the case? The z scores are compelling, but the models themselves are woefully underdeveloped—that is, they are misspecified. The *pseudo-R^2* suggests that this model does not even explain 2 percent of the variance in the outcome. And this makes sense: we are trying to explain the outcome with merely *one* variable, race. What sort of variables could also logically go into this model?

ORDINAL OUTCOMES: THE ORDERED LOGIT

The same logic that underlies both binary and multinomial logit models is employed in ordered logit models, with one important twist. With ordered logit, we are running regression models on categorical variables that we can rank—what we call ordinal variables. Thus there is an *implied* distance between the rankings: infractions are less serious than misdemeanors, which are less serious than felonies. What that distance is is, of course, arbitrary. A lack of mathematically meaningful distance between categories is the hallmark of ordinal variables and the characteristic that most distinguishes them from continuous outcomes. Even Likert scales are not continuous in the technical sense of the term. For example, if we ask police officers to rank their job satisfaction using a Likert scale of 1 = not satisfied and 3 = completely satisfied, we may be tempted to say an officer who ranks her satisfaction as 3 is three times more satisfied as an officer who ranks his satisfaction as 1, but we would be incorrect to do so. Ordinal variables are still categorical, which means the only math we can really perform is to say that x percent of officers are completely satisfied compared to y percent of officers who are not satisfied with their jobs.

What makes ordinal regression unique from other GLMs is that it makes use of this *implied* distance. Specifically, when creating the logit link for the criterion—that is, when converting the categorical outcome to a hypothetical continuous outcome—the model projects an estimated linearity that it assumes underlies the ranked categories. This is visually represented in Figure A-5 below. The top row represents the actual ordinal variable, moving from least satisfied to most satisfied. The bottom row represents the conversion to a hypothetical continuous variable. Note that there are "cutoff" points, represented by dashed horizontal lines, that coincide with the original categorical variable. These cutoff points are extremely important when modeling an ordered criterion and are typically represented by the Greek letter tau: τ.

For any ordered logit model, there are a number of τ's (cutoff points) equal to the number of categories. Each represents the distance, in estimated continuous units, between one category and the next. The reason why there are only two cutoff points listed in Figure A-5 is because the first cutoff, τ_0, is our referent point in the same sense that in binary or multinomial regression we need a referent category. τ_0 represents the space from negative infinity ($-\infty$) to τ_1. Like dummy variables, the cutoff points will actually be entered into the GLM equation and included in the computer printout. Before we talk about how to understand their coefficients, let's take a look at a computer example.

The ordered logit model in Table A-3 is measuring how likely an officer is to be satisfied with his job given certain demographic and professional characteristics, using the Likert scale described above. There are several dummy and interaction variables in the equation, including race (the referent category is white), gender (the referent category is male), and gender × race (the referent categories are white males and black males, respectively). The model also includes dummy variables for

FIGURE A-5
Projected continuous
variable underlying
an ordinal variable

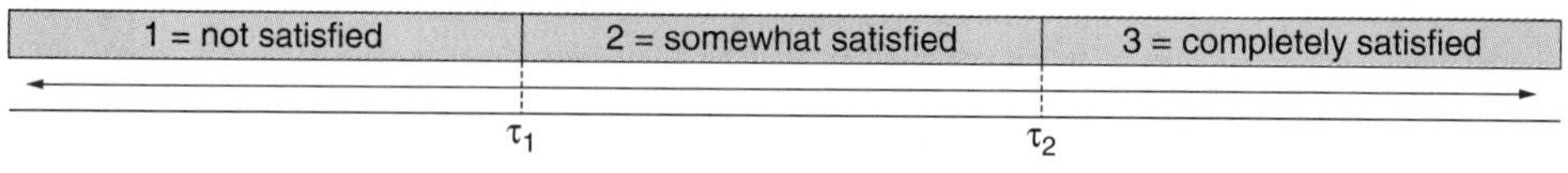

| 1 = not satisfied | 2 = somewhat satisfied | 3 = completely satisfied |

τ_1 $\qquad\qquad$ τ_2

TABLE A-3. *An Example of an Ordered Logit Model*

Iteration 0: log likelihood = −164.63581
Iteration 1: log likelihood = −151.48067
Iteration 2: log likelihood = −151.16418
Iteration 3: log likelihood = −151.16258
Iteration 4: log likelihood = −151.16258

Ordered logistic regression	Number of obs = 177
	LR chi2(10) = 26.95
	Prob > chi2 = 0.0027
Log likelihood = −151.16258	Pseudo-R2 = 0.0818

Satisfied	OR	SE B	Z	SIG Z
Black	1.97452	1.04007	1.29	0.197
Hispanic	2.39969	1.21006	1.74	0.083
Female	1.01558	0.614	0.03	0.98
FemHisp	1.35077	1.22568	0.33	0.74
FemBlck	1.4105	1.26567	0.38	0.701
Detail	0.98742	0.35917	−0.03	0.972
Admn	2.66739	1.47262	1.78	0.076
Detective	4.05177	1.95348	2.9	0.004
Sergeant	2.75587	1.33561	2.09	0.036
Age*	1.08644	0.04222	2.13	0.033
/cut1	−1.3305	0.35957		
/cut2	1.88913	0.37933		

*Mean centered.

an officer's job, with patrol chosen as the referent category, and a continuous variable representing their age in years. Note that this printout has the same pattern we observed for the previous two GLMs: iterations, a chi square test, and a pseudo-R^2. Based on what you've learned so far, how well does the model fit the data?

Note that the coefficients also follow the same pattern. This time, we've asked the computer to automatically calculate our odds ratios. We can see that females are more likely than males to be satisfied and that those on details are less likely than those on patrol (our referent category) to be satisfied. Otherwise, no other variables are statistically significant. Incidentally, can you figure out how to return ORs to b coefficients? If we arrive at odds ratios by raising e to the power of b, we simply reverse the process by taking the *natural log* of the odds ratio. Taking the *log* of any number transforms its base. And the *natural log* specifically transforms the number to base e. Thus the natural log (typically abbreviated as ln) of our female dummy variable is $ln(1.01558) = 0.015$. This makes sense: the b coefficient is linear, and b of 0.015 suggests little movement, just as an odds ratio of 1.01558 suggests poor odds.

You should immediately note two new rows in Table A-3 not present in our other GLM printouts: "/cut1" and "/cut2." As you probably figured out, these represent our τ's. How are they interpreted? The short answer is *carefully*. These coefficients describe the likelihood of the associated categorical outcome. Thus, "/cut1" is used to determine the probability of *somewhat satisfied*, and "/cut2" is used to determine the probability of *completely satisfied*. In essence, they are the tools we use to arrive back at our original scale—categorical. The math involved can be quite complex, and the options available in a statistical package can be equally overwhelming (for example, you can choose from among the minimum and maximum probability, the average probability, etc.). For now, we believe you have the tools to grasp what an ordered logit model is intuitively trying to convey, and that's enough. Future classes should clarify how we move from τ to predicted probability for each category.

COUNT OUTCOMES: HEAVILY SKEWED DISTRIBUTIONS

Thus far we have discussed regression models with categorical dependent variables. Now, we turn our attention to regression models that use limited dependent variables, specifically *count* criteria. Outcomes that are count are, perhaps, technically continuous, but their behavior is distinct. Truly continuous variables have a normal distribution; count variables do not. Rather, they tend to be heavily skewed toward the right, as in Figure A-1. This breaks a primary assumption of normality of the LM. Count models' underlying function is different from the GLMs we have so far encountered: whereas categorical regression models convert a nonnormally distributed outcome to a linearly distributed outcome, count models apply a completely different distribution—one that reflects their heavily skewed nature.

In truth, there are *several* count models. Which one an analyst chooses is largely governed by the extremity of the criterion's skew. We will briefly consider three such models: the Poisson, the negative-binomial, and the zero-inflated count models. Each of these assumes a count outcome, such as the number of times someone violated parole or the number of police officers in a city. (You may think that this latter variable would be normally distributed, considering how large some police agencies are. But you must remember that the average number of police officers per capita is only around 2.4.) The "base" distribution, so to speak, for count models is the **Poisson distribution**. A Poisson distribution is appropriate when the mean and standard deviation are roughly equal. If they are unequal, such that the standard deviation is vastly larger than the mean, then we have what is called an overdispersed model, and we must use the **negative-binomial distribution**, which compensates for the heavier skew of an overdispersed distribution. (Incidentally, there is a statistic available to determine whether a distribution is overdispersed, called the dispersion parameter. This means that researchers do not have to "eyeball" whether a distribution is skewed.)

Finally, for samples that have a large number of 0's, we use **zero-inflated models**. Having a lot of zeros reduces variation, which makes uncovering statistical significance difficult (because of type II error). The number of UCR Index crimes a person has committed is a good example of what would amount to be a zero-inflated model: most people have not committed larceny (well, at least not beyond petty theft, which, unfortunately, is likely included in the larceny-theft category), homicide, rape, aggravated assault, burglary, robbery, auto theft, or an arson. Zero-inflated models are extremely time consuming and complex, both logically and in terms of the math. We therefore leave it to another book to teach you how to run and interpret such models. It is enough for now that you are aware that such statistical solutions exist for highly skewed models with lots of zeros.

We now turn our attention to Table A-4, which is an example of a Poisson model. This is a simple model, to help us keep things straight. We are regressing our variable—number of crimes committed, or *crime*—on *gpa*, *iq*, and *sex* (referent category is 0 = male). As with the previous models, we have our iterations, a chi square test, and a pseudo-R^2. Additionally we have *b* coefficients, standard errors, *z* scores, and probability tests. Is this a good fitting model? Which variables are statistically significant? Which best increases the likelihood of committing more offenses?

If you got stuck on that last question, look back over the previous models. How did you standardize the coefficients for the other GLMs? You'll do the same thing here: exponentiate the coefficient by raising *e* to the *b*. Thus, for the only statistically significant coefficient available, *gpa*, the odds ratio that someone with a higher GPA

TABLE A-4. *An Example of a Poisson Model*

Iteration 0: log likelihood = −882.70577				
Iteration 1: log likelihood = −882.70577				

Poisson regression		Number of obs = 400		
		LR chi2(3) = 241.38		
		Prob > chi2 = 0.0000		
Log likelihood = −882.70577		Pseudo-R2 = 0.1203		

crime	B	SE B	Z	SIG Z
gpa	0.56436	0.03665	15.4	0.000
sex	0.00513	0.03346	0.15	0.878
iq	0.00063	0.00113	0.56	0.578
_cons	0.58769	0.16393	3.59	0.000

would actually engage in *more* criminal behavior is $e^{0.5644}$ =1.758. You might be wondering why we are not creating dummy variables for GPA. After all, it represents a categorical variable, where 0 = F, 1 = D, 2 = C, 3 = B, and 4 = A. Although this is true, it is also true that GPA is an *average*. Rather than thinking in terms of A–F, think in terms of the average score across all classes. This in effect creates a

FIGURE A-6
gpa's distribution

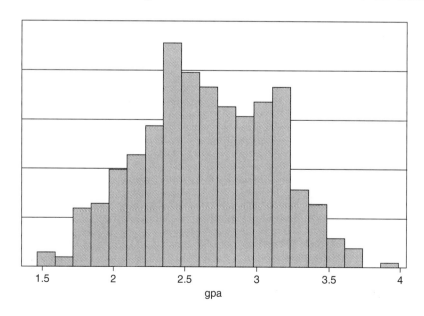

continuously behaving variable. In our example, *gpa* has a mean of 2.65 and a standard deviation of 0.46 and a basically normal distribution, as seen in Figure A-6. There is an important lesson here: as much as we like rules of thumb, much of statistics are educated and informed judgment calls (recall our discussion about what is and is not a strong correlation coefficient, for example, from chapter 11).

SUMMARY

This appendix has provided a brief overview of four important generalized linear models: binary logit models, multinomial logit models, ordered logit models, and count models, including negative-binomial and Poisson models. These models are important because so many of the variables we use in criminology and criminal justice use dependent variables that align most closely with these statistical models. The math underlying these statistical models is quite complex—but not so complex that you cannot understand the basic functions. What's more, you now have all the tools necessary to interpret and start exploring the generalized linear models. If you are interested in learning more, we suggest two books. First, if you are worried about your math, consider John Fox's (2009) *A Mathematical Primer for Social Statistics*. Second, for the best and most accessible text on these generalized linear models, we recommend J. Scott Long's (1997) *Regression Models for Categorical and Limited Dependent Variables*.

REFERENCES

Fox, J. (2009). *A mathematical primer for social scientists*. Thousand Oaks, CA: Sage.

Long, J. C. (1997). *Regression models for categorical and limited dependent variables*. Thousand Oaks, CA: Sage.

Appendix B

A Brief Primer on Statistical Software

In this primer, we introduce you to what are arguably the four most popular statistical packages that criminologists and criminal justicians use: SPSS, SAS, Stata, and R. For each package, we discuss their general user interface, strengths and weaknesses, costs, and available resources. Among the three of us, we have ample experience in all four software packages (collectively, more than 50 years of experience). Throughout this book, we have purposely avoided using one statistical package in our examples because, despite voices to the contrary, there simply is no standard statistical package used among social scientists. Although it may be true that most undergraduate students are introduced to statistical software through SPSS, most graduate students (and therefore professors and analysts) will eventually branch out into other statistical packages as the need arises. The fact of the matter is that although most statistical software can do almost everything an analyst may want, it may not do it as well, as easily, or as elegantly as other software. Pursuant to our secondary goal of preparing undergraduate students for graduate-level statistical work, we therefore use this appendix to make you aware of what statistical software is out there and why you may (or may not) want to use one over the other.

SPSS

SPSS is currently owned by IBM. Prior to that, it was developed and owned by its namesake, SPSS, Inc. SPSS stands for Statistical Package for the Social Sciences. This nomenclature is somewhat anachronistic because SPSS is popular across many fields of study, not just those considered social sciences. SPSS is probably the most popular statistical software at the university level, particularly for undergraduate students and entry-level graduate students. This is likely because of its longevity and its graphical user interface (GUI), which, in some ways, mirrors more familiar software programs, such as spreadsheets and databases. SPSS's GUI is its most distinctive feature. The program divides into three essential windows, with a fourth "optional" window (although in all reality, this fourth window can easily replace two of the three essential windows, as you will see momentarily). The two main windows are called Data View and Variable View. As the names suggest, users can see all data under the Data View window; it basically works like a spreadsheet program with limited functionality. The Variable View window delineates the variable attributes: names, labels, construction, etc. These two graphical issues are useful visual tools that, in the end, possess little functionality. Almost all of the functions are accessed via the menus or via the fourth "optional" window: the Syntax window.

Unlike almost all other statistical packages, SPSS uses a Syntax model to communicate with the software—most packages use what's better called a command language. Syntax is a string of command codes that tell SPSS what to do with the data. The user can type these codes directly into the Syntax window and run functions from there in lieu of running them through the menus. A typical SPSS syntax call for an independent *t* test might look like this:

```
t-test groups = gender(0 1)
        /variables = crime.
```

When run, this syntax will ask SPSS to run a *t* test comparing mean crime rates between men and women. Some syntax can be more involved than this, however. For example, a typical OLS regression might look like this:

```
regression variables = crime gender iq lsc
        /dependent = crime
        /method = enter.
```

Can you figure out which variable is regressing onto which predictors from the syntax above ("lsc" refers to low self-control)? The strength of the Syntax window is that it helps the user *not* to rely on the default options, which, when using the more user-friendly menu system, is likelier to happen (more on this in the following paragraph). After the menus have been accessed or code inputted, SPSS will provide extensive output in the Output window. The output window provides a history of what the analyst has asked SPSS to do, as well as the actual results in table form.

The strengths of SPSS lie in its ubiquity and apparent user-friendliness. Although we do not agree that SPSS is *the* standard for social science statistics, even for undergraduates, it is certainly the one that almost everyone knows, even if only on a superficial level. This makes it easier for researchers to collaborate and for students to move from one school to another—say from their undergraduate institute to their graduate institute. The native GUI of SPSS is also appealing to new users because, as we've pointed out, it mirrors the look and feel of other data-drive programs that are not inherently statistics based, particularly those associated with spreadsheets or databases. We note, however, that this user-friendliness is more apparent than real: at some point, students must venture from the comfortable point-and-click environment of the GUI and begin playing around in the Syntax window. SPSS syntax is less user-friendly than the GUI, of course, and can be intimidating. The difficulty of learning and working with SPSS Syntax has been mitigated in recent software iterations, but it remains a weak point of SPSS. This is related to what we think is the most important weakness of SPSS: By providing such a vast and capable GUI, SPSS pushes users toward "the default" options. Granted, sometimes these default options are based on convention and to that end are acceptable. But convention is not always appropriate in every given situation. At least with the Syntax, users must think about the choices that they are making with much more deliberateness than they would if only relying on the mouse. All and all, it has been our observation that students can and almost always do make the jump from the GUI to the Syntax with relatively little growing pains. Nevertheless, it is something that anyone thinking of moving toward statistical software should be aware of.

SAS

The second software program we want to introduce you to is SAS. SAS stands for the appropriately named Statistical Analysis Software. Although SAS may not be the standard in criminology and criminal justice, it is the standard among college business programs and among incorporated businesses. Like SPSS, therefore, SAS has a wealth of resources available to those who want to use it. SAS is quite old: it has been around since the 1960s. Developed at North Carolina State University, within 10 years it moved to its own corporation, the SAS Institute. SAS (along with R, see below) is an incredibly intimidating piece of software for the uninitiated, in no small part because of the feature that most distinguishes it: namely, how to ask SAS to do, well, anything. Like SPSS, in SAS you code in a sequence of steps for the program to follow all at once; SAS asks you to type in "procedure" commands, one by one, filling in the options as you go. Continuing our examples from above, here's how you'd ask SAS to run a *t* test between the crime rates of men and women:

```
proc ttest data="c:\data";
class gender;
var crime;
run;
```

Until you type in "run;" and hit enter, SAS waits for you to finish filling in all the options, even after you've hit enter at the end of each line. Although there is a GUI add-on for SAS, it is rarely used. Most work is done using the "proc" command. Here's the regression example from above:

```
proc reg data="c:\data";
model crime = gender iq lsc;
run;
```

Note how SAS literally writes out a formula: *crime = gender iq lsc*. This is one of the best parts for learning any command language: it helps you grasp exactly what the statistic is trying to do.

The procedure commands that SAS employs are a two-edged sword. In one way, they are anything from intuitive to those not familiar with programming language. But for those who are, or who are willing to take the time to learn SAS's programming language, SAS becomes an incredibly powerful tool—and one that is almost as flexible as R. SAS can do many types of analyses, including the most sophisticated out there, with relative elegance and simplicity. For example, it is one of the best choices for running the now in-vogue propensity score matching statistics. Also, because it lacks the multiple window system of SPSS, it is, in the end, easier to use. But SAS's steep learning curve and business focus have kept it beyond most criminal justice and criminology researchers.

STATA

Stata, created in the mid-1980s by StataCorp, is a powerful and versatile statistical package. The name "Stata" is an amalgam of "statistics" and "data." Stata works with a single window that is by default divided into four frames: one for output, one for commands, one for the list of variables, and another that keeps a logged history of all commands entered by the user. Users can adjust these frames as desired. Stata provides users with the option of using menus, like SPSS, or via typed in commands, similar yet distinct from SAS. The menu system has a slightly higher learning curve than that of SPSS, which can be understood as a benefit because users must be aware of exactly why they are doing what they are doing. In other words, it's more difficult to just "accept the default," which consequently pushes users to be better statisticians. The command prompt works in a way that is reminiscent of DOS or Unix: the user types in a string of words that tells Stata what to do. As soon as she hits the "enter" key, Stata runs the command. Like SAS, this has the advantage of helping the user know what's going on, but the language is not as explicit as SAS. It is, however, much more economical. For example, to call for a *t* test, we would type in the following command:

  ttest crime, by(gender)

And for a regression:

  regression crime gender iq lsc

A few things should be noted about the regression command. First, note that it is simply *assumed* that the first variable is the criterion. Second, because of its economy, Stata can make do with abbreviations. For example, we could just as correctly (and more easily) have called for this regression by typing in

  reg crime gender iq lsc

(Indeed, assuming that we had no other variables in our data set, we could also call for *reg c g i l*). Stata is a powerful tool and, after a certain rather steep learning curve, intuitive and elegant. One of its most noteworthy strengths is how customizable it is. Not only can users change visual preferences in turns of the GUI and the frames, but also they can change how the output is displayed. For example, an analyst can use a command option when calling for a regression that creates a table with *b* and *Beta* coefficients, standard errors, probabilities, and the ever ubiquitous "stars" (recall the journal tables we've displayed throughout the textbook). Perhaps most importantly, there are a number of freely available "add-ons" that have been independently developed that allow a wide range of options for social scientists. It is for this reason that Stata has become one of the preferred software packages for running what are known as multilevel mixed models and panel analyses.

R

The statistical program R is far from user-friendly. What it lacks in ease of use, however, it more than makes up for in flexibility, sophistication, and power. In short, it is the best statistical program out there for any function you are seeking. That's why R is popular among social scientists, hard scientists, educators, cartographers, and everyone in between. It is not really an exaggeration to say that if it can be done, R does it. For the student willing to deal with R's seemingly insurmountable learning curve, the view from the summit is endless. (One of the authors, while in graduate school, spent a three-day weekend locked in his office, refusing to leave until he had "figured out" R. He succeeded in learning how to open a file in R.)

With the base program, R has no GUI. Rather, it only has a command prompt. (A GUI add-on is available, however—see below for more information on this.) It is quite striking to open R up for the first time and be presented with nothing more than ">". It doesn't get any easier once you realize that there are multiple ways to do the same thing. This is because R is a completely open source—a GNU project based on the statistical language S. What this means, practically, is that you have several options from multiple programmers to do the same thing. For example, to run the *t* test from above, you could do either of the following commands:

```
t.test(y~x)
t.test(y,x)
```

To be frank, running simple statistics in R is sometimes frustrating. For example, to get essential and normally easily run frequency statistics, it is easier to download a special package designed for psychologists (*psych*). Because of R's GNU nature, users can create special "packages" designed to do specific things, from simple correlation matrices to complex spatial analytics. All of these are available free and with documentation. And it is all quite overwhelming, but the online R community is outstandingly helpful, and more statistical books are being written solely with R in mind, including code and links to specific R packages.

One of the greatest advantages of R is that it can read anything—whether the data were originally created in SPSS, Excel, or Notepad. What's more, you can *save* anything. For example, to run a multiple regression, you would use the following command (again, extending the example from above):

```
lm(crime~gender+iq+lsc)
```

You can save the *entire model output* and then *manipulate it in future commands* by saving it thusly:

   model1<-lm(crime~gender+iq+lsc)

Why might you want to do this? Let's say you run two regression models: the one above and this one:

   model2<-lm(crime~gender+iq+strain)

where "strain" measures certain stressors on the participant. Having saved the output, you can now compare the models to see if they behave equally well by calling for an *F* test:

   anova(model1,model2)

Being able to save output opens up a world of possibilities for statistics.

Let's look at that formula for OLS regression again and note the following things. First, it does not call for "reg" or "regression" like Stata; rather, it calls for *lm*, which stands for linear model. You might recall from the second half of this book and Appendix A that the LM is a family of statistics that each act the same. Thus, the call for an ANOVA is also *lm* because both regression and ANOVA belong to the LM family (the *anova* command specifically calls for an *F* test, as above). Second, note that the formula is just that, a formula: it is saying that a criterion is equal to the sum of its predictors. Compare the command for a regression above with the traditional regression formula:

$$y = \beta_0 + \Sigma(\beta_p X_p) + \epsilon$$

Can you see the connection between the two? In this fashion, R makes sure that you really do know what you're doing when running statistics.

Probably the best place to start with R is the website Quick R, by Robert Kabacoff (http://www.statmethods.net/), and John Fox's (2002) *An R and S-Plus Companion to Applied Regression*. Given that R is free and is where statistical analysis is trending in all the social sciences, it is worth the time to learn it.

CONCLUSION

The purpose of this primer was merely to provide you with an idea of what sorts of statistical software is out there and, in our opinion, most popular. There is much,

much more, however. For example, many criminologists and criminal justicians use MatLab or HLM. These statistical programs are specific in their purposes—which is quite common. If one is interested in spatial analysis, for example, one could use the various spatial packages created for R or download GeoDa. For SEM, one could use a package for SPSS or something like LISREL. It really all comes down to what you want to do, the level of flexibility you need, and the time and patience you possess. Admittedly, most packages do the same thing (at least, for basic probabilistic statistics—this is not true when we start running more sophisticated statistics, such as factor analysis); it's a matter of some doing it better or more economically than others. According to at least one study (published by Alan Acock in 2005 in the *Journal of Marriage and Family*), although SAS may have the widest variety of analytical functions, it is far from the easiest when compared to Stata and SPSS—although even these can be expanded through free add-ons, as mentioned above.

Regardless of which you choose, the key is to learn by doing. In fact, as you start to run statistics on a regular basis, you'll quickly learn how common it is to have to run them again and again and again—because you forgot one simple step, or something isn't quite working correctly, or something else you'd never expect. In this process, the Internet, with its multitude of help forums and YouTube videos, becomes essential. The amount of help available is one factor in determining which package you could use—but so is price point. SAS, SPSS, and Stata may be available from your university, but for personal use, they are exceptionally expensive. R, on the other hand, is completely free. This is only one reason why we believe that R is one package you should absolutely have somewhere in your statistical software repertoire.

REFERENCE

Fox, J. (2002). *An R and S-Plus companion to applied regression*. Thousand Oaks, CA: Sage.

Table of z Scores and Area under the Normal Curve

z/SD	0.00	0.01	0.02	0.03	0.04	0.05	0.06	0.07	0.08	0.09	
0.0	0.0000	0.0040	0.0080	0.0120	0.0160	0.0199	0.0239	0.0279	0.0319	0.0359	0.0
0.1	0.0398	0.0438	0.0478	0.0517	0.0557	0.0596	0.0636	0.0675	0.0714	0.0753	0.1
0.2	0.0793	0.0832	0.0871	0.0910	0.0948	0.0987	0.1026	0.1064	0.1103	0.1141	0.2
0.3	0.1179	0.1217	0.1255	0.1293	0.1331	0.1368	0.1406	0.1443	0.1480	0.1517	0.3
0.4	0.1554	0.1591	0.1628	0.1664	0.1700	0.1736	0.1772	0.1808	0.1844	0.1879	0.4
0.5	0.1915	0.1950	0.1985	0.2019	0.2054	0.2088	0.2123	0.2157	0.2190	0.2224	0.5
0.6	0.2257	0.2291	0.2324	0.2357	0.2389	0.2422	0.2454	0.2486	0.2517	0.2549	0.6
0.7	0.2580	0.2611	0.2642	0.2673	0.2704	0.2734	0.2764	0.2794	0.2823	0.2852	0.7
0.8	0.2881	0.2910	0.2939	0.2967	0.2995	0.3023	0.3051	0.3078	0.3106	0.3133	0.8
0.9	0.3159	0.3186	0.3212	0.3238	0.3264	0.3289	0.3315	0.3340	0.3365	0.3389	0.9
1.0	0.3413	0.3438	0.3461	0.3485	0.3508	0.3531	0.3554	0.3577	0.3599	0.3621	1.0
1.1	0.3643	0.3665	0.3686	0.3708	0.3729	0.3749	0.3770	0.3790	0.3810	0.3830	1.1
1.2	0.3849	0.3869	0.3888	0.3907	0.3925	0.3944	0.3962	0.3980	0.3997	0.4015	1.2
1.3	0.4032	0.4049	0.4066	0.4082	0.4099	0.4115	0.4131	0.4147	0.4162	0.4177	1.3
1.4	0.4192	0.4207	0.4222	0.4236	0.4251	0.4265	0.4279	0.4292	0.4306	0.4319	1.4
1.5	0.4332	0.4345	0.4357	0.4370	0.4382	0.4394	0.4406	0.4418	0.4429	0.4441	1.5
1.6	0.4452	0.4463	0.4474	0.4484	0.4495	0.4505	0.4515	0.4525	0.4535	0.4545	1.6
1.7	0.4554	0.4564	0.4573	0.4582	0.4591	0.4599	0.4608	0.4616	0.4625	0.4633	1.7
1.8	0.4641	0.4649	0.4656	0.4664	0.4671	0.4678	0.4686	0.4693	0.4699	0.4706	1.8
1.9	0.4713	0.4719	0.4726	0.4732	0.4738	0.4744	0.4750	0.4756	0.4761	0.4767	1.9
2.0	0.4772	0.4778	0.4783	0.4788	0.4793	0.4798	0.4803	0.4808	0.4812	0.4817	2.0
2.1	0.4821	0.4826	0.4830	0.4834	0.4838	0.4842	0.4846	0.4850	0.4854	0.4857	2.1
2.2	0.4861	0.4864	0.4868	0.4871	0.4875	0.4878	0.4881	0.4884	0.4887	0.4890	2.2
2.3	0.4893	0.4896	0.4898	0.4901	0.4904	0.4906	0.4909	0.4911	0.4913	0.4916	2.3
2.4	0.4918	0.4920	0.4922	0.4925	0.4927	0.4929	0.4931	0.4932	0.4934	0.4936	2.4
2.5	0.4938	0.4940	0.4941	0.4943	0.4945	0.4946	0.4948	0.4949	0.4951	0.4952	2.5
2.6	0.4953	0.4955	0.4956	0.4957	0.4959	0.4960	0.4961	0.4962	0.4963	0.4964	2.6
2.7	0.4965	0.4966	0.4967	0.4968	0.4969	0.4970	0.4971	0.4972	0.4973	0.4974	2.7
2.8	0.4974	0.4975	0.4976	0.4977	0.4977	0.4978	0.4979	0.4979	0.4980	0.4981	2.8
2.9	0.4981	0.4982	0.4982	0.4983	0.4984	0.4984	0.4985	0.4985	0.4986	0.4986	2.9
3.0	0.4987	0.4987	0.4987	0.4988	0.4988	0.4989	0.4989	0.4989	0.4990	0.4990	3.0
3.1	0.4990	0.4991	0.4991	0.4991	0.4992	0.4992	0.4992	0.4992	0.4993	0.4993	3.1
3.2	0.4993	0.4993	0.4994	0.4994	0.4994	0.4994	0.4994	0.4995	0.4995	0.4995	3.2
3.3	0.4995	0.4995	0.4995	0.4996	0.4996	0.4996	0.4996	0.4996	0.4996	0.4997	3.3
3.4	0.4997	0.4997	0.4997	0.4997	0.4997	0.4997	0.4997	0.4997	0.4997	0.4998	3.4
3.5	0.499767										
3.6	0.499841										
3.7	0.499892										
3.8	0.499928										
3.9	0.499952										
4.0	0.499968										
4.1	0.499979										
4.2	0.499987										
4.3	0.499991										
4.4	0.499995										
4.5	0.499997										
4.6	0.499998										
4.7	0.499999										
4.8	0.499999										
4.9	0.500000										

An example of ~ +1z area under the normal curve

z scores/standard deviation

Distribution of *t*

df	One-Tailed Test α / Two-Tailed Test α	0.10 / 0.20	0.05 / 0.10	0.025 / 0.05	0.01 / 0.02	0.005 / 0.01	0.0005 / 0.001	df
1		3.078	6.314	12.706	31.821	63.657	636.619	1
2		1.886	2.920	4.303	6.965	9.925	31.598	2
3		1.638	2.353	3.182	4.541	5.841	12.941	3
4		1.533	2.132	2.776	3.747	4.604	8.610	4
5		1.476	2.015	2.571	3.365	4.032	6.859	5
6		1.440	1.943	2.447	3.143	3.707	5.959	6
7		1.415	1.895	2.365	2.998	3.499	5.405	7
8		1.397	1.860	2.306	2.896	3.355	5.041	8
9		1.383	1.833	2.262	2.821	3.250	4.781	9
10		1.372	1.812	2.228	2.764	3.169	4.587	10
11		1.363	1.796	2.201	2.718	3.106	4.437	11
12		1.356	1.782	2.179	2.681	3.055	4.318	12
13		1.350	1.771	2.160	2.650	3.012	4.221	13
14		1.345	1.761	2.145	2.624	2.977	4.140	14
15		1.341	1.753	2.131	2.602	2.947	4.073	15
16		1.337	1.746	2.120	2.583	2.921	4.015	16
17		1.333	1.740	2.110	2.567	2.898	3.965	17
18		1.330	1.734	2.101	2.552	2.878	3.922	18
19		1.328	1.729	2.093	2.539	2.861	3.883	19
20		1.325	1.725	2.086	2.528	2.845	3.850	20
21		1.323	1.721	2.080	2.518	2.831	3.819	21
22		1.321	1.717	2.074	2.508	2.819	3.792	22
23		1.319	1.714	2.069	2.500	2.807	3.767	23
24		1.318	1.711	2.064	2.492	2.797	3.745	24
25		1.316	1.708	2.060	2.485	2.787	3.725	25
26		1.315	1.706	2.056	2.479	2.779	3.707	26
27		1.314	1.703	2.052	2.473	2.771	3.690	27
28		1.313	1.701	2.048	2.467	2.763	3.674	28
29		1.311	1.699	2.045	2.462	2.756	3.659	29
30		1.310	1.697	2.042	2.457	2.750	3.646	30
40		1.303	1.684	2.021	2.423	2.704	3.551	40
60		1.296	1.671	2.000	2.390	2.660	3.460	60
120		1.289	1.658	1.980	2.358	2.617	3.373	120
∞		1.282	1.645	1.960	2.326	2.576	3.291	∞

Distribution of F when $\alpha = 0.05$

df_2 (within)	df_1 (between)										df_2 (within)
	1	2	3	4	5	6	8	12	24	∞	
1	161.4	199.5	215.7	224.6	230.2	234.0	238.9	243.9	249.0	254.3	1
2	18.51	19.00	19.16	19.25	19.30	19.33	19.37	19.41	19.45	19.50	2
3	10.13	9.55	9.28	9.12	9.01	8.94	8.84	8.74	8.64	8.53	3
4	7.71	6.94	6.59	6.39	6.26	6.16	6.04	5.91	5.77	5.63	4
5	6.61	5.79	5.41	5.19	5.05	4.95	4.82	4.68	4.53	4.36	5
6	5.99	5.14	4.76	4.53	4.39	4.28	4.15	4.00	3.84	3.67	6
7	5.59	4.74	4.35	4.12	3.97	3.87	3.73	3.57	3.41	3.23	7
8	5.32	4.46	4.07	3.84	3.69	3.58	3.44	3.28	3.12	2.93	8
9	5.12	4.26	3.86	3.63	3.48	3.37	3.23	3.07	2.90	2.71	9
10	4.96	4.10	3.71	3.48	3.33	3.22	3.07	2.91	2.74	2.54	10
11	4.84	3.98	3.59	3.36	3.20	3.09	2.95	2.79	2.61	2.40	11
12	4.75	3.88	3.49	3.26	3.11	3.00	2.85	2.69	2.50	2.30	12
13	4.67	3.80	3.41	3.18	3.02	2.92	2.77	2.60	2.42	2.21	13
14	4.60	3.74	3.34	3.11	2.96	2.85	2.70	2.53	2.35	2.13	14
15	4.54	3.68	3.29	3.06	2.90	2.79	2.64	2.48	2.29	2.07	15
16	4.49	3.63	3.24	3.01	2.85	2.74	2.59	2.42	2.24	2.01	16
17	4.45	3.59	3.20	2.96	2.81	2.70	2.55	2.38	2.19	1.96	17
18	4.41	3.55	3.16	2.93	2.77	2.66	2.51	2.34	2.15	1.92	18
19	4.38	3.52	3.13	2.90	2.74	2.63	2.48	2.31	2.11	1.88	19
20	4.35	3.49	3.10	2.87	2.71	2.60	2.45	2.28	2.08	1.84	20
21	4.32	3.47	3.07	2.84	2.68	2.57	2.42	2.25	2.05	1.81	21
22	4.30	3.44	3.05	2.82	2.66	2.55	2.40	2.23	2.03	1.78	22
23	4.28	3.42	3.03	2.80	2.64	2.53	2.38	2.20	2.00	1.76	23
24	2.26	3.40	3.01	2.78	2.62	2.51	2.36	2.18	1.98	1.73	24
25	4.24	3.38	2.99	2.76	2.60	2.49	2.34	2.16	1.96	1.71	25
26	4.22	3.37	2.98	2.74	2.59	2.47	2.32	2.15	1.95	1.69	26
27	4.21	3.35	2.95	2.73	2.57	2.46	2.30	2.13	1.93	1.67	27
28	4.20	3.34	2.95	2.71	2.56	2.44	2.29	2.12	1.91	1.65	28
29	4.18	3.33	2.93	2.70	2.54	2.43	2.28	2.10	1.90	1.64	29
30	4.17	3.32	2.92	2.69	2.53	2.42	2.27	2.09	1.89	1.62	30
40	4.08	3.23	2.84	2.61	2.45	2.34	2.18	2.00	1.79	1.51	40
60	4.00	3.15	2.76	2.52	2.37	2.25	2.10	1.92	1.70	1.39	60
120	3.92	3.07	2.68	2.45	2.29	2.17	2.02	1.83	1.61	1.25	120
∞	3.84	2.99	2.60	2.37	2.21	2.09	1.94	1.75	1.52	1.00	∞

Distribution of F when $\alpha = 0.01$

					df_1 (between)						
df_2 (within)	1	2	3	4	5	6	8	12	24	∞	df_2 (within)
1	4052	4999	5403	5625	5764	5859	5981	6106	6234	6366	1
2	98.49	99.01	99.17	99.25	99.30	99.33	99.36	99.42	99.46	99.50	2
3	34.12	30.81	29.46	28.71	28.24	27.91	27.49	27.05	26.60	26.12	3
4	21.20	18.00	16.69	15.98	15.52	15.21	14.80	14.37	13.93	13.46	4
5	16.26	13.27	12.06	11.39	10.97	10.67	10.27	9.89	9.47	9.02	5
6	13.74	10.92	9.78	9.15	8.75	8.47	8.10	7.72	7.31	6.88	6
7	12.25	9.55	8.45	7.85	7.46	7.19	6.84	6.47	6.07	5.65	7
8	11.26	8.65	7.59	7.01	6.63	6.37	6.03	5.67	5.28	4.86	8
9	10.56	8.02	6.99	6.42	6.06	5.80	5.47	5.11	4.73	4.31	9
10	10.04	7.56	6.55	5.99	5.64	5.39	5.06	4.71	4.33	3.91	10
11	9.65	7.20	6.22	5.67	5.32	5.07	4.74	4.40	4.02	3.60	11
12	9.33	6.93	5.95	5.41	5.06	4.82	4.50	4.16	3.78	3.36	12
13	9.07	6.70	5.74	5.20	4.86	4.62	4.30	3.96	3.59	3.16	13
14	8.86	6.51	5.56	5.03	4.69	4.46	4.14	3.80	3.43	3.00	14
15	8.68	6.36	5.42	4.89	4.56	4.32	4.00	3.67	3.29	2.87	15
16	8.53	6.23	5.29	4.77	4.44	4.20	3.89	3.55	3.18	2.75	16
17	8.40	6.11	5.18	4.67	4.34	4.10	3.79	3.45	3.08	2.65	17
18	8.28	6.01	5.09	4.58	4.25	4.01	3.71	3.37	3.00	2.57	18
19	8.18	5.93	5.01	4.50	4.17	3.94	3.63	3.30	2.92	2.49	19
20	8.10	5.85	4.94	4.43	4.10	3.87	3.56	3.23	2.86	2.42	20
21	8.02	5.78	4.87	4.37	4.04	3.81	3.51	3.17	2.80	2.36	21
22	7.94	5.72	4.82	4.31	3.99	3.76	3.45	3.12	2.75	2.31	22
23	7.88	5.66	4.76	4.23	3.94	3.71	3.41	3.07	2.70	2.26	23
24	7.82	5.61	4.72	4.22	3.90	3.67	3.36	3.03	2.66	2.21	24
25	7.77	5.57	4.68	4.18	3.86	3.63	3.32	2.99	2.62	2.17	25
26	7.72	5.53	4.64	4.14	3.82	3.56	3.29	2.96	2.58	2.13	26
27	7.68	5.49	4.60	4.11	3.78	3.56	3.26	2.93	2.55	2.10	27
28	7.64	5.45	4.57	4.07	3.75	3.53	3.23	2.90	2.52	2.06	28
29	7.60	5.42	4.54	4.04	3.73	3.50	3.20	2.87	2.49	2.03	29
30	7.56	5.39	4.51	4.02	3.70	3.47	3.17	2.84	2.47	2.01	30
40	7.31	5.18	4.31	3.83	3.51	3.29	2.99	2.66	2.29	1.80	40
60	7.08	4.98	4.13	3.65	3.34	3.12	2.82	2.50	2.12	1.60	60
120	6.85	4.79	3.95	3.48	3.17	2.96	2.66	2.34	1.95	1.38	120
∞	6.64	4.60	3.78	3.32	3.02	2.80	2.51	2.18	1.79	1.00	∞

Distribution of Chi Square (χ^2)

df	0.995	0.975	0.9	0.5	0.1	0.05	0.025	0.01	0.005	0.001	df
					ALPHA LEVELS						
1	0.000	0.001	0.016	0.455	2.706	3.841	5.024	6.635	7.879	10.828	1
2	0.010	0.051	0.211	1.386	4.605	5.991	7.378	9.210	10.597	13.816	2
3	0.072	0.216	0.584	2.366	6.251	7.815	9.348	11.345	12.838	16.266	3
4	0.207	0.484	1.064	3.357	7.779	9.488	11.143	13.277	14.860	18.467	4
5	0.412	0.831	1.610	4.351	9.236	11.070	12.833	15.086	16.750	20.515	5
6	0.676	1.237	2.204	5.348	10.645	12.592	14.449	16.812	18.548	22.458	6
7	0.989	1.690	2.833	6.346	12.017	14.067	16.013	18.475	20.278	24.322	7
8	1.344	2.180	3.490	7.344	13.362	15.507	17.535	20.090	21.955	26.124	8
9	1.735	2.700	4.168	8.343	14.684	16.919	19.023	21.666	23.589	27.877	9
10	2.156	3.247	4.865	9.342	15.987	18.307	20.483	23.209	25.188	29.588	10
11	2.603	3.816	5.578	10.341	17.275	19.675	21.920	24.725	26.757	31.264	11
12	3.074	4.404	6.304	11.340	18.549	21.026	23.337	26.217	28.300	32.909	12
13	3.565	5.009	7.042	12.340	19.812	22.362	24.736	27.688	29.819	34.528	13
14	4.075	5.629	7.790	13.339	21.064	23.685	26.119	29.141	31.319	36.123	14
15	4.601	6.262	8.547	14.339	22.307	24.996	27.488	30.578	32.801	37.697	15
16	5.142	6.908	9.312	15.338	23.542	26.296	28.845	32.000	34.267	39.252	16
17	5.697	7.564	10.085	16.338	24.769	27.587	30.191	33.409	35.718	40.790	17
18	6.265	8.231	10.865	17.338	25.989	28.869	31.526	34.805	37.156	42.312	18
19	6.844	8.907	11.651	18.338	27.204	30.144	32.852	36.191	38.582	43.820	19
20	7.434	9.591	12.443	19.337	28.412	31.410	34.170	37.566	39.997	45.315	20
21	8.034	10.283	13.240	20.337	29.615	32.671	35.479	38.932	41.401	46.797	21
22	8.643	10.982	14.041	21.337	30.813	33.924	36.781	40.289	42.796	48.268	22
23	9.260	11.689	14.848	22.337	32.007	35.172	38.076	41.638	44.181	49.728	23
24	9.886	12.401	15.659	23.337	33.196	36.415	39.364	42.980	45.559	51.179	24
25	10.520	13.120	16.473	24.337	34.382	37.652	40.646	44.314	46.928	52.620	25
26	11.160	13.844	17.292	25.336	35.563	38.885	41.923	45.642	48.290	54.052	26
27	11.808	14.573	18.114	26.336	36.741	40.113	43.195	46.963	49.645	55.476	27
28	12.461	15.308	18.939	27.336	37.916	41.337	44.461	48.278	50.993	56.892	28
29	13.121	16.047	19.768	28.336	39.087	42.557	45.722	49.588	52.336	58.301	29
30	13.787	16.791	20.599	29.336	40.256	43.773	46.979	50.892	53.672	59.703	30
31	14.458	17.539	21.434	30.336	41.422	44.985	48.232	52.191	55.003	61.098	31
32	15.134	18.291	22.271	31.336	42.585	46.194	49.480	53.486	56.328	62.487	32
33	15.815	19.047	23.110	32.336	43.745	47.400	50.725	54.776	57.648	63.870	33
34	16.501	19.806	23.952	33.336	44.903	48.602	51.966	56.061	58.964	65.247	34
35	17.192	20.569	24.797	34.336	46.059	49.802	53.203	57.342	60.275	66.619	35

(Continued)

	ALPHA LEVELS										
df	0.995	0.975	0.9	0.5	0.1	0.05	0.025	0.01	0.005	0.001	df
36	17.887	21.336	25.643	35.336	47.212	50.998	54.437	58.619	61.581	67.985	36
37	18.586	22.106	26.492	36.336	48.363	52.192	55.668	59.893	62.883	69.346	37
38	19.289	22.878	27.343	37.335	49.513	53.384	56.896	61.162	64.181	70.703	38
39	19.996	23.654	28.196	38.335	50.660	54.572	58.120	62.428	65.476	72.055	39
40	20.707	24.433	29.051	39.335	51.805	55.758	59.342	63.691	66.766	73.402	40
41	21.421	25.215	29.907	40.335	52.949	56.942	60.561	64.950	68.053	74.745	41
42	22.138	25.999	30.765	41.335	54.090	58.124	61.777	66.206	69.336	76.084	42
43	22.859	26.785	31.625	42.335	55.230	59.304	62.990	67.459	70.616	77.419	43
44	23.584	27.575	32.487	43.335	56.369	60.481	64.201	68.710	71.893	78.750	44
45	24.311	28.366	33.350	44.335	57.505	61.656	65.410	69.957	73.166	80.077	45
46	25.041	29.160	34.215	45.335	58.641	62.830	66.617	71.201	74.437	81.400	46
47	25.775	29.956	35.081	46.335	59.774	64.001	67.821	72.443	75.704	82.720	47
48	26.511	30.755	35.949	47.335	60.907	65.171	69.023	73.683	76.969	84.037	48
49	27.249	31.555	36.818	48.335	62.038	66.339	70.222	74.919	78.231	85.351	49
50	27.991	32.357	37.689	49.335	63.167	67.505	71.420	76.154	79.490	86.661	50
51	28.735	33.162	38.560	50.335	64.295	68.669	72.616	77.386	80.747	87.968	51
52	29.481	33.968	39.433	51.335	65.422	69.832	73.810	78.616	82.001	89.272	52
53	30.230	34.776	40.308	52.335	66.548	70.993	75.002	79.843	83.253	90.573	53
54	30.981	35.586	41.183	53.335	67.673	72.153	76.192	81.069	84.502	91.872	54
55	31.735	36.398	42.060	54.335	68.796	73.311	77.380	82.292	85.749	93.168	55
56	32.490	37.212	42.937	55.335	69.919	74.468	78.567	83.513	86.994	94.461	56
57	33.248	38.027	43.816	56.335	71.040	75.624	79.752	84.733	88.236	95.751	57
58	34.008	38.844	44.696	57.335	72.160	76.778	80.936	85.950	89.477	97.039	58
59	34.770	39.662	45.577	58.335	73.279	77.931	82.117	87.166	90.715	98.324	59
60	35.534	40.482	46.459	59.335	74.397	79.082	83.298	88.379	91.952	99.607	60
61	36.301	41.303	47.342	60.335	75.514	80.232	84.476	89.591	93.186	100.888	61
62	37.068	42.126	48.226	61.335	76.630	81.381	85.654	90.802	94.419	102.166	62
63	37.838	42.950	49.111	62.335	77.745	82.529	86.830	92.010	95.649	103.442	63
64	38.610	43.776	49.996	63.335	78.860	83.675	88.004	93.217	96.878	104.716	64
65	39.383	44.603	50.883	64.335	79.973	84.821	89.177	94.422	98.105	105.988	65
66	40.158	45.431	51.770	65.335	81.085	85.965	90.349	95.626	99.330	107.258	66
67	40.935	46.261	52.659	66.335	82.197	87.108	91.519	96.828	100.554	108.526	67
68	41.713	47.092	53.548	67.335	83.308	88.250	92.689	98.028	101.776	109.791	68
69	42.494	47.924	54.438	68.334	84.418	89.391	93.856	99.228	102.996	111.055	69
70	43.275	48.758	55.329	69.334	85.527	90.531	95.023	100.425	104.215	112.317	70
71	44.058	49.592	56.221	70.334	86.635	91.670	96.189	101.621	105.432	113.577	71
72	44.843	50.428	57.113	71.334	87.743	92.808	97.353	102.816	106.648	114.835	72
73	45.629	51.265	58.006	72.334	88.850	93.945	98.516	104.010	107.862	116.092	73
74	46.417	52.103	58.900	73.334	89.956	95.081	99.678	105.202	109.074	117.346	74
75	47.206	52.942	59.795	74.334	91.061	96.217	100.839	106.393	110.286	118.599	75
76	47.997	53.782	60.690	75.334	92.166	97.351	101.999	107.583	111.495	119.850	76
77	48.788	54.623	61.586	76.334	93.270	98.484	103.158	108.771	112.704	121.100	77
78	49.582	55.466	62.483	77.334	94.374	99.617	104.316	109.958	113.911	122.348	78
79	50.376	56.309	63.380	78.334	95.476	100.749	105.473	111.144	115.117	123.594	79
80	51.172	57.153	64.278	79.334	96.578	101.879	106.629	112.329	116.321	124.839	80

(Continued)

df	0.995	0.975	0.9	0.5	0.1	0.05	0.025	0.01	0.005	0.001	df
					ALPHA LEVELS						
81	51.969	57.998	65.176	80.334	97.680	103.010	107.783	113.512	117.524	126.083	81
82	52.767	58.845	66.076	81.334	98.780	104.139	108.937	114.695	118.726	127.324	82
83	53.567	59.692	66.976	82.334	99.880	105.267	110.090	115.876	119.927	128.565	83
84	54.368	60.540	67.876	83.334	100.980	106.395	111.242	117.057	121.126	129.804	84
85	55.170	61.389	68.777	84.334	102.079	107.522	112.393	118.236	122.325	131.041	85
86	55.973	62.239	69.679	85.334	103.177	108.648	113.544	119.414	123.522	132.277	86
87	56.777	63.089	70.581	86.334	104.275	109.773	114.693	120.591	124.718	133.512	87
88	57.582	63.941	71.484	87.334	105.372	110.898	115.841	121.767	125.913	134.745	88
89	58.389	64.793	72.387	88.334	106.469	112.022	116.989	122.942	127.106	135.978	89
90	59.196	65.647	73.291	89.334	107.565	113.145	118.136	124.116	128.299	137.208	90
91	60.005	66.501	74.196	90.334	108.661	114.268	119.282	125.289	129.491	138.438	91
92	60.815	67.356	75.100	91.334	109.756	115.390	120.427	126.462	130.681	139.666	92
93	61.625	68.211	76.006	92.334	110.850	116.511	121.571	127.633	131.871	140.893	93
94	62.437	69.068	76.912	93.334	111.944	117.632	122.715	128.803	133.059	142.119	94
95	63.250	69.925	77.818	94.334	113.038	118.752	123.858	129.973	134.247	143.344	95
96	64.063	70.783	78.725	95.334	114.131	119.871	125.000	131.141	135.433	144.567	96
97	64.878	71.642	79.633	96.334	115.223	120.990	126.141	132.309	136.619	145.789	97
98	65.694	72.501	80.541	97.334	116.315	122.108	127.282	133.476	137.803	147.010	98
99	66.510	73.361	81.449	98.334	117.407	123.225	128.422	134.642	138.987	148.230	99
100	67.328	74.222	82.358	99.334	118.498	124.342	129.561	135.807	140.169	149.449	100

Glossary

Addition Rule: A rule of probability used to calculate the probability of one of several events occurring. It takes the general form of $P(A|B) = P(A) + P(B)$.

Alpha Level: The probability that our statistics are representative of the population parameters.

Alternative (H_1): Opposite of the null hypothesis. If the sample results can be shown not to be a function of sampling error, we can reject the null hypothesis. Also called the *research hypothesis*.

Analysis of Variance (ANOVA): A statistical model that allows us to compare the means between two or more categories.

Antecedent Variable: A variable that precedes both the dependent and the independent variables in time, but associated with the overall causal model.

Association: When two or more variables are related, such that as one changes, we observe a change in the other(s).

Between-Group Variance: The variance that is explained by the grouped or categorized independent variable.

Binary Variable: Also called a *dichotomous variable*. A categorical variable in which there are only two options.

Binomial Distribution: The frequency of the joint probabilities of two events. Generally normally distributed.

Categorical Variable: A variable that is not continuous; a variable that can only be described in terms of categories with no mathematical characteristics, such as "black, white, or Asian."

Census: Data on an entire population; that is, a complete tabulation of some characteristics of interest from all elements in a population.

Central Limit Theorem: A complex theorem on which all probability statistics are based; it allows us to make a conclusion about a population based on a sample. Further, it suggests that as our sample sizes increase in size, their distribution approaches normality, even if the population itself is not normally distributed.

Chi Square: One of a number of tests of significance and measures of association known as nonparametric statistics.

Chi Square Distribution: A positive distribution whose shape is entirely determined by the degrees of freedom; it becomes more symmetrical as the degrees of freedom increase and begins to look like the normal curve when *df* is greater than 30.

Chi Square Test of Independence: A test of significance that is used for categorical data in the form of frequencies or proportions.

Classical Probability: Probability based on *a priori* knowledge of all possible outcomes. Outcomes each have an equal numerical chance of occurring.

Conceptual Definition: A statement that relates our understanding of what any given variable "is" to another person.

Conditional Distribution: A distribution wherein the distribution of frequencies of the first variable depends on the distribution of frequencies of the second variable.

Conditional Odds: Odds that depend on the presence of the independent variable.

Confidence Interval (CI): A range of values constructed around a statistic. Usually takes the form of "a value of x, $\pm p$."

Constant: Any "variable" that does not vary from case to case.

Contingency Coefficient (C): A measurement of effect size appropriate for nominal and ordinal variables having more than two categories. One limitation is that its upper range depends on the size of the table (i.e., it is unstandardized).

Continuous Variable: A variable that can theoretically take on any value between two points on a scale and be classified according to the magnitude and quantity of their characteristics.

Control Variable: Any variable that is not of interest to the researcher, but necessary to include in both the research design and statistical models so that all variation can be explained and threats to internal validity can be avoided.

Correlation: A measurement of association for two continuous variables that describes the strength and the direction of the relationship. Pearson's r is the most common correlation coefficient.

Count Data: Data that are enumerated from 0 to infinite that literally *count* the occurrence of something. Typically, count data distributions are heavily skewed to the right, with many 0's and 1's.

Covariance: The joint variation of two sets of scores from their respective means; the more the two variables covary, the stronger their statistical relationship will be.

Criterion Variable: A term used in regression to describe the dependent variable.

Critical Value: See *alpha level*.

Curves: A term used to describe the histograms of continuous variables.

Data (singular Datum): A set of numerical scores relating to the phenomenon under investigation; a piece of numerical information we can combine with other pieces of numerical information and submit this collection of datum to statistical analysis.

Deductive: A logical process wherein the researcher considers specific cases in light of general propositions.

Degrees of Freedom (df): Restrictions placed on data that indicate the number of ways the data can vary; usually the size of the sample(s) minus the number of parameters being estimated.

Dependent Variable: A variable that *depends* on the value of another variable or variables for its own values; a variable that is affected by independent variables.

Descriptive Statistics: Information that can be organized and presented in simple and direct ways; univariate statistics that do not involve any inferences or generalizations.

Deviation Score: A raw score minus the distribution's mean.

Dichotomous Variable: A variable with only two options, e.g., "yes or no."

Discrete Variables: Variables that are not numerical, but descriptive (i.e., nominal and ordinal). See *Categorical Variable*.

Distribution: A way to arrange data by frequency; often visualized as a histogram.

Effect Size: A way to measure how closely two variables are related.

Efficient Estimate: A statistic with minimal variance that expresses maximum information.

Empirical Probability: Probability that is calculated using observations rather than *a priori* knowledge.

Error: The degree to which our estimate is off; the extent to which our statistics do not reflect the parameter.

Error Sum of Squares: The final total error in an ANOVA model.

Explanation: Whenever a relationship between two variables is spurious due to the presence of an antecedent third variable.

F distribution: A test for the significance of the ANOVA variance ratios; varies in shape according to the number of degrees of freedom used in calculation and begins to look something like the normal curve as *df* increases; always remains positively skewed.

F ratio: Used in ANOVA models; describes the ratio of the *mean square within* to the *mean square between*.

First-Order Partial Relationship: An operation that examines the bivariate relationship between the independent and dependent variables under one control variable.

Fitting the Line: Drawing a straight line through the cluster of dots on a scatterplot so that the line comes as close as possible to touching every dot. Also known as a "regression line."

Frequency Distribution: Arranging the data according to category and frequency. See also *distribution*.

Frequency Table: A tabular explanation of a frequency distribution, such that the number of occurrences for each category is enumerated.

Gamma: An effect size that ranges between −1.0 and +1.0 for categorical variables; compares similar pairs of scores with dissimilar pairs, but ignores tied pairs.

Generalized Linear Model: A suite of statistical equations, each of which attempts to convert a nonlinear dependent variable to a linear distribution and then applies the linear model.

Grand Mean: The mean of the means of all groups in an ANOVA.

Histograms: A graphed distribution which helps us visualize a frequency distribution.

Hypothesis: A testable statement about the relationship between or among the variables that are to be studied.

Hypothesis Testing: The process of calculating the probability that we can recreate any hypothesized relationships by mere chance.

Independent Variable: The variable on which the dependent variable "depends" for its values; it is considered to vary "randomly."

Inferential Statistics: Statistical techniques that enable us to make inferences or generalizations about a large group of subjects or objects called a population on the basis of data taken from a subset of that population called a sample.

Interpretation: A term used in some statistical textbooks to describe a mediating relationship: an outcome that occurs when the initial relationship between two variables is rendered nonsignificant by an intervening third variable.

Interquartile Range (IQR): The score of the 75th percentile minus the score of the 25th percentile in a distribution.

Interval Estimate: A range of values within a sample estimating a range of values in a population; in contrast to a *point estimate*.

Interval Level: Variables that can be classified and ranked, but also have equal units of measurement between classes; interval-level variables are distinguished from ratio-level variables by the absence of an absolute zero.

Kurtosis: A measure of the relative peakedness of a curve. It is measured using a scale where the closer to 0.0 the distribution is, the more normal is its kurtosis. If a curve's kurtosis is positive, the curve is more peaked or narrow than the normal curve; if it is negative, it is flatter than the normal curve.

Lambda: An asymmetrical measure of association with values ranging between 0.0 and 1.0; it is best suited to distributions in which both variables are measured at the nominal level. It is also useful for gaining a grasp of the concept of *proportional reduction in error* because it uses the general formula for PRE.

Leptokurtic Curve: A curve that is tall and thin relative to the theoretical normal curve, indicating a small amount of variation around the mean.

Levels of Measurement: The way a variable is measured; either *categorically* (nominal or ordinal) or *continuously* (ratio and interval).

Logistic Regression: A probabilistic statistical model that is used to predict a binary outcome; part of the family of statistical models known as the *generalized linear model*.

Main Effect: The non-interactive effect of one variable on another variable, net of controls.

Mean: A measure of central tendency that most of us think about when we hear the term *average*; the average of a distribution of scores.

Mean Square (*MS*): The ANOVA term for variance.

Means of Means: The mean of the distribution of sample means.

Measure of Association: A statistic that quantifies the degree to which two variables are related, linked, or associated. Chi square and Pearson's *r* are the most common.

Measures of Dispersion: A family of statistics that indicates the degree to which values within a distribution differ from each other; most commonly the standard deviation, but also the range, variance, and variation.

Median (*Md*): A score in a data array that divides the distribution into two equal parts; the middle score of a set of scores that have been arranged from lowest to highest.

Mediating Relationship: Used to describe the relationship between two variables that can be explained by the presence of a third, intervening variable. Also see *interpretation*.

Mesokurtic Curve: A curve with a normal scatter of observations about its mean (i.e., a normal curve's kurtosis).

Misspecification: The omission of crucial explanatory variables from the model.

Mode (*Mo*): The score that occurs most frequently in a distribution of scores. It is possible to have more than one mode in a frequency distribution; in such cases the distribution is bimodal or even multimodal.

Moderating Relationship: Used to describe the relationship between two variables that can be explained by the presence of a third, preceding variable. Also see *explanation*.

Multiple Correlation Coefficient: The combined effects of a set of independent variables on the dependent variable; it can give us an idea of how well the statistical model fits the data; often referred to as a goodness-of-fit statistic (e.g., R^2).

Multiple Regression: Sometimes referred to as multivariate regression. This is a basic tool for evaluating the overall dependence of a variable on a set of independent variables.

Multiplication Rule: A rule of probability used to calculate the probability of several events co-occurring. It takes the general form of $P(A \text{ and } B) = P(A)P(B)$.

Necessary and Sufficient Cause: A cause that (a) must be present for the effect to occur and (b) is the only cause needed for the effect to occur.

Necessary Cause: A cause or condition that must be present for an effect to follow; if A is not present, there is no known incident in which B has occurred.

Negative Association: A relationship where the values of two variables move in opposite directions but in relation to each other. Thus as one variable increases, the other variable would decrease. Sometimes called an inverse relationship or association.

Negative-Binomial Distribution: A count distribution appropriate for hypothesis testing; especially appropriate when the distribution is overdispersed.

Nominal Level: A level of measurement for purely categorical variables where the values have no mathematical qualities nor can they be ranked.

Nominal Outcome: Any outcome that can be measured at the nominal level. Unlike binary outcomes, which are a subset of nominal outcomes, nominal outcomes can take on more than two categories.

Nonparametric: A statistic that does not ultimately consider the population.

Nonparametric Test: A less restrictive hypothesis test when compared to parametric tests, but also less powerful than parametric tests and with a slightly larger probability of type II error. Appropriate for when nothing can be assumed about the population under examination.

Normal Curve: The graphical representation, in histogram form, of a perfectly symmetrical distribution where the mean, mode, and median are all equal and where the skew is equal to 0.

Normal Distribution: A perfectly symmetrical distribution where the mean, mode, and median are all equal and where the skew is equal to 0.

Null Hypothesis (H_0): A test of no difference and the standard against which all hypothesis tests are run. The "goal" of hypothesis testing is to see whether one is able to reject the probability of the null hypothesis as being true.

Odds Ratio: An easy way to interpret odds; literally, the odds of an event occurring against the odds of another event occurring (or of the first event not occurring). The most common standardized coefficient in the generalized linear model.

One-Tailed Test: Also called a "directional test." Conducted when there are theoretical reasons for expecting a difference in a particular direction. Less conservative than two-tailed hypothesis tests.

Operational Definition: The definition of a concept in terms of how it is to be measured.

Operationalization: A variable's *operational definition*.

Ordinal Level: A categorical level of measurement where each category can be rank ordered, but there is no intrinsic mathematical distance between the categories.

Ordinal Outcome: An outcome that is ordinal in its level of measurement.

Paired Cases: Cases in a data set that are somehow attached to other cases (e.g., observations taken at time 1 and time 2 on the same person on the same variable).

Parameters: A measurable value of a population; typically unknown but estimated via statistics.

Partial Correlation: An estimate of the correlation between two variables in a population with the effects of one or more other variables controlled for, or partialed out (i.e., the correlation between y and x uncontaminated by v, w, and so on); tends to eliminate overlap and gives us a more valid association between the variables.

Partial Gamma: Similar to a partial correlation but for tabular data; obtained by combining separate computations from each of several conditional tables into a single measure of association.

Pearson Correlation Coefficient (r): A way to measure the strength of association between two continuous variables. Standardized between -1 and $+1$ and shows both strength and direction of the association.

Percentages: The most basic way to standardize raw numbers for comparison. Typically is calculated by dividing a part by its whole and then multiplying this by 100.

Platykurtic Curve: A curve that is wide and flat relative to the theoretical normal curve, indicating a great deal of variation around the mean.

Point Estimate: A singular value from a sample estimating a singular value in a population; as opposed to an *interval estimate*.

Poisson Distribution: A count distribution used for the generalized linear model; appropriate when the count is not overdispersed (i.e., when the standard deviation is not larger than the mean).

Population: A large group of subjects or objects about which a researcher wishes to make inferences using statistics.

Positive Association: A relationship where the values of two variables move in the same direction in relation to each other, such that as one increases, so too does the other, or as one decreases, so too does the other.

Predictor Variable: A term used to describe independent and control variables in a regression equation.

Probabilistic Statistics: A method for inferring facts about a population from a sample using the rules of probability.

Probability: The likelihood of an event occurring.

Proportional Reduction in Error (PRE): The reduction of errors made as we move from predicting scores on the dependent variable without knowing the distribution of the independent variable, to predicting scores on the dependent variable knowing how the independent variable is distributed.

Range: The simplest measure of dispersion, often measured as the difference between the lowest and highest scores in the distribution. Sometimes 1 is added to this value; other times it is presented descriptively, as "the range is n to p."

Ratio Level: A continuous level of measurement that is distinguished not only by having meaningful distances between each unit, but also by having an absolute 0. All mathematical operations are possible with ratio level data.

Regression: A suite of statistical techniques that help us partial out the effects or association of multiple variables on a single variable.

Regression Line: A line drawn between the joint distribution (i.e., a *scatterplot*) of two variables in such a way as to come closest to all co-occurring points.

Regression Slopes: The b coefficients in a regression equation, also known as the algebraic "rise and run"; indicate how much the dependent variable will change on average given a one unit change in the independent variable.

Reliability: The consistency with which repeated measures produce the same results across time and observers.

Replication: In statistical parlance, whenever a mediating or moderating relationship can be ruled out because the relationship between the independent and dependent variables does not change whenever a third variable is introduced.

Residuals: The error made in predicting the dependent variable when we have knowledge of the distribution of the independent variable.

Robust: A statistical model is *robust* if it can yet provide accurate results even when its assumptions are violated.

Sample: A subset of the population.

Sample Statistics: Numbers used to estimate population parameters, typically using probability statistics.

Sampling Distribution of Means: A frequency distribution of all possible unique sample means of a constant sample size that we could draw from the same population.

Sampling Error: The difference between a sample statistic and its corresponding population parameter.

Sampling Frame: An exhaustive list of all members of the population that have an equal probability of being selected.

Scatterplot: A graphical representation of the strength of association between two variables.

Scheffé Test: A method of determining which means differ in an ANOVA model; it is the most conservative method because it yields fewer significantly different pairs than other methods; further, it is the most versatile method because it can be used with unbalanced designs.

Second-Order Partial Relationship: An operation that examines the basic bivariate relationship under the conditions of two control variables.

Second-Order Partials: The coefficient derived from a *second-order partial relationship*.

Simple Random Sampling: The ideal method of achieving representativeness in a sample.

Skewed: The degree to which a distribution leans to the left or right. Curves that are skewed are not considered normal.

Slope: The vertical distance divided by the horizontal distance between any two points on the line. In regression, typically understood as the *b* coefficient.

Somer's *d*: An asymmetrical measure of association that is more restrictive than other similar measures in that it takes into account pairs that are tied on the dependent variable.

Spearman's Rank Order Correlation (rho): A measurement of association that is ideal for two variables with values that have been ordered into ranks on a case-by-case basis. Rho ranges from −1 to +1.

Specification: In statistical parlance, a relationship between variables that is being driven by a third variable that the researcher can manipulate.

Spuriousness: Occurs when the relationship between the independent and dependent variables is explained away by either an intervening or an antecedent third variable.

Standard Deviation: The average deviation score from the mean among all values in a distribution.

Standard Error: The standard deviation of the sampling distribution; it represents error resulting from sampling variation and is equal to the sample standard deviation divided by the square root of the sample size.

Standard Error of the Estimate: A statistic for assessing the accuracy of predictions; informs you of the average prediction error in predicting *y* from *x*.

Standard Normal Curve: A special case of the normal distribution curve that has a mean of zero and a standard deviation of 1.

Standardize: To render a number comparable to other numbers of different scales.

Standardized Beta: A coefficient used in regression models that indicates how many standard deviations the dependent variable changes given a one standard deviation change in an independent variable.

Standardized Partial Regression Slope: Indicates the average standard deviation change in the dependent variable associated with a standard deviation change in the independent variable, holding constant all other variables in the equation.

Standardized Slope: Indicates the change (increase or decrease) in the dependent variable in standard deviation units per standard deviation change in the independent variable; allows for a determination of which predictor has the strongest impact on the criterion. The standard way of measuring strength of association in regression; typically assigned the Greek letter β.

Statistics: Numbers that allow us to analyze, evaluate, and summarize large quantities of data and that represent some form of reality; in addition, statistics allow us to rule out the possibility that any relationship we might observe between two variables is actually chance.

Stratified Random Sampling: Subdivides a heterogeneous population into homogeneous subsets (*strata*) and randomly selects cases from each subset as in simple random sampling. Particularly useful when one wants to oversample a marginalized or small population.

Sufficient Cause: A cause or condition that by itself is able to produce an event; if other causal agents are needed to augment the nominated cause, it is not a sufficient cause.

Sum of Squares: A measure of dispersion calculated by summing the distribution's squared deviation scores.

Suppressor Variable: A variable that hides the true relationship between variables.

***t* test:** A basic parametric test of the difference between two means on a single variable.

Tau *b*: A nonparametric measurement of association that is even more restrictive than Somer's *d*; it includes pairs tied on the independent variable but not on the dependent variable and pairs tied on the dependent variable but not on the independent variable; it is appropriately used when the number of rows and columns in a table is equal.

Total Sum of Squares: The total value of all squared deviation scores from the grand mean in an ANOVA.

Two-Tailed Test: Also known as a nondirectional test. A hypothesis test conducted when researchers have no theoretical reason to believe that one group should have a mean greater or less than the other. More conservative (and conventional) than the one-tailed test.

Two-Way ANOVA: An ANOVA model that examines the partial effects of two independent variables on the dependent variable.

Type I error: Also known as alpha (α) error; wrongly rejecting a true null hypothesis.

Type II error: Also known as beta (β) error; failing to reject a false null hypothesis.

Unbiased Estimate: A statistic that is equal to the population parameter it estimates.

Unexplained Variance: Also called the sum of squared residuals. The variation in the dependent variable that cannot be explained even with knowledge of the independent variable.

Unit of Analysis: What a researcher is analyzing (often with probabilistic statistics) as opposed to what they are observing.

Unstandardized Partial Regression Slope: A coefficient that indicates the amount of change in the dependent variable per unit change in the independent variable, controlling for the effects of all other independent variables in the equation.

Validity: How well measures derived from an operation reflect a concept; we essentially ask ourselves the question, are we measuring what we intend to measure?

Variables: Observations that we can measure that refer to anything that can change in value from case to case (that is, can vary).

Variance: The difference in the values from case to case.

Within-Group Variance: The unexplained variance that results from the proportion of the variance that cannot be accounted for by one's group; that is, the variance that exists within a group is independent of any influence outside of that group. This variance is considered random.

Yates's Correction for Continuity: Used to calculate chi-square whenever expected values drop below 5 for any cell in the "expected" table.

Y-Intercept/Constant: The point at which the slope intersects the y-axis.

Z score: A method of tying the theoretical probability distribution to empirical raw scores. Equal to standard deviation scores.

Zero-Inflated Model: A count model that is appropriate for samples that have a large number of 0's.

Zero-Order Relationship: A relationship between two variables without any control variables.

Formula Index

3-1   Mean (*see page 44*).

$$\bar{x} = \frac{\Sigma x}{n}$$

where $\bar{x}$ = sample mean
   Σ = sum of
   x = represents each individual value in the set of values
   n = sample size (the total number of values to be summed)

3-2   Population standard deviation formula (*see page 52*).

$$\sigma = \sqrt{\frac{\Sigma(x - \mu)^2}{N}}$$

where N = number of cases (the population)
   x = each individual score
   Σ = sum of
   μ = population mean

3-3   Sample standard deviation formula (*see page 53*).

$$s = \sqrt{\frac{\Sigma(x - \bar{x})^2}{n-1}}$$

where $\bar{x}$ = sample mean
   n = sample size

3-4   Sample standard deviation computational formula (*see page 56*).

$$s = \sqrt{\frac{\Sigma x^2 - (\Sigma x)^2 / n}{n-1}}$$

where Σx^2 = sum of the squared individual scores

$(\Sigma x)^2$ = sum of the individual scores squared

n = sample size

3-5   Coefficient of variation (CV) (*see page 60*).

$$CV = \frac{s100}{\bar{X}}$$

where s = standard deviation

$\bar{X}$ = mean

3-6   Index of qualitative variation (IQV) (*see page 60*).

$$IQV = \frac{k(N^2 - \Sigma f^2)}{N^2(k - 1)}$$

where k = number of categories

N = number of cases

Σf^2 = sum of the squared frequencies

4-1   Probability (*see page 67*).

$$P(\text{A}) = \frac{\text{number of ways the event can occur}}{\text{total number of possible outcomes}}$$

4-2   Joint probability of independent events (*see page 68*).

$$P(\text{AB}) = P(\text{A}) \times P(\text{B})$$

4-3   Joint probability of dependent events (*see page 69*).

$$P(\text{AB}) = P(\text{A}) \times P(\text{B}|\text{A})$$

where A and B are independent events

$P(\text{B}|\text{A})$ is the probability of B, given A has already occurred

4-4   Addition rule for two independent outcomes (*see page 71*).

$$P(A \text{ or } B) = P(A) + P(B)$$

where A and B are independent events

4-5   Addition rule for non–mutually exclusive occurrences (*see page 72*).

$$P(A \text{ or } B) = P(A) + P(B) - P(A \text{ and } B|A)$$

P(A and B|A) is the probability of A and B, given A has already occurred

4-6   Combinations (*see page 77*).

$$_nC_r = \frac{N!}{r! \,(N - r)!}$$

where C = number of combinations
   N = number of trials
   r = number of successes

4-7   Permutation (*see page 78*).

$$_nP_r = \frac{N!}{r!(N - r)!} p^r q^{n-r}$$

where p = probability
   $q = 1 - p$
   N = number of trials
   r = number of successes

4-8   Normal curve (*see page 83*).

$$Y = \frac{1}{\sigma\sqrt{2\pi}} e^{-(x-\mu)^2/2\sigma^2}$$

where μ = mean
   σ = standard deviation

4-9   *Z* scores for a single score (*see page 86*).

$$z = \frac{x - \bar{x}}{s}$$

where x = a value
 $\bar{x}$ = sample mean
 s = sample standard deviation

4-10   Converting a *z* score to a raw score (*see page 90*).

$$x = (z)(s)$$

where x = raw score
 s = sample standard deviation
 z = person's z score

5-1   Combinations of samples from a population (*see page 100*).

$$C = \frac{N!}{n!(N - n)!}$$

where N = size of population
 n = size of sample

5-2   Standard error (*see page 105*).

$$\sigma_{\bar{x}} = \frac{s}{\sqrt{N}}$$

where N = sample size
 s = sample standard deviation

5-3   Confidence intervals (*see page 108*).

$$CI = \bar{x} \pm z \left(\frac{s}{\sqrt{n}} \right)$$

where CI = confidence interval

$\bar{x}$ = sample mean

s = sample standard deviation

z = z score (usually 1.96)

5-4   Sample size (*see page 111*).

$$n = \left[\frac{(z)(\sigma)}{e} \right]^2$$

where z = desired level of confidence

σ = population standard deviation estimated from sample s

e = desired accuracy, as measured by the amount of error we are willing to accept

6-1   *Z* scores for groups of scores (*see page 119*).

$$z = \frac{\bar{x} - \mu}{\sigma / \sqrt{n}}$$

where $\bar{x}$ = sample mean

μ = population mean

$\sigma / \sqrt{n}$ = standard error

6-2   Computing *t* (*see page 126*).

$$t = \frac{\overline{X}_1 - \overline{X}_2}{\sqrt{\frac{(N_1 - 1)S_1{}^2 + (N_2 - 1)S_2{}^2}{(N_1 - 1)(N_2 - 1)}} \sqrt{\frac{N_1 + N_2}{(N_1)(N_2)}}}$$

where $\overline{X}_1$ = mean for group 1

$\overline{X}_2$ = mean for group 2

N_1 = sample size for group 1

N_2 = sample size for group 2

S_1 = standard deviation for group 1

S_2 = standard deviation for group 2

6-3   Computing t for correlated (dependent) means (*see page 130*).

$$t = \frac{\bar{x}_1 - \bar{x}_2}{\sqrt{\dfrac{\Sigma D^2 - \dfrac{(\Sigma D)^2}{n}}{n(n-1)}}}$$

Where $\bar{x}_1$ = mean for time 1
$\bar{x}_2$ = mean for time 2
D = difference
n = sample size

6-4   Calculating t with unequal variances (*see page 132*).

$$t = \frac{\bar{X}_1 - \bar{X}_2}{\sqrt{\dfrac{s_1{}^2}{N_1 - 1} + \dfrac{s_2{}^2}{N_2 - 1}}}$$

where $\bar{X}_1$ = mean for group 1
$\bar{X}_2$ = mean for group 2
s_1 = standard deviation for group 1
s_2 = standard deviation for group 2
N_1 = sample size for group 1
N_1 = sample size for group 2

6-5   Eta squared (*see page 133*).

$$\eta^2 = \frac{t^2}{t^2 + df}$$

where t^2 = t calculated squared
df = degrees of freedom

7-1   ANOVA F (*see page 149*).

$$F = \frac{MS_{between}}{MS_{within}}$$

where MS = mean square
 MS_{between} = mean square between variance
 MS_{within} = mean square within variance

7-2 Total sum of squares (*see page 150*).

$$SS_{\text{total}} = \Sigma\left(x - \bar{x}_t\right)^2$$

where $\bar{x}_t$ = total or grand mean

7-3 Total sum of squares computational formula (*see page 150*).

$$SS_{\text{total}} = \Sigma x_t^2 - \frac{\left(\Sigma x_t\right)^2}{n_t}$$

where Σx_t^2 = sum of the squared x scores totaled over all groups
  $\left(\Sigma x_t\right)^2$ = square of the sum of the x scores totaled over all groups

7-4 Total sum of squares (alternate formula; *see page 152*).

$$SS_{\text{total}} = SS_{\text{between}} + SS_{\text{within}}$$

where SS_{between} = between sum of squares
 SS_{within} = within sum of squares

7-5 Between sum of squares (*see page 152*).

$$SS_{\text{between}} = \Sigma\left[\frac{\left(\Sigma x_g\right)^2}{n_i}\right] - \frac{\left(\Sigma x_t\right)^2}{n_t}$$

where $\dfrac{\Sigma\left(\Sigma x_g\right)^2}{n_i}$ = the square of the sum of the x scores in each group

n_i = the number of observations in each group

$\left(\Sigma x_t\right)^2$ = the square of the sum of the x scores totaled over all groups

7-6 Mean square between variance (*see page 154*).

$$MS_{\text{between}} = \frac{SS_{\text{between}}}{df_{\text{between}}}$$

where SS_{between} = between sum of squares

df_{between} = between degrees of freedom

7-7 Mean square within variance (*see page 154*).

$$MS_{\text{within}} = \frac{SS_{\text{within}}}{df_{\text{within}}}$$

where SS_{within} = within sum of squares

df_{within} = within degrees of freedom

7-8 Scheffé test (*see page 157*).

$$C = \left[\sqrt{(k-1)(F_{\text{critical}})}\right]\left[\sqrt{\frac{1}{n_1} + \frac{1}{n_2}(MS_{\text{within}})}\right]$$

where k = number of groups

n_1 and n_2 = sample size of the contrasting groups

7-9 Explained sum of squares (*see page 161*).

$$SS_{\text{explained}} = \Sigma\left[\frac{(\Sigma x_a)^2}{n_c}\right] - \left[\frac{(\Sigma x_b)^2}{n_t}\right]$$

where Σx_a = sum of all values *by group*

n_c = number of cases in each group

Σx_b = sum of all values *across the groups*

n_t = total sample size of all cases

7-10 Degrees of freedom for interaction effects (*see page 164*).

$$df = (r-1)(c-1)$$

where r = number of row

c = number of columns

8-1 Chi square (*see page 181*).

$$\chi^2 = \Sigma\frac{(O-E)^2}{E}$$

where O = frequencies we observe

E = frequencies we would expect given only chance

8-2   Expected frequency (*see page 182*).

$$E = \frac{(\text{Column marginal } n)(\text{Row marginal } n)}{\text{total } n}$$

where n = sample size

8-3   Yates's correction for continuity (*see page 186*).

$$\chi^2_{corrected} = \Sigma \frac{(|O - E| = 0.5)^2}{E}$$

where O = frequencies we observe
E = frequencies we would expect given only chance

8-4   Phi (*see page 188*).

$$\phi = \sqrt{\frac{\chi^2}{n}}$$

where χ^2 = chi square
n = sample size

8-5   Contingency coefficient (*see page 191*).

$$C = \sqrt{\frac{\chi^2}{\chi^2 + n}}$$

where χ^2 = chi square
n = sample size

8-6   Cramer's V (*see page 192*).

$$V = \sqrt{\frac{\chi^2}{n(k-1)}}$$

where χ^2 = chi square
n = sample size
k = the number of rows or columns

9-1   Proportional reduction in error (PRE) (*see page 204*).

$$PRE = \frac{\text{errors using rule 1} - \text{errors using rule 2}}{\text{errors using rule 1}}$$

9-2   Lambda (λ) (*see page 204*).

$$\lambda = \frac{E_1 - E_2}{E_1}$$

where E_1 = errors using rule 1
E_2 = errors using rule 2

9-3   Total pairs possible (*see page 206*).

$$total\ pairs = \frac{n(n-1)}{2}$$

Where n = the sample size

9-4   Gamma (γ) (*see page 210*).

$$\gamma = \frac{N_s - N_d}{N_s + N_d}$$

where N_s = number of similar pairs
N_d = number of dissimilar pairs

9-5   Somer's d (*see page 213*).

$$d = \frac{N_s - N_d}{N_s + N_d + T_y}$$

where N_s = number of similar pairs
N_d = number of dissimilar pairs
T_y = values multiplying the value of the target cell by all tied cases

9-6   Tau b (*see page 215*).

$$b = \frac{N_s + N_d}{\sqrt{(N_s + N_d + T_y)(N_s + N_d + T_x)}}$$

where N_s = number of similar pairs
N_d = number of dissimilar pairs
T_y, T_x = values multiplying the value of the target cell by all tied cases

9-7   Test tau b for significance (*see page 216*).

$$z = \frac{b}{\sqrt{\dfrac{4(r+1)(c+1)}{9nrc}}}$$

where b = Tau b

   r = number of rows

   c = number of columns

9-8   Odds (*see page 217*).

$$\text{odds} = \frac{P}{Q}$$

where P = probability of an event occurring

   Q = probability of an event not occurring

9-9   Odds ratio (*see page 218*).

$$OR = \frac{A/C}{B/D}$$

9-10   Yule's Q (*see page 219*).

$$Q = \frac{AD - BC}{AD + BC}$$

9-11   Yule's Q using odds ratio (*see page 219*).

$$Q = \frac{OR - 1}{OR + 1}$$

where OR = odds ratio

9-12   Spearman's rank order correlation (rho) (*see page 222*).

$$r_s = 1 - \frac{6(\Sigma D^2)}{N(N^2 - 1)}$$

where N = number of paired observations

   ΣD^2 = sum of the squared differences

9-13   Significance testing for rho (*see page 222*).

$$t = r_s \sqrt{\frac{n-2}{1-r_s^2}}$$

where r_s = rho
n = sample size

10-1   Partial gamma (*see page 248*).

$$\gamma_p = \frac{\Sigma N_s - \Sigma N_d}{\Sigma N_s + \Sigma N_d}$$

where ΣN_s = similar pairs summed across all conditional tables
ΣN_d = dissimilar pairs summed across all conditional tables

11-1   Regression slopes (*see page 260*).

$$b = \frac{\text{vertical distance}}{\text{horizontal distance}} = \frac{y_1 - y_2}{x_1 - x_2}$$

11-2   Equation for a straight line (*see page 262*).

$$a = \bar{y} - b\bar{x}$$

where a = intercept
b = slope

11-3   The slope b (*see page 267*).

$$b = \frac{SS_{yx}}{SS_x}$$

where SS_{yx} = sum of squares of the cross-products of y and x
SS_x = sum of squares of x

11-4   Computing b (*see page 267*).

$$b = \frac{N\Sigma XY - (\Sigma X)(\Sigma Y)}{N\Sigma X^2 - (\Sigma X)^2}$$

where ΣXY = sum of products of paired values
ΣX = sum of x values
ΣX^2 = sum of squared x values

ΣY = sum of y values

N = number of pairs of values

11-5 Pearson correlation coefficient (*see page 270*).

$$r = \frac{N\Sigma XY - (\Sigma X)(\Sigma Y)}{\sqrt{[N\Sigma X^2 - (\Sigma X)^2][N\Sigma Y^2 - (\Sigma Y)^2]}}$$

where ΣXY = sum of products of paired values

ΣX = sum of x values

ΣX^2 = sum of squared x values

ΣY = sum of y values

ΣY^2 = sum of squared y values

N = number of pairs of values

11-6 Covariance (*see page 271*).

$$\text{COV}(XY) = \frac{\Sigma XY - \dfrac{(\Sigma X)(\Sigma Y)}{n}}{n-1}$$

where ΣXY = sum of products of paired values

ΣX = sum of x values

ΣY = sum of y values

n = sample size

11-7 Significance testing for Pearson's r (*see page 276*).

$$t = r\sqrt{\frac{n-2}{1-r^2}}$$

where r = correlation coefficient

n = sample size

11-8 critical r (*see page 277*).

$$r = \frac{t_{\text{critical}}}{t^2_{\text{critical}} + df}$$

where t = critical t value

df = degrees of freedom

11-9   Standard error of r (*see page 278*).

$$s_r = \frac{1 - r^2}{\sqrt{n}}$$

where r = correlation coefficient
n = sample size

11-10   Regression slope (*see page 278*).

$$b = r \left[\frac{s_x}{s_y} \right]$$

where r = correlation coefficient
s_x = standard deviation of x
s_y = standard deviation of y

11-11   Standardized beta (*see page 279*).

$$\beta = b \left[\frac{s_x}{s_y} \right]$$

where b = slope
s_x = standard deviation of x
s_y = standard deviation of y

11-12   Standard error of estimate (*see page 280*).

$$s_{y.x} = \sqrt{\frac{\Sigma(y - y')^2}{n - 2}}$$

where y = observed y value
y' = predicted y value
n = sample size

11-13   Confidence intervals (*see page 283*).

$$CI = b \pm tSE_b$$

where b = slope
t = critical t
SE_b = standard error of b

12-1   Partial correlation (*see page 292*).

$$r_{yx.v} = \frac{r_{yx} - (r_{yv})(r_{xv})}{\sqrt{1-r_{yv}^2}\sqrt{1-r_{xv}^2}}$$

where r_{yx} = total correlation between two variables y and x
$\quad r_{yv}$ = total correlation between two variables y and v
$\quad r_{xv}$ = total correlation between two variables x and v

12-2   Significance testing for partial correlation (*see page 293*).

$$t = \frac{r_{yx.v}\sqrt{n-q-2}}{\sqrt{1-r_{yx.v}^2}}$$

where $r_{yx.v}$ = correlation between variables y and x controlling for v
$\quad n$ = sample size
$\quad q$ = number of variables held constant

12-3   Second-order partials (*see page 296*).

$$r_{yx.vw} = \frac{r_{yx.v} - (r_{yw.v})(r_{xw.v})}{\sqrt{1-r_{yx.v}^2}\sqrt{1-r_{xw.v}^2}}$$

where $r_{yx.v}$ = correlation between variables y and x controlling for v
$\quad r_{xw.v}$ = correlation between variables x and w controlling for v

12-4   Multiple correlation coefficient (*see page 297*).

$$R_{y.xv} = \sqrt{\frac{r_{yx}^2 + r_{yv}^2 - 2r_{yx}r_{yv}r_{xv}}{1-r_{xv}^2}}$$

where r_{yx} = total correlation between variables y and x
$\quad r_{yv}$ = total correlation between variables y and v
$\quad r_{xv}$ = total correlation between variables x and v

12-5   Regression formula (*see page 299*).

$$y = b_0 + \Sigma b_p x_p + e$$

where y = dependent variable, or the criterion
$\quad b_0$ = a from the bivariate regression equation, that is, the constant
$\quad\quad$ or y-intercept

b_p = slope for a given independent variable (or predictor) p

x_p = value of a predictor p

e = error or residuals, as discussed in the previous chapter

12-6   Unstandardized partial regression slope (*see page 300*).

$$b_p = \left[\frac{S_y}{S_x}\right]\left[\frac{r_{yx} - (r_{yv})(r_{vx})}{1 - r_{vx}^2}\right]$$

where b_p = partial slope of v on y

s_y = standard deviation of y

s_x = standard deviation of x

r_{yv} = zero-order correlation between y and v

r_{yx} = zero-order correlation between y and x

r_{vx} = zero-order correlation between v and x

12-7   Standardized slope (β) (*see page 302*).

$$\beta_p = b_p\left[\frac{s_v}{s_y}\right]$$

where b_p = partial slope of v on y

s_y = standard deviation of y

s_v = standard deviation of v

12-8   Standardized beta (*see page 302*).

$$\beta_{yv.x} = b_{yv.x}\left[\frac{s_x}{s_y}\right]$$

where $\beta_{yv.x}$ = standardized partial beta

$b_{yv.x}$ = unstandardized partial b

12-9   Standard error of estimate (*see page 305*).

$$S_{y.xvw} = \sqrt{\frac{SS_{residual}}{df}}$$

where $SS_{residual}$ = residual sum of squares

df = degrees of freedom

12-10   Adjusted R^2 (*see page 306*).

$$\text{adjusted } R^2 = 1 - (1 - R^2)\frac{n-1}{n-k-1}$$

where k = number of predictors

n = sample size

$R^2 = R$ squared

A-1   Generalized linear model (*see page 319*).

$$\eta = \beta_0 + \Sigma\beta_p X_p + \epsilon$$

where β_0 = intercept

β_p = regression slop

ϵ = error term

X = the value of a variable

η = a non-linear outcome, the "link" term

Index